Longman

G000066394

English Structure Practice

Gordon Drummond

English Sentence Patterns and multi-level practice
exercises with grammar notes

Longman Group Limited
London

*Associated companies, branches and representatives
throughout the world*

© Longman Group Limited

First published 1972

ISBN 0 582 52438 5

Printed in Great Britain by J. W. Arrowsmith Ltd Bristol

CONTENTS

(Levels: E = Elementary, I = Intermediate, A = Advanced)

iv

TO THE TEACHER

The purpose of this book is to provide adult students with intensive aural/oral training in the common grammatical patterns of English. It may be used in conjunction with a course book.

The material is grouped into 'elementary', 'intermediate' and 'advanced' levels, and there is a corresponding increase in lexical variety as the exercises become more demanding. Key structures and words are returned to again and again as the exercises proceed.

How to Use the Drills—a Suggested Procedure

1. The teacher points out the important feature(s) of the structure to be learnt or the exercise to be done—he may use a chalkboard or some other visual aid for this.

2. With students' books open, the teacher reads out the examples and selects individual students to read out the example responses.

3. If the exercise is to be done 'aural/oral' only, the students now close their books and the teacher starts the practice by reading the example responses aloud once more and then continuing with the numbered sentences for the students to give their responses. A typical exercise which may be done in this way is No. 24.

   If the exercise is to be done 'visual-aural/oral' (e.g. Ex. 22), the students keep their books open when forming their responses and follow the 'read and look up to speak' method. It is important for the students to address some-one when speaking, and not to speak to the book. Exercises done in this way may then be repeated with students' books closed, the teacher adopting the technique explained above.

4. For further reinforcement the students may now give their own examples, basing these on the structure being prac-tised.

5. The exercise may be done in writing as homework, and may also be repeated orally by students working together in pairs outside the class, or in the language laboratory.

6. In certain exercises (e.g. Nos. 26 and 94) the teacher may

exchange places with the students so that they can have oral practice with his side of the 'conversation'.

7. For revision at a later date, exercises previously done may be repeated, but with students' books closed.

Stress and Intonation

An utterance is more than a mere arrangement of words with the appropriate inflexions in a grammatically 'correct' order. An essential part of every utterance is the intonation—the tune—and the stress pattern which produces the rhythm.

In the notes in this book there is frequent reference to sentence stress and intonation. Such notes are mainly for teachers but intermediate and advanced students should find them helpful in many cases. The symbols which are used to show stress and intonation are listed following the phonetic symbols on page (viiia).

The stress-tone pattern suggested for an utterance is usually one of many possible patterns. It is even likely that the pattern symbolised will not be exactly the same as the stress and intonation to be heard on the tape, since native English speakers vary greatly in this respect according to the context, the situation, their mood and feelings about these things, and their own personality. In using symbols to suggest stress and intonation this book seeks to present a neutral pattern which students can safely use in most circumstances.

The Language

The kind of language practised is for the most part that of easy informal modern conversation. A few exercises at the higher levels offer more formal English for the use of students who want to engage in serious discussion, debating and even lecturing, but notes will always indicate such departures from the informal registers.

The extremely colloquial is avoided, and students should avoid the use of the slang and the more colourful expressions of their native-English-speaking contemporaries. Expressions of this kind are apt to be ephemeral and suddenly 'date' the speaker, and the gayest idiom is likely to sound quaint on the lips of a speaker who retains any flavour of 'foreign accent'. To convince himself of this the student has only to hear or imagine a foreign speaker of his own mother tongue uttering the very latest student slang.

On the other hand, it is not possible to catch the rhythm of spoken English without the use of the contractions, weak forms and neutral vowels of conversation, and it is the rhythm which will tell the student whether his utterance is acceptable when he reaches the stage of 'feeling' whether what he is about to say is English or not. For this reason the transcriptions in the notes show such contractions and informal pronunciation wherever a native speaker would employ them.

Notes:

1. Oral drills are best done with students sitting in a semi-circle facing the teacher, or along the three sides of a square. The teacher is seated and his book placed in such a way that he has only to glance down momentarily to see the oral stimulus he is to give. He delivers the utterance either by speaking to the class generally before selecting one of the students to respond (random selection method) or by speaking directly to the student who is to give the response.

2. The exercise should begin slowly and build up gradually to normal conversational speed. The students will need time to gain confidence in using structures unfamiliar to them. This does not mean that the teacher should at any time speak more slowly than usual or distort in any way the natural rhythm, stress-pattern and intonation of his utterances.

3. Many of the simpler, shorter responses may be given in chorus (e.g. Exs. 9 and 24).

4. Although students may prepare drills that they are to do the following day, ideally they should learn new words by hearing them pronounced, rather than by reading them. The teacher may therefore select words from exercises to be done next and say these to his class, at the same time illustrating their meaning.

5. Exercises requiring longer or more complex responses should be done in writing and corrected by the teacher before aural/oral practice is attempted.

6. To provide variety in the practice, different exercise techniques are employed: transformational grammar, question and answer, substitution, sentence completion, word insertion, sentence linking, etc.

7. Wall charts or pictures are useful for indicating the lexical

items introduced in some of the elementary exercises. They may also be used to reinforce a structure being practised.

8. Oral drills help to ensure accurate comprehension and speech, but do not produce conversational continuity. To obtain this, the teacher should write his own suitable dialogues, have these duplicated so that each student can have a copy, and then practise them round the class until they can be spoken by the students without referring to the printed word. The effective classroom is not so far removed from the theatre as many people might think.

How to Select the Material

If this book is used in conjunction with a course book, it is a simple matter to select an exercise or group of exercises practising the grammatical point being studied (consult the Index or the Contents).

Some teachers, however, especially those giving summer and short courses, or perhaps 'brush-up' sessions, may wish to devote the greater part of their lesson time to oral drilling. If this is the case, it is recommended that exercises are chosen from different sections at the required level. A sample selection would be one exercise taken from Tenses, another from Anomalous Finites ('Special' Verbs), a third from Adjectives and a fourth from Quantity Determinatives. The next day would see a fairly rapid revision of these exercises (done with students' books closed) followed by the next exercise at that level in each of the same four sections, or alternatively other patterns from other sections.

Abbreviations in the text

Cf.	*Confer* (Compare)
U.S.	United States
U.N.	United Nations
ad(vert)	advertisement
TV	television
St	Saint or Street
pl	plural
vb	verb
adj.	adjective
n	noun
pro.	pronoun

The author has found the following books extremely useful:

A. S. Hornby	— A Guide to Patterns and Usage in English (O.U.P.)
H. E. Palmer	— The Teaching of Oral English (Longman)
A. J. Thomson and A. V. Martinet	— A Practical English Grammar (O.U.P.) 2nd edition
Michael West	— Essays on Language Teaching (Longman)
Charles C. Fries Robert Lado	— An Intensive Course in English (English Language Institute, University of Michigan)
Charles C. Fries	— Teaching and Learning English as a Foreign Language (E.L.I., Univ. of Mich.)
Brian Kelly	— An Advanced English Course
D. Abercrombie	— Problems and Principles (Longman)
W. Stannard Allan	— Living English Structure (Longman)

He would like to thank the English Language Institute of the University of Michigan for their suggestion that certain of their instructional devices should be adopted. Thanks are also due to J. R. L. and the editorial staff of Messrs Longman, who gave valuable advice and help.

The English Alphabet

		Name			*Name*
A	a	/ei/	N	n	/en/
B	b	/biː/	O	o	/əu/
C	c	/siː/	P	p	/piː/
D	d	/diː/	Q	q	/kjuː/
E	e	/iː/	R	r	/ɑː/
F	f	/ef/	S	s	/es/
G	g	/dʒiː/	T	t	/tiː/
H	h	/eitʃ/	U	u	/juː/
I	i	/ai/	V	v	/viː/
J	j	/dʒei/	W	w	/ˈdʌbljuː/
K	k	/kei/	X	x	/eks/
L	l	/el/	Y	y	/wai/
M	m	/em/	Z	z	/zed/

The Sounds of English

The phonetic symbols are those used in the *English Pronouncing Dictionary* (EPD) by Daniel Jones, 13th edition (revised by A. C. Gimson). The consonants are:

/p/	as in	*p*ea /piː/	/f/	as in	*f*ew /fjuː/
/b/	,,	*b*ay /bei/	/v/	,,	*v*iew /vjuː/
/t/	,,	*t*ea /tiː/	/θ/	,,	*th*in /θin/
/d/	,,	*d*ay /dei/	/ð/	,,	*th*en /ðen/
/k/	,,	*k*ey /kiː/	/s/	,,	*s*o /səu/
/g/	,,	*g*ay /gei/	/z/	,,	*z*oo /zuː/
/tʃ/	,,	*ch*eap /tʃiːp/	/ʃ/	,,	*sh*ow /ʃəu/
/dʒ/	,,	*j*ump /dʒʌmp/	/ʒ/	,,	plea*s*ure /ˈpleʒə/
/l/	,,	*l*ot /lɔt/	/h/	,,	*h*ot /hɔt/
/r/	,,	*r*ot /rɔt/	/m/	,,	hi*m* /him/
/w/	,,	*w*ill /wil/	/n/	,,	te*n* /ten/
/j/	,,	*y*es /jes/	/ŋ/	,,	lo*ng* /lɔŋ/

The following table shows three different ways of representing the vowel sounds. The first column shows the simplest form of the International Phonetic Alphabet. Here called 'Simple IPA', it is the system used for example in *An International Reader's Dictionary* by Michael West. The second column gives the system used in this book; it is used in the *Advanced Learner's Dictionary of Current English* (ALD) by Hornby,

Gatenby and Wakefield as well as in the *EPD*. The last column gives a more complex system; one book using a system like this is *An Introduction to the Pronunciation of English* by A. C. Gimson.

Vowel Number	Keyword	Simple IPA	EPD/ALD	Gimson
1	bead	iː	iː	iː
2	bid	i	i	ɪ
3	bed	e	e	e
4	bad	a	æ	æ
5	barred	aː	ɑː	ɑː
6	pot	o	ɔ	ɒ
7	bought	oː	ɔː	ɔː
8	put	u	u	ʊ
9	boot	uː	uː	uː
10	bud	ʌ	ʌ	ʌ
11	bird	əː	əː	ɜː
12	'cupboard /ˈkʌbəd/	ə	ə	ə
13	make	ei	ei	eɪ
14	home	əu/ou	əu/ou	əʊ/oʊ
15	like	ai	ai	aɪ
16	town	au	au	ɑʊ
17	noise	oi	ɔi	ɔɪ
18	peer	iə	iə	ɪə
19	pair	eə	ɛə	ɛə
20	poor	uə	uə	ʊə

(As shown in the table, the first element of vowel 14 can be transcribed as either /ə/ or /o/. In this book, this vowel is always /əu/.)

A hyphen - is used to separate the syllables when two vowels occur together, for example in *playing* /ˈplei-iŋ/.

Intonation and stress are shown together by tonetic stress-marks. Any of these marks indicates that the following syllable is stressed, while its shape and position indicates the intonation that is used:

'	high level tone	ˌ	low level tone
ˋ	falling tone	ˊ	rising tone
	˅	falling-rising tone	

The falling-rising tone can occur on a single syllable, as in:

he might /hi ˅might/

Or the fall can come on one syllable and the rise on a later one, as in:

there might have been /ðə ˋmait əv ˌbiːn/

Where a syllable requires special emphasis, it is shown by repeating the symbol thus:

"	emphatic high level tone	ˌˌ	emphatic low level tone
ˎ	emphatic falling tone	ˈˈ	emphatic rising tone
	ˎˊ	emphatic falling-rising tone	

The symbol ‾ comes before a high tone that is not stressed. If this symbol is not present, all unstressed syllables before the first stress have a low tone.

DEMONSTRATIVE PRONOUNS AND ADJECTIVES

SINGULAR	PLURAL
This	**These**
That	**Those**

Notes:
(i) Generally speaking, nearer things are demonstrated with **this** and **these**; things farther away with **that** and **those**.

    EXAMPLES:

    This man (here) is John Smith.

    That man (over there) is Peter Brown.

    These men (here) are managers.

    Those men (over there) are workers.

(ii) Demonstratives are often used to express a contrast:

    EXAMPLES:

    This car is mine, and **that** car is John's.

    These students are French, and **those** students are German.

(iii) For the singular, use **this** or **that**.
For the plural, use **these** or **those**.

    EXAMPLES:

    This/that   is a pen.

    These/those are pens.

---

1 Demonstratives*   E

Touch (for this) *or point to* (that) *the items named:*

1. This is a table.	8. That's a picture.
2. That's a chair.	9. This is a page.
3. This is a desk.	10. That's a word.
4. That's a book.	11. This is a sentence.
5. This is a notebook.	12. That's a letter.
6. That's a dictionary.	13. This is a newspaper.
7. This is a chalkboard.	14. That's a pen.

* It is recommended to use real objects, wall-charts or pictures drawn on the chalkboard when doing this and similar exercises.

15. This is a pencil.	23. This is a man.
16. That's a window.	24. That's a woman.
17. This is a door.	25. This is a student.
18. That's a nail.	26. That's a watch.
19. This is a curtain.	27. This is a cigarette.
20. That's a carpet.	28. That's a lighter.
21. This is a room.	29. This is a match.
22. That's a key.	30. That's a car.

QUESTION	ANSWER
What's **this**?	**It**'s a table.
What's **that**?	**It**'s a chair.

Notes:
(i) What's /wɔts/ = What is. It's /its/ = It is.

(ii) General questions (for Yes/No answers) are formed by inverting the subject and the verb *be*.

> EXAMPLES:
> *This is* . . . becomes *Is this* . . . ?
>
> *That is* . . . becomes *Is that* . . . ?

---

2 Demonstratives   E

To contrast this *and* that, *respond as shown:*

pen and pencil   STUDENT A: **Here's a pen and there's a pencil.**

           STUDENT B: **This is a pen and that's a pencil.**

table and desk   STUDENT C: **Here's a table and there's a desk.**

           STUDENT D: **This is a table and that's a desk.**

1. pen and pencil	8. notebook and dictionary
2. curtain and carpet	9. wall and corner
3. table and desk	10. door and window
4. cigarette and lighter	11. letter and page
5. chair and table	12. book and newspaper
6. picture and chalkboard	13. man and woman
7. house and hotel	14. word and sentence

15. watch and key
16. lighter and match
17. newspaper and letter
18. book and magazine
19. student and teacher
20. dictionary and course book

---

3 Demonstratives   E

To practise what's that? *respond as shown:*

pen	STUDENT A: **What's that?**
	STUDENT B: **It's a pen.**
book	STUDENT C: **What's that?**
	STUDENT D: **It's a book.**
key	STUDENT E: **What's that?**
	STUDENT F: **It's a key.**

1. pencil
2. letter
3. watch
4. magazine
5. dictionary
6. notebook
7. newspaper
8. cigarette
9. lighter
10. postcard
11. envelope
12. ring
13. tape
14. record
15. record-player
16. tape-recorder

MY AND YOUR

Is this **your** newspaper?   Yes, it is.
That's **my**   newspaper.

---

4 Demonstratives   E

To practise this *and* that, my *and* your, *respond as shown:*

Is this your book?	**Yes, it is.**	**That's my book.**
Is this your chair?	**Yes, it is.**	**That's my chair.**
Is this your newspaper?	**Yes, it is.**	**That's my newspaper.**

1. Is this your pen?
2. Is this your chair?
3. Is this your key?
4. Is this your car?
5. Is this your book?
6. Is this your magazine?
7. Is this your watch?
8. Is this your lighter?

3

9. Is this your letter?
10. Is this your newspaper?
11. Is this your dictionary?
12. Is this your ring?
13. Is this your room?
14. Is this your cigarette?
15. Is this your notebook?
16. Is this your record?
17. Is this your postcard?
18. Is this your bedroom?
19. Is this your flat?
20. Is this your house?

Isn't

Is this your newspaper? No, it **isn't**.
That **isn't** my newspaper.

Note:
The negative of **is** is **is not** (**isn't**).

---

5 Demonstratives   E

To practise isn't *with demonstratives, respond as shown:*

Is this your book?	**No, it isn't.**	**That isn't my book.**
Is this your chair?	**No, it isn't.**	**That isn't my chair.**
Is this your newspaper?	**No, it isn't.**	**That isn't my newspaper.**

(*Continue with Nos.* 1–20 *in Ex.* 4.)

---

6 Demonstratives   E

These are — /ˈðiːzə/. Those are — /ˈðəuzə/.

Touch (**these**) or point to (**those**) the items named:

1. These are books.
2. Those are letters.
3. These are keys.
4. Those are windows.
5. These are pens.
6. Those are notes.
7. These are socks.
8. Those are shoes.
9. These are stockings.
10. Those are notebooks.
11. These are newspapers.
12. Those are magazines.
13. These are dictionaries.
14. Those are matches.
15. These are cigarettes.
16. Those are knives.
17. These are forks.
18. Those are spoons.
19. These are plates.
20. Those are cups.

QUESTION	ANSWER
What are **these**?	**They**'re books.
What are **those**?	**They**'re pens.

Notes:

(i) What are——? /ˈwɔtə/. **They're** /ðeə/.

(ii) Use the word **they** for the plural.

(iii) For the regular plural of a noun add
   the sound /s/, spelt *s*—stamp*s*, envelope*s*
or the sound /z/, spelt *s*—letter*s*, postcard*s*
or the sound /iz/, spelt *s* or *es*—sentence*s*, glass*es*

---

7 Demonstratives   E

To contrast these *and* those, *respond as shown:*

   books and notebooks
    STUDENT A: **Here are some books and there are some notebooks.**
    STUDENT B: **These are books and those are notebooks.**
   pens and pencils
    STUDENT C: **Here are some pens and there are some pencils.**
    STUDENT D: **These are pens and those are pencils.**

1. stamps and envelopes
2. letters and postcards
3. magazines and newspapers
4. matches and cigarettes
5. words and sentences
6. men and women
7. shoes and socks
8. shirts and ties
9. knives and forks
10. mirrors and cupboards
11. stockings and skirts
12. sheets and blankets
13. sweaters and jackets
14. TV sets and radios
15. records and tapes
16. rulers and rubbers
17. glasses and bottles
18. tables and chairs
19. boxes and suitcases
20. buses and trains

---

8 Demonstratives   E

To practise What are those? *respond as shown:*

  notes   STUDENT A: **What are those?**
           STUDENT B: **They're notes.**

glasses STUDENT C: **What are those?**
STUDENT D: **They're glasses.**
letters STUDENT E: **What are those?**
STUDENT F: **They're letters.**

1. cups	5. notes	9. cigarettes	13. records
2. shoes	6. stockings	10. matches	14. tapes
3. socks	7. lighters	11. parcels	15. coins
4. stamps	8. postcards	12. suitcases	16. telephones

9 Demonstratives E

To practise affirmative questions with these, *and answers with* those, *respond as shown:*

Are these your books?
Yes, they are.   Those are my books.
Are these your shoes?
Yes, they are.   Those are my shoes.
Are these your keys?
Yes, they are.   Those are my keys.

1. Are these your cigarettes?
2. Are these your matches?
3. Are these your records?
4. Are these your magazines?
5. Are these your newspapers?
6. Are these your postcards?
7. Are these your stamps?
8. Are these your letters?
9. Are these your photographs?
10. Are these your notebooks?
11. Are these your notes?
12. Are these your tapes?
13. Are these your keys?
14. Are these your friends?
15. Are these your cheques?
16. Are these your tablets?
17. Are these your clothes?
18. Are these your tickets?
19. Are these your brushes?
20. Are these your suitcases?

Aren't

Are these your cigarettes?　No, they **aren't**.
Those **aren't**　my　cigarettes.

Note:
The negative of **are** is **are not** (**aren't**). /ɑːnt/

10　Demonstratives　　　　　　　　　　　　　　E

To practise aren't *with demonstratives, respond as shown*:

Are these your books?
No, they aren't.　Those aren't my books.
Are these your shoes?
No, they aren't.　Those aren't my shoes.
Are these your keys?
No, they aren't.　Those aren't my keys.
Continue with Nos. 1–20 in Ex. 9.

11　Demonstratives　　　　　　　　　　　　　　E

---

*To practise singular/plural, change the sentences in Ex. 1 into
the plural.*

This is a table.　**These are tables.**
That's a chair.　**Those are chairs.**
This is a desk.　**These are desks.**
Continue with Nos. 4–30.

12　Demonstratives　　　　　　　　　　　　　　E

---

*To practise plural/singular, change the sentences in Ex. 6 into
the singular.*

These are books.　**This is a book.**
Those are letters.　**That's a letter.**
These are keys.　**This is a key.**
　Continue with Nos. 4–20.

TELLING THE TIME

Notes:
(i) It is helpful to have a large clock-face with easily moved hands to demonstrate the different times.

(ii) When the number of minutes is not exactly divisible by 5, the word "minutes" is used:

It's twenty-five to four.
It's twenty-four *minutes* to four.

---

13 Telling the Time E

To practise asking for and telling the time. Students ask and answer the questions:

5.00	**What's the time ?**	**It's five o'clock.**
6.30	**What's the time ?**	**It's half past six. (Six thirty)**
4.15	**What's the time ?**	**It's (a) quarter past four.**
		(Four fifteen)
3.45	**What's the time ?**	**It's (a) quarter to four.**
		(Three forty-five)

1. 3.20	5. 6.30	9. 2.50	13. 9.15	17. 5.55	21. 7.20
2. 4.40	6. 7.10	10. 8.10	14. 11.00	18. 6.15	22. 2.02
3. 2.00	7. 12.45	11. 9.50	15. 1.30	19. 1.35	23. 5.17
4. 5.25	8. 1.25	12. 10.05	16. 4.45	20. 3.50	24. 6.48

---

14 Time E

To practise common situations involving giving the time. Respond as shown:

breakfast	STUDENT A :	**What time's breakfast ?**
	STUDENT B :	**It's at eight o'clock.**
lunch	STUDENT C :	**What time's lunch ?**
	STUDENT D :	**It's at one o'clock.**
the train (3.45)	STUDENT E :	**What time's the train ?**
	STUDENT F :	**It's at three forty-five.**

1. breakfast
2. morning break
3. lunch
4. afternoon break
5. dinner
6. the plane (8.55)

7. the bus (2.20)
8. the train (4.45)
9. the meeting (11.15)

10. the concert (6.30)
11. the film (10 p.m.)
12. the lecture (11 a.m.)

TENSES

Active Voice:

The Future:	She **will**	**do**	it tomorrow.
Continuous:	She **will be**	**doing** it tomorrow.
The Future Perfect:	She **will have done**	it by tomorrow.
The Simple Present:	She	**does**	it every day.
Continuous:	She **is**	**doing** it now.
The Present Perfect:	She **has**	**done** it.
Continuous:	She **has been doing** it for many years.
The Simple Past:	She	**did**	it yesterday.
Continuous:	She **was**	**doing** it yesterday.
The Past Perfect:	She **had**	**done** it before I arrived.
Continuous:	She **had been doing** it before I arrived.

The exercises that follow give practice in the Active Voice.
The Passive Voice will be found in Exercises 234 to 239.

VERB 'be'—PRESENT TENSE

15 Verb **'be'**   E

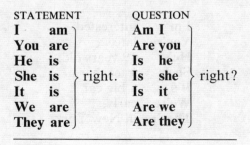

STATEMENT		QUESTION	
I	**am**	**Am I**	
You	**are**	**Are you**	
He	**is**	**Is he**	
She	**is**	right.	**Is she**	right?
It	**is**	**Is it**	
We	**are**	**Are we**	
They	**are**	**Are they**	

Preliminary exercise, to relate person to verb.

I	**I am.**
he	**He is.**
they	**They are.**

1. we	8. you	14. they	20. the boy
2. she	9. he	15. he	21. the men
3. it	10. she	16. they	22. you and I
4. they	11. it	17. you	23. the idea
5. you	12. we	18. Mary	24. the girl
6. I	13. John	19. we	25. John and
7. they			Mary

---

16 Verb 'be'   E

Relating person to verb in question form.

I	**Am I?**
he	**Is he?**
they	**Are they?**

Continue with Nos. 1–25 in Ex. 15.

---

17 Verb 'be'   E

I'm	interested.
You're	late.
He's	19 years old.
She's	a teacher.
It's	a big car.
We're	early.
They're	in New York.

Note:
The contracted forms above represent: **I am**, **you are** (singular and plural), **he is**, **she is**, **it is**, **we are**, **they are**.

To practise forming questions and short answers.

She's interested.   STUDENT A: **Is she interested ?**
                      STUDENT B: **Yes, she is.**
You're right, John.   STUDENT C: **Am I right ?**
                      STUDENT D: **Yes, you are.**
We're happy.   STUDENT E: **Are you happy ?**
                      STUDENT F: **Yes, we are.**

1. They're Italian.
2. He's English.
3. I'm tired.
4. You're right, Mary.
5. She's French.
6. He's cold.
7. Mary's 19 today.
8. John's here.
9. She's a doctor.
10. He's a teacher.
11. She's lazy.
12. I'm late.
13. He's from Spain.
14. They're German.
15. It's ready.
16. We're comfortable.
17. You're late, John and Mary.
18. He's American.
19. She's Swiss.
20. It's a Swiss stamp.
21. He's an actor.
22. She's an actress.
23. They're foreigners.
24. You're early, Mary and Jane.
25. I'm busy.
26. He's angry.
27. She's nice.
28. I'm right.
29. They're wrong.
30. He's clever.

11

NEGATIVE STATEMENT	QUESTION	
I'm **not** right.	**Aren't I**	right?
You're **not** interested.	**Aren't you**	interested?
He's **not** a doctor.	**Isn't** **he**	a doctor?
She's **not** here.	**Isn't** **she**	here?
It's **not** important.	**Isn't** **it**	important?
We're **not** late.	**Aren't we**	late?
They're not in London.	**Aren't they**	in London?

Notes:

(i) **Aren't I?** is an exception. It is idiomatic.

(ii) Alternative statement forms are: **you aren't, he isn't, she isn't, it isn't, we aren't, they aren't.**

To practise the negative form, make questions from the following:

He isn't there.	STUDENT A:	**Isn't he there ?**
	STUDENT B:	**No, he isn't.**
She's not clever.	STUDENT C:	**Isn't she clever ?**
	STUDENT D:	**No, she isn't.**
I'm not tired.	STUDENT E:	**Aren't you tired ?**
	STUDENT F:	**No, I'm not.**

1. She's not Spanish.
2. He isn't intelligent.
3. They're not new.
4. I'm not happy.
5. She isn't in New York.
6. He isn't French.
7. They aren't here.
8. It's not ready.
9. You're not early.
10. It isn't correct.
11. We aren't comfortable.
12. You aren't right.
13. He's not English.
14. We're not interested.
15. I'm not an engineer.
16. She's not married.
17. It isn't difficult.
18. They're not from Germany.
19. She isn't over 21.
20. It isn't very good.

THE PRESENT CONTINUOUS

Introductory notes:
(i) The present continuous tense is used to indicate:

(a) a temporary action in progress at the present moment (see the examples in the box below).
(b) a future arrangement.

> EXAMPLES:
> I *am visiting* Mexico *next week*.
>
> She *is leaving* for New York *tomorrow*.

(c) a temporary activity not necessarily proceeding at the present moment.

> EXAMPLES:
> They *are building* a new school over there. (said at 10 p.m. on the site)
>
> We *are having* central heating installed.

(d) the constant repetition of an event (with *always* or a similar adverbial).

> EXAMPLES:
> Mary is *always* smoking.
>
> John is *continually* making mistakes.

(ii) Some verbs are not normally used in continuous tenses. See the section on non-conclusive verbs.

I	'm learning	English	
You	're having	a lesson	
He	's watching	TV	
She	's working	in Paris	now.
It	's raining	hard	
We	're studying	here	
They	're writing	letters	

13

19 ELEMENTARY

(a) *To practise the present continuous, respond as shown:*

Mary—learn English
  STUDENT A: **What's Mary doing ?**
  STUDENT B: **She's learning English.**
John—have a drink
  STUDENT C: **What's John doing ?**
  STUDENT D: **He's having a drink.**
they—come to class
  STUDENT E: **What are they doing ?**
  STUDENT F: **They're coming to class.**

1. you—learn English
2. Sally—speak to Peter
3. they—go into the hotel
4. Susan—study
5. Paul—watch TV
6. the girls—play a record
7. Paul—help Betty
8. the men—dance
9. the man—look at Anne
10. Sally—sleep
11. the women—wash clothes
12. the woman—clean the room
13. Alice—do homework
14. the child—play
15. the children—make a noise
16. Harry—read a book
17. Bob—take a walk
18. Mary—have a swim
19. the boys—do nothing
20. they—listen to the radio

(b) *To practise asking questions, respond as shown:*

Susan (sleep—read)
  STUDENT A: **Is Susan sleeping ?**
  STUDENT B: **No, she isn't. She's reading.**
Paul (read—write)
  STUDENT C: **Is Paul reading ?**
  STUDENT D: **No, he isn't reading. He's writing.**

1. Don (type—dictate)
2. Susan (speak—listen)
3. Paul (get dressed—wash)
4. Bob (watch TV—have a meal)
5. Mr Brown (shave—have a shower)
6. Gordon (have a rest—go to work)
7. Sally and Betty (get up—go to bed)
8. John and Adrian (play golf—tennis)
9. Bob (do his work—look out of the window)
10. Richard (have a cup of tea—a cup of coffee)
11. John (go to the supermarket—department store)
12. Susan (go to the shops—come back from the shops)

---

20 The Present Continuous   E

To practise relating occupations to present activities, respond as shown:

Paul's a teacher.
   STUDENT A: **What's he doing now?**
   STUDENT B: **He's teaching now.**
Sue's a journalist. (write)
   STUDENT C: **What's she doing now?**
   STUDENT D: **She's writing an article now.**

1. Jean's a typist.
2. Betty's a dancer.
3. Len's a bus-driver.
4. Sue's a tennis-player.
5. Jim and Bob are teachers.
6. David's an author. (write)
7. Paul's a dentist. (extract)
8. Gordon's a salesman. (sell)
9. Betty's a housewife. (clean)
10. Michael's a doctor. (examine)
11. Sheila's a secretary. (answer)
12. Mary and Jim are tourists. (visit)

---

21 The Present Continuous   EI

To contrast the present continuous with the past continuous, respond as shown:

John was living in Mexico.
John was living in Mexico, but he's not living there now.

Mary wasn't waiting for Peter.
Mary wasn't waiting for Peter, but she's waiting for him now.

1. Paul wasn't having fun.
2. I was reading that novel.
3. Harry was enjoying himself.
4. They weren't learning a lot.
5. You weren't paying attention.
6. Rosemary was writing a letter.
7. Sheila wasn't living in Canada.
8. Harold was carrying some luggage.
9. Paul was taking a computer course.
10. John wasn't thinking about his job.
11. Mr and Mrs Smith were having a meal.
12. Betty wasn't listening to Mr Hammond.
13. Paul was trying to repair his scooter.
14. All the workers were planning to leave.
15. Those two firms weren't making a profit.

---

22 The Present Continuous I

To practise using always, continually *and* constantly *to indicate an incessant action, respond as shown:*

Does your car break down? (always)
Yes. It's always breaking down.

Does Barbara speak to herself? (constantly)
Yes. She's constantly speaking to herself.

Do the other students ask for help? (continually)
Yes. They're continually asking for help.

1. Does John smoke? (always)
2. Does Jim watch TV? (always)
3. Do the girls laugh? (always)
4. Does Tom work late? (constantly)
5. Does Steve complain? (constantly)
6. Does Richard tell lies? (always)
7. Does Sheila hurt herself? (always)
8. Does Henry have accidents? (always)

9. Do the boys miss meals? (continually)
10. Does Tom get into trouble? (constantly)
11. Does Susan interrupt you? (continually)
12. Does Betty listen to pop music? (always)
13. Does Gordon make mistakes? (continually)
14. Does Barbara fall downstairs? (constantly)
15. Does Jane talk about herself? (constantly)
16. Does Betty argue with people? (continually)
17. Does Robert say the wrong thing (constantly)
18. Does Sally change her boy-friend? (always)
19. Does Helen find fault with John? (continually)
20. Does Jean spill coffee down her dress? (always)

VERB 'be'—PAST TENSE

STATEMENT		QUESTION	
I was		Was I	
You were		Were you	
He was		Was he	
She was	early **yesterday**.	Was she	early **yesterday**?
It was		Was it	
We were		Were we	
They were		Were they	

Note:
Was and **were** have weak forms:

	STRONG FORM	WEAK FORM
was	/wɔz/	/wəz/
were	/wɜː/	/wə/

The weak forms are usual in the affirmative when the word is unstressed and a stress follows:

I was there.   The boys were in London.
/ai wəz ˋðɛə/   /ðə ˈbɔiz wərin ˋlʌndn/

They are not common in questions, where the strong form is heard even when **was** or **were** does not have sentence stress:

Was I wrong?   Were they right?
/wɔz ai ˌrɔŋ/   /wɜː ðei ˌrait/

17

(a) *Preliminary exercise to relate person to verb in statements.*

I	**I was.**
he	**He was.**
they	**They were.**

Continue with Nos. 1–25 of Ex. 15.

(b) *Relating person to verb in question form.*

I	**Was I?**
he	**Was he?**
they	**Were they?**

Continue with Nos. 1–25 of Ex. 15.

---

24 Verb **be**—past tense   E

To practise forming questions with was *and* were, *respond as shown:*

John was here last week.	**Was John here last week?** Yes, he was.
Jim was at home yesterday.	**Was Jim at home yesterday?** Yes, he was.
You were late last night.	**Were we late last night?** Yes, you were.

1. We were late this morning.
2. I was in New York last week.
3. Bill was at home last night.
4. You were early this morning.
5. Sheila was in Austria last year.
6. They were in Tokyo two weeks ago.
7. Bob was upstairs a few minutes ago.
8. They were in their bedroom an hour ago.
9. I was in the town at 5 p.m. yesterday.
10. John was in the north of Spain last year.
11. Richard was on the phone half an hour ago.
12. They were on holiday on the 10th of August.
13. Gordon was at the club at 10 o'clock last night.
14. John was in the newspaper shop several hours ago.
15. Betty and Sheila were in the TV room just now.

NEGATIVE STATEMENT		QUESTION	
I **was not**		**Wasn't** I	
You **were not**		**Weren't** you	
He **was not**		**Wasn't** he	
She **was not**	early	**Wasn't** she	early
It **was not**	**yesterday**.	**Wasn't** it	**yesterday?**
We **were not**		**Weren't** we	
They **were not**		**Weren't** they	

Note:

Wasn't = was not, weren't = were not.
/'wɔznt/ /wəz'nɒt/ /'wɜːnt/ /wə'nɒt/

The —**n't** forms of verbs nearly always have sentence stress:

Wasn't he early?—He certainly **wasn't** late.
/'wɔznt hi ˌɜːli/   /hi 'sɜːtnli 'wɔznt ˈleit/

To practise the negative form, respond as shown:

They were home late.	**They weren't home late.**
Weren't they?	**No, they weren't.**
Anne was at the theatre.	**Anne wasn't at the theatre.**
Wasn't she?	**No, she wasn't.**
I was early this morning.	**You weren't early this morning.**
Wasn't I?	**No, you weren't.**

1. Bob was on the phone.
2. Richard was at the shops.
3. They were in the TV room.
4. I was in bed before 11 p.m.
5. Philip was in the restaurant.
6. Anne and Sally were very busy.
7. Caroline was in Spain last year.
8. Mary was in that chair yesterday.
9. Peter was at the cinema last week.
10. The radio was on during the morning.
11. Mr Brown was at the office yesterday.
12. Sue was at the hairdresser's at 3 p.m.
13. Allan was in hospital for an operation.
14. The directors were at the hotel before me.
15. The newspapers were on the table last night.

THE PAST CONTINUOUS

Introductory notes:
(i) The past continuous tense is used to indicate:
    (a) an action in progress at the past time stated or implied (see the examples in the box below).
    (b) an action in the past begun before, and still in progress at the beginning of, another past action.

> EXAMPLES:
> Paul *was working* when Susan telephoned.
>
> John *was watching* TV when Mary came in.
>
> The boys went to the library while the girls *were preparing* lunch.
>
> Mary wrote some letters while the children *were having* their afternoon nap.

    (c) two actions going on simultaneously in the past.

> EXAMPLES:
> I *was singing* while Peter *was dancing*.
>   (Cf. I sang while Peter danced.)
>
> Tom *was working* while Sue *was relaxing*.
>   (Cf. Tom worked while Sue relaxed.)

    (d) reported (indirect) speech.

> EXAMPLE:
> John said, 'I'm coming.'
>
> John said (that) he *was coming*.

(ii) Some verbs are not normally used in continuous tenses. See the section on non-conclusive verbs.

What **were** you **doing** at 8 p.m. last night?
I **was reading** a book.
What **was** John **doing** at 1 p.m. yesterday?
He **was having** lunch.
What **were** you **doing** at 9 p.m. last night?
We **were going** to the cinema.

(a) *To practise and contrast* was(n't) *and* were(n't) *in statements and questions, respond as shown:*

The children weren't swimming at 4 p.m. (tea)
Weren't they?
No, they weren't.
What were they doing at 4 p.m.?
They were having a cup of tea.

I wasn't studying at 9.30 last night. (TV)
Weren't you?
No, I wasn't.
What were you doing at 9.30 last night?
I was watching TV.

1. I wasn't typing at 11 a.m. (lesson)
2. Mary wasn't cooking at midday. (friends)
3. We weren't having a meal at 7 p.m. (rest)
4. The girls weren't working at 9 p.m. (TV)
5. I wasn't having dinner at 8 p.m. (newspaper)
6. You weren't listening to me earlier. (window)
7. Jim wasn't writing a letter at 6 p.m. (novel)
8. I wasn't getting dressed at 8 a.m. (sleep)
9. John wasn't helping Mary after lunch. (garden)
10. I wasn't going into the town at 2 p.m. (tennis)
11. Peter wasn't having lunch at 1 p.m. (coffee)
12. They weren't going to class at 9 a.m. (breakfast)
13. David wasn't driving to work at 10 a.m. (suitcase)
14. Richard wasn't speaking to Helen at 10 p.m. (radio)
15. The boys weren't watching the match at 3 p.m. (beer)

(b) *The past continuous may be used with time expressions such as 'all day', 'the whole evening', 'the entire week'. To practise these, respond as shown. Stress the italicised words.*

Was Betty lying in bed *all* morning? (at 11)
Well, she was still lying in bed at 11 o'clock.

Were the girls doing nothing the *whole* evening? (at 9)
Well, they were certainly doing nothing at 9 o'clock.

21

1. Was Tom working *all* evening? (at 8)
2. Was Sheila ironing *all* afternoon? (at 3)
3. Was Paul travelling the *whole* day? (at 5)
4. Was Tom playing tennis *all* morning? (at 11.30)
5. Were they watching the film *all* the time? (at 9)
6. Was Bob looking for Joe the *whole* day? (at 5)
7. Were the boys playing golf *all* day yesterday? (at 4)
8. Was Jim writing the book *all* last month? (on the 25th)
9. Was Paul playing cards the *entire* evening? (at 10)
10. Was Gordon reading his paper *all* afternoon? (at tea-time)
11. Were they building that school *all* last year? (in October)
12. Was Joe preparing for his exam *all* last week? (on Thursday)
13. Was Tom working for that firm *all* last month? (on the 27th)
14. Was Bob planning his trip the *entire* day? (at dinner-time)
15. Was Sally learning English the *whole* of last year? (in November)

---

27 The Past Continuous   I

To practise this tense with 'during', 'while' *and* 'when' (*see also Ex.* 196).

What was Bob doing during the meeting? (notes)
He was taking notes (during the meeting).

What were you doing when the phone rang? (bath)
I was having a bath (when the phone rang).

What was Susan doing while John was in Canada? (Jim)
She was going out with Jim (while John was in Canada).

1. What were you doing while I was out? (newspaper)
2. What was Mary doing when her friends called? (baby)
3. What was Sally doing when George telephoned? (dressed)
4. What was the manager doing during the morning? (letters)
5. What was Mrs Jones doing when her husband got in? (guests)

6. What were the others doing when Bob came down-stairs? (chat)
7. What was the salesman doing during the afternoon? (retailers)
8. What was Richard doing while Susan was packing? (air tickets)
9. What were the children doing when Tom opened the door? (noise)
10. What were the employers doing during the strike? (negotiations)
11. What was Helen doing when Tom asked her to go out? (housework)
12. What was John doing while Mary was at the doctor's? (eye-test)
13. What were Mr and Mrs Brown doing during their holiday? (Europe)
14. What was Sue doing when Jim arrived outside her room? (make-up)
15. What was Jim trying to do when the car in front accelerated? (overtake)

THE SIMPLE PRESENT

Introductory note:
   The simple present tense is used to express:

 (i) habits and repeated actions.

   EXAMPLES:
   He *starts* work at 9 a.m. every day.

   We *go* to the United States every year.

   Susan always *arrives* on time.

(ii) general statements.

   EXAMPLES:
   John *likes* Mary.

   The boys *enjoy* playing golf.

   Mary *prefers* coffee to tea.

(iii) known facts of a permanent nature.

EXAMPLES:
The sun *rises* in the east.

Men *retire* at the age of 65.

The Rhine *flows* through Germany.

(iv) part of a future programme.

EXAMPLES:
Sally *leaves* tomorrow.

The new students *arrive* on Monday.

Peter *sails* for Japan next Wednesday.

STATEMENT			QUESTION			
I	**like**	⎫	**Do**	I	**like**	⎫
You	**like**	⎪	**Do**	you	**like**	⎪
He	**likes**	⎪	**Does**	he	**like**	⎪
She	**likes**	⎬ beer.	**Does**	she	**like**	⎬ beer?
It	**likes**	⎪	**Does**	it	**like**	⎪
We	**like**	⎪	**Do**	we	**like**	⎪
They	**like**	⎭	**Do**	they	**like**	⎭

Notes:
(i) In the affirmative of regular verbs the 3rd person singular of this tense has the added sound /s/, /z/, or /iz/, spelt *s* or *es*.

(ii) The 3rd person singular question indicator is **does**. Other persons take **do**. These auxiliaries have weak forms, /dəz/, and /du/, /də/, /d/. They are used when the word does not carry sentence stress.

EXAMPLES:
Does John like beer?
/dəz 'dʒɔn 'laik ˌbiə/

Do you like this beer?
/dju 'laik ðis ˌbiə/

but Does he really like it?
/'dʌz hi ˌriəli laik it/

---

28 ELEMENTARY

(a) *Preliminary exercise to relate person to verb.*

24

I	**I do.**
he	**He does.**
they	**They do.**

Continue with Nos. 1–25 of Ex. 15.

(b) *Relating person to verb in question form.*

I	**Do I?**
he	**Does he?**
they	**Do they?**

Continue with Nos. 1–25 of Ex. 15.

---

29 The Simple Present   E

(a) *To practise questions with* do.

I teach every day.	**Do you teach every day?**	Yes, I do.
They like tea.	**Do they like tea?**	Yes, they do.
You arrive early.	**Do I arrive early?**	Yes, you do.

1. I drive a car.
2. You know a lot of words.
3. I take classes every day.
4. They study at night.
5. I want to eat now.
6. We know John.
7. I go to bed early.
8. I have regular holidays.
9. They speak French.
10. I wear a watch.
11. We watch TV.
12. I shop at the supermarket.
13. I sleep well.
14. You speak well.
15. They read a lot.
16. I understand.
17. They walk in the park.
18. I need a drink.
19. You come to class on time.
20. I get up at 8 o'clock.

(b) *To practise questions with* Does.

John likes coffee.	**Does John like coffee?**	Yes, he does.
Mary prefers tea.	**Does Mary prefer tea?**	Yes, she does.

He speaks German.
Does he speak German?   Yes, he does.

1. She has classes in English.
2. The car goes well.
3. He tries to work hard.
4. It eats grass.
5. Peter has breakfast at 8 a.m.
6. Mr Brown wants a drink.
7. Mrs Smith knows Canada.
8. Mary studies after lunch.
9. Susan speaks two languages.
10. Bob takes a newspaper.
11. Paul uses a typewriter.
12. He arrives late.
13. She watches TV.
14. It flies fast.
15. John reads novels.
16. He walks to work.
17. She loves Peter.
18. He wants a coffee.
19. Tom understands English.
20. Peter goes by bus.

---

30 The Simple Present   E

(a) *To force a choice between* do *and* does.

I like coffee.
Do you like coffee?   Yes, I do.
Mary knows John.
Does Mary know John?   Yes, she does.
They need a car.
Do they need a car?   Yes, they do.

1. Peter drives a car.
2. I go dancing.
3. Ben knows New York.
4. They speak Italian.
5. Harry comes early.
6. Mary eats a lot of fruit.
7. I work in the evening.
8. Philip types well.
9. I understand.
10. He wants some soap.
11. Lucy needs help.
12. She rides a scooter.
13. I listen to the radio.
14. He travels by air.

15. Peter likes tea.
16. You speak well.
17. He gets up late.

18. She wakes up early.
19. They have a late lunch.
20. I read short stories.

(b) *Giving short answers* (do *and* does) *and complete statements.*

Do you want any help?	**Yes, I do.**	**I want some help.**
Does Mary like John?	**Yes, she does.**	**She likes John.**
Do they need a car?	**Yes, they do.**	**They need a car.**

1. Do you want a drink?
2. Does he ask questions?
3. Do I speak slowly?
4. Does she live here?
5. Do they know the answer?
6. Does the bus come late?
7. Do we get off here?
8. Does Mary speak English?
9. Do Bob and Jim know him?
10. Does John use a camera?
11. Does Sally like London?
12. Do the men work hard?
13. Does David drive fast?
14. Do you need a holiday?
15. Does the club open late?
16. Do the women shop early?
17. Do you want to come?
18. Does Paul want to come?
19. Do you want Paul to come?
20. Does Mary want Paul to come?

---

31 The Simple Present   E

This is a substitution exercise for further practice with do *and* does.

Do you want to speak English?
Do you want to speak English?
Peter
Does Peter want to speak English?
understand English
Does Peter want to understand English?

they
Do they want to understand English?

1. need	17. buy a book
2. you	18. you
3. she	19. Richard
4. speak English	20. record
5. you	21. you
6. want	22. he
7. have a coffee	23. see Mary
8. Peter	24. you
9. watch TV	25. speak to Mary
10. you	26. John
11. Anne	27. they
12. the play	28. go for a drive
13. they	29. Henry
14. go into town	30. a walk
15. you	31. you
16. she	32. stop now

---

32 The Simple Present   E

To contrast the simple present with the present continuous tense.
Ask a question about now.

Mary reads books in English.
Is she reading a book in English now?   Yes, she is.
John writes letters to Mary.
Is he writing a letter to Mary now?   No, he isn't.

1. They speak Spanish.	11. John and Harry smoke.
2. Sheila comes to class.	12. Betty listens to the radio.
3. Mary cooks for John.	13. Peter watches TV.
4. Don swims in the sea.	14. Edward teaches English.
5. Betty uses a typewriter.	15. Don has coffee.
6. Bob has a long holiday.	16. You speak English well.
7. Patricia sleeps in class.	17. John goes to New York.
8. Peter eats at home.	18. Bob does his work.
9. Jim thinks about Sally.	19. Susan helps her mother.
10. Jane cleans the rooms.	20. George drives to the office.

28

NEGATIVE STATEMENT		QUESTION		
I	don't		Don't	I
You	don't		Don't	you
He	doesn't		Doesn't	he
She	doesn't	swim well.	Doesn't	she	swim well?
It	doesn't		Doesn't	it
We	don't		Don't	we
They	don't		Don't	they

To practise making negative statements, disagree with the following:

You speak well.	**I don't speak well.**
Don't you?	**No, I don't.**
Peter reads a lot.	**Peter doesn't read a lot.**
Doesn't he?	**No, he doesn't.**
They want a lot of money.	**They don't want a lot of money.**
Don't they?	**No, they don't.**

1. Sue writes home every week.
2. You know everybody here.
3. We come to class every day.
4. She needs a new pen.
5. They like their teacher.
6. Lucille wants to go now.
7. Harry owes John a lot.
8. Peter eats too much.
9. Sally cooks for her husband.
10. I speak too fast.
11. That shop sells books.
12. Don often borrows money.
13. Sally saves her money.
14. Harry drinks too much.
15. Bob speaks Russian.
16. Mary wants to hire a car.
17. John always arrives late.
18. Jim gets up after John.
19. Joe pays all his bills.

20. I always arrive early.
21. She travels a lot by air.
22. They go to the best shops.
23. Jim lends Bob his car.
24. John borrows money from Bob.
25. Sally spends a lot.
26. They often write home.
27. Helen uses a tape-recorder.
28. Robert wears pyjamas.
29. You understand the word.
30. They have a bath every day.

---

34 The Simple Present   E

To practise forming questions, respond as shown:

I don't want to go.	**Don't you want to go?**
	No, I don't.
Mary doesn't like David.	**Doesn't Mary like David?**
	No, she doesn't.
You don't know the answer.	**Don't I know the answer?**
	No, you don't.

1. They don't know this town.
2. He doesn't pay attention.
3. Mary doesn't wake up early.
4. I don't want to see that film.
5. She doesn't speak English.
6. He doesn't smoke.
7. John doesn't sleep well.
8. I don't know Peter.
9. Sally doesn't need any help.
10. She doesn't eat very much.
11. I don't speak Russian.
12. They don't want that book.
13. He doesn't like his car.
14. I don't understand.
15. She doesn't arrive late.

16. I don't want a drink now.
17. He doesn't want anything.
18. We don't have a lot of rain.
19. Mary doesn't like flying.
20. I don't want to stop.

---

35 The Simple Present EI

To contrast the affirmative and the negative, respond as shown:

Do you know Helen and Susan?
I know Helen, but I don't know Susan.

Do they play tennis on Fridays and Saturdays?
They play tennis on Fridays, but they don't play on Saturdays.

Does Ken listen to Bach and Beethoven?
He listens to Bach, but he doesn't listen to Beethoven.

1. Do you know Mary and Jane?
2. Does Paul see Sally and Alice?
3. Do you use a car and a bicycle?
4. Does John have lunch and dinner?
5. Does Betty love Gordon and Peter?
6. Does David own a house and a flat?
7. Does Harry speak French and Spanish?
8. Does Philip travel by air and by sea?
9. Does Henry smoke cigarettes and a pipe?
10. Do John and Mary visit Madrid and London?
11. Do you read newspapers and comics?
12. Does Bill have holidays at home and abroad?
13. Does Peter go to the cinema and the theatre?
14. Does Jim do business in New York and Toronto?
15. Do Mr and Mrs Jones need a TV set and a radio?
16. Do you keep books in your room and in your suitcase?
17. Do they watch TV at the hotel and at Bob's house?
18. Does Elizabeth own a tape-recorder and a record-player?
19. Does Barry have classes on weekdays and at the weekends?
20. Do you listen to the radio in the evening and in the afternoon?

THE SIMPLE PAST

Introduction

The simple past tense is used to indicate past actions or states. Past time adverbials often accompany this tense.

> EXAMPLES:
>
> Peter *saw* the film *last night*.
>
> I *came* to this country *three weeks ago*.
>
> Steve *was* here *for a month last year*.
>
> The two men *were promoted in July*.
>
> Mary *stayed* in Canada *during the summer*.
>
> Harry *got up when Sally came in*.
>
> I *set* the table *while Anne got (was getting) the meal ready*.
>
> I *drank* all the milk in one gulp.

The exercises to follow concentrate on the verb, and simple contexts are presented. More intensive work with adverbials will be found in Exs. 194–197.

The Simple Past Tense

Regular Verbs

STATEMENT			QUESTION		
I	work**ed** well		**Did** I	work well	
You	stud**ied**		**Did** you	study	
He	want**ed** a drink	yesterday.	**Did** he	want a drink	yesterday?
She	us**ed** the car		**Did** she	use the car	
It	rain**ed**		**Did** it	rain	
We	need**ed** John		**Did** we	need John	
They	play**ed** tennis		**Did** they	play tennis	

Note:
Regular verbs fall into three groups:

(a) Past form adds the sound /d/:	(b) Past form adds the sound /t/:	(c) Past form adds the sound /id/:
arrived	washed	needed
married	looked	wanted
ordered	danced	wasted
rubbed	stopped	fitted

(a) *To practise the regular verbs in statements. Pronounce the past form distinctly.*

I use a pen.	**I used a pen.**
I cook dinner.	**I cooked dinner.**
I wait for John.	**I waited for John.**

1. I look at Mary.
2. I smoke.
3. I need a stamp.
4. I expect to go.
5. I dance well.
6. I start the car.
7. I stop going.
8. I walk to work.
9. I watch TV.
10. I work at home.
11. I like the film.
12. I ask questions.
13. I help myself.
14. I finish my work.
15. I reach the end.
16. I prefer to stay.
17. I receive a card.
18. I thank him.
19. I remember her.
20. I touch her hand.
21. I wash my face.
22. I try to open it.
23. I lock the door.
24. I answer the card.
25. I notice her.
26. I intend to go.
27. I clean the room.
28. I enjoy coming.
29. I follow Susan.
30. I trust Henry.
31. I turn on the tap.
32. I relax after work.
33. I stay at the hotel.
34. I measure the windows.
35. I call at his house.
36. I post the letters.
37. I repeat the word.
38. I love Marion.
39. I move to London.
40. I visit Betty.
41. I advise David.
42. I doubt her honesty.
43. I join the club.
44. I wish to see John.
45. I want to be early.

(b) *Further practice with the regular verbs. Ask questions and give the answers as shown:*

I use a pen.	STUDENT A: **Did you use a pen?**
	STUDENT B: **Yes, I used a pen.**
I cook dinner.	STUDENT C: **Did you cook dinner?**
	STUDENT D: **Yes, I cooked dinner.**
I wait for John.	STUDENT E: **Did you wait for John?**
	STUDENT F: **Yes, I waited for John.**

(Continue with Nos. 1 to 45 in (a) above.)

33

The Simple Past Tense
Irregular Verbs

STATEMENT				QUESTION			
I	**spoke**	to her		**Did** I	**speak**	to her	
You	**wrote**	a letter		**Did** you	**write**	a letter	
He	**went**	away		**Did** he	**go**	away	
She	**had**	a cold	yesterday.	**Did** she	**have**	a cold	yesterday?
It	**ate**	the food		**Did** it	**eat**	the food	
We	**saw**	the film		**Did** we	**see**	the film	
They	**did**	the work		**Did** they	**do**	the work	

37 ELEMENTARY

(a) *To practise the irregular verbs in statements.*

I do my homework.   **I did my homework.**

I have a car.   **I had a car.**

I go to New York.   **I went to New York.**

1. I see Peter.	19. I feel well.
2. I get a present.	20. I take a train.
3. I know John.	21. I keep a pet.
4. I speak to Mary.	22. I shake hands.
5. I read the book.	23. I leave early.
6. I write a letter.	24. I stand up.
7. I put on my coat.	25. I meet Mary.
8. I eat at 1 p.m.	26. I wear a suit.
9. I begin at 9 a.m.	27. I sleep well.
10. I swim in the sea.	28. I hold a party.
11. I run for the bus.	29. I tear my coat.
12. I forget his name.	30. I sit down.
13. I give her a pen.	31. I say "Hello."
14. I bring my books.	32. I choose a gift.
15. I buy some shoes.	33. I lend her a pen.
16. I catch a cold.	34. I find the money.
17. I teach Susan.	35. I spend a lot.
18. I sell my car.	36. I let the cat go.

34

37. I lose my watch.
38. I think about her.
39. I tell her to come.
40. I learn the words.
41. I understand him.

42. I send a letter.
43. I break a window.
44. I build a wall.
45. I throw it away.

(b) *Further practice with the irregular verbs. Ask questions and give answers as shown:*

I do my homework. STUDENT A: **Did you do your home-work?**

STUDENT B: **Yes, I did my homework.**

I have a car. STUDENT C: **Did you have a car?**

STUDENT D: **Yes, I had a car.**

I go to New York. STUDENT E: **Did you go to New York?**

STUDENT F: **Yes, I went to New York.**

Continue with Nos. 1 *to* 45 *in* (a) *above.*

---

38 The Simple Past   EI

To practise the question form, ask about Mary:

John went to Panama.
STUDENT A: **Did Mary go to Panama?**
STUDENT B: **Yes, she did.**

John arrived on Monday.
STUDENT C: **Did Mary arrive on Monday?**
STUDENT D: **Yes, she did.**

John saw Paul in London.
STUDENT E: **Did Mary see Paul in London?**
STUDENT F: **Yes, she did.**

1. John had a cigarette.
2. John looked at George.
3. John came to class late.
4. John went dancing last night.
5. John got a present from Sandra.
6. John wrote a letter before class.
7. John knew Jim before he came here.
8. John forgot to ask the man his name.

9. John put on a coat before going out.
10. John spoke to Anne in the TV room.
11. John had dinner very late last night.
12. John read the letter before breakfast.
13. John took a business management course.
14. John ran down the road to catch the bus.
15. John made a lot of unnecessary mistakes.
16. John gave Jim some help with his homework.
17. John learnt some English before coming here.
18. John bought something for his flat yesterday.
19. John caught a cold after swimming in the sea.
20. John remembered to bring his books yesterday.

---

39 The Simple Past EI

To contrast present and past, respond as shown:

Sally's always catching colds. (last week)
   STUDENT A: **Did she catch a cold last week?**
   STUDENT B: **Yes, she did.**

I write some letters every day. (yesterday)
   STUDENT C: **Did you write any letters yesterday?**
   STUDENT D: **Yes, I did.**

1. Jane teaches English. (last year)
2. I know John. (before he came here)
3. Peter often sees Mary. (last night)
4. Mary uses the phone. (a minute ago)
5. Joe has a cup of tea. (this morning)
6. John finishes work early. (yesterday)
7. Anne often calls on Susan. (last week)
8. Peter usually sleeps well. (last night)
9. I usually leave before Bob. (last Friday)
10. Sally feels all right. (yesterday)
11. Betty has a nap before dinner. (yesterday)
12. That firm sells thirty cars a week. (last week)
13. Bob lends Jim some money every week. (last week)
14. Michael often looks in his dictionary. (just now)
15. Mary rings us up when she wants to talk. (yesterday)
16. Sue cleans the rooms every morning. (yesterday morning)

17. Paul often comes at 9 o'clock. (the day before yesterday)
18. Mr White lets Helen stay out late every night. (last night)
19. I usually stay at the best hotels. (last time you went abroad)
20. I pay my bills at the end of the month. (the end of last month)

---

40 The Simple Past   I

To practise irregular verbs, give affirmative answers to the following questions:

Did you understand him? (speak)
Yes. He spoke English.

Did John have a birthday recently? (get)
Yes. He got some nice presents.

Did you go to the cinema last night? (see)
Yes. I saw a very good film.

1. Did Mary feel cold? (put on)
2. Did Bob work too quickly? (make)
3. Did you visit the bookstall? (buy)
4. Did Peter embarrass Susan? (forget)
5. Did John go to the restaurant? (have)
6. Did you nearly miss the bus? (run)
7. Did Jim speak to John yesterday? (say)
8. Did Paul visit a bar last night? (drink)
9. Did Richard get rid of his old car? (sell)
10. Did Elizabeth have a restful night? (sleep)
11. Did Gordon give his friend the news? (write)
12. Did John meet the managing director? (speak)
13. Did Mary do any work in the train? (read)
14. Did David go out without a jacket on? (catch)
15. Did Paul understand the homework all right? (do)
16. Did Philip dress properly for the wedding? (wear)
17. Did Patrick have an accident while skiing? (break)
18. Did Marion do a lot of shopping yesterday? (spend)
19. Did Sally put on a lot of weight last year? (become)
20. Did Peter remember that it was Anne's birthday? (give)

The Simple Past

Negative

41 ELEMENTARY/INTERMEDIATE

NEGATIVE STATEMENT			QUESTION		
I	**didn't** buy it		**Didn't** I	buy it	
You	**didn't** work		**Didn't** you	work	
He	**didn't** stay long		**Didn't** he	stay long	
She	**didn't** know that	yesterday.	**Didn't** she	know that	yesterday?
It	**didn't** bite you		**Didn't** it	bite you	
We	**didn't** go		**Didn't** we	go	
They	**didn't** come		**Didn't** they	come	

Note:
  Didn't = did not.
  /'didnt/

To practise the negative form, use the word(s) in brackets to form a negative statement.

Bill and Bob took some cake. (bread)
They didn't take any bread.

George went into the bedroom. (lounge)
He didn't go into the lounge.

Peter saw Jim outside the cinema. (chemist's)
He didn't see him outside the chemist's.

1. I sat on the chair. (sofa)
2. Peter found his wallet. (money)
3. Jill broke her watch. (necklace)
4. Jim wanted to see the zoo. (park)
5. Philip chose a Ferrari. (Cadillac)
6. Peter repeated the word. (sentence)
7. Mr Smith loved his secretary. (wife)
8. Alice sent Paul a postcard. (letter)
9. Jack visited Betty last night. (Mary)
10. I advised Bob to buy a car. (scooter)
11. John stood up when Mary came in. (Sue)

12. The men built a hotel. (block of flats)
13. John asked Peter a question. (for help)
14. The girls enjoyed the party. (ride home)
15. The dog followed Jim into the shop. (bank)
16. John wore a suit to the concert. (the dance)
17. Sally lost her glasses at the theatre. (ring)
18. I told Tom to remain a bachelor. (get married)
19. Paul understood the first question. (the second)
20. Dick waited for me outside my room. (in the hall)

---

42 The Simple Past   I

Asking questions with didn't.

John didn't see Mary last night. (not at the party)
   Didn't he?
   No, he didn't.
   Why didn't he see her?
   Because she wasn't at the party.

I didn't pay the bill. (incorrect)
   Didn't you?
   No, I didn't.
   Why didn't you pay it?
   Because it was incorrect.

1. I didn't go swimming yesterday. (cold)
2. Richard didn't enjoy his steak. (tough)
3. John didn't do any work yesterday. (tired)
4. Jim didn't get any sleep last night. (noisy)
5. Bob didn't feel well yesterday. (have a cold)
6. Paul didn't lend Tom his car. (use it himself)
7. Harry didn't drink any of the wine. (too sweet)
8. Peter's first wife didn't love him. (no presents)
9. Gordon didn't telephone Susan yesterday. (forget)
10. Jim didn't play golf yesterday. (weather uncertain)
11. Don didn't do his homework last night. (feel lazy)
12. David didn't watch TV last night. (nothing good on)
13. Mary didn't ask anybody the way when she got lost (shy)
14. Peter didn't go to New York last week. (have to be here)
15. Mary didn't say anything when John spoke to her.
    (angry)

16. Lucy didn't pay attention in class. (not like the teacher)
17. I didn't get to the station early enough. (car break down)
18. Tom didn't find the play very interesting. (not understand)
19. Helen didn't write any letters last night. (want to watch TV)
20. David didn't want Bill to see Lucy any more. (see her himself)

---

43 The Simple Past   I

Practise with 'What did—do?' *Respond as shown:*

Paul—last night (cinema)
  STUDENT A: **What did Paul do last night?**
  STUDENT B: **He went to the cinema.**

you—last night
  STUDENT A: **What did you do last night?**
  STUDENT B: **I visited some friends.**

1. Bob—last night (bar)
2. you—last night
3. Mary—on the beach (sunbathe)
4. you—on the beach
5. Tom—at the station (ticket)
6. you—at the station
7. Jim—at the office (work)
8. you—at the office
9. Susan—after tea (bath)
10. you—after tea
11. Joe—last Friday (go racing)
12. you—last Friday
13. John—at the club (dinner)
14. you—at the club
15. Anne—during the lesson (sleep)
16. you—during the lesson
17. John—last Saturday (tennis)
18. you—last Saturday
19. Mary—at the party (talk)
20. you—at the party

THE PRESENT PERFECT

Introductory notes:

The present perfect tense is used:

(i) to refer to a completely past action or state where no indication is given as to the time it occurred.

> EXAMPLES:
> I *have been* to Canada.
>> (Cf. I was in Canada two years ago.)
>
> John *has visited* the United States.
>> (Cf. John visited the United States in 1971.)

(ii) to indicate an action or state, beginning in the past, which is not completed at the time of speaking.

> EXAMPLES:
> I *have used* that car for years. (I still use it.)
>
> Tom *has been* ill since Monday. (He's still ill.)

(iii) to refer to the present or future result of a past action or experience.

> EXAMPLES:
> Tom *has been* ill. He can't play football today.
>
> My car *has broken down*. I shall have to walk.

The interest here is more in the result than in the reason.

(iv) with certain adverbials which add 'time' information.

> EXAMPLES:
> John has not been to Scotland *before*.
>
> Richard has *just* sold his car.

Compare the following two sentences:

(a) Have you been to Mexico?
(b) Have you been to the shops?

In (a) the listener must decide if the speaker means 'in your life' (Have you *ever* been to Mexico?). In (b) the speaker is interested in a very recent action.

Cf. { Paul has *gone* to Miami. (He's not here now.)
{ Paul has *been* to Miami. (in his life)

I	**have(n't) sold** my car.
You	**have(n't) seen** the film.
He	**has(n't) gone** to Bolivia.

She **has(n't)** **done** her work.
It **has(n't)** **been** cold.
We **have(n't)** **had** breakfast.
They **have(n't)** **read** the book.

---

44 The Present Perfect   E

(a) *To practise the present perfect with* ever, *respond as shown:*

write a book
    STUDENT A: **Have you ever written a book?**
    STUDENT B: **Yes, I have.**   or: **No. I haven't.**

work in a bank
    STUDENT C: **Have you ever worked in a bank?**
    STUDENT D: **Yes, I have.**   or: **No. I haven't.**

go to Miami
    STUDENT E: **Have you ever been to Miami?**
    STUDENT F: **Yes, I have.**   or: **No. I haven't.**

1. go to Trinidad
2. ride a horse
3. drink Vodka
4. play golf
5. go to New York
6. visit Ireland
7. do any cooking
8. have a pet
9. go to Canada
10. be in the army
11. do any skiing
12. use a computer
13. go to China
14. have a bad cold
15. sail a boat
16. drive a racing car
17. be in a TV studio
18. hear the opera 'Carmen'
19. have any driving lessons
20. be married
21. see a painting by Picasso
22. spend a holiday in Bermuda

42

23. attend a political meeting
24. read any of Shakespeare's plays

(b) *To practise forming complete statements, respond as shown :*

write a book
    STUDENT A : **I've written a book.**
    STUDENT B : **Have you?**
    STUDENT A : **Yes, I have.**

work in a bank
    STUDENT C : **I've never worked in a bank.**
    STUDENT D : **Haven't you?**
    STUDENT C : **No, I haven't.**
Continue with 1–24 of Ex. 44*a.*

---

45 The Present Perfect EI

To practise the present perfect with before, *respond as shown :*

Shall we go to the market? (be)
No. I've been there before.
or **Yes. I've never been there before.**

Would you like to see that film? (see)
No. I've seen it before.
or **Yes. I haven't seen it before.**

  1. Shall we go to the museum? (be)
  2. Shall we do this exercise? (do)
  3. Shall we try this restaurant? (be)
  4. Shall we go to the next town? (be)
  5. Shall we visit the art gallery? (be)
  6. Do you want to hear that record? (hear)
  7. Shall we stay at the Harbour Hotel? (stay)
  8. Would you like to try this fruit? (try)
  9. Do you want to climb the hill today? (do)
10. Would you like to borrow this book? (read)
11. Do you want to go on the pleasure boat? (be)
12. Would you like to see this Ibsen play? (see)
13. Would you like one of those ice-creams? (have)
14. Would you like to hear Tom play the guitar? (hear)
15. Would you like to try one of these cigarettes? (have)

Use ever *in your questions, and emphasise the* have/has *in your answers:*

Bob—Argentina (Chile)
   STUDENT A: **Has Bob ever been to Argentina?**
   STUDENT B: **No, he hasn't, but he** *has* **been to Chile.**

they—Spanish food (Italian)
   STUDENT C: **Have they ever had Spanish food?**
   STUDENT D: **No, they haven't, but they** *have* **had Italian food.**

John—football (tennis)
   STUDENT E: **Has John ever played football?**
   STUDENT F: **No, he hasn't, but he** *has* **played tennis.**

1. Bill—Paris (Rome)
2. James—Turin (Milan)
3. Peter—Picasso (Dali)
4. Sally—Shakespeare (Ibsen)
5. Jill—Italian food (French)
6. Alice—tennis (table-tennis)
7. Susan—the museum (art gallery)
8. Anne and Helen—Germany (Holland)
9. Gordon—music by Beethoven (Bach)
10. Henry—the United States (Canada)
11. Mrs Thomas—John (John's brother)
12. Helen—holiday in Germany (Austria)
13. Mr and Mrs Smith—Madrid (Barcelona)
14. Harry and Helen—Chinese food (Indian)
15. Pat—a bad accident (a slight accident)

Compare these two questions:

Have you **read** a newspaper **today?**
Did you **read** a newspaper **yesterday?**

To contrast have . . . *and* did . . . *as shown above. Ask two questions.*

been for a walk
    STUDENT A: **Have you been for a walk today?**
    STUDENT B: **Yes, I have.**   or: **No, I haven't.**
    STUDENT A: **Did you go for a walk yesterday?**
    STUDENT B: **Yes, I did.**   or: **No, I didn't.**

done any work
    STUDENT C: **Have you done any work today?**
    STUDENT D: **Yes, I have.**   or: **No, I haven't.**
    STUDENT C: **Did you do any work yesterday?**
    STUDENT D: **Yes, I did.**   or: **No, I didn't.**

1. written any letters
2. done any reading
3. learnt anything
4. bought anything
5. been out of the house
6. watched TV
7. done any driving
8. had any cigarettes
9. been swimming
10. seen a newspaper
11. been for a walk
12. spoken any English

Yet and **Already**

---

48 The Present Perfect   I

Have you been to London **yet**?
No, I haven't been to London **yet**.
or: Yes, I have **already** been to London.

Note:
Yet is used with negatives and questions in this pattern. You will sometimes find **yet** placed before the main verb (*I haven't* yet *been to London*).

To practise yet *and* already, *respond as shown:*

Have you been to New York? (Miami)
No, I haven't been to New York yet, but I've already been to Miami.

Has Peter done his essay? (précis)
No, he hasn't done his essay yet, but he's already done his précis.

Has Susan learnt how to use a computer? (adding-machine)
No, she hasn't learnt how to use a computer yet, but she's already learnt how to use an adding-machine.

1. Has John told Sheila? (Sally)
2. Have they read the book? (play)
3. Has David spoken to Steve? (Helen)
4. Has Jim been to Scotland? (Ireland)
5. Has Sally telephoned Harry? (David)
6. Has Susan done the shopping? (hair)
7. Has John polished his car? (wash)
8. Have Bob and Anne met John? (Richard)
9. Have they bought the records? (tapes)
10. Has John had a letter from Mary? (Sue)
11. Has Mary driven John's car? (Sheila's)
12. Has Peter visited Hong Kong? (Singapore)
13. Have Jim and Sally seen Mr Smith? (Paul)
14. Has Bob been to the local cinema? (theatre)
15. Has Mary worn her new skirt? (dress)

Recently

---

49 The Present Perfect   I

Have you sold any pictures **recently**?
No, I haven't sold any **recently**.

When was the last time you sold any?
I sold some **two months ago**.

Notes:
(i) **Recently** may be used with tenses other than the present perfect.

EXAMPLES:
Bob came back from New York very **recently**.

He said he had **recently** been to Australia.

(ii) **Recently** may be replaced by **lately**.

To practise **recently,** *respond as shown:*

Has Bob watched any TV plays recently? (10 days)
No, he hasn't watched any recently.

When was the last time he watched one?
He watched one ten days ago.

Have the fishermen caught anything recently? (an hour)
No, they haven't caught anything recently.

When was the last time they caught anything?
They caught something an hour ago.

1. Has Jim read a newspaper recently? (a week)
2. Has Sue done any shopping recently? (5 days)
3. Has Philip bought anything recently? (3 days)
4. Have the men had a holiday recently? (a year)
5. Has Bob read any good books recently? (a month)
6. Has Betty telephoned anybody recently? (4 days)
7. Has anybody telephoned Betty recently? (2 weeks)
8. Has Mary been to the theatre recently? (3 weeks)
9. Has anybody given Paul any help recently? (a week)
10. Has David spoken to the manager recently? (a month)
11. Has Bob taken Jill to the cinema recently? (2 months)
12. Have the other students been out recently? (a week)
13. Has David given anybody a present recently? (2 years)
14. Has Richard been out to dinner recently? (6 months)
15. Has Elizabeth been to any parties recently? (3 months)
16. Have the men asked for more money recently? (3 years)
17. Has Bob's car given him any trouble recently? (a month)
18. Has Jim been to the hairdresser's recently? (a long time)
19. Have the other students done any work recently? (a week)
20. Has Jim given anybody a lift in his car recently? (2 weeks)

Just

50 ELEMENTARY/INTERMEDIATE

What has Peter **just** done?
He has **just** opened the window.
(He opened the window **just** now.)

To practise **just** *with the present perfect tense.*

47

you—begin the exercise
> STUDENT A: **What have you just done?**
> STUDENT B: **We've just begun the exercise.**

Peter—light a cigarette
> STUDENT C: **What has Peter just done?**
> STUDENT D: **He's just lit a cigarette.**

Sally—post the letters
> STUDENT E: **What has Sally just done?**
> STUDENT F: **She's just posted the letters.**

1. Mary—wake up
2. the ship—sail
3. Anne—meet Lucy
4. Mr Smith—get up
5. Bob—ring John up
6. the pilot—take off
7. Harry—borrow a pen
8. Susan—say goodbye
9. Mary—get into a taxi
10. you—look at Number 9
11. Bill—put on his coat
12. John—buy a newspaper
13. John—have a cup of tea
14. Jim—shake hands with Bob
15. the passengers—embark
16. the chairman—speak
17. Mrs Harvey—lay the table
18. Susan—bring back my books
19. the secretary—type a letter
20. the guide—close the museum
21. the children—hide from Jane
22. Betty—put out her cigarette
23. Mary—tear up John's letters
24. the teacher—give a dictation
25. the postman—deliver a parcel
26. the cricketer—hit the ball
27. Jimmy—get rid of his old car
28. the doctor—feel John's pulse
29. the student—finish the novel
30. the judge—take away Sheila's driving licence

The present perfect continuous tense is used to indicate an action or state that extends from the past to the present moment, is still in progress, and may also continue into the future.

EXAMPLES:

Tom *has been thinking* about Mary all day. (and is still thinking about her)

Sally *has been waiting* for a letter from John. (and is still waiting)

I *have been hearing* a lot about John during the past few weeks.

Peter *has been drinking* heavily all evening.
   (Cf. Peter has drunk ten whiskies this evening.)

The continuous action need not be in progress now:

Joe has been working all morning and *now he's having lunch*.

I have been swimming all day and *now I'm tired*. (I'm no longer swimming.)

Two common adverbials of time used with this tense are **since** . . . and **for** . . .

I   **have been** learning English   **for**   a number of years.
She **has** **been**   living in London **for**   several months.

I   **have been** learning English   **since** 1969.
She **has** **been**   living in London **since** March.

Note:

The word **for** in this pattern introduces a statement of **length of time**. The word **since** introduces a statement of **the time of commencement** of the action.

(a) *To practise the present perfect continuous. Choose between* since *and* for.

John is learning English. (2 years)
   STUDENT A: **How long has he been learning English?**
   STUDENT B: **He's been learning it for two years.**

Bob works in Washington. (1967)
   STUDENT C: **How long has he been working in Washington?**
   STUDENT D: **He's been working there since 1967.**

1. Jim comes to class. (2 weeks)
2. Jane wears glasses. (15 years)
3. I'm reading that book. (a week)
4. John takes Betty out. (Christmas)
5. Gordon's lying in bed. (breakfast)
6. Barbara's studying English. (1 year)
7. Harry works in New York. (last March)
8. Paul's playing table-tennis. (an hour)
9. Harry's speaking to Joan. (she came in)
10. David's reading his paper. (ten minutes)
11. Peter's swimming in the pool. (it opened)
12. Jean's waiting for Philip. (half an hour)
13. Richard's staying at that hotel. (10 days)
14. Gordon's walking in the garden. (9 o'clock)
15. Ian plays football professionally. (6 months)
16. Tom's thinking of getting married. (he met Sue)
17. Philip's studying. (the beginning of the year)
18. George lives in Barcelona. (the last ten years)
19. Tom's buying clothes now. (a quarter of an hour)
20. Bob's attending the conference. (the last 3 days)

(b) *Further practice with* since *and* for.

Mary's been waiting here since it began to rain.
Then she's been waiting here for ten minutes. (It began to rain ten minutes ago.)

I haven't seen John for three days.
Then you haven't seen him since Friday. (It's now Monday.)

Jim's been studying economics for six months.
Then he's been studying it since January. (It's now June.)

1. Robert's been out sailing since 7 a.m.
2. Sally's been working hard for a fortnight.
3. I haven't seen a good film for three months.
4. I haven't had any letters since last Saturday.
5. Jim hasn't played golf since this course began.
6. Mary's been smoking continuously since breakfast.
7. Susan hasn't attended a meeting for fifteen years.
8. John's been wearing the same suit for ten days now.
9. That car's been standing there since last Wednesday.
10. They've been coming here since the first of the month.
11. Jane hasn't spoken to any of her friends for four days.

50

12. Paul hasn't stopped talking since he got up at 8.30 a.m.
13. Bob's been staying at Mary's house for the last six days.
14. George hasn't done any homework since he joined the group.
15. Paul hasn't heard from his family since he arrived on the tenth of last month.

---

52 The Present Perfect   I

To contrast the past tense and the present perfect tense + since.

Did John see Susan last week?
Yes. He saw Susan last week, but he hasn't seen her since.

Did Peter go to Scotland five years ago?
Yes. He went to Scotland five years ago, but he hasn't been there since.

Did David do any reading the night before last?
Yes. He did some reading the night before last, but he hasn't done any since.

1. Did John do any flying last year?
2. Did Alice read a novel last month?
3. Did Sally go skiing two years ago?
4. Did Robert come to class last week?
5. Did Bill have a cold two months ago?
6. Did Henry go to any dances last year?
7. Did Jim see a good film six weeks ago?
8. Did the car go well when you bought it?
9. Did Harry take any exams three years ago?
10. Did Peter buy a new car when he got married?
11. Did Jim forget Anne's birthday five years ago?
12. Did George do any work when he first came here?
13. Did Gordon have Italian food when he was in Rome?
14. Did Peter have an accident in his car last month?
15. Did Bob go to the night-club when it first opened?
16. Did John want to marry Mary when he first met her?
17. Did David give his wife a present three months ago?
18. Did Elizabeth use her car when she did her shopping?
19. Did Paul turn up late for work the week before last?
20. Did Steve make a lot of mistakes in his English when he started learning?

THE PAST PERFECT

Introductory notes:

(i) The past perfect is a 'before past' tense, i.e. it is used to indicate an action that was completed before another action occurred.

> EXAMPLES:
>
> Bob studied English after he *had learnt* French.
>
> Sue bought a car after she *had passed* her test.

(ii) As the past equivalent of the present perfect tense it may also be used for an action continuing at the past time referred to.

> EXAMPLE:
>
> They *had lived* next door for five years when they first spoke to us.

(iii) The past perfect is often found in reported speech.

> EXAMPLES:
>
> Tom said he *had telephoned* John.
>
> Mary told me that she *hadn't been* there before.

(iv) Other conjunctions may be used.

> EXAMPLES:
>
> John went into the army *as soon as* he had finished his studies.
>
> Mary got married again *when* she hadn't heard from her husband for seven years.

See Ex. 55b for practice with 'time' conjunctions.

(v) The importance of the correct use of tenses can be seen when comparing the following sentences:

> When I arrived, the family *had* (already) *sat* down to lunch.
> When I arrived, the family *sat* down to lunch.

In the first sentence, the family were on their chairs when I arrived. In the second, the family waited for me to arrive before sitting down.

Cf. { John asked me why I *had come* so early.
{ John asked me why I *came* so early.

In the first sentence, I came early on that particular occasion. In the second, I had the habit of coming early.

The boys came after they **had** **had** a cup of tea.
Joe didn't go until he **had** **spoken** to Tom.

Elizabeth knew that John **hadn't seen** the film.
On learning that she **hadn't passed** the exam, Jane burst into tears.

53 ELEMENTARY/INTERMEDIATE

Use the past perfect tense to rephrase the following, as shown:

Bob had a cup of tea and then started work.
After Bob had had a cup of tea he started work.

John finished his English course and then went home.
After John had finished his English course he went home.

I looked up Mary's phone number and then rang her up.
After you'd looked up Mary's phone number you rang her up.

1. Elizabeth got up and then got dressed.
2. Jill typed the letter and then posted it.
3. Peter tried out the car and then bought it.
4. Sally saw the mistake and then rubbed it out.
5. Jim visited Rome and then decided to live there.
6. Susan made breakfast and then sat down to eat it.
7. I heard the news and then knew what was going on.
8. I turned on the TV and then pulled the curtains.
9. John saw the film and then told Peter all about it.
10. Sally packed her suitcases and then rang for a taxi.
11. Bob read the book and was then able to speak about it.
12. Paul had a coffee and then went back to the classroom.
13. I parked the car and then noticed the 'no parking' sign.
14. The businessman had lunch and then left for the airport.
15. Sue washed the dishes and then cleaned the kitchen floor.
16. Harry got into the car and then opened the door for Susan.
17. Mary lit the fires and then relaxed in a comfortable chair.
18. We got to the station and then found out the train was late.
19. John broke the window and then had to pay for it to be mended.
20. Mary had an accident in the car and then decided to keep quiet about it.

This tense may be used to indicate that the 'before past' action was in progress prior to the time stated or implied.

EXAMPLES:
When I went to the room, I could see that someone *had been lying* on the bed.
  (Cf. I could see that someone *was lying* . . .)

Bob noticed that Mary *had been crying*.
  (she was no longer crying when he saw her)

The action may still have been in progress.

EXAMPLES:
I knew that George *had been having* trouble with his car. (and was still having trouble with it)

When Sally finally left her house, Paul *had* already *been waiting* outside the cinema for an hour. (he still had to wait a further 20 minutes before she arrived)

We could see that John	**had**	**been running.**
I felt tired because I	**had**	**been working** hard.
Rosemary said that she	**hadn't been sleeping** well.	
Sally told me that she	**hadn't been living** at home.	

(a) *To practise the past perfect continuous in reported speech, respond as shown:*

the shopkeeper say—have his premises redecorated
  STUDENT A: **What did the shopkeeper say?**
  STUDENT B: **He said (that) he'd been having his premises redecorated.**

the doctor tell you—examine a patient
  STUDENT C: **What did the doctor tell you?**
  STUDENT D: **He told me (that) he'd been examining a patient.**

  1. the chef say—get the meal ready
  2. the salesman say—call on retailers
  3. the swimmer tell you—get warmed up
  4. the electrician say—replace a fuse

5. the chairman say—consider my promotion
6. the mechanic tell you—repair the brakes
7. the director say—attend a Board meeting
8. the housewife tell you—do the washing-up
9. the architect tell you—plan the new factory
10. the children say—play with the boy next door
11. the pilot say—bring the aeroplane in to land
12. the student say—have extra lessons every week
13. the hotelier say—expect the guests to stay on
14. the designer tell you—choose the right pattern
15. the driver tell you—wait for the lights to change
16. the publisher say—have an argument with the author
17. the buyer tell you—have trouble choosing products
18. the teacher say—prepare the lessons for the next day
19. the author tell you—think about the title for his book
20. the air-hostess say—prepare the passengers for take-off

(b) *Further practice with the past perfect continuous. This is a substitution exercise.*

Tom knew that Bob had been resting.

	Tom knew that Bob had been resting.
I	**I knew that Bob had been resting.**
found out	**I found out that Bob had been resting.**
slacking	**I found out that Bob had been slacking.**
that Tom	**I found out that Tom had been slacking.**

1. was told
2. driving
3. we were told
4. swimming
5. I could see
6. working hard
7. someone told me
8. us
9. had not
10. using the language lab
11. that Mary
12. Susan said
13. paying attention
14. I knew that
15. had been
16. waiting for John
17. that Helen
18. found out
19. seeing
20. staying in London
21. had not
22. lying to me
23. I was glad to know
24. going to parties
25. sorry to hear
26. feeling well
27. we knew
28. sleeping
29. had been
30. staying up late

To practise and contrast affirmative and negative, respond as shown:

skirt/blouse
What did Mary say about the skirt and the blouse?
She said she'd bought the skirt, but hadn't bought the blouse.

Peter/Jim
What did John say about Peter and Jim?
He said he'd been in touch with Peter, but hadn't been able to contact Jim.

New York/Chicago
What did the tourists say about New York and Chicago?
They said they'd liked New York, but hadn't had a very good time in Chicago.

1. tennis/golf
2. letters/homework
3. cinema/theatre
4. Peter/Paul
5. book/play
6. jacket/trousers
7. breakfast/lunch
8. Scotland/Ireland
9. hospital/operation
10. bed/sleep
11. fire/lights
12. Sally/Susan
13. sauna/shower
14. food/wine
15. bank/office
16. house/flat
17. car/motorbike
18. cigar/pipe
19. dentist/teeth
20. ring/watch
21. suitcase/trunk
22. reservation/ticket
23. instructions/machine
24. holiday/weather
25. Italy/Spain
26. language/literature
27. museum/art gallery
28. ship/hovercraft
29. beds/washing-up
30. waste-paper basket/ dustbin

55b The Past Perfect   A

To practise the past perfect tense with adverbials of time introduced by a variety of conjunctions and prepositions. Decide how the following should be made into complete sentences. You may need to rearrange the order of ideas, and you may need to use the inversion pattern shown and practised in Ex. 193.

The race started. My horse threw its jockey. (hardly)

Hardly had the race started when my horse threw its jockey.

or **The race had hardly started when my horse threw its jockey.**

Henry spent the money. He borrowed some more from Tom. (once)

Once Henry had spent the money, he borrowed some more from Tom.

Mary went to Ireland. John found out. He followed her there. (on)

On finding out that Mary had gone to Ireland, John followed her there.

1. The phone rang twice. Sally answered it. (not until)
2. The decision was taken. There was no going back. (once)
3. Tom took the money. Bob came home. He found out. (only after)
4. Joe left the oven door open. Sue saw it. She was angry. (when)
5. Anne was able to do the exercise. The teacher explained it to her. (when)
6. Helen could take down shorthand. She went to a secretarial college. (once)
7. George prepared himself for bad news. He was told that he had won. (hardly)
8. Tom was once in prison. His manager was told about it. He dismissed him. (on)
9. Bill checked all his figures a second time. He found the error. (only after)
10. Bob made a mistake. He found out. It was too late to rectify it. (by the time)
11. Paul gave the dictionary to Mary. He got it from the next room. (as soon as)
12. Joe thought seriously about buying the house. He looked over it carefully. (not until)
13. Peter made the mess. We knew who it was. We were able to make him clean it up. (once)

14. The firm became insolvent. Jim learnt about this. He got another job without delay. (on)
15. Dick was granted a rise in salary. Tom heard about this. He put in for one himself. (no sooner)
16. Paul was once unfaithful to Mary. She found out. She told him to leave the house. (when)
17. Joe was selected for the appointment. He heard about it. He rushed home to tell Helen. (immediately)
18. Bob was chosen to represent his country. He learnt this from Peter. Bob said that the selectors had made the right decision. (on)
19. Mary saw the film herself. She complained to the cinema manager that she had never been so disgusted in her life. (only when)
20. Richard didn't do the job properly. George told him this. He took absolutely no notice of him. (when)

THE FUTURE

We may divide the future forms into two groups:
(i) those forms which express future activities or states.

> EXAMPLES:
> The election will take place soon. ⎫
> I shall* be forty in a week's time. ⎪
> There will be time to have dinner. ⎬ Simple Future
> Shall* I know the results soon? ⎪
> Paul won't be here tomorrow. ⎭
>
> I shall* be seeing you next week.—Future Continuous
>
> We shall* have finished by 4 p.m.—Future Perfect

(ii) those forms which may express certain ideas in addition to future activities or states.

EXAMPLES	special meaning
I'm going to visit Bob tomorrow.	(intention)
It's going to rain.	(probability or likelihood)
I'm visiting Bob tomorrow.	(arrangement or plan)
I leave for New York on Monday.	(part of a schedule)
You're to fill in the form as instructed.	(command)
John's to be met at the airport.	(arrangement or plan)
Jill's sure/certain to come.	(certainty)

With *will* or *shall*:

I will help you, with pleasure.	(willingness)
Shall I call a taxi for you?	(offer of service)
Will you please move your car?	(request)
I will sue you if you try to blackmail me.	(threat)
You shall have the book tomorrow.	(promise)
I won't give it to you—it's mine!	(refusal)
That will be Jim at the door.	(conjecture or likelihood)
I can and I will pass that examination.	(determination)
Won't you come in?	(invitation)

It is important to recognise when a special interpretation is being placed on *shall* or *will*. However, the contexts in which these words are found usually indicate the meanings quite clearly.

Note:
(*i) *Shall* is usual for the 1st person singular and plural; *will* is usual for 2nd and 3rd persons (but see (ii) above).

(ii) The following contractions should be noted:

will = 'll (for 1st, 2nd and 3rd persons)
will not = won't /waʊnt/
shall not = shan't /ʃɑːnt/

(iii) The strong form of *shall* is pronounced /ʃæl/; the weak (unstressed) form is pronounced /ʃl/.

---

56 ELEMENTARY

To practise and contrast shall *and* will, *respond as shown:*

Mary will be here tomorrow. How about John?
He will be here tomorrow too.

Bob will see that film tonight. What about you?
I/We shall see that film tonight too.

1. John will leave tomorrow. How about Alice?
2. Anne will fly to New York. What about Peter?
3. David will study hard tonight. What about you?
4. Mary will use her car tomorrow. What about John?
5. Sally will pay the rent on time. How about Steve?
6. Bob will watch TV this evening. What about you?
7. Paul will come to class tomorrow. What about Jim?
8. Tom will feel better after a rest. What about you?

9. Gordon will buy a new car soon. How about Richard?
10. John will have a haircut this week. What about Tom?
11. Helen will do her homework tonight. What about you?
12. I shall speak to Sheila later today. How about you?
13. Anne will have lunch early tomorrow. How about Paul?
14. John will take a taxi to the station. What about Jim?
15. I shall have my car washed tomorrow. How about Betty?

---

57 The Future   EI

To practise the 'll *contraction, respond as shown:*

Mary hasn't prepared today's lesson yet. (later)
She'll prepare it later.

George hasn't done his homework yet. (this evening)
He'll do it this evening.

You haven't seen the film on at the cinema yet. (soon)
I/We'll (go and) see it soon.

1. Helen hasn't written home yet. (tomorrow)
2. Peter hasn't called on Mary yet. (tonight)
3. Anne hasn't got up yet. (in an hour's time)
4. George hasn't sold his car yet. (next week)
5. You haven't read your newspaper yet. (later)
6. You haven't decorated your flat yet. (soon)
7. You haven't been to Scotland yet. (next year)
8. Sheila hasn't come to class yet. (next Monday)
9. Rosemary hasn't had anything to eat yet. (soon)
10. Sandra hasn't read that book yet. (this evening)
11. Barbara hasn't taken up tennis yet. (next summer)
12. Alice hasn't got any new clothes yet. (next week)
13. The girls haven't cleaned my room yet. (8 o'clock)
14. Richard hasn't shaved yet. (in half an hour's time)
15. You haven't had a rise in salary yet. (next month)
16. John hasn't started to learn English yet. (next week)
17. Sandra hasn't had a holiday yet. (in two weeks' time)
18. You haven't been to the United States yet. (next year)
19. Harry hasn't bought Sarah a present yet. (later today)
20. Peter hasn't written to his girl-friend yet. (tomorrow)

To contrast shall/shan't *and* will/won't, *respond as shown:*

Will you put the word in, or will you leave it out?
I shall put the word in; I shan't leave it out.

Will Jim get hold of a typewriter, or will he get rid of one?
Jim will get hold of a typewriter; he won't get rid of one.

1. Will the car keep going, or will it break down?
2. Will the plan come off, or will it fall through?
3. Will you ring George up, or will you call on him?
4. Will you take on the job, or will you turn it down?
5. Will John turn the TV down, or will he turn it up?
6. Will you get up at 8 a.m., or will you turn in then?
7. Will Paul put on his jacket, or will he take it off?
8. Will you pay some money in, or will you draw some out?
9. Will you get away at 9 p.m., or will you get back then?
10. Will Peter do up his room, or will he leave it as it is?
11. Will John hold on, or will he hang up? (on the telephone)
12. Will you take the books away, or will you bring them back?
13. Will Mary stay away from John, or will she go out with him?
14. Will you keep on with this exercise, or will you give it up?
15. Will Jane stay up until midnight, or will she go to bed early?
16. Will you be able to keep up with John, or will you fall behind?
17. Will Sally run after the bus, or will she wait for the next one?
18. Will you have Peter do the job, or will you get David to do it?
19. Will Mary get on the boat at Hong Kong, or will she get off there?
20. Will Harry give the kittens away, or will he let Sally keep them?
21. Will Bob get over that cold, or will he take a turn for the worse?
22. Will you have to go to the party, or will you be able to get out of it?

23. Will you have to get down to some hard work, or will you be able to take it easy?
24. Will you be able to put me up for the night, or will you have to book me into a hotel?
25. Will you try and find out what happened yourself, or will you get in touch with the police?

---

59 The Future I

To practise the present continuous used as a future. Answer the following questions in the negative, and make a contrast statement in the affirmative.

Are you having an interview tomorrow? (next week)
No, I'm not having an interview tomorrow. I'm having one next week.

Is Peter going home by sea? (air)
No, he's not going home by sea. He's going home by air.

1. Is Bill eating here this evening? (at home)
2. Is Mary going out with John tonight? (Paul)
3. Is Philip going to bed early tonight? (late)
4. Is Bob going to work by bus tomorrow? (train)
5. Is John coming to class tomorrow? (next week)
6. Are you spending the evening with Susan? (Mary)
7. Are you staying at the Royal Hotel tonight? (Ritz)
8. Are you spending the weekend in the town? (country)
9. Are they getting a new car soon? (some time next year)
10. Is Jim doing his homework this evening? (something else)
11. Are Harry and Susan going to the cinema tonight? (theatre)
12. Are you having dinner at a Chinese restaurant tonight? (here)
13. Are the others spending the evening playing cards? (watch TV)
14. Are you meeting a business acquaintance this evening? (friend)
15. Is Mary seeing the doctor tomorrow night? (the following night)

To practise the simple present used as a future. Read the following passage carefully and then answer the questions below:

Paul has made up an itinerary for his trip. He leaves Paris on Monday, arrives at London Airport in the afternoon, takes a taxi to his hotel and books in. On Tuesday he catches the 10.40 a.m. train from Waterloo Station and gets to Southampton at 12.10 p.m. He joins a coach tour of the New Forest after lunch, and in the evening attends a dinner arranged by his agent. On Wednesday he looks over the local factory, has lunch with the Mayor and then returns to London by the 3.45 p.m. train. He spends the night in London and flies back to Paris the next morning. The following day he prepares his report for the board.

1. When does Paul leave Paris?
2. Which English airport does he fly to?
3. How does he get to his hotel?
4. What does he do when he gets to his hotel?
5. Which train does he catch on Tuesday?
6. Which station does he leave from?
7. What time does he get to Southampton?
8. What does he do after lunch on Tuesday?
9. What does he do on Tuesday evening?
10. Which day does he look over the new factory?
11. Who does he have lunch with on Wednesday?
12. How does he get back to London on Wednesday?
13. Where does he spend Wednesday night?
14. How does he get back to Paris on Thursday?
15. How does he spend the following day?

---

61 The Future Continuous   I

Two common uses of the future continuous are:
(i) to indicate an activity or state that will cover the whole of a future time period.

EXAMPLES:
Gordon *will be living* in Mexico (all) next year.
We *shall be watching* TV all (during the whole) evening.

(ii) to indicate an activity or state that will occur at a certain point or period of time, and will also precede and follow it.

EXAMPLES:

Tom *will be looking* over the new house at 4 p.m.

My husband *will be working* in the garden when I get back from the shops.

To practise the future continuous, respond as shown:

Sally—at 6 p.m. (have dinner)
STUDENT A: **What will Sally be doing at 6 p.m.?**
STUDENT B: **She'll be having dinner at 6 p.m.**

John—tomorrow morning (work)
STUDENT C: **What will John be doing tomorrow morning?**
STUDENT D: **He'll be working tomorrow morning.**

1. Peter—all day Sunday (play golf)
2. Sheila—all next term (learn English)
3. Sally—all next week (take her exams)
4. John—all day tomorrow (write letters)
5. Bob—during the evening (see Elizabeth)
6. David—at 6 p.m. tomorrow (wash the car)
7. Jane—at 9 a.m. tomorrow (do the housework)
8. Tom—at 3 p.m. tomorrow (have his interview)
9. Mr Brown—this time tomorrow (pack his bags)
10. Joe—in an hour's time (drive to the airport)
11. Mary—during the summer (tour the United States)
12. Jim—while Jane's getting dinner ready (watch TV)
13. Tom—every afternoon next week (have extra lessons)
14. Jim—while Mary's getting out the cups (make coffee)
15. Marion—the whole evening (talk about her boy-friend)

---

62 The Future Perfect I

The use of the future perfect indicates that an activity in the future will be completed *by* a certain time, or will include (and may continue beyond) that time.

EXAMPLES:
John *will have had* dinner by 8 p.m. (completed)

(Cf. John *will have* dinner before 8 p.m.)

I *shall have got* my car back from the garage by Saturday. (completed)

Mary *will have been* here a year on the 16th of March (and will stay a further year). (uncompleted)

A continuous act, which may or may not be completed, may be represented by the future perfect continuous.

EXAMPLES:

Paul *will have been learning* English for three years (completed) when he leaves the school.

I *shall have been living* in London for six months (uncompleted) by the time Mary comes back from New York.

To practise the future perfect, respond as shown:

John's already gone, but has Peter? (9 p.m.)
Not yet, but he'll have gone by 9 p.m.

Mary's already phoned, but has Sally? (day's over)
Not yet, but she'll have phoned before the day's over.

Paul's already read the book, but has Helen? (you want it)
Not yet, but she'll have read it by the time you want it.

1. David's already woken up, but has Sally? (tea-time)
2. Jim's already thought of the answer, but has Don? (long)
3. Peter's already made up his mind, but has Paul? (tomorrow)
4. Anne's already been out with Jim, but has Sue? (she leaves)
5. Allan's already seen the specialist, but has Betty? (Friday)
6. Bob's already caught Jane up, but has Mary? (the end of term)
7. John's already tried out the car, but has Robert? (dinner-time)
8. Paul's already given up smoking, but has Jim? (he's much older)
9. John's already run out of money, but has Bob? (the end of the week)
10. Bob's already got rid of his old typewriter, but has Paul? (Monday)
11. Steve's already taken out insurance, but has Don? (he's twenty-one)

65

12. Jane's already done her housework, but has Betty?
(Harry gets home)
13. The goods have already gone, but has the invoice?
(the ship sails)
14. Tom's already signed the contract, but has Jim?
(the manager comes)
15. The manufacturers have already put up their prices, but
have the retailers? (the end of the year)

---

63 Future Ability and Obligation IA

(a) *To elicit a response with* 'll be able to, *respond as shown:*

The exam may take place here. (sit for it)
We'll be able to sit for it if it does.

Peter and Joe may come here tomorrow. (see Anne)
They'll be able to see Anne if they do.

Jim may make the recording this evening. (use it tomorrow)
I'll be able to use it tomorrow if he does.

1. George may do up his flat. (sell it)
2. Elizabeth may look up the word. (spell it)
3. Bob and Jim may visit Australia. (look Tom up)
4. The weather may clear up soon. (go for a picnic)
5. John may get away in time. (keep his appointment)
6. Jim may pay back the money soon. (borrow some more)
7. Gordon may go on learning English. (speak it better)
8. Richard may carry on working hard. (afford a holiday)
9. The suppliers may deliver the car soon. (drive to work)
10. I may find out what happened. (decide what action to
take)
11. Sandra may look after the children. (go out for the
evening)
12. Betty may take her library book back. (take out another
one)
13. Anne may have the children at her house. (keep an eye
on them)
14. Allan may get himself a new dictionary. (throw away his
old one)

15. The neighbours may turn down their radio. (hear the news on ours)

(b) *To elicit a response with* 'll have to, *respond as shown:*

I don't know if Bob wants to use the bathroom. (get in the queue)
If he does, he'll have to get in the queue.

I don't know if Jim and Tom want tomorrow off. (have a good excuse)
If they do, they'll have to have a good excuse.

I don't know if Sue wants to arrange a meeting. (take it up with Jim)
If she does, she'll have to take it up with Jim.

1. . . . if Bob wants to put Jean up. (ask his parents)
2. . . . if Sheila wants to buy a car. (arrange a loan)
3. . . . if John and Mary want to see the sights. (hurry)
4. . . . if Sally wants to get on with Helen. (be more polite)
5. . . . if the drivers behind want to overtake. (get a move on)
6. . . . if Paul wants to get over his cold quickly. (stay in bed)
7. . . . if Bill wants to come round this evening. (see Mary first)
8. . . . if Joe wants to call off the meeting. (phone everybody up)
9. . . . if Paul wants to see Jane off. (go to the airport with her)
10. . . . if Bob wants to give Jim a lift. (pick him up at the office)
11. . . . if Sheila wants to try on the dress. (use the fitting-room)
12. . . . if the workers want to make up for lost time. (work overtime)
13. . . . if John wants to take on the job. (get in touch with the firm)
14. . . . if Peter and David want to contact Tom. (go round to his flat)
15. . . . if Jane wants to get her own back. (ask Tom to give her a hand)

(c) *To contrast* shan't/won't be able to *and* shan't/won't have to, *respond as shown:*

You've written the essay. (stay in tonight)
Yes, I've written the essay, so I shan't have to stay in tonight.

Mary's already done the cleaning. (do it later)
Yes, Mary's already done the cleaning, so she won't have to do it later.

John's ill in bed. (come to class tomorrow)
Yes, John's ill in bed, so he won't be able to come to class tomorrow.

You haven't got any free time this evening. (help you)
No, I haven't got any free time this evening, so I shan't be able to help you.

1. You've hired a car. (walk)
2. Jim's just taken a 'pep' pill. (sleep)
3. Mary's promised to see Peter. (see Paul)
4. I've seen Mary once today. (see her again)
5. Jane's got a front-door key. (be home early)
6. I have plenty of money on me. (go to the bank)
7. John has some work to do. (go out this evening)
8. You haven't got a TV set. (watch the programme)
9. I have my own typewriter. (use the office machine)
10. Mary hasn't got Peter's phone number. (ring him up)
11. Gordon hasn't brought his camera. (take any pictures)
12. I've just been to the dentist. (go again for six months)
13. You've already got an overdraft. (borrow any more money)
14. You've just filled the tank. (stop at any filling stations)
15. Bob's just had his car serviced. (have it done again just yet)

---

64 The Future   IA

This is a substitution exercise to contrast different ways of expressing the future.

I shall be here tomorrow.   **I shall be here tomorrow.**
John   **John will be here tomorrow.**

intends	**John intends to be here tomorrow.**
go to London	**John intends to go to London tomorrow.**
is going	**John's going to London tomorrow.**
night	**John's going to London tomorrow night.**
staying in	**John's staying in London tomorrow night.**

1. arrives
2. leaves
3. Paris next Friday
4. will be leaving
5. the country
6. I'll
7. am going
8. be early tomorrow
9. Mary
10. in future
11. not to be late
12. you
13. won't
14. I
15. again
16. take the exam
17. be taking
18. Peter
19. be able to
20. we
21. have to
22. Sally
23. see John
24. will see Tom
25. next month
26. have seen (by)
27. they're seeing
28. coming back
29. we'll be
30. Susan
31. working hard
32. need to
33. all next week
34. stay at home
35. we'll have to
36. I shan't
37. Bob

THE ARTICLES

Introductory notes:
(i) **A** or **an** (the indefinite article) is used:
   (a) before a singular countable noun when it is mentioned for the first time, and if it does not represent any particular person or thing.

   EXAMPLES:
   I can see **a** man.   I want **an** orange.

   (b) with a noun complement, including names of professions.

   EXAMPLES:
   She is **a** teacher.   She is **an** old woman.

   He is **a** doctor.   He is **a** good man.

   (c) before names of people. This implies that the speaker does not know exactly who the person is or was.

EXAMPLES:

There was **a** Mr Smith here during the summer.

There's **an** Allan Brown living upstairs now.

(d) before nouns which are used as countable nouns (see page 75) although they may usually be uncountable.

EXAMPLES:

I had **an** interesting experience last night.
(Cf. Experience is sometimes expensive.)

John has **a** weakness for pretty women.
(Cf. Weakness is often held in contempt.)

This is **a** tea I think you'll like.
It's **an** ink which will never wash out.

a is used before a word beginning with a consonant sound; **an** is used before a word beginning with a vowel sound.

EXAMPLES:

A house   **A** student

An hour /ən ˈauə/   **An** egg

A university /ə juːniˈvəːsiti/

An honest one /ən ˈɔnist wʌn/

(ii) **The** (the definite article) is used:

(a) before a noun which refers to the same person(s) or thing(s) as in a previous use.

EXAMPLES:

She was wearing **a** hat. **The** hat was bright red but rather old.

He received **some** letters and cards. **The** letters were from relations.

(b) before a noun used in a particular sense.

EXAMPLES:

The sun (the only one)

The floor (the only one in sight)

The man who delivers the milk

The milkman

The is pronounced /ði/ before a word beginning with a vowel sound, /ðə/ before a word beginning with a consonant sound.

---

65 The Articles   E

Note:
In this pattern the articles never carry sentence stress.

I have **a** house and **a** flat.   **The** house is in India
He had two sons and **a** daughter. **The** sons were in Zambia.

To contrast a/an (*or* some) *and* the. *Use the word(s) in brackets in your sentence.*

I have a radio and a TV set. (here)
The radio is here.

Tom has an apple and an orange. (in his hand)
The apple is in his hand.

Bob has some fruit and some nuts. (delicious)
The fruit is delicious.

  1. Mary has a flat and a house. (modern)
  2. I have a car and a bicycle. (in the car-park)
  3. Peter has some papers and some books. (today's)
  4. Susan has a boat and a caravan. (in the harbour)
  5. Jane has a telegram and a letter. (from her aunt)
  6. Bob has a camera and some films. (in the cupboard)
  7. I have a magazine and some paperbacks. (over there)
  8. Sue has some new shoes and some boots. (in that box)
  9. Mary has a cigarette and a cocktail. (in the ashtray)
10. You have some letters and a postcard. (from my family)
11. We have some notebooks and a dictionary. (very useful)
12. Helen has a dress and a trouser suit. (in her wardrobe)
13. Mary has some luggage and some parcels. (at the station)
14. Paul has some suitcases and a wooden box. (under his bed)
15. Tom has some old trousers and some new ones. (in that drawer)

---

66 The Articles   I

The history   of Spain   is interesting.
The coffee   I like best   comes from Brazil.

To practise the *with nouns used in a particular sense, respond as shown:*

(a) History can be interesting. (of Spain)
    The history of Spain is interesting.

Pictures may be well painted. (in that exhibition)
The pictures in that exhibition are well painted.

1. Girls can be beautiful. (in that show)
2. Tea can be refreshing. (grown in Ceylon)
3. Roads can be dangerous. (in that country)
4. Architecture may be impressive. (of St Paul's)
5. Anxiety may be difficult to hide. (of a mother)
6. Opposition can be annoying. (of ignorant people)
7. Shop assistants can be very helpful. (in Macey's)
8. Stamps may be very valuable. (in that collection)
9. People can be difficult to please. (in that firm)
10. Music can be inspiring. (of my favourite composer)
11. Children may be very intelligent. (at that school)
12. Students may be dissatisfied. (at that university)
13. Typewriters may be old-fashioned. (in that office)
14. Ideas can be ridiculous. (expressed in that article)
15. Houses can be very expensive to buy. (in that street)

(b) There's coffee from different countries. (like best)
The coffee I like best is from Brazil.

There are films about very many subjects. (dislike most)
The films I dislike most are about animals.

Continue with the following, expressing your own opinion:

1. There's wall-paper of different designs. (want)
2. There's bread from different bakers. (prefer)
3. There's honey of very many kinds. (really like)
4. There's petrol of a large number of brands. (use)
5. There are films of many different kinds. (like to see)
6. There's pudding of a good many varieties. (hate most)
7. There are girls of all shapes and sizes. (like least)
8. There's beer of a great many different varieties. (prefer)
9. There are people of many different temperaments. (like best)
10. There are English lessons of several kinds. (enjoy most)
11. There are books of many descriptions. (find most interesting)
12. There are pop programmes from various stations. (like best)
13. There seem to be cars of a good many different colours. (like best)

14. There are newspaper articles about all sorts of things. (never read)
15. There seem to be ices of all sorts of different flavours. (like least)

---

67 The Articles A

(a) Certain nouns may be both countable and uncountable and this will affect the use of articles.

EXAMPLES:

A cat has nine **lives.**
Life teaches many things.
Such **a life** wouldn't interest me.
The life of Shakespeare is interesting.

Complete the following by using the word given, as shown:

crime	(a) Jim committed	**Jim committed a crime.**
	(b) was premeditated	**The crime was premeditated.**
	(c) I'm interested in	**I'm interested in crime.**
	(d) is on the increase	**Crime is on the increase.**
	(e) of violence are on the increase	**Crimes of violence are on the increase**

1. exercise
   (a) did me good
   (b) it's new
   (c) in that book are easy
   (d) is good for you

2. experience
   (a) it was valuable
   (b) of a lifetime
   (c) I didn't enjoy
   (d) I've had a lot of
   (e) is often of value

3. art
   (a) Bob has a knowledge of
   (b) it's a work
   (c) selling is
   (d) she knows of love

4. food
   (a) milk is
   (b) should never be overcooked
   (c) that Mary buys is the best
   (d) I like good

5. noise
   (a) Jim hates
   (b) John made
   (c) was unbearable
   (d) can make people neurotic
   (e) I heard strange

6. marriage
   (a) is nearly as common as divorce

(b) of Mrs Brown was a disaster

(c) there are broken

(d) it was a convenience

7. life/death

(a) what!

(b) in London is hectic

(c) of a butterfly is short

(d) begins at forty

(e) life ends in

(f) of a great man is a tragedy

8. success/failure

(a) is important

(b) Jim wants to be

(c) of your scheme is assured

(d) nothing succeeds like

(e) the opposite of success is

(f) nobody wants to be

9. time

(a) these are bad

(b) I've got

(c) has come to go

(d) is money

(e) I had to spare

(f) I had of my life

(g) is up

(h) he had to see me

(i) have good

(b) The previous exercise showed that certain nouns may be used both with and without articles. In this exercise you are to give a definition of the nouns shown below, and to do this no article is needed.

hope	power	virtue	life
love	pride	charity	laughter
beauty	honesty	discretion	necessity
patience	experience	marriage	patriotism

Answer the following questions. Each sentence you make will be a well-known saying.

What is money?	**Time is money.**
What doesn't pay?	**Crime doesn't pay.**
What's the best policy?	**Honesty is the best policy.**

1. What corrupts?
2. What's a virtue?
3. What begins at home?
4. What begins at forty?
5. What's only skin-deep?
6. What's an institution?
7. What is its own reward?
8. What comes before a fall?

74

10. What makes the world go round?
11. What's the mother of invention?
12. What's the better part of valour?
13. What's the name we give to our mistakes?
14. What's the last refuge of the scoundrel?
15. What springs eternal (in the human breast)?

NOUNS

Preliminary notes:

(i) *Common* nouns divide into *countable* and *uncountable*.
Countable means that the thing named by the noun exists in units which can be counted, e.g. 'I've got *a* typewriter (one), *some* pencil*s* (more than one) and *two* book*s*.' You use **a/an** with singular countable nouns only, and only countable nouns have plurals.

In the sentence 'I have plenty of milk, but not enough sugar' the words 'milk' and 'sugar' are *uncountable*. You do not use **a/an** with *uncountable* nouns, and they have no plural form.

Certain nouns may be either *countable* or *uncountable*.

EXAMPLES:
I want **a   cake**. (countable)
I want **some cake**. (uncountable)
I want **some cakes**. (countable)

I'd like **a   pie**. (countable)
I'd like **some pie**. (uncountable)
I'd like **some pies**. (countable)

It is important to remember that English words cannot be treated as belonging to fixed categories. A grammatical term can be applied to a word only in connection with its function in a particular sentence.

(ii) A *proper* noun denotes a particular place or person, or a title.

EXAMPLES:
John   The House of Commons   New York
Mr Smith   The Government   Hamlet

(iii) An *abstract* noun denotes a quality.

EXAMPLES:
Happiness is difficult to achieve.
Sheila is looking for *love*.
Jim has no *strength*.

(iv) A *collective* noun denotes a number of people or things considered as a unit.

EXAMPLES:

a *crowd* of people   a *gang* of youths
a *team* of players   a *group* of students
a *mob* of rioters   a *bunch* of flowers
a *swarm* of bees   a *suite* of furniture
a *flock* of birds   a *pack* of hounds
a *pack* of cards   a *board* of directors
a *panel* of experts   a *pile* of stones

(v) Certain nouns indicate a person's sex.

EXAMPLES:

husband   boy   host
wife   girl   hostess

(vi) The following nouns do not indicate the person's sex:

guest	parent	student	lawyer
patient	person	worker	cousin
doctor	people	driver	engineer
child	teacher	writer	dentist

---

68 A/An and Some   E

To contrast a/an *and* some. *Respond as shown:*

table   **I want a table.**
milk   **I want some milk.**
books   **I want some books.**
bed   **I want a bed.**

1. chair
2. water
3. picture
4. pencil
5. beer
6. notebook
7. match
8. cigarettes
9. whisky
10. newspaper
11. meat
12. plate
13. knife
14. soup
15. fork
16. fish
17. spoon
18. egg
19. orange
20. tea
21. ice-cream
22. fruit

23. apples	32. holiday
24. cream	33. wine
25. roll	34. cup of coffee
26. cheese	35. cups of coffee
27. cheque	36. wool
28. bread	37. glass of wine
29. money	38. food
30. cushion	39. help
31. answer	40. bottle of sauce

---

69 Masculine/Feminine forms EI

Give the feminine form for the following:

(a)
(1) boy	(5) uncle	(9) prince
(2) brother	(6) nephew	(10) gentleman
(3) man	(7) son	(11) waiter
(4) father	(8) king	(12) host

(b)
(1) actor	(5) bachelor	(9) male
(2) steward	(6) Mr (2)	(10) bridegroom
(3) hero	(7) manager	(11) sir
(4) heir	(8) landlord	(12) widower

---

70 Abstract Nouns EI

Cf. { How large are those shoes?
     { What's the size of those shoes?

Notice that the noun *size* is quite different from the adjective *large*. In other cases there is a clear relation, e.g. *width—wide*; *strength—strong*.

To practise 'irregular' abstract nouns, respond as shown:

It's a wide river, isn't it?
I don't know the width of the river.

The water's hot, isn't it?
I don't know the temperature of the water.

It's a strong rope, isn't it?
I don't know the strength of the rope.

1. The boy's tall, isn't he?
2. It's a fast car, isn't it?
3. The river's deep, isn't it?
4. It's a high mountain, isn't it?
5. The suit's expensive, isn't it?
6. The suitcase is heavy, isn't it?
7. The shoes are large, aren't they?
8. It's a long piece of wood, isn't it?
9. It's an old piece of furniture, isn't it?
10. It's a long way to the next town, isn't it?

---

71 Abstract Nouns   I

Here are examples of how 'regular' abstract nouns are formed:

with **ness**:	whiteness	with **ency**:	fluency
with **ence**:	intelligence	with **hood**:	childhood
or **ance**:	avoidance	with **ship**:	friendship
with **ion**:	information	with **dom**:	freedom
with **y**:	honesty	with **ism**:	criticism
with **ity**:	probability	with **itude**:	gratitude
with **ment**:	agreement		

To practise forming abstract nouns, respond as shown:

Is Sally kind to animals? (show)
Yes. She shows kindness to animals.

Does the job completely satisfy Peter? (give)
Yes. It gives him complete satisfaction.

1. Is Tom's essay promising? (show)
2. Does George encourage Tom? (give)
3. Is John confident? (have a lot of)
4. Is Joe very patient? (have a lot of)
5. Is Tom very ambitious? (have a lot of)
6. Does it please Mary to see John? (give)
7. Is John talented? (have a great deal of)
8. Is Bob respectful to his manager? (show)
9. Did Paul feel helpless? (have a feeling of)
10. Was Sally very reluctant to go? (show great)
11. Is John very energetic? (have a great deal of)
12. Is Paul very sensible? (possess a great deal of common)

(a) *Further practice with abstract nouns, respond as shown:*

Does the chair support your back? (give—to)
Yes. It gives support to my back.

Did John have to force Bob to help him? (use)
Yes. He had to use force to get Bob to help him.

Did the girls entertain the troops? (provide—for/with)
Yes. They provided the troops with entertainment.
Yes. They provided entertainment for the troops.

1. Was the paper very informative? (give a lot of)
2. Is George a very able person? (have tremendous)
3. Is Mary interested in music? (show considerable)
4. Was Mr Brown afraid when the lion got out? (show)
5. Was Henry very tactful? (show a considerable amount)
6. Does Tom know a lot about aeroplanes? (have a good— of)
7. Is Tom free to do as he likes? (have a great deal of)
8. Is Gordon experienced enough to sail that boat? (have)
9. Was Tom enthusiastic about the play? (show great— for)
10. Did Betty have to persuade Jim to get out of bed? (use)
11. Is Richard intelligent enough to know what to do? (have)
12. Does his job make Tom feel insecure? (give a feeling of)
13. Was Mary courageous during the storm? (show considerable)
14. Did the barn shelter the walkers when it rained? (provide)
15. Is Paul interested in the firm's progress? (take a great deal of)

(b) *Rephrase the following sentences by using abstract nouns, and form adjectives from the bracketed nouns:*

Jim's cautious. (advisability)
His caution's advisable.

Caroline's happy. (importance)
Her happiness is important.

John concentrated. (necessity)
His concentration was necessary.

1. Jim performed. (memory)
2. Anne hesitated. (nature)
3. It's legal. (uncertainty)
4. Mary acted. (deliberation)
5. Philip's ignorant. (pathos)
6. Henry's stupid. (irritation)
7. John was rejected. (surprise)
8. Harry's persevering. (fantasy)
9. Susan was poor. (incredibility)
10. Richard was punished. (severity)
11. David's inconsistent. (annoyance)
12. Susan was prepared. (thoroughness)
13. Rosemary was angry. (justification)
14. Elizabeth's extravagant. (notoriety)
15. Steve was recognised. (inevitability)

NOUN CLAUSES

Here is an example of a noun clause:

A: 'Do you know **what I said about her?'**
B: 'No. What did you say about her?'

The clause **what I said about her** functions as a noun, the object of the verb 'know'.

Below are examples of two noun clause patterns:

1. Do you know	**who**		borrowed my car?
Do you know	**what**		happened last night?
Do you know	**which**	car	belongs to Richard?
Do you know	**how many**	people	came to the party?
2. Do you know			
who*	I		saw last night?
Do you know			
what	John		said to Sheila?
Do you know			
whose	book	you	took?
Do you know			
how much	money	Susan	needs?

Notes:
(i) Alternative question introductions are:

Do you remember . . .?   Can you explain . . .?
Do you understand . . .?   Did you ask . . .?
Do you believe . . .?   Could you repeat . . .?
Did you recognise . . .?   Can you tell me . . .? etc.

(ii) Here are possible negative replies:

I don't know . . .   I haven't the faintest/slightest idea . . .
I have no idea . . .   I'm afraid I can't tell you/say . . .

(iii) *Some speakers use the form **whom**, but it is becoming the
exception rather than the rule.

---

73 Noun Clauses   EI

(a) *Notice how infinitives are used in the following:*
    Do you know **what to do, where to go** or **how to travel**?

*To practise the use of infinitives in the equivalents of noun
clauses, respond as shown:*

Did Peter intend to travel *by air*?
He didn't know how to travel.

Do Bob and Mary intend *to get married*?
They don't know what to do.

Does Sally intend to leave *on Wednesday*?
She doesn't know when (which day) to leave.

1. Did Jim intend to go *to Canada*?
2. Does Gordon intend *to see Harry*?
3. Do you intend *to have a holiday*?
4. Did John intend to ask for *a lot*?
5. Does Robert intend *to do his work*?
6. Did Alice intend to use *Bob's* room?
7. Did John intend to live *in New York*?
8. Does Steve intend to buy *ten* records?
9. Does David intend to travel *by train*?
10. Does Peter intend to get up *at 7 a.m.*?
11. Did Jane intend to see Paul *every week*?
12. Does Sheila intend to go out with *Peter*?
13. Does John intend to stay *for three weeks*?

81

14. Does Betty intend *to resign from her firm*?
15. Does Jim intend to speak to *Jean* about it?
16. Did Paul intend to drive *twenty kilometres*?
17. Did Susan intend to give away her *blue* dress?
18. Did Sheila intend to have her holiday *at home*?
19. Does Betty intend to give her boy-friend *a car*?
20. Did Joe intend to arrive *on the 1st of the month*?

(b) *To practise and contrast the two types of clause shown above, respond as shown:*

Who is that man?
I don't know who he is.

What's Peter's surname?
I've no idea what it is.

Where does John come from?
I haven't the faintest idea where he comes from.

Who took my pen?
Don't ask me who took it. I haven't the slightest idea.

1. How old is George?
2. Who took John's car?
3. When did Peter arrive?
4. Where does Gordon live?
5. Where do they have lunch?
6. Why does Bob buy two papers?
7. What did Sue cook for dinner?
8. Which of those books is Peter's?
9. Whose car is that near the house?
10. What time did the programme start?
11. How long did Bob stay at the party?
12. How far is it from here to New York?
13. What time will Jim leave for Toronto?
14. What happened when Jim didn't turn up?
15. How many cigarettes did Rosemary have?
16. How long was the film on TV last night?
17. Who decided when all the guests should go?
18. How does Mary travel to her place of work?
19. How often does Allan take his family abroad?
20. How much time does Joe spend on his homework?

Answer the following questions as shown:

Bob went to New York last month. Do you know why?
No, I don't know why Bob went to New York last month.

I said something to you. Did you understand it?
No, I'm sorry. I didn't understand what you said to me.

Something happened at the office yesterday. Do you know
   what it was?
**No, I'm afraid I don't know what happened at the office
   yesterday.**

1. Gordon's very old. Do you know how old?
2. That man says a lot. Do you believe him?
3. I said something just now. Can you repeat it?
4. Philip spoke to a lady. Did you see who it was?
5. John went to Canada last year. Can you explain why?
6. Jim came home late. Do you remember what time it
   was?
7. Someone cleaned the rooms. Can you tell me who it
   was?
8. One of the firm's agents called. Do you know which
   one?
9. A car has broken down outside. Do you know whose it
   is?
10. Elizabeth went out with someone. Do you know who it
    was?
11. Someone drove Jim to the station. Do you know who it
    was?
12. I want to watch the film. Do you know what time it
    starts?
13. John said something just now. Can you tell me what it
    was?
14. Bob goes to the cinema a lot. Have you any idea how
    often?
15. One of those actors is English. Can you tell me which
    one?
16. Someone rang me up while I was out. Did Jim say who
    it was?

17. There were a lot of people there. Can you tell me how many?
18. One of the men has lost his passport. Do you know which one?
19. You saw John a short while ago. Do you remember when it was?
20. There's some money in that account. Can you tell me how much?
21. Mary has a lot of friends in Australia. Do you know how many?
22. Those books belong to someone. Can you tell me whose they are?
23. Jim hurt his leg last week. Have you any idea how it happened?
24. A lot of people live in that city. Could you tell me how many?
25. English spelling is difficult. Have you asked anyone why this is so?

---

75 Noun Clauses   I

Further practice.

What's Peter's first name?
   STUDENT A: **Do you know what his first name is?**
   STUDENT B: **I've no idea what it is.**

Who's got my magazine?
   STUDENT C: **Have you any idea who's got his magazine?**
   STUDENT D: **I don't know who's got it. Why ask me?**

Where does John have dinner?
   STUDENT E: **Can you tell me where he has dinner?**
   STUDENT F: **I haven't the slightest idea where he has it.**

1. When must Mr Jones take his holiday?
2. How many pairs of shoes did Mary buy?
3. What do Peter and Paul like to drink?
4. When will Sally's brother arrive here?
5. What did Richard lend George yesterday?
6. How long has Jane been studying English?
7. How often does Bill think about the exam?
8. How much will it cost me to fly to Canada?
9. Where does John like to spend his holidays?

10. What did Robert go to his room for just now?
11. What does that hotel charge for a single room?
12. How long ago did Mr and Mrs Brown get that car?
13. Which of the two films did Betty enjoy the most?
14. How soon must Barbara go back to her own country?
15. How long did Rosemary stay at the party last night?
16. How many cigarettes does Peter get through in a day?
17. Who did Sheila meet in the town yesterday afternoon?
18. What time did David finish his breakfast this morning?
19. Whose house are the interior decorators working on now?
20. How much did Bob spend while he was in Miami last month?

---

76 Noun Clauses   I

Use the word(s) in brackets to introduce your clause, as shown:

Was Paul late getting home? (what time)
I don't know what time he got home.

Did John go to the office? (where)
I don't know where he went.

Will Mary watch TV this evening? (what)
I don't know what she'll do this evening.

(a) 1. Was Peter at the meeting? (who)
    2. Is Mary speaking to *David*? (who)
    3. Is Harry having a meal now? (what)
    4. Is David's birthday in June? (when)
    5. Is that Peter's typewriter? (whose)
    6. Did John come because of Mary? (why)
    7. Was Jim going to telephone *Jill*? (who)
    8. Did David take the 1 p.m. train? (which)
    9. Will Bob be driving to the station? (how)
  10. Has *Peter* gone on holiday with Bill? (who)
  11. Did Bob leave the car in the street? (where)
  12. Did Jim go to the theatre last night? (what)
  13. Will *Anne* invite Gordon to the party? (who)
  14. Has Mary bought that book for *her mother*? (who)
  15. Will John be having three assistants? (how many)

(b) As (a) above (further practice).
1. Did Mary pay a lot for that dress? (how much)
2. Is the swimming pool near here? (how far away)
3. Does Mary want to have English lessons? (what)
4. Did Helen spend the evening with *George*? (who)
5. Has John gone to Canada on business? (what—for)
6. Is Paul going into the town for a haircut? (why)
7. Did Bill come on a Friday? (which day of the week)
8. Will Mary be arriving in a few minutes? (how soon)
9. Does this book cost more than that one? (how much)
10. Will there be plenty of seats available? (how many)
11. Is the flat large enough for six people? (how large)
12. Was the exam very important for Bob? (how important)
13. Did Jim first meet Betty in the United States? (where)
14. Was John late for class because of a traffic jam? (why)
15. Will David read psychology at university? (what subject)

---

77 Noun Clauses   A

Notes:
(i) Where there is a lack of certainty the following may be used:

> I'm not sure . . .   I'm not certain . . .
> I can't say for sure . . . I'm not positive . . .

(ii) might have /'mait həv/ or /'maitəv/
Use one of the above introductions in your answer:

Did Peter come on Wednesday, or on Thursday?
I'm not sure (on) which day he came. He might have come on Wednesday, and then again he might have come on Thursday.

Are there thirty people at the meeting, or are there more?
I'm not positive how many people there are at the meeting. There might be thirty, and there might be more.

Has Paul taken the chair away, or has he left it in the house?
I'm not certain what Paul's done with the chair. He might have taken it away; on the other hand he might have left it in the house.

1. Is that Betty I can see over there, or is it Mary?
2. Did the match go on for two hours, or for three hours?
3. Did Elizabeth lay the table, or was it Susan who did it?

4. Has Peter gone to New York by air, or has he gone by sea?
5. Is Mary going to marry John, or is she going to marry Bob?
6. Has David been to London twice, or has he been three times?
7. Did the men do the job in the morning, or in the afternoon?
8. Do John and Mary go to class every day, or every other day?
9. Is it this book the critics recommended, or is it that one?
10. Was Sheila born in Switzerland, or was she born in Austria?
11. Will there be a strike now, or will there be one next week?
12. Were there twenty people on the plane, or were there more?
13. Did Sally swim one kilometre, or was it a greater distance?
14. Did Paul need a month to learn English, or did he need longer?
15. Did Bob stay away because he was ill, or because of laziness?
16. Is it six hundred kilometres from here to the border, or is it further?
17. Has John got a headache, or has he got a broken leg? (use: suffer from)
18. Did Sheila spend three weeks in Osaka, or did she stay there for four weeks?
19. Is Bob going to the United States for a visit, or to live there permanently?
20. Does Bob prefer to go out in the evening, or does he prefer to do something else?

NOUN PATTERNS

---

78 ELEMENTARY

Noun pattern A: noun + *to*-infinitive

EXAMPLES:

I have a   **train to catch.**

I've got some   **shopping to do.**

There's a   **meal to prepare.**

To practise the above pattern, respond as shown:

see someone
>STUDENT A: **Are you going to see someone?**
>STUDENT B: **Yes. I have someone to see.**

pack a suitcase
>STUDENT C: **Are you going to pack a suitcase?**
>STUDENT D: **Yes. I have a suitcase to pack.**

1. do an exercise	11. do some washing-up
2. make an appointment	12. buy some presents
3. iron a shirt	13. make a phone call
4. catch a bus	14. write some letters
5. do some shopping	15. send a telegram
6. do some work	16. do some painting
7. pay a bill	17. meet a friend
8. say something	18. catch a train
9. read a book	19. learn some words
10. catch a plane	20. do some gardening

---

79 Noun patterns   I

Noun pattern B: noun + *for* + (pro)noun + *to*-infinitive

Note:
There are really two patterns here:

(i) Here are some   **problems for Richard to solve.**
    I've found a   **book for Elizabeth to read.**

(ii) I'll find an   **opportunity for John to meet** Mary.
     It was a   **treat for the children to play** on the beach.

in (i) the noun (*problems*, *book*) is the object of the *to*-infinitive.
In (ii) the noun (*opportunity*, *treat*) is not the object of the *to*-infinitive.

88

To practise pattern (i), *respond as shown:*

There's a good film. We can see it.
There's a good film for us to see.

Here's a problem. Paul can solve it.
Here's a problem for Paul to solve.

1. Here's a letter. You can read it.
2. Netball is a good game. Girls can play it.
3. It's a good company. A young man can join it.
4. I've bought some ice-cream. The boys can eat it.
5. John had a question. The professor could answer it.
6. Here are some good steaks. The cook can grill them.
7. I've got a puzzling situation. They can explain it.
8. He brought home a beautiful fur coat. His wife could wear it.
9. There are some really difficult questions. We must answer them.
10. The teacher produced some interesting subjects. We could discuss them.

To practise (ii), *respond as shown:*

We couldn't swim in the pool. There was no opportunity.
There was no opportunity for us to swim in the pool.

Someone should open a new factory here. There's a need.
There's a need for someone to open a new factory here.

11. Paul should leave. Mary says it's time.
12. Susan didn't believe John. There was no reason.
13. Paul couldn't check the accounts. There was no time.
14. Tom isn't coming home straight away. Jane's in no hurry.
15. Jim didn't go into a long explanation. There was no need.
16. You'll be able to come later. There'll be an opportunity.
17. Bob heard that he'd failed his exam. It was a disappointment.
18. Rosemary needn't accept what Richard says. There's no reason.
19. Sally can't drive Joe's car. He's been trying to get insurance.
20. Bob should be sent to New York without delay. I've given orders.

(a) Noun pattern C: noun + *that*-clause

EXAMPLES:

There's little **hope (that) they'll be found.**

I had no **idea (that) you'd write.**

There's no **proof (that) he's been here.**

To practise the above pattern, respond as shown:

I had no idea . . .   of your interest in crime.
I had no idea (that) you were interested in crime.

There's no doubt . . .   of Bob's concern about the case.
There's no doubt (that) Bob's concerned about the case.

There's no certainty . . .   of the criminal being found.
There's no certainty (that) the criminal will be found.

Note:
It is better not to omit the word *that* after the words marked with an asterisk [*].

1. There's evidence* . . .
      of foul play.
2. There were indications* . . .
      of there having been an argument.
3. There were signs . . .
      of a struggle.
4. There's little proof . . .
      of Gordon's innocence.
5. There's no hope . . .
      of the case being solved quickly.
6. There was no sign* . . .
      of Betty having been in the park.
7. There's a possibility . . .
      of another person being involved.
8. There's no likelihood* . . .
      of the murderer's getting away.
9. Mary had no proof . . .
      of Jim's being at home.
10. It was the thought* . . .
      of Jim's guilt that worried Mary.

11. Sally had proof . . .
   of Jim's involvement in the case.
12. There was no evidence* . . .
   of Bob's having committed the crime.
13. Mary now has evidence* . . .
   of Jim's having hidden the weapon.
14. There's no certainty . . .
   of her being able to find it now.
15. There's little likelihood* . . .
   of anybody being convicted.

(b) Noun pattern D: noun + preposition + (pro)noun or gerund

EXAMPLES:

Mary has a **hatred of spiders.**

John asked a **question about the test.**

There was no **way of stopping** Peter.

To practise the above pattern, respond as shown:

What made John angry? (Mary was *pleased* to see Peter.)
(It was) Mary's pleasure at seeing Peter.
What makes Jim spend so much time in Tokyo? (He *loves* Japan.)
(It's) his love of Japan.

1. What makes Jim stay away from women? (He *distrusts* them.)
2. What made Peter irritated? (Sally *chose* modern furniture.)
3. What enables Bob to enjoy himself in Rome? (He speaks *fluent* Italian.)
4. What makes Don so popular? (He *respects* other people's opinions.)
5. What proved to Mary that John loved her? (He was *delighted* when he saw her again.)
6. What kept their marriage from breaking up? (Anne *believed* in Henry's honesty.)
7. What made Jim give up driving? (He was *afraid* of being involved in a road accident.)
8. What's making Gordon into a nervous wreck? (He's *anxious* about the results of the exam.)
9. What gave Peter the job? (He was *quick* to work out the answer to the problem.)

10. What made Sheila cry out in alarm? (She was *surprised* to find a stranger in her kitchen.)
11. What made Betty decide to throw a party? (She was *successful* in passing her driving test.)
12. What led Peter to study for a degree in Economics? (He was *interested* in financial matters.)
13. What made Sally drop the coffee-pot? (She was *astonished* to see John back from the office so early.)
14. What prevents Richard from enjoying circuses? (He's *disgusted* when he sees performing animals.)
15. What put Sandra into a bad temper? (She was *disappointed* when she couldn't hear the 'Blue Flames' pop group.)

---

81 Noun Patterns   A

Noun pattern E: noun (+ preposition) + conjunctive + phrase or clause.

EXAMPLES:

We've received no **news about what the directors are planning to do next.**

The **problem of how it's to be done** must be solved.

Please give me some **advice about where to go for my holiday.**

Notes:

(i) The first sentence above can be expressed 'We have received no news **as to** (or **concerning**) what the directors are planning to do next.' **As to** is often found in this pattern.

(ii) The conjunctive **whether** is often used in this pattern.

EXAMPLES:

John is in some doubt (as to) **whether** the party will be held.

I have no idea **whether** Peter will be here or not.

To practise the above pattern, answer the questions as shown:

What has John been doing? Did Peter give an account?
No, Peter didn't give an account of what John has been doing.

What happened to the computer? Is there any doubt?
Yes, there is some doubt as to what happened to the computer.

How long will David be away? Have you any information?
No, I have no information about how long David will be away.

1. Who did the job? Is there any doubt?
2. What should I do? Can you give me any advice?
3. Who caused the accident? Is there any certainty?
4. Which firm is the best? Have you any information?
5. Where will the dance take place? Have you any news?
6. What did John go to New York for? Have you any idea?
7. Who will come first in the exam? Is there any question?
8. How is Mary doing at school? Did Paul show any interest?
9. Who did Jim drive to the airport? Isn't there some doubt?
10. What have they been discussing? Can you give me a summary?
11. When will the boat be leaving? Have you received notification?
12. What should I say at the meeting? Should I take special care?
13. What time will the plane be in? Have you received any news?
14. How many people were involved in the robbery? Have the police any evidence?
15. How much will the cost of living rise next year? Is there any indication?

PRONOUNS

82 ELEMENTARY

The book is for **me**.	**I**	need it.
The book is for **you**.	**You**	need it.
The book is for **him**.	**He**	needs it.
The book is for **her**.	**She**	needs it.
The book is for **us**.	**We**	need it.
The book is for **them**.	**They**	need it.

Notes:
(i) The personal pronouns in subject form are: **I, you, he, she, it, we, you, they**. (**You** is singular or plural.)

The personal pronouns in object form are: **me, you, him, her, it, us, you, them**. (**You** is singular or plural.)

(ii) You will find the possessive pronouns on page 104.

(iii) In English **we**, **us**, **our**, **ours** may include the person(s) spoken to. Whether it does so or not is usually clear from the context.

To practise using the personal pronouns, start your response with the pronoun that answers the pronoun in the stimulus:

The book is for us.
You need it.   (or: We need it.—see Note iii).

The house is for him.
He needs it.

The magazine is for you.
I need it.   (or: We need it.)

1. The flat is for me.
2. The bed is for her.
3. The TV set is for us.
4. The picture is for them.
5. The newspaper is for you.
6. The shirt is for him.
7. The magazine is for them.
8. The lesson is for you.
9. The drink is for me.
10. The present is for us.
11. The sweater is for her.
12. The wine is for them.
13. The cigarette is for him.
14. The book is for you.
15. The pencil is for me.
16. The watch is for her.
17. The ring is for you.
18. The gin is for us.
19. The tie is for him.
20. The whisky is for them.

---

83 Personal Pronouns   E

Further practice.

(a) *Replace the nouns with pronouns:*

Mary likes John.   **She likes him.**

I want to see Mary.   **I want to see her.**

Harry likes Joe and Bob.   **He likes them.**

1. John likes Susan.
2. Mary has the answer.
3. Mrs Jones is with Jim.
4. The girl has the books.
5. Peter is studying English.
6. The key is under the table.
7. Sally can make her own bed.

8. Sarah can help the children.
9. The boy can see Miss Roberts.
10. Mr Smith wants to see Sheila.
11. Betty is with George and Paul.
12. George and Anne are on the bus.
13. The book is with Mr and Mrs Brown.
14. Richard is in front of the TV set.
15. Henry and John are outside the hotel.

(b) *To contrast the personal pronouns with the possessive adjectives, respond as shown:*

you—book
STUDENT A: **Have you got your book with you?**
STUDENT B: **Yes, I've got my book with me.**

he—letter
STUDENT C: **Has he got his letter with him?**
STUDENT D: **Yes, he's got his letter with him.**

she—car
STUDENT E: **Has she got her car with her?**
STUDENT F: **Yes, she's got her car with her.**

1. you—notebook	11. she—father
2. she—pen	12. they—tickets
3. they—books	13. you—dictionary
4. he—radio	14. she—typewriter
5. she—money	15. he—records
6. you (pl.)—newspapers	16. you—raincoat
7. she—camera	17. she—handbag
8. they—suitcases	18. they—luggage
9. you—friends	19. he—tape-recorder
10. he—scooter	20. you (pl.)—cars

One and **It**

84 ELEMENTARY

QUESTION	ANSWER
Have you got **a book**?	Yes, I've got **one**.
Have you got **your book**?	Yes, I've got **it**.

Note:

One in this pattern represents '*a* + noun'. It is used where we do not wish to repeat the noun.

It in this pattern represents a noun naming a particular thing or idea.

Cf. $\begin{cases} \text{I have \textbf{one} book.} \\ \text{I have \textbf{a} book.} \end{cases}$

To contrast one *and* it.

Have you got a pen?	**Yes, I've got one.**
Have you got your pen?	**Yes, I've got it.**
Has he got a magazine?	**Yes, he's got one.**
Has he got his magazine?	**Yes, he's got it.**

1. Have you got a camera?
2. Have you got your camera?
3. Has Peter got a car?
4. Has Peter got his car?
5. Have you got your cup of tea?
6. Have you got a cup of tea ?
7. Have you got your notebook?
8. Have you got a notebook?
9. Has Mary got a dictionary?
10. Has Mary got her dictionary?
11. Have you got your passport?
12. Has John got a passport?
13. Has Peter got a letter?
14. Has Peter got his letter?
15. Have they got a suitcase?
16. Has Allan got his suitcase?
17. Has Susan got a newspaper?
18. Have you got your newspaper?
19. Has Richard got a drink?
20. Has Brian got his drink?

One and **Ones**

85 ELEMENTARY/INTERMEDIATE

Situation: You see some oranges that you like and you speak to the shop-assistant:

I want		**one**.
I want	that	**one**.
I want	a	big juicy **one**.
I want	the	big juicy **one**.
I want	this	big juicy **one**.

I want		big juicy **ones**.
I want	these	**ones**.
I want	the	big juicy **ones**.
I want	those	big juicy **ones**.
I want one	of the	big juicy **ones**.
I want some	of these	big juicy **ones**.

Notes:

(i) The pronouns **one** and **ones** are often placed after the demonstrative adjectives when there is selection or comparison.

EXAMPLES:

I like that clock.	I'll have that **one**.
This peach looks ripe.	Let me have this **one**.
Those oranges look juicy.	Give me those **ones**.*
I want to take these shirts.	Pack these **ones**.*

*Some people feel that it is unnecessary to say 'these ones', 'those ones'. They say: **Give me those. Pack these.**

(ii) If the demonstrative adjective is followed by an adjective, it is usual to say **one** or **ones**.

EXAMPLES:

Look at that large sweater in the window. I'm talking about that **green one**.

Can you see those expensive women's magazines on the bookstall? They are near those **cheap ones**.

(iii) **One's** (the possessive adjective) is occasionally used.

EXAMPLES:

It is not a good idea to spend all **one's** time thinking about food.

One's duty in life is to help others.

(a) *To practise and contrast the above structures, respond as shown: This is a substitution exercise.*

I should like a green one.
I should like a green one.

pink
I should like a pink one.

the
I should like the pink one.

ones
I should like the pink ones.

one of
I should like one of the pink ones.

1. the silver one	11. small	21. the
2. a	12. one of	22. one of
3. these	13. some	23. those
4. that	14. a	24. cheap
5. the	15. red	25. this
6. those	16. those	26. these
7. automatic	17. the	27. some of
8. an	18. that	28. long-playing
9. this	19. comfortable	29. that
10. these	20. these	30. one of

(b) *For further practice with* one *and* ones *ask questions and respond as shown:*

books (this)
STUDENT A: **Which of these books would you like?**
STUDENT B: **I should like this one.**

apples (some—these small)
STUDENT C: **Which of these apples would you like?**
STUDENT D: **I should like some of these small ones.**

sweaters (one—the large)
STUDENT E: **Which of these sweaters would you like?**
STUDENT F: **I should like one of the large ones.**

1. envelopes (some—the small)
2. dictionaries (that English)
3. magazines (one—these weekly)

4. suitcases (this yellow)
5. newspapers (one—the daily)
6. pairs of shoes (these black)
7. beds (that double)
8. souvenirs (one—those glass)
9. brushes (the stiff)
10. records (one—the long-playing)
11. cushions (one—those soft)
12. chairs (one—the metal)
13. diaries (the pocket-sized)
14. typewriters (the portable)
15. jackets (this leather)
16. notebooks (the pink)
17. eggs (some—those brown)
18. TV sets (one—the colour*)
19. hats (that purple)
20. washing-machines (the front-loading)

* Note **colour** is used here as an adjective.

Some and **Any**

---

86 ELEMENTARY

QUESTION	ANSWER
Have you got **any** matches?	Yes, I've got **some** (matches).
	No, I haven't got **any** (matches).
Have you got **a** match?	Yes, I've got **one**.
	No, I haven't got **one**.

To practise some *and* any, *and to contrast* some *and* any *with* one, *respond as shown:*

they—coffee	STUDENT A:	**Have they got any coffee?**
	STUDENT B:	**Yes, they've got some.**
	or:	**No, they haven't got any.**
she—match	STUDENT C:	**Has she got a match?**
	STUDENT D:	**Yes, she's got one.**
	or:	**No, she hasn't got one.**

1. she—money	11. you—new clothes
2. he—car	12. they—sister
3. they—cigarettes	13. you—work to do
4. you—dictionary	14. he—newspaper
5. she—stamps	15. she—brothers
6. you—English friends	16. you—petrol
7. they—sugar	17. we—beer
8. you—scissors	18. they—boat
9. he—milk	19. she—stockings
10. she—double bed	20. you—butter

Notes:

(i) As a general rule, use **some** in affirmative statements, use **any** in questions and negative statements. But compare:

A. Do you want any bread?—a question, not an invitation; the answer may be 'Yes, I do.' or 'No, I don't.'

B. Would you like some bread?—an invitation to have some; the answer will probably be 'Yes, I should like some.'

(ii) **Some** and **any** function as pronouns as well as adjectives. As a pronoun, *some* is pronounced /sʌm/; as an adjective without special emphasis it is usually /sm/.

(iii) These two words form the following common compounds:

somebody (someone) something somewhere
anybody (anyone) anything anywhere

(See Exercises 87 and 88.)

THE INDEFINITE PRONOUNS

87 INTERMEDIATE

I saw	**something**	in the garden.
I didn't see	**anything**	in the room.
I saw	**nothing**	in the room.
I saw	**somebody (someone)**	in the car.
I didn't see	**anybody (anyone)**	in the taxi.
I saw	**nobody (no one)**	in the taxi.

Notes:

(i) Indefinite pronouns stand alone or may be followed by adjectives.

EXAMPLES:

I got **something** (interesting) for my birthday.

I didn't see **anything** (nice) in the shop.

There was **nothing** (cheap) on the counter.

(ii) **Nothing** and **not . . . anything** have the same general meaning. **Nobody** and **not . . . anybody** have the same general meaning.

(iii) These pronouns may be followed by a *to*-infinitive as adjunct.

EXAMPLES:

She was looking for **something to do**.

Isn't there **anything to sit** on?

(iv) They take the '*for* + (pro)noun + *to*-infinitive' pattern. See B(i) page 88.

EXAMPLES:

There was **nothing for him to drink**.

He will bring **something for you to eat**.

(v) *Who*- or *that*-clauses may be added.

EXAMPLES:

There was **nothing (that) I could say**.

He ate **anything (that was) put in front of him**.

I could find **no one who could do it**.

To practise the above patterns, respond as shown:

Is there anyone in Room 200? (Room 201)
Yes, there's somebody in Room 200, but there's nobody in 201.

Didn't you see anything in the boat? (the water)
No, I didn't see anything in the boat, but I saw something in the water.

1. Is there anything I can do for you? (John)
2. Was there anyone in the waiting-room? (surgery)
3. Is there anything wrong with your car? (Robert's)
4. Is there anything good on TV tonight? (the cinema)
5. Is there anybody to fetch from the station? (airport)
6. Is there anything I can buy for you in the town? (Bob)
7. Was there anyone interesting at the dance? (the party)
8. Don't you know anybody to ask to the party? (to dinner)

101

9. Didn't you see anyone go into the bank? (the Post Office)
10. Is there anyone here who wants to play tennis? (football)
11. Doesn't anyone know the answer to Question 2? (Question 3)
12. Is there anything good on at the cinema now? (the theatre)
13. Will there be anything to do tomorrow afternoon? (evening)
14. Is there anyone in Bob's class on holiday now? (ill in bed)
15. Isn't there anybody here who wants to discuss Philosophy? (Politics)

---

88 Indefinite Pronouns and Adverbs   IA

Note the indefinite adverbs: 'somewhere', 'nowhere', and 'anywhere'. Respond as shown:

Who can mend my watch?
There isn't anyone here who can mend your watch.
or   **No one here can mend your watch.**

What shall we do tomorrow afternoon?
There isn't anything to do tomorrow afternoon.
or   **There's nothing to do tomorrow afternoon.**

Where can Paul stay the night?
There isn't anywhere for him to stay the night.
or   **There's nowhere for him to stay the night.**

1. What can I do to help?
2. Who will make the tea?
3. Where can Paul sit down?
4. What can Bob have to eat?
5. Who can I complain to?
6. Who can answer the question?
7. What shall we do this evening?
8. Where can we hold the discussion?

9. Where can we buy a cup of coffee?
10. Who can we ask for information?
11. What shall we watch on TV tonight?
12. Where can Jim have a game of tennis?
13. Who can Sally take to the station?
14. Where shall I put the empty suitcases?
15. What should Bob and Jim do for homework?

POSSESSION

Possession may be indicated in the following ways:

This is **my** house. (possessive adjectives)
This house is **mine**. (possessive pronouns)
That's Peter**'s*** car. (adding 's to singular nouns)
These are the boys' books. (adding (') to plural nouns)
I'm at the end **of** the book. (using 'of')
We saw Mary and Anne**'s*** flat. (showing joint ownership)
Bob**'s*** and Tom**'s*** cars are here.

(showing separate ownership)

* Pronunciation is important here. It is necessary to add the
sound /s/, /z/ or /iz/, spelt 's in each case, to a singular noun
naming a person or living creature. Plural nouns of the same
type ending with s add an apostrophe but no extra sound.

FURTHER EXAMPLES:
The **cat's** /kæts/ eyes; a **man's** /mænz/ socks; a **fish's**
/ˈfiʃiz/ tail; Alice's /ˈælisiz/ books; **Dickens's** /ˈdikinziz/
novels.

The **students'** /ˈstjuːdnts/ books; their **teachers'** /ˈtiːtʃəz/
cars; (but) **children's** /ˈtʃildrənz/ games.

Certain nouns besides those for living beings also have this
form.

EXAMPLES:
A **week's** work; the **sun's** rays.

The following words also indicate possession: 'to possess',
'to own', 'to have', 'to have got', 'to belong to', 'owner',
'belongings'.

POSSESSIVE ADJECTIVES	POSSESSIVE PRONOUNS
This is **my** house.	This house is **mine.**
This is **your** house.	This house is **yours.**
This is **his** house.	This house is **his.**
This is **her** house.	This house is **hers.**
This is **our** house.	This house is **ours.**
This is **their** house.	This house is **theirs.**

Note:
The possessive adjectives are: my, your, his, her, its, our, your, their.
(**Your** is singular or plural.)
The possessive pronouns are: mine, yours, his, hers, ours, yours, theirs. (**Yours** is singular or plural.)

To practise and contrast the possessive adjectives and pronouns, respond as shown:

This is my book.	**This book's mine.**
That's your house.	**That house is yours.**
These are our shoes.	**These shoes are ours.**
Those are her papers.	**Those papers are hers.**

1. That's her dictionary.
2. This is my overcoat.
3. These are our suitcases.
4. That's her watch.
5. Those are their keys.
6. This is her newspaper.
7. That's his parcel.
8. These are our letters.
9. Those are your postcards.
10. This is my camera.
11. These are our drinks.
12. Those are your flowers.
13. This is my sweater.
14. That's her house.
15. These are his spectacles.
16. Those are their magazines.
17. This is our flat.

18. That's your brush.
19. These are her stockings.
20. Those are their cars.

90 **Whose** E

QUESTION		ANSWER
Whose pen	is that?	It's **mine.**
or **Whose**	is that pen?	
Whose money	is this?	It's **Peter's.**
or **Whose**	is this money?	
Whose cards	are these?	They're **his.**
or **Whose**	are these cards?	
Whose cars	are those?	They're **Bob's** and **John's.**
or **Whose**	are those cars?	

To practise asking and answering questions with whose, *respond as shown:*

car—Peter	STUDENT A:	**Whose car is that?**
	STUDENT B:	**It's Peter's.**
house—us	STUDENT C:	**Whose house is this?**
	STUDENT D:	**It's ours.**
shoes—him	STUDENT E:	**Whose shoes are those?**
	STUDENT F:	**They're his.**
stamps—Harry	STUDENT G:	**Whose stamps are these?**
	STUDENT H:	**They're Harry's.**

1. books—Bill
2. camera—John
3. towel—Anne
4. pyjamas—me
5. soap—you
6. shirts—us
7. handbag—her
8. purse—Mary
9. house—them
10. stamps—us
11. writing—Bob
12. radio—Allan
13. bed—Jane
14. bottle—us
15. books—you
16. envelopes—him
17. hat—Mr Johnson
18. suitcase—her
19. chocolates—Bob
20. notebook—me
21. magazines—David
22. fruit—us

23. cup—him
24. caravan—them
25. letters—her
26. records—Tom

27. bag—Alice
28. typewriter—me
29. glass—him
30. sweater—her

---

91 Possession   I

To practise and contrast the 's, s' and the of form of the possessive:

Betty. Has her husband come home?
Yes, Betty's husband has come home.

That dress. Do you know the price?
No, I don't know the price of that dress.

There was a delay. Was it for an hour?
Yes, there was an hour's delay.

(a)   1. Mary. Is her car outside?
      2. The flat. Do you know the owner?
      3. The book. Does Jim know the value?
      4. Whisky. Did you see a bottle there?
      5. The passage. Is the room at the end?
      6. Sally. Does her father collect coins?
      7. That car. Isn't the price prohibitive?
      8. This camera. Is the lens a good one?
      9. The association. Is it for the students?
     10. This book. Are the contents interesting?
     11. This TV set. Is the tuning easy?
     12. Philip. Is his chair next to Elizabeth's?
     13. The newspaper. Was the article on Page 2?
     14. John. Did his business collapse last year?
     15. That yacht. Is its owner a millionaire?

(b) As (a) above (further practice).

      1. The house. Is the kitchen at the back?
      2. John did some work. Was it for one day?
      3. The tree. Was John sitting in the shade?
      4. George. Was his coat hanging on the door?
      5. His shoes. Doesn't John remember the size?
      6. The town. Is the High Street in the centre?
      7. Rosemary. Will her holiday start next week?

106

8. Peter. Has his wife gone away for a few days?
9. Mary. Did her brother break his leg yesterday?
10. The newspapers. Were they for the hotel guests?
11. The house. Was Jane standing in the front room?
12. Your coat. Isn't there a small hole in the back?
13. That scooter. Does it belong to Gordon and David?
14. The girl-friends. Were they waiting for Bob and Tom?
15. One of my friends. Is it his intention to visit Rome?

---

92 Possession   I

Use a noun clause to answer the following, as shown:

Whose book is this? (whose)
I don't know whose book that is.

Whose shares are these? (own)
I don't know who owns those shares.

Whose house is that? (belong)
I don't know who that house belongs to.

1. Whose car is this? (belong)
2. Whose money is that? (own)
3. Whose room is that? (whose)
4. Whose ring is that? (owner)
5. Whose office is this? (whose)
6. Whose watch is that? (belong)
7. Whose bed is that? (whose)
8. Whose tie is this? (belong)
9. Whose pen is that? (owner)
10. Whose key is this? (whose)
11. Whose sweater is this? (whose)
12. Whose radio is that? (belong)
13. Whose magazine is this? (owner)
14. Whose flat is that? (own)
15. Whose tapes are these? (whose)
16. Whose books are those? (belong)
17. Whose typewriter is that? (whose)
18. Whose dogs are these? (owner)
19. Whose socks are those? (whose)
20. Whose newspaper is this? (own)

There is and **There are**

There is	a woman on the beach.
There are	some houses on the hill.
There was	a boy in the garden.
There were	some men on the lawn.

Note:
There + **finite** indicates the existence of somebody or something.

To practise the above pattern with the present tense, respond as shown:

I want some fruit. (table)
There's some on the table.

Jim wants a taxi. (station)
There's one by the station.

Mary wants an orange. (bowl)
There are some in that bowl.

1. John wants some tea. (pot)
2. I want a typewriter. (desk)
3. Jim wants some water. (table)
4. Peter wants a chair. (corner)
5. We want some stamps. (machine)
6. I want a tape-recorder. (shop)
7. I want a tobacconist's. (cinema)
8. Bob wants some sugar. (sideboard)
9. Susan wants a suitcase. (basement)
10. Peter wants some drawing-pins. (tin)
11. I want a single room. (second floor)
12. Mary wants to use a telephone. (hotel)
13. I want to find a post office. (street)
14. Tom wants a good dictionary. (bookshop)
15. Jim wants to find a chemist's. (grocer's)

To contrast present and past, form questions as shown:

There are some new students today. (last week)
Were there any new students last week?
Yes, there were.

There's someone near the bus-stop. (ten minutes ago)
Was there anyone near the bus-stop ten minutes ago?
No, there wasn't.

1. There are some guests in the hotel. (last month)
2. There's a good play on TV tonight. (last night)
3. There's something wrong with my radio. (yesterday)
4. There are a lot of people at the bar. (an hour ago)
5. There are some newspapers in the cupboard. (yesterday)
6. There's somebody in the bathroom. (twenty minutes ago)
7. There are some mistakes in John's homework. (yesterday)
8. There's someone living in that flat now. (two years ago)
9. There's a concert on the radio this evening. (last night)
10. There's a good film on at the cinema tonight. (last week)
11. There's a policeman opposite the bank. (five minutes ago)
12. There's something wrong with the computer. (earlier today)
13. There are some houses for sale in that street. (a month ago)
14. There are some people in the office. (just before it closed)
15. There's a taxi waiting by the station. (when you wanted one)
16. There's someone studying in the next room. (a short while ago)
17. There's somebody waiting outside in the hall. (ten minutes ago)
18. There are some ships in the harbour. (the day before yesterday)

19. There are some dirty cups and saucers in the sink. (last night)
20. There are a lot of people at the meeting. (the week before last)

---

95 There is/There are I

For further practice in asking questions with there, *respond as shown:*

There isn't time for another drink. (get home)
Isn't there?
No, there isn't.
Why isn't there time?
Because we've got to get home.

There wasn't anybody there when I arrived. (holiday)
Wasn't there?
No, there wasn't.
Why wasn't there anybody there?
Because everybody was on holiday.

1. There aren't any flights today. (fog)
2. There weren't any papers left. (late)
3. There wasn't anybody working. (holiday)
4. There aren't any letters. (post not come)
5. There wasn't a car available. (all booked)
6. There won't be any buses tomorrow. (strike)
7. There isn't any news. (Susan not telephoned)
8. There isn't a doctor available. (out on call)
9. There won't be any trains for hours. (a hold-up)
10. There isn't anything to drink. (supplies not come)
11. There wasn't a typewriter in the office. (repaired)
12. There weren't any dictionaries in the shop. (sold out)
13. There isn't anybody at the reception desk. (coffee break)
14. There wasn't enough beer to go round. (not enough ordered)
15. There won't be a talk on TV tonight. (programme cancelled)

To practise there *with modal verbs* + *perfect infinitive, respond as shown:*

Have there been any complaints? (can't)
There can't have been any complaints.

Was there anybody in the other room? (might)
There might have been somebody in the other room.

Were there any students sitting for the exam? (could)
There could have been some students sitting for the exam.

1. Was there any trouble there? (needn't)
2. Was there anybody on the roof? (couldn't)
3. Were there any seats available? (mightn't)
4. Was there a message for me earlier? (might)
5. Was there a fire in the building? (couldn't)
6. Have there been any visitors recently? (must)
7. Was there steak on the menu last night? (ought)
8. Was there a letter for you this morning? (should)
9. Were there any shops open yesterday evening? (won't)
10. Was there anybody in the office on Saturday? (shouldn't)
11. Were there many mistakes in Gordon's homework? (wouldn't)
12. Was there anybody in the TV room late last night? (might)
13. Were there any newspapers on sale yesterday morning? (must)
14. Has there been a change of government there recently? (can't)
15. Have there been any demands for a shorter working week? (could)

Practise also the conversational short answer.
Have there been any complaints? (can't)
There can't have been.
    /ðə `kɑːntəv ˌbiːn/ —certainty

Was there anybody in the other room? (might)
There might have been.
    /ðə `maitəv ˌbiːn/ —uncertainty

111

ADJECTIVES

STATEMENT	QUESTION
The lesson is **good**.	Is the lesson **good**?
The books are **interesting**.	Are the books **interesting**?
The girl is **young**.	Is the girl **young**?

Notes:

(i) Adjectives never have plural forms.

(ii) The adjectives in the table above are part of the predicate: they complete a statement or a question about the subject, with a verb such as **be, seem, look**:

EXAMPLES:
That girl **is beautiful**.
She **looks clever**.
She **seems intelligent**.

(iii) Most adjectives of this kind can also be used attributively, and then they come before the noun.

EXAMPLES:
That's a **beautiful** girl.

She looks a **clever** girl.

She appears to be an **intelligent** girl.

To practise adjective position in questions, change the statements to questions:

The books are interesting.
STUDENT A: **Are the books interesting?**
STUDENT B: **Yes, they are.**

The coffee is hot.
STUDENT C: **Is the coffee hot?**
STUDENT D: **Yes, it is.**

The food is ready.
STUDENT E: **Is the food ready?**
STUDENT F: **Yes, it is.**

1. The car is fast.
2. The clock is slow.
3. The question is right.
4. The answers are wrong.
5. The room is warm.
6. The water is cold.
7. The weather is bad.
8. The food is good.
9. The books are easy.
10. The exercise is difficult.
11. The road is long.
12. The lesson is short.
13. The towels are new.
14. The hotel is old.
15. The shirt is large.
16. The rooms are small.
17. The lessons are interesting.
18. The book is boring.
19. The record is cheap.
20. The camera is expensive.
21. The man is old.
22. The woman is young.
23. The bed is comfortable.
24. The chair is hard.

---

98 Adjectives   E

(a) *Give the opposite adjective to the one shown:*

This room's warm.	**That room's cold.**
That train's fast.	**This train's slow.**
These bottles are empty.	**Those bottles are full.**
Those people are generous.	**These people are selfish.**

1. These shoes are clean.
2. That child's tall.
3. Those houses are old.
4. That woman's old.
5. These cakes are large.
6. That boy's strong.
7. Those girls are late.
8. That road's wide.
9. This story's true.
10. Those cases are light.
11. That child's noisy.
12. This exercise is easy.
13. These women are beautiful.
14. Those sentences are long.
15. That girl's intelligent.
16. These cigarettes are mild.
17. This tie's expensive.
18. Those people are polite.
19. That answer's right.
20. These programmes are interesting.

(b) *Choose suitable adjectives for the nouns given:*

pen   **This pen's new; that one's old.**
shoes   **These shoes are clean; those are dirty.**
suit   **That suit's expensive; this one's cheap.**
people **Those people are friendly; these are unfriendly.**

1. girls	21. door
2. men	22. radio
3. exercise	23. furniture
4. letters	24. overcoat
5. child	25. stockings
6. car	26. people
7. boy	27. watch
8. women	28. answer
9. house	29. questions
10. children	30. bicycle
11. hotel	31. skirts
12. clock	32. sweaters
13. fire	33. window
14. newspapers	34. coin
15. light	35. suitcases
16. TV set	36. drink
17. TV programme	37. flowers
18. dictionary	38. music
19. cigarettes	39. dancers
20. umbrella	40. raincoat

---

99 Adjectives   I

Disagree with the following, as shown:

John's popular.   **No, he's unpopular.**
Mary's right.   **No, she's wrong.**
The book was useful.   **No, it was useless.**

(a)
1. The road was wide.	8. Philip's honest.
2. The verb's regular.	9. My plan's practical.
3. John's modest.	10. Harry was pleased.
4. Henry was satisfied.	11. Lucy's experienced.
5. Jimmy was certain.	12. The drug was harmful.
6. Sarah's respectful.	13. Paul was adventurous.
7. Peter was friendly.	14. The firm's solvent.

114

15. John's mature.
16. Paul's sensible.
17. The plan's perfect.
18. Paul was coherent.
19. The action was legal.
20. The statement was valid.
21. The meal was satisfying.
22. Jim is professional.

23. The action was effective.
24. Peter's innocent.
25. The dog was infected.
26. The food was edible.
27. Mary's sensitive.
28. The drink was sweet.
29. Harry was suitable.
30. The road was passable.

(b) As (a) above (further practice).

1. Paul was affected.
2. Mary's sane.
3. Bob's cooperative.
4. Sarah was competent.
5. John was careful.
6. The star's visible.
7. The writing's legible.
8. I was conspicuous.
9. The piano was movable.
10. The car's serviceable.
11. John's eligible.
12. The drink was alcoholic.
13. The tool's essential.
14. The film's meaningful.
15. The party was organised.

16. The set was complete.
17. The test's simple.
18. My plan's superior.
19. The child was legitimate.
20. The story was believable.
21. The results were tangible.
22. The signs were favourable.
23. David was helpful.
24. The substance is organic.
25. The trunk's accompanied.
26. The book's worthless.
27. The people are civilised.
28. The judge was interested.
29. The arrangements were adequate.
30. Her illness is chronic.

---

100 Adjectives   I

Further practice with adjectives in the pre-noun position. Respond as shown:

Mrs. Brown—generous
  STUDENT A: **Can you describe Mrs Brown?**
  STUDENT B: **She's a very generous lady.**

novel—historical
  STUDENT C: **Can you describe the novel?**
  STUDENT D: **It's a historical novel.**

house—semi-detached
  STUDENT E: **Can you describe the house?**
  STUDENT F: **It's a semi-detached house.**

1. furniture—antique	11. newspaper—daily
2. car—sports	12. examination—oral
3. bed—double	13. flat—self-contained
4. John—intelligent	14. typewriter—portable
5. hotel—central	15. Peter—good-looking
6. wallpaper—plain	16. table—folding
7. magazine—illustrated	17. region—industrial
8. film—horror	18. river—fast-flowing
9. story—detective	19. town—country
10. school—comprehensive	20. Tom—hard-working

---

101 Adjectives   I

The pattern 'adverb + participle + noun' is common.

EXAMPLES:
That businessman's well known.
He's a   **well known businessman.**

This club's properly administered.
It's a   **properly administered club.**

Note:
Students have probably been taught that a hyphen is used when a combination like *well-known*, used attributively, is written. The hyphen is not wrong; it means that one of the components loses (some of) its stress—/ə 'welnəun /mæn/. But it is not necessary unless there might be ambiguity—and since we do not say 'a well man', there can be no ambiguity in the example given here. No hyphen should be used in writing 'a **properly administered** club' /ə 'prɔpəli əd'ministəd ˋklʌb/.

To practise the above pattern, give the alternative form as shown:

That man's well educated.
Yes. He's a well educated man.

This room's comfortably furnished.
Yes. It's a comfortably furnished room.

1. That woman's well dressed.
2. That bread was freshly baked.
3. This man's well built.

116

4. That worker's highly paid.
5. This boy's well behaved.
6. That woman's dearly loved.
7. This voter's well informed.
8. This play's cleverly written.
9. This party's well organised.
10. That building's badly positioned.
11. That flat's nicely furnished.
12. This meal's well prepared.
13. That house is well preserved.
14. This woman's highly respected.
15. That holiday was well deserved.
16. This actor's greatly admired.
17. That woman's happily married.
18. This house is well designed.
19. That doctor's fully qualified.
20. That explanation's totally inadequate.

NOUNS FUNCTIONING AS ADJECTIVES

102 ELEMENTARY/INTERMEDIATE

a room with a bath	a bathroom
a table for dinner	a dinner-table
a teacher of English	an English teacher

Notes:
  (i) Certain words which are usually nouns can function as attributive adjectives and can form word combinations.

  (ii) In writing, these combinations may be:

    (a) connected   (**bathroom**)
    (b) hyphenated (**dinner-table**)
    (c) separated   (**English teacher**)

It is not possible to give absolute rules about this, and the student must rely on a good dictionary, but modern British–English practice is generally:

(1) If the two parts are given equal attention, so that both have sentence stress, they are written or printed as two words:

Write to the **county council**.
/ðə ˈkaunti ˈkaunsl/

He collects **model aircraft**.
/ˈmɔdl ˈɛəkrɑːft/

(2) If the main attention is on the first part, it carries the major sentence stress, and a hyphen is commonly used:

Try a model in the **wind-tunnel**.
/ðə ˈwind‚tʌnl/

It has become usual to print this as two words without the hyphen when

(a) there is a degree of stress on the second part, and
(b) the person reading it will not misunderstand:

Try a model in the **wind tunnel**.

Take it to the **Post Office**.
/ðə ˈpəust ˈɔfis/

The reader must understand from the context whether, for example, the writer of

He's an **English teacher**.

means a teacher of English /ən ˈiŋgliʃ ‚tiːtʃə/ or an Englishman who is a teacher /ən ˈiŋgliʃ ˈtiːtʃə/.

(3) If the combination is in very common use so that it is spoken with only one major stress and no pause, it is likely to be written as one word: **teaspoon** /ˈtiːspuːn/, **headache** /ˈhedeik/, **seasickness** /ˈsiːsiknis/. But this is less common in British English than in American English.

(iii) Notice the difference in meaning between:

It's a **milk bottle**. (It's empty.)
/ə ˈmilk ˈbɔtl/

It's a **bottle of milk**. (It's full.)
/ə ˈbɔtl əv ˈmilk/

To practise nouns functioning as adjectives, respond as shown:

(a) *In 1–30 the combination in the answer always has major sentence stress on the first part.*

room—bed   STUDENT A: **What kind of room is it?**
            STUDENT B: **It's a bedroom.**

table—card   STUDENT C: **What sort of table is it?**
            STUDENT D: **It's a card-table.**

bottle—milk   STUDENT E: **What kind of bottle is it?**
            STUDENT F: **It's a milk bottle.**

1. room—class
2. book—note
3. board—chalk
4. coat—rain
5. set—radio
6. bottle—whisky
7. garden—flower
8. case—book
9. work—home
10. knife—fruit
11. packet—cigarette
12. house—fashion
13. book—telephone
14. cover—typewriter
15. case—suit
16. spoon—dessert
17. post—lamp
18. book—grammar
19. set—TV
20. knife—fish
21. chair—arm
22. case—brief
23. bag—hand
24. work—house
25. button—shirt
26. review—book
27. forecast—weather
28. cover—bed
29. box—telephone
30. view—sea

(b) *In 31–40 the combination in the answer has sentence stress on both parts.*

He lives in a fine old *house in the country*.
He lives in a fine old country house.

He sells paving stones for *paths in gardens*.
He sells paving stones for garden paths.
     (Notice the singular form of **garden**.)

31. Sandhurst is a college for *officers for the army*.
32. He's painting *the door of his garage*.
33. I'm particularly fond of *pies with apples in them*.
34. Once a year Mrs Hammond goes to see the *shops in London*.
35. I'm afraid *seats in the theatre* are becoming very expensive.

36. That fine building houses the *library belonging to the city*.
37. My son is interested in *travel through space*.
38. He's even invented his own *vehicle for the moon*.
39. I don't really like looking at other people's *albums of photographs*.
40. And I get terribly bored with their *photographs in colour*.

(c) *Read 41–50 aloud, trying to use a natural rhythm and sentence stress, especially for the combinations printed in italics.*

41. Have you ever been in a *London fog*?
42. In a bad fog you really need a *gas-mask*.
43. We couldn't find the way to the *railway station*.
44. You couldn't even see the *street lamps*.
45. We waited for ages for the *Brighton express*.
46. In the *station car park* I looked for the *family car*.
47. The *headlamps* only lit up the *fog particles*.
48. I was glad to see the glow of *firelight* in the *kitchen window*.
49. There was a cheerful fire in the *dining-room fireplace*.
50. There's nothing like *old-world home comforts*.

ADJECTIVE EQUIVALENTS

103 INTERMEDIATE

The man		told me a story.
The man	**at the bar**	told me a story.
The hotel		is in the High Street.
The hotel	**in the High Street**	is the best.
The woman		showed me the way.
The woman	**near the Post Office**	showed me the way.

Note:
The prepositional phrases in the above examples function as adjective equivalents, i.e. they act as modifiers, limiting the meaning of the noun they follow.

To practise the use of prepositional phrases with the subject, respond as shown:

The woman got first prize. She's across the road.
The woman across the road got first prize.

The man wants to borrow the record-player. He's at the door.
The man at the door wants to borrow the record-player.

1. The bank's open late. It's on the corner.
2. The jacket costs too much. It's on the counter.
3. The man's the new teacher. He's in the next room.
4. A man asked me for a match. He was near the cinema.
5. The woman's a doctor. She's in the car over there.
6. The shop sells TV sets. It's next to the chemist's.
7. A woman got out of the taxi. She was in a blue dress.
8. A girl took my temperature. She was in a white uniform.
9. The supermarket's shut. It's next to the post office.
10. The car caused an accident. It was opposite the station.
11. The fire was left on all night. It's in the classroom.
12. The service-station's open. It's at the end of the road.
13. The men cleaned all the carriages. They were in the train.
14. The children are playing table-tennis. They're in the basement.
15. The people are looking for bargains. They're in the department store.

---

104 Adjectives   I

Note:
Prepositional phrases may be adjective equivalents (modifiers) limiting nouns in other parts of the sentence besides the subject.

EXAMPLES:
I met a man **in a grey suit**.

I saw an old woman **with a suitcase**.

(a) *To practise placing the modifier before or after the noun, respond as shown:*

Jim will buy some shoes. (leather)
Jim will buy some leather shoes.

I want to know the name of the girl. (red dress)
I want to know the name of the girl in the red dress.

1. I want a camera. (Japanese)
2. That's the man. (broken leg)
3. I spoke to the woman. (suitcase)
4. How much is the book? (yellow cover)
5. I bought a number of ties. (woollen)
6. The policeman arrested the man. (gun)
7. I don't want that coat. (large collar)
8. Mary has never met the boy. (brown suit)
9. I gave the money to the woman. (pink hat)
10. Where can I find a lawyer? (honest and efficient)
11. Mary arranged for us to have a meal. (well cooked)
12. Why don't you find a girl-friend? (plenty of money)
13. Peter followed the girl into the shop. (mini-skirt)
14. Jane was looking for the socks. (the holes in them)
15. Peter asked the man for a typewriter. (reconditioned)

(b) *This is a substitution exercise to give further practice with modifiers.*

I want the car.	**I want the car.**
green	**I want the green car.**
leather upholstery	**I want the green car with the leather upholstery.**
fast	**I want the fast green car with the leather upholstery.**
large boot	**I want the fast green car with the large boot.**
luggage-rack	**I want the fast green car with the luggage-rack.**

1. the blue van
2. sliding doors
3. sunshine roof
4. sports car
5. radio
6. two-seater
7. the car

8. air-conditioning
9. flat
10. central heating
11. I'd like
12. built-in wardrobes
13. top-floor
14. the new house

15. the big garage
16. two-car
17. country
18. woods at the back
19. kitchen
20. we'll buy
21. lovely view
22. the old house
23. I'll have the room
24. private bath
25. ground-floor

26. shower and toilet
27. double bed
28. large
29. the room
30. newly-decorated
31. modern furniture
32. period
33. the suite (of rooms)
34. the man wants
35. brown suit
36. suitcase

---

105 Adjective Equivalents   I

The boy		is my brother.
The boy	on the chair over there	is my brother.
The boy	**sitting on the chair over there**	is my brother.

Note:
The prepositional phrase is preceded by an —ing form (present participle) 'sitting'. This adds further information to the adjective equivalent.

To practise using an —ing form + prepositional phrase to modify the noun in the subject, respond as shown:

The play's by Shakespeare. It's lying on the table.
The play lying on the table is by Shakespeare.

The car's mine. It's standing outside the front door.
The car standing outside the front door is yours.

The man's a doctor. He's having lunch at the next table.
The man having lunch at the next table is a doctor.

1. The smoke's dirty. It's rising from that chimney.
2. The boy should do well. He's working at that desk.
3. The computer's a new one. It's now being delivered.
4. The child's very noisy. He's playing in the garden.
5. The girl's a secretary. She's having dinner with me.
6. The man's trying to escape. He's hiding in the wood.
7. The student wants to watch TV. He's arguing with Tom.
8. The girl's always late. She's arriving at the door now.

9. The man's the manager. He's selling a car in the show-room.
10. The man's a famous musician. He's practising in that room.
11. The girl's my sister. She's putting on make-up in the hall.
12. The woman's Mrs Smith. She's speaking to Bob on the stairs.
13. The car used to be Tom's. It's now lying on the scrap-heap.
14. The patient's very ill. He's being examined in that cubicle.
15. The man has an urgent appointment. He's speaking on the phone.
16. The hotel will be very modern. It's being built near the airport.
17. The director's in a good mood. He's practising golf in his office.
18. The maid will be away next week. She's making the bed in your room.
19. The man's a politician. He's thumping the table in front of the TV cameras.
20. The man can't find anywhere to park. He's driving past the end of the road.

ADJECTIVE CLAUSES—Relative Pronouns

Preliminary notes:
In considering adjective clauses (also called relative clauses) it is important to be quite clear about the kind of English (the 'register') involved. The nature of our **spoken** English varies with the circumstances and the person or people we are speaking to; the nature of our **written** English varies with the purpose of our writing. The student should therefore be warned that the following division into **informal** and **formal** is an oversimplification.

informal—Most **spoken** English
Written English which is intentionally familiar in style

formal— English **written** for serious purposes
Speech-making and other speaking on important occasions

(i) In **informal** English—signalled (I) in examples below:
  (1) *Defining* relative clauses are common. Non-defining clauses are very uncommon.
  (2) *Contact* clauses (omitting relative pronouns) are usual.
  (3) The relative pronouns **whom** and **which** are not frequently used. Their use with a preposition (e.g. **to whom, of which**) is most uncommon.

(ii) In **formal** English—signalled (F) in examples below:
  (1) Both *defining* and *non-defining* relative clauses are used.
  (2) In very formal English there is still a tendency to avoid end-preposition constructions and therefore to use clauses introduced by preposition + pronoun (**to whom, in which** etc.).

Defining Relative Clauses

People:	A. The man	**who**	repaired my car is good at his job.	(I)
	B. The woman		you met last night is an air-hostess.	(I)
	C. The man		you told me **about** is on holiday in Rome.	(I)
	D. The girl	**whose**	photograph you saw just now is not here.	(I)
Things:	A. The car	**that**	won the race was driven by Jim Marshall.	(I)
	B. The book		Bob gave me was very interesting.	(I)
	C. The music		we listened **to** last night was by Beethoven.	(I)
	D. The car		*with the yellow top belongs to me.	(I)

Notes:
  (i) We use the word 'defining' since the relative clause actually defines the person or thing referred to by the noun that precedes it. Without this relative clause the person or thing remains unidentified.

  (ii) There is no pause after the noun preceding the defining clause, and there is no change of pitch in its stressed syllable.

That's the *man who found it*.   (I)
/ˈðæts ðə ˈmæn (h)uːˈfaund it/

The *man who found it is* over there. (I)

/ðə ˈmæn (h)uː ˈfaʊnd ɪts ˈəʊvə ˈðɛə/

(In writing, the headword and clause are not separated by a comma.)

(iii) In informal English the group marked (*) is preferable to the relative clause. **With** is also employed in similar sentences with people, e.g. The girl **with** the red hair is standing by the bar.

(iv) It is useful to distinguish between the four types: A, B, C and D. (To be found also in the non-defining relatives below.)

A. Subject first.   C. With preposition.
B. Object first.   D. Possessive.

(v) Alternative connectives for the above are:

	PEOPLE	THINGS
A.	**that**	**which**
B.	**that**	**that/which**
C.	**that**	**that/which**
D.	—	**that has/which has**

Non-defining Relative Clauses

People:

A. The world greatly admires Shakespeare, **who** wrote many plays, and **who** lived in England. (F)

B. She spent many happy holidays in Greece with Peter, **whom** she had first met in Athens. (F)

C. Room 501 is that of the sales manager, **to whom** a 50-hour week is nothing out of the ordinary. (F)

D. Mary was introduced to Mr Smith, **whose** book on education had been so well received by the critics. (F)

Things:

A. They had worked very hard on the house, **which** now looked much better decorated. (F)

B. The Chairman had recently been to Russia, **which** he described in detail in a lecture. (F)

C. He tried very hard to obtain the position, **to which** was attached a very high salary with many fringe benefits. (F)

D. Sherlock Holmes opened the bottle, the label **of which** declared the contents to be whisky. (F)

Note:
We use the word 'non-defining' because the relative clause merely offers further information about the word preceding it. Without the relative clause we would still know who or what is referred to.

There is a complete intonation pattern before the non-defining clause, with a pitch change (often a fall-rise) in the noun it modifies:

The portrait is of Elizabeth Taylor, who was the star of 'Antony and Cleopatra'.
/ðə ˈpɔːtrit iz əv iˈlizəbəθ ˈteiləˈhuː wəz ðə ˈstɑːrəv ˈæntəni ən kliəˈpætrə/

Elizabeth Taylor, who acted in 'Antony and Cleopatra', judged the competition. (F)
/iˈlizəbəθ ˈteilə huː ˈæktid in ˈæntəni ən kliəˌpætrə ˈdʒʌdʒd ðə kɔmpiˈtiʃn/

In these examples the non-defining clause is parenthetic. It could be shown in brackets:

Elizabeth Taylor (who acted in Antony and Cleopatra) judged the competition.

But the usual punctuation has commas, as shown above, to represent the breaks in intonation pattern.

---

106 Defining Relative Clauses I

To practise the 'subject first' pattern. Choose between who *and* that.

The man's good at his job. He repaired my radio.
The man who repaired your radio is good at his job.

The car was driven by Jim Brown. It won the race.
The car that won the race was driven by Jim Brown.

1. People aren't trusted. They tell lies.
2. The car was Jim's. It went into the ditch.
3. The film was 'The Victors'. It made Mary cry.
4. The ship was carrying a cargo of buses. It sank.
5. The girl's an air hostess. She helped you just now.
6. The man knows a lot about roses. He does my garden.
7. The man was the hotel manager. He put up that notice.
8. The assistant is off duty now. She served you before.
9. The man's a company director. He arranged the meeting.

10. The plane had come from New York. It had just arrived.
11. The woman's married to an architect. She wrote that book.
12. The newspaper was 'The Times'. It reported the news first.
13. The woman's outside the supermarket. She stole your purse.
14. The salesman has left this firm. He sold you that TV set.
15. The newspaper article was about the accident. It upset John.
16. The man's on the stage now. He was responsible for the play.
17. The man wanted to know where you were. He rang up last night.
18. The idea will make us a lot of money. It came to me just now.
19. The violinist was exceptional. He played at the concert hall.
20. The book's called 'Love Affair'. It pleased the critics most.

---

107 Defining Relative Clauses   I

To practise the 'object first' pattern. Use a contact clause.

The book was very interesting. Bob gave it to me.
The book Bob gave you was very interesting.

The woman's a computer programmer. I met her last night.
The woman you met last night is a computer programmer.

1. The train was the 1.45 p.m. Peter missed it.
2. The car was no good. You wanted me to buy it.
3. The flat has five rooms. John intends to rent it.
4. The student's passed his exams. David taught him.
5. The drug didn't help Peter. Dr Jones prescribed it.
6. The boy hasn't come back. I sent him to the grocer's.
7. The film was suitable for children. I let Paul see it.
8. The car had two detectives in it. John was watching it.
9. The club didn't provide tennis facilities. Sue joined it.

10. The man's gone on holiday. David advised John to see him.
11. The houses are very expensive. Bob wanted to inspect them.
12. The girl was wearing a grey dress. Tom remembers her best.
13. The girl's in Richard's office. John wants to take her out.
14. The case had all my things in it. The porter has mislaid it.
15. The diamond ring's not genuine. William gave it to his wife.
16. The woman was an old school friend. Alice met her yesterday.
17. The man was no longer at the hotel. John wanted to meet him.
18. The exercise is all wrong. We did it for homework last night.
19. The man was a sales representative. I took him into the shop.
20. The money should be spent on food. George spends it on drink.

---

108 Defining Relative Clauses I

To practise the 'prepositional' pattern (C). Use a contact clause.

The music was by Mozart. We listened to it last night.
The music you listened to last night was by Mozart.

The man's away in the United States. I told you about him.
The man you told me about is away in the United States.

1. The chair's not safe. You're sitting on it.
2. The boy never turned up. Sally waited for him.
3. The woman's a model. Gordon was looking at her.
4. The firm's gone bankrupt. I warned you about it.
5. The woman's here now. You were talking about her.
6. The girl's getting engaged. I gave a party for her.
7. The job's now done. I've been helping Peter with it.
8. The hotel used to be a palace. Betty's staying at it.
9. The camera wasn't worth buying. I was saving up for it.

10. The bus was the wrong one. Rosemary was running after it.
11. The man's the new manager. The chairman's talking to him.
12. The car's been stolen. Richard spent all that money on it.
13. The man's left for Miami. Jim was to get in touch with him.
14. The noise is from the flat above. Tom's complaining about it.
15. The boy's a student. Barbara's driving to the school with him.
16. The position's already been filled. Bob and Tom applied for it.
17. The woman's married with three children. Mary's smiling at her.
18. The money's been found. Sally and Caroline were looking for it.
19. The town will soon be full of tourists. We've just passed through it.
20. The man's the Secretary-General of the U.N. Robert was reading about him.

109 Defining Relatives   I

To practise the 'possessive' pattern (D), respond as shown:

The car belongs to me. It has a yellow top.
The car with the yellow top belongs to you.

The girl's not here. You saw her photograph just now.
The girl whose photograph I saw just now is not here.

1. The boat belongs to George. It has red sails.
2. The woman's in hospital now. John hit her car.
3. That's the newspaper. It has the best editorial.
4. That's the man. You'll be attending his lectures.
5. The bottle has shampoo in it. It has a green label.
6. That's the boy. His father made a fortune out of oil.
7. I want to buy the car. It has power-assisted steering.
8. The shirt's waiting to be cleaned. It has a green stain.

9. That's the man. You saw his photograph in the news-paper.
10. That's a picture of the man. You'll be visiting his house.
11. The house should fetch a good price. It has central heating.
12. That's the woman. Her son got an honours degree at university.
13. The police want to interview the man. His flat was broken into.
14. That's the woman. Her husband sailed round the world single-handed.
15. The chair's been taken to the repair shop. It has a broken leg.

---

110 Non-defining Relative Clauses   A

Use non-defining relative clauses to combine the following sentences:

The s.s. Unsinkable sank without trace. It was carrying 1,500 passengers.

The s.s. Unsinkable, which was carrying 1,500 passengers, sank without trace. (F)

The chairman of the company did not know the answer to the question. He had just come out of a Board meeting.

The chairman of the company, who had just come out of a Board meeting, did not know the answer to the question. (F)

The man outside the cinema got in contact with the police. His car had been stolen.

The man outside the cinema, whose car had been stolen, got in contact with the police. (F)

Richard Smith spoke to Peter about his plans. Peter had already met him several times before.

Richard Smith, whom Peter had already met several times before, spoke about his plans. (F)

Continue with the following. ( ) shows the point at which you are expected to add the clause. You should remember, however, that

131

a long clause between subject and main verb is usually avoided in English, even in formal style.

1. Sheila telephoned her sales manager ( ). He had given her the wrong instructions.
2. The clock in the hall ( ) suddenly became erratic. It had been accurate for years.
3. The man at the door ( ) said 'Thanks' and went off. David had given him some money.
4. The bottles containing drugs ( ) were nowhere to be found. They had been purchased only that morning.
5. The businessman in the lounge ( ) finally became impatient. He had been waiting for an hour.
6. The woman on the boat ( ) said she felt safer going by sea. Her husband was flying home.
7. The hospital patient in Ward 10 wanted to see his wife ( ). She was in Ward 11.
8. Mary explained the situation to Sally ( ). She knew that Sally would not be greatly offended.
9. The engineer at the workshop ( ) gave the little boy a sweet. He had children of his own.
10. The typewriter at the office ( ) was not as good as David's. The office machine had been bought cheaply.
11. The man in the orange sweater ( ) asked Jane out to dinner. She had helped to push his car to get it started.
12. The lady at the office party ( ) invited John to her house. He had never met her before.
13. Sally called at the newspaper office to see Tom Brown ( ). His article on the future of the town had irritated her.
14. Bob tried to purchase the painting 'Sea Rescue' ( ). It had once been in the possession of a relative of his.
15. The woman in the sea ( ) cried out to Peter for assistance. Her face could only just be seen.
16. The hotel guests ( ) went to the shop to buy their own papers. Their free copies had failed to arrive.
17. Sally interviewed Andrew Jones ( ). His employers were thinking of sending him to South America.
18. Jim called on Mary Jones ( ). She was just getting ready to go away for the weekend.
19. Paul wants to meet Susan Smith ( ). Her book on the history of music has just been published.
20. The pilot of the 'plane ( ) prepared for an emergency landing. He had already radioed his position.

Notes:
(i) **Which** may introduce a non-defining clause referring to a complete statement.

EXAMPLES:
He had a holiday in Mexico, **which** made him feel much better.   (I/F)

Mary failed her exams, **which** made her father very angry. (I/F)

Intonation varies with context but there is a complete statement pattern before **which**, e.g.
/hi hæd ə ˈhɔlədi in ˈmeksikəul witʃ ˈmeid him ˌfiːl ˌmʌtʃ ˈbetə/

(ii) **Which** and **whom** may occasionally be preceded by the prepositions **to** and **of**, but other prepositions are more common (especially with **which**).

EXAMPLES:
Peter spent the evening playing cards, **after which** he went home.   (F)

John lives at the Bridge Hotel, **near which** there is a well-known night-spot.   (F)

Whom (and **whose**) may also be preceded by certain prepositions, but this is rarely found in the spoken language.

EXAMPLES:
Don often saw Mary, **for whom** he had the greatest respect. (F)

This is John Brown, **without whom** (or: **without whose help**) I should never have succeeded.   (F)

(iii) **Which** and **whom** may be preceded by certain linking phrases.

EXAMPLES:
John had intended to spend his holiday in Spain, **instead of which** he decided to go to Italy.   (F)

I invested my savings in two public companies, **both of which** promptly went into liquidation.   (F)

Paul spoke to a lot of students, **none of whom** he had seen before.   (F)

There were six girls dancing, **each of whom** had made her own dress.   (F)

Other linking phrases are:

as a result of	neither of	because of
in addition to	either of	many of
on account of	(a) few of	some of
in spite of	every one of	all of

133

To practise the above patterns, respond as shown:

Jim didn't do the homework. This was silly of him.
Jim didn't do the homework, which was silly of him.

Bob spoke to two people. They wanted to buy his car.
Bob spoke to two people, both of whom wanted to buy his car.

Tom made a good impression. He got the job.
Tom made a good impression, as a result of which he got the job.

1. It began to rain heavily. The wind rose.
2. John stole from Jim. He was sent to prison.
3. Bob missed classes. He managed to pass his exam.
4. The firm went bankrupt. I found myself out of work.
5. Tom had arranged to go to Canada. He went to America.
6. I interviewed two workers. They could have·done the job.
7. I met two students. They couldn't understand anything.
8. The dog went into quarantine. I had to leave it behind.
9. Bob met a number of people. He didn't know any of them.
10. Sandra hurt herself. She went on instructing her class.
11. I looked at the pullovers. They had price-tags attached.
12. Betty spoke to the guests. She'd met many of them before.
13. Joe won a lot on a horse. This gave him an overall profit.
14. Elizabeth went to her sister's party. She then went to bed.
15. Richard played the records. He intended to buy some of them.
16. The exam was difficult for the students. Few managed to pass.
17. John got a rise in salary. This was exactly what he'd wanted.
18. The lecturer gave a lot of facts. Paul understood all of them.
19. Susan showed me some photos. I'd seen every one of them before.
20. Sheila should have gone to university. She emigrated to Australia.

Notes:
 (i) The possessive relative pronoun **whose** may be used with phrases such as **for the sake of**, **on behalf of**, etc.

> EXAMPLES:
> One of the firm's directors addressed the Board, **on whose behalf** he had previously spoken to the unions in order to effect a wage settlement.   (F)
>
> The child welfare officer brought in Tom and Mary, **for whose sake** their mother had decided not to leave home.   (F)

(ii) The 'preposition + relative pronoun' pattern may be replaced by the relative adverbs **when** and **where** (and sometimes **why**).

> EXAMPLES:
> Four o'clock is **when** I usually have a cup of tea.   (I)
> (Cf. . . . the time **at which** . . .)   (F)
>
> The office is **where** I spend most of my time.   (I)
> (Cf. . . . the place **at which** . . .)   (F)

Whereupon (meaning 'upon which' or 'as a consequence of which') may be used.

> EXAMPLE:
> Richard was told to leave the house, **whereupon** he packed his bags and took a taxi to the station.   (F)

Further practice with relatives:

Henry gave a lecture on Psychology. Susan was not the slightest bit interested in this subject.
Henry gave a lecture on Psychology, a subject in which Susan was not the slightest bit interested.

Sally will come on Tuesday. I shall be at home on that day.
Sally will come on Tuesday, when I shall be at home. (On which day).

Jim went to visit the Smiths. The Council had placed young Jimmy and Sarah in their care.
Jim went to visit the Smiths, in whose care the Council had placed young Jimmy and Sarah.

The students sat down at the examination desks. The papers were handed round.
The students sat down at the examination desks, whereupon the papers were handed round.

1. The demolition team knocked down a wall. The whole building collapsed.
2. Harry fell down the stairs. Sheila burst out laughing at the sight.
3. Mary went back to the church. She and John had been married there.
4. Peter dressed for dinner at eight o'clock. He usually had an appetite by this time.
5. Mary was handed the bill. When she received it she took out her purse.
6. James spoke to the owner of the house. He (James) had just thrown a ball over his wall.
7. Paul played golf from two to six p.m. Susan was doing the housework during this time.
8. The Government may decide to open an investigation. In this case Jim will have to go to Washington.
9. Jim wanted to discuss Economics. Helen knew absolutely nothing about this subject.
10. David met Jane's husband, Harry. Jane had left her well-paid employment for his (Harry's) sake.
11. John joined a new firm, Electrical Industries Ltd. He was to work for them for five years.
12. I visited a very old town. The name of it escapes me for the moment.
13. The headmaster talked the matter over with the head of the department. The results of the exam would depend on her teaching ability.
14. The factory manager reprimanded the foreman. The machine-tool had been damaged beyond repair through his (the foreman's) incompetence.
15. The Secretary-General of the U.N. addressed the Committee. He had previously spoken to the President on their behalf.

ADJECTIVE PATTERNS

113 ELEMENTARY

Adj. pattern A: **it** + be + adj. + **to**-infinitive

EXAMPLES:
It's suitable to wear.
It's safe   to drive.
It's simple   to use.

(a) *To practise the above pattern, with* it *in object relation to the* to-*infinitive, respond as shown:*

Is it ready? (use)	**Yes, it's ready to use.**
Is it exciting? (watch)	**Yes, it's exciting to watch.**
Is it good? (eat)	**Yes, it's good to eat.**

1. Is it cheap? (buy)
2. Is it interesting? (read)
3. Is it easy? (find)
4. Is it dangerous? (eat)
5. Is it hard? (learn)
6. Is it nice? (drink)
7. Is it safe? (handle)
8. Is it heavy? (lift)
9. Is it funny? (watch)
10. Is it awkward? (carry)
11. Is it easy? (undo)
12. Is it delightful? (watch)
13. Is it expensive? (run)
14. Is it difficult? (play)
15. Is it wonderful? (listen to)
16. Is it pleasant? (hear)
17. Is it exciting? (see)
18. Is it useful? (have)
19. Is it simple? (understand)
20. Is it handy? (use)

(b) Do not confuse the pattern in (a) with one in which **it** is in subject relation to the **to**-infinitive.

It's	likely	to happen
	sure	to explode
	certain	to disappear
	unlikely	to go away

Make sentences from the substitution table (16 are possible).

---

114 Adjective Patterns   EI

Adj. pattern B: (pro)noun + be + adj. + **to**-infinitive

EXAMPLES:
I   was **afraid to go** there.
You were **ashamed to be seen.**
Jim's   **glad to be** of help.

(a) *To practise the above pattern, respond as shown:*

Did you meet Peter? (determined)
Yes. I was determined to meet him.

Did you ring Anne up? (afraid)
No. I was afraid to ring her up.

Did you hear that Mary had come? (glad)
Yes. I was glad to hear that she'd come.

1. Did you see John with Anne? (amused)
2. Did you look in the cupboard? (scared)
3. Did you get a card from Sally? (amazed)
4. Did you do the exercise once? (content)
5. Did you help Peter? (glad—use 'able to')
6. Did you let Sheila use your room? (happy)
7. Did you see that David was here? (pleased)
8. Did you accept the invitation? (delighted)
9. Did you see Sandra at the party? (relieved)
10. Did you tell Anne where you'd been? (ashamed)
11. Did you get the present I sent you? (thrilled)
12. Did you hear that John was very ill? (shocked)
13. Did you hear Jane had got married? (astonished)
14. Did you see the stain on your coat? (horrified)
15. Did you know that Peter was coming? (interested)
16. Did you hear Mary wanted to meet you? (flattered)
17. Did you see that Sheila had failed? (disappointed)
18. Did you leave the dance early? (sorry—use 'have to')
19. Did you find you could remember the words? (surprised)
20. Did you hear that you were to be promoted? (gratified)

Note:
Most of the responses to the above could end with the infinitive particle *to*:

Did you meet Peter?—Yes. I was determined to.
Did you ring Anne up?—No. I was afraid to.

See also Exercise 293.

(b) *Further practice with pattern B above.*

Tell me something you'd be glad to hear.
I'd be glad to hear (that) my English was better.

Tell me someone you'd be glad to see.
I'd be glad to see Mary.

Tell me someone you'd be . . .
1. glad to see
2. prepared to help
3. willing to entertain
4. disappointed to miss
5. proud to know
6. thrilled to meet
7. interested to speak to
8. excited to go out with
9. astonished to see
10. happy to provide accommodation for

Tell me something you'd be . . .
11. glad to hear
12. afraid to do
13. angry to find out
14. disappointed to hear
15. sorry to see
16. delighted to receive
17. relieved to hear
18. excited to see
19. keen to do
20. amused to watch

---

115 Adjective Patterns I

Notice the anticipatory **it** in the following examples. The pronoun represents the whole of the **to**-infinitive phrase.

Tom finds **it hard** to believe the rumour.

She considered **it stupid** to start so early.

To practise this pattern and to add further practice in pattern B, respond as follows:

Paul finished the job. He found it difficult.
Paul found it difficult to finish the job.

Bob doesn't have to go home by sea. He's happy.
Bob's happy not to have to go home by sea.

John saw his picture in the paper. He was pleased.
John was pleased to see his picture in the paper.

1. I was away from home. I found it strange.
2. Bob's not seen the cathedral yet. He's keen.
3. We left the party early. We found it necessary.
4. Peter doesn't know the exam results. He's anxious.
5. I heard Susan's voice in the next room. I was relieved.
6. Jim knew he was to represent his country. He was pleased.
7. John didn't lend David his car. He found it inconvenient.
8. I heard that Susan's in trouble again. I was disturbed.
9. I have to tell you that we can't go out tonight. I'm sorry.
10. Mary learnt that Jim was getting married. She was surprised.
11. Alice is leaving for New York in an hour. She will be ready.
12. Betty will collect the car later. She will find it possible.
13. Bob wants to speak English very well. He finds it difficult.
14. I heard that nobody had been killed in the crash. I was glad.
15. Susan was told not to smoke. She thought it unusual.

---

116 Adjective Patterns   I

(a) Adj. pattern C: **it** + be + **—ing** + **to**-infinitive

EXAMPLES:
It was **amusing to see** Mary in that hat.
It's **thrilling to watch** that show.
It was **exciting to speak** to the producer.

Note:
The **it** in this pattern is anticipatory, representing the whole of the *to*-infinitive phrase. (See Exs. 137–140.)

To practise the above pattern, respond as shown:

What was surprising? (Paul at church)
It was surprising to see Paul at church.

What's frustrating? (traffic)
It's frustrating to be held up in traffic.

140

What's irritating? (able to remember her name)
It's irritating not to be able to remember her name.

1. What was thrilling? (the match)
2. What was horrifying? (that story)
3. What's irritating? (our team lose)
4. What's exciting? (the West Indies)
5. What's fascinating? (Helen dancing)
6. What's frustrating? (unable to help)
7. What was surprising? (Paul with Jane)
8. What was amusing? (John imitating Paul)
9. What was infuriating? (the train had gone)
10. What's annoying? (you're on the wrong road)
11. What's interesting? (Gordon's been promoted)
12. What was flattering? (Susan wanted to see me)
13. What's amazing? (Sally out of hospital so soon)
14. What's shocking? (the change in Jim's appearance)
15. What was frightening? (the fire spreading so quickly)

Practise also the short answer beginning with (not/to).

What was surprising? (Paul at church)

To see Paul at church.
/tə ˈsiːˈpɔːl ət ˈtʃɜːtʃ/

What's irritating? (able to remember her name)
Not to be able to remember her name.
/ˈnɔt tə bi ˈeibl tə riˈmembə hə ˈneim/

(b) Adj. pattern D: **it** + be + adj. + **for** + (pro)noun + **to**-infinitive

EXAMPLES:
It's   **inconvenient for us to leave** now.
It will be **better for John not to see** Mary tonight.
It was   **difficult for you to come** to a decision.

Note:
The **it** is anticipatory. (See also Ex. 137.)

To practise the above pattern, respond as shown:
Will John benefit from studying at university? (useful)
Yes. It will be useful for John to study at university.

Was Richard able to attend the concert? (impossible)
No. It was impossible for Richard to attend the concert.

141

Did Anne have to take the exam all over again? (necessary)

Yes. It was necessary for Anne to take the exam all over again.

1. Will you be able to see David? (possible)
2. Is Sheila often back home by 6 p.m.? (usual)
3. Was Bob able to have the day off? (impossible)
4. Will Jim have to be at the meeting? (necessary)
5. Does Pat often buy a new hat on pay-day? (common)
6. Did Jim have difficulty in writing the book? (easy)
7. Will it cheer Steve up to see Elizabeth again? (good)
8. Does Bob normally pick Anne up at her house? (unusual)
9. Can Sandra stay out late at a dance tonight? (all right)
10. Can you speak English without making mistakes? (difficult)
11. Will Peter benefit from doing the work by himself? (better)
12. Can the management improve industrial relations? (difficult)
13. Did Bob need to ask for any help with his work? (unnecessary)
14. Did Gordon have to attend the interview yesterday? (necessary)
15. Does Elizabeth prefer to have her holiday now? (more convenient)

---

117 Adjective Patterns   IA

Adj. pattern E: **it** + be + adj. + **of** + (pro)noun + **to**-infinitive.

EXAMPLES:

It was   **good of you to help** me with my work.
It's   **nice of Mary to offer** to help.
It will be **wrong of John to sell** the house.

Note:
The **it** is anticipatory. (See also Ex. 138.)

To practise the above pattern, respond as shown:

You were wrong to slap Jane's face just now.
Yes, it was wrong of me to slap Jane's face.

142

Peter's stupid to miss class so often.
Yes, it's stupid of Peter to miss class so often.

Bob was optimistic to imagine he'd be chosen for the team.
Yes, it was optimistic of Bob to imagine he'd be chosen.

1. Bill's sensible to arrange for an investigation.
2. You were careless to forget to write that letter.
3. Paul was clever to guess what I was thinking about.
4. Harry was stupid to think that he could outwit John.
5. Richard was impudent to expect me to lend him money.
6. The children were brave to go there alone in the dark.
7. George will be prudent to take out additional insurance.
8. Richard was idiotic to take the boat out in that weather.
9. John was foolish to expect Mary to accept his explanation.
10. David was cowardly to have run away when Mary needed help.
11. Sally will be wise to discuss the matter with her husband.
12. Betty was thoughtless not to have realised David would come.
13. Jim's wrong to think he can take it easy *and* pass his exams.
14. Bob was inconsiderate not to have anticipated Pat's reaction.
15. Jim will be unwise to take on that job without asking for further details.

---

118 Adjective Patterns   IA

Adj. pattern F: adj. + **that**-clause

EXAMPLES:
I'm   **glad (that) you've been able to come.**
Sally's **happy (that) John likes her.**
Jim was **anxious (that) Mary should enjoy the party.**

To practise the above pattern, respond as shown:

Are you sorry about the accident?
Yes, I'm sorry (that) I caused the accident.

Are you sure about the radio?
Yes, I'm sure (that) the radio's working all right now.

Are you worried about Sally?
Yes, I'm worried (that) something's happened to Sally.

1. Are you glad about the car?
2. Are you happy about the job?
3. Are you sure about the time?
4. Are you confident about John?
5. Are you angry about the delay?
6. Are you certain about the cost?
7. Are you annoyed about the noise?
8. Are you sorry about the mistake?
9. Are you positive about the strike?
10. Are you confident about the plan?
11. Are you worried about the future?
12. Are you optimistic about the race?
13. Are you certain about the homework?
14. Are you anxious about the operation?
15. Are you surprised about the weather?

---

119 Adjective Patterns   A

Adj. pattern G: adj. + preposition + (pro)noun or gerund
(—**ing**).

EXAMPLES:
Bob was **afraid of being beaten.**
Jim's **ashamed of his action.**
John's been **successful in business.**

To practise the above pattern, respond as shown:

Was John very upset when he failed his test? (angry)
Yes. He was angry at/about having failed his test.

Doesn't Mary like walking home alone in the dark? (afraid)
No. She's afraid of the dark.

144

Does Jim admire his son for his ability? (proud)
Yes. He's proud of his son.   (or . . . **of his son's ability.)**

1. Does Bill make a lot of spelling mistakes? (good)
2. Are smoking and drinking unhealthy activities? (bad)
3. Doesn't Richard mind working by himself? (accustomed)
4. Does Jim get annoyed when he's kept waiting? (not used)
5. Does Sue want to have Bob sit next to her? (apprehensive)
6. Did Bob find the address he was looking for? (successful)
7. Do you want to know how David made a profit? (interested)
8. Does Helen like to be taken out on Sunday evenings? (fond)
9. Did John panic when Sally didn't turn up? (really worried)
10. Were you surprised when share prices fell so low? (shocked)
11. Isn't John quite the worst actor you've ever seen? (hopeless)
12. Wasn't Jim able to solve the problem without help? (incapable)
13. Does Bob have to see that all the lights are out? (responsible)
14. Is Elizabeth waiting for the results to come through? (anxious)
15. Does Sue feel uncomfortable when people stare at her? (not used)
16. Doesn't Mary mind when people speak to her in bad English? (used)
17. Didn't Anne know anything about the stain on her dress? (unaware)
18. Does Mary object to having lessons in the afternoon? (quite happy)
19. Did Mary ignore Jim when he paid her compliments? (not interested)
20. Does Bob like to have Jane wait on him hand and foot? (accustomed)

120 ELEMENTARY

To practise forming regular and irregular plurals, respond as shown:

John used a match.
Mary used two matches.   (Regular)

John saw a man.
Mary saw two men.   (Irregular)

John went to a party.
Mary went to two parties.   (Regular)

1. John had a glass.
2. John visited a country.
3. John had a tooth out.
4. John used a box.
5. John saw a woman.
6. John visited a church.
7. John talked to a lady.
8. John saw a mouse.
9. John ate a tomato.
10. John used a knife.
11. John got a kiss.
12. John met a housewife.
13. John saw a foot.
14. John met a child.
15. John has a hobby.
16. John spoke to a man.
17. John used a match.
18. John saw a bus.
19. John held a party.
20. John bought a brush.
21. John put up a shelf.
22. John moved a piano.
23. John caught a fish.
24. John met someone.

121 Irregular Plurals   I

The following form their plural irregularly:

analysis	criterion*	bureau*
memorandum*	phenomenon	formula*
datum	crisis	medium*

*Note:
These have also regular plural forms which have achieved respectability in certain contexts, but use the irregular forms in this exercise.
Answers are on page 434.

Choose the correct word for each of the following and give the plural form:

1. . . . are facts given.
2. . . . are observed events.
3. . . . are decisive moments.
4. . . . are channels of communication.
5. . . . are notes to assist the memory.
6. . . . are standards or means of judging.
7. . . . are offices for the transaction of business.
8. . . . are general expressions for solving problems.
9. . . . are separations of things into their parts or components.

QUANTITY DETERMINATIVES

It is useful to divide certain determinatives into two groups: those used with countable nouns, and those with uncountable nouns. Compare the parts of the table below:

COUNTABLE (affirmative)		UNCOUNTABLE (affirmative)	
	a lot of		**a lot of**
	lots of		**lots of**
	plenty of		**plenty of**
	many		
There are	**enough** pens here.	There is	**enough** tea here.
	several		
	some		**some**
	a few		**a little**
	few		**little**
	no		**no**
COUNTABLE (negative)		UNCOUNTABLE (negative)	
	a lot of		**a lot of**
	many		**much**
There aren't	**enough** pens here.	There isn't	**enough** tea here.
	any		**any**

Notes:
 (i) The determinatives above (sometimes known as 'quantitative adjectives') describe either **quantity** or **number**.

(ii) Other determinatives to describe **number** are:
    a number of   a fair number of
    a large number of   a considerable number of
    hardly any

     Other determinatives to describe **quantity** are:
    a large quantity of   a good deal of
    a considerable quantity of   a great deal of
    a small/large amount of   a bit of
    hardly any

(iii) Compare: She has **a few** friends.   (probably sufficient)
                   She has   **few** friends.*   (certainly insufficient)
                   She has **a little** money.   (probably sufficient)
                   She has   **little** money.*   (certainly insufficient)

    (*Rather formal)

(iv) We often use **only** and **just** with **a few** and **a little**.

      EXAMPLES:
      I have **just a few** friends.
      I have **only a little** time.

(v) Notice how **much** is used:
      I don't have **much** free time. (a negative sentence)
      Do you have **much** free time? (an interrogative sentence)
      Yes, I've **plenty of** time. (**Much** cannot be used here)
      I like chocolate **very much**.
      Much time was lost during the strike.*
      Much of what you have said is irrelevant.*
      How **much** money have you got on you?—Not **much**.

    (*Rather formal)

(vi) The majority of the demonstratives function as pronouns as well as adjectives.

      EXAMPLES:
      Do you have **plenty of** free time?
      No. I don't have **much**. (I have only **a little**.)

      Have you got any chocolates?
      Yes. I've got **some**. (I've got **a few**.)

(vii) Certain of these determinatives function as adverbs.

      EXAMPLES:
      I speak English **a little**.   (I speak **a little** English.)
      I go to New York **a lot**.   (**I often** go to New York.)

(viii) **No** may be used alone or compounded as follows:

> I have **none**. (**None** is a pronoun meaning **not one**.)
> I have **nothing** to read,
> > **nobody** (**no one**) to speak to and
> > **nowhere** to go.

---

122 Quantity

The quantity determinatives can be divided into three groups:

(a) **A lot of, many, much, plenty of, etc.**
(b) **A few, a little, some, not much, not many, etc.**
(c) **No, not . . . any** (and the **no**-compounds **none, nothing, nobody**)

In this exercise a situation is given for Paul, and this will contain a word or phrase taken from one of the above three groups. Use a word or phrase drawn from each of the other groups to speak about John and Mary. Give Mary the larger number or quantity.

Paul's got a lot of friends.
> STUDENT A: **Mary's got a few friends.**
> STUDENT B: **John's got no friends.**

Paul knew no English.
> STUDENT C: **Mary knew a lot of English.**
> STUDENT D: **John knew a little English.**

1. Paul's got a lot of plans.
2. Paul hasn't got much (money).
3. Paul's got a little time.
4. Paul knows a lot about music.
5. Paul hasn't got any books.
6. Paul hasn't got any milk.
7. Paul needed a little help.
8. Paul's car has no petrol in it.
9. Paul knows nothing about art.
10. Paul had a little whisky.
11. Paul doesn't have much patience.
12. Paul wrote a few letters.
13. Paul makes many mistakes.
14. Paul drank a lot of beer.
15. Paul's got a few (friends).

16. Paul knows a little about Bob.
17. Paul's got a little (sense).
18. Paul knows a lot about cars.
19. Paul made a lot of money.
20. Paul saw a few people.
21. Paul spoke to nobody.
22. Paul took some photographs.
23. Paul had a little (trouble).
24. Paul didn't have much to do.
25. Paul had a lot to buy.

---

123 Quantity EI

To practise how much, *respond as shown:*

petrol   STUDENT A: **How much is petrol?**
             STUDENT B: (gives the price per litre)

oranges   STUDENT C: **How much are oranges?**
             STUDENT D: (gives the price per unit or kilo)

car (that)   STUDENT E: **How much is that car?**
             STUDENT F: (gives the price)

1. milk
2. newspapers
3. beer
4. cigarettes
5. whisky
6. bread
7. butter
8. oil
9. sugar
10. apples (those)
11. house (this)
12. car (that)
13. camera (the)
14. bananas (these)
15. shoes (those)
16. dictionary (the)
17. wine (that)
18. tape-recorder (the)
19. tapes (the)
20. record-player (that)
21. records (those)

---

124 Quantity I

To practise how much *and* how many. *Give both question and answer as shown:*

chairs—room (enough)
    STUDENT A: **How many chairs are there in the room?**
    STUDENT B: **There are enough chairs in the room.**

money—on you (plenty of)

STUDENT C: **How much money have you got on you?**
STUDENT D: **I've got plenty of money on me.**

1. sugar—bowl (a little)
2. people—crowd (a lot of)
3. time—homework (not much)
4. times—read that book (a few)
5. bread—lunch (a lot of)
6. petrol—car (not enough)
7. newspapers—table (not many)
8. magazines—bookstall (hardly any)
9. water—jug (enough)
10. bottles—doorstep (several)
11. milk—bottle (a little)
12. hotels—village (any)
13. room—suitcase (no)
14. rooms—hotel (a few)
15. mistakes—homework (very few)
16. intelligence—Bob (hardly any)
17. records—Don (lots)
18. friends—Bill (not many)
19. money—account (not much)
20. damage—car (a lot of)

Practise also the conversational short answers.

STUDENT A: **How many chairs are there in the room?**
STUDENT B: **There are enough,** or even: **enough.**
STUDENT C: **How much money have you got on you?**
STUDENT D: **I've got plenty.** or even: **plenty.**

---

125 Quantity   I

Answer the following questions with suitable quantity expressions, and follow these with short comments giving further information. (Choose your own expressions; the ones given in brackets are merely a guide.)

How many books have you got? (only a few)
Only a few—a course book and two dictionaries.

How much money have you got on you? (only a little)
Only a little—about five new pence.

Do you do much walking? (very little)
Hardly any—just at weekends.

Have you got enough time? (ample)
Yes, plenty—about an hour.

1. Do you have many hobbies? (not many)
2. How much do newspapers cost here? (not much)
3. Have you been to the club many times? (a few)
4. Does Jim spend much time swimming? (not a lot)
5. Does Barbara spend much on cosmetics? (not much)
6. Does Tom spend much time with Sally? (very little)
7. Do you meet many English people here? (just a few)
8. How many times has Rosemary been absent? (not many)
9. Do you spend much time at the races? (only a little)
10. How much time do you spend on your homework? (enough)
11. Have you had many letters from home yet? (quite a few)
12. Were there many people at the party last night? (lots)
13. Do you make many mistakes in your English? (only a few)
14. How many times have John and Mary had lunch here? (many)
15. How much does it cost to hire a car here? (rather a lot)

Both and All

With plural countable nouns	**Both** women	stayed for tea.	**All** men	tell lies.
	Both the women	stayed for tea.	**All** the men	had tea late.
	Both of the women	stayed for tea.*	**All** of the men	had tea late.*
	The women **both**	stayed for tea.	The men **all**	had tea late.
With uncountable nouns			**All** the milk	boiled over.
			All of the milk	boiled over.*
			The milk **all**	boiled over.
With 'be' and anomalous finites	**Both** women	were hungry.	{ **All** men	are liars.
			{ **All** milk	is nourishing.
	Both the women	were hungry.	**All** the milk	was sour.
	Both of the women	were hungry.	**All** of the milk	was sour.*
	The women were **both** hungry.		The milk was **all** sour.	
With pronouns	**Both** of us	stayed for tea.	{ **All** of them	had tea late.
			{ **All** of it	boiled over.
	We **both**	stayed for tea.	They **all**	had tea late.
	We were **both** hungry.		{ They were **all** angry.	
			{ It was **all** sour.	

Notes:
 (i) Sentences marked (*) in the table usually have a special meaning and are perhaps less common than the others.

 (ii) **Both** and **all** usually have sentence stress.

> We both stayed for tea.
> /wi ˈbəuθ ˈsteid fə ˈtiː/

> It was all sour.
> /it wəz ˈɔːl ˈsauə/ or /it wəz ˈɔːl ˈsauə/

(iii) Be careful of **all** + negative verb form. You may mean **none**.

> **All** the committee members are not here.
>   (= only some of them are here)
> **None of** the committee members are here.

In the same way, avoid **both** + negative verb when you mean **neither**.
(See also Ex. 205.)

---

126 ELEMENTARY/INTERMEDIATE

(a) *To practise using* both *and* all, *respond as shown:*

Do you both drink whisky?
Yes. Both of us do (we both do).

Will you all be going?
Yes. All of us will (we all will).

Did they both see John?
Yes. Both of them did (they both did).

Can they all speak English?
Yes. All of them can (they all can).

1. Can they both swim?
2. Did they all know the answer?
3. Must you both go?
4. Should they all be studying?
5. Have you both been away?
6. Were they all in class?
7. Did they both speak to John?

8. Must they all take the exam?
9. Can they both speak Russian?
10. Will you all be coming back?
11. Have they both finished?
12. Did you all visit the city?
13. Were they both late for work?
14. Will you all get up early?
15. Can they both come to lunch?
16. Do you all like to study?
17. Did they both have a walk?
18. Have they all been swimming?
19. Will you both have coffee now?
20. Do you all want to stop?

(b) *Further practice with* both *and* all.

Did the two boys come?
Yes. They both came.

Will the three girls go?
Yes. They'll all go.

1. Can the two men help?
2. Did the four women sing?
3. Have the two parcels gone?
4. Were the five books sent?
5. Must the two boys leave?
6. Will the six letters be sent?
7. Have the two papers arrived?
8. Can the three sisters dance?
9. Did the two postcards go?
10. Do the four men play golf?
11. Were the two rooms cleaned?
12. Did the ten teams play?
13. Have the two houses been sold?
14. Are the three flats vacant?
15. Were the two bottles full?
16. Have the four visitors come?
17. Can the two men drive?
18. Were the four cars repaired?
19. Did the two banks open?
20. Are the three women going to speak?

Every(one/thing)

127 Everyone and Everything   EI

Examples of the use of **everyone (everybody)** and **everything**:

Everyone knows Peter.
Everybody likes Harry.
Everything is all right.

To contrast the above words, respond as shown:

Who went to the party?	**Everybody did.**
What's wrong with your car?	**Everything is.**
Who knows the answer?	**Everyone does.**
What's fallen out of the suitcase?	**Everything has.**

 1. What's gone wrong?
 2. Who made you angry?
 3. What was the matter?
 4. Who did the homework?
 5. Who's read this book?
 6. Who wants dinner early?
 7. Who's gone to the cinema?
 8. Who's coming to the party?
 9. What's the matter with it?
10. Who can answer the question?
11. Who'll see Mary at the dance?
12. What's the matter with the car?
13. Who saw John off at the station?
14. What went wrong with the typewriter?
15. What's gone wrong with the hair-dryer?

128 ELEMENTARY/INTERMEDIATE

To contrast everyone (everybody) *with* all, *respond as shown. This is a substitution exercise.*

Everyone came.	**Everyone came.**
all the people	**All the people came.**
the students	**All the students came.**
have homework to do	**All the students have homework to do.**
everybody	**Everybody has homework to do.**

155

1. everyone	13. everyone
2. enjoys travelling	14. wants to learn English
3. all tourists	15. all businessmen
4. everybody	16. everybody
5. a holiday	17. to earn more money
6. all workers	18. all the workers
7. everyone	19. everyone
8. watches TV	20. avoid making mistakes
9. all the students	21. all students
10. everybody	22. speak English well
11. knows John	23. everybody
12. all the visitors	24. is interested in

129 INTERMEDIATE

Compare **each** and **every** with **all**:
> **Each** and **every** imply a number of persons or things that are considered individually (**each** is more individual than **every**).
> **All** implies a number of persons or things that are considered as a group.

EXAMPLES:
Each man was given his individual assignment.
Every man was given an assignment.
All the men were given assignments.

To practise and contrast each, every *and* all, *respond as shown.*
This is a substitution exercise.

Every student knows	
the answer.	**Every student knows the answer.**
all	**All the students know the answer.**
each	**Each student knows the answer.**
is studying hard	**Each student is studying hard.**
all the girls	**All the girls are studying hard.**
every	**Every girl is studying hard.**

1. all	9. use the library
2. come to class	10. each boy
3. every	11. has bought a car
4. wearing a new dress	12. all
5. all	13. every
6. each	14. each student
7. arrives early	15. took an exam
8. all	16. all

17. every
18. has a problem
19. all
20. have their own rooms
21. each
22. made a short speech
23. all

24. every
25. does exercises
26. all
27. have to buy books
28. their own
29. each
30. be interviewed

---

130 INTERMEDIATE/ADVANCED

Although **everyone** always means 'every person', **every one** may mean 'every person' or 'every object'. The word 'single' may be used for emphasis.

EXAMPLES:

He interviewed **everyone (everybody)**.
He interviewed **every one** of the applicants.
He interviewed **every single one** of the applicants.

A: We saw   **everything** in the city.
B: Did you see **every** museum?
A: Yes, we saw **every one** of them.
B: Not   **every one!**
A: Yes,   **every single one!**

Each may be adjectival or pronominal:

Each student has a book.	(adjectival use)
Each (one) has a book.	(pronominal use)
Each (one) of the students has a book.	(pronominal use)

Sometimes **each**, like **all** and **both**, follows (and is in apposition to) a plural (pro)noun. Notice the number of the verb in such cases:

The men **each** carry a suitcase.
They have **each** carried their suitcases for thirty kilometres, haven't they?

Each is used adverbially in such sentences as:

The men carried two suitcases **each**.
Oranges are 2 pence **each**.

To practise using the above words, use the word or phrase in brackets to replace all *in the following:*

We were all late. (everyone)
Everyone was late.

They all come. (each one of)
Each one of them comes.

You are all right. (every one of)
Every one of us is right.

We all know the answer. (each of)
Each of us knows the answer.

The students have all bought the wrong newspaper. (every)
Every student has bought the wrong newspaper.

1. All the glasses were broken. (every)
2. All the men at the party had cars. (each)
3. The fast trains have all gone. (every one)
4. We all tried out the new guitar. (everyone)
5. We have met all the people here. (everybody)
6. The guests have all been introduced. (each of)
7. The visitors all had a large breakfast. (each)
8. All the rooms have been cleaned. (every one of)
9. All the rooms were specially prepared. (each of)
10. All the tourists signed the visitors' book. (every)
11. We are all working hard just at present. (everyone)
12. All the hotels were uncomfortable. (every single one)
13. We all admire Jim for his charity work. (every one of)
14. All the girls there have their own flats. (each one of)
15. The women all have to take samples of the new butter. (each of)

Either and Neither

131 INTERMEDIATE/ADVANCED

Examples of how these words are used:

Either book is suitable.	(adjectival use)
Either (one) is suitable.	(pronominal use)
Either (one) of the books is suitable.	(pronominal use)

Neither job is easy.	(adjectival use)
Neither (one) is easy.	(pronominal use)
Neither (one) of the jobs is easy.	(pronominal use)

Both these words indicate *two* people or objects. **Either** means 'one *or* the other', **neither** means 'not one *nor* the other.' (See Exs. 132 and 205).

The exercise to follow includes practice in the use of **neither** with a verb in the affirmative form, but students should remember that

Where are the ships? I **can** see **neither** of them.

is rather more formal than

Where are the ships? I **can't** see **either** of them.

To contrast, respond as shown:

Which of those two houses did Jim buy? (neither)
(He bought) neither (of them).

Which of the two books did Mary choose? (not-either)
She didn't choose either (of them).

Can I have the mono recording, or must I have the stereo?
(either)
(You can have) either (of them).

1. Which of the two suits did Richard buy? (neither)
2. Which of those two films did Mary see? (not-either)
3. Can we invite Sheila, or must we invite Susan? (either)
4. Which of those two magazines was Paul reading?
(neither)
5. Which of the two letters did Sally throw away? (not-either)
6. Would Sue like to marry Bob, or would she prefer Jim?
(either)
7. Which of the two new employees will John promote?
(not-either)
8. Which of the two clubs in the town does Steve visit?
(neither)
9. Can I do business with Tom, or must I deal with Paul?
(either)
10. Does David recommend this newspaper, or that one?
(not-either)
11. Which of those two magazines did Jim choose for
Tom? (neither)
12. Can we call on Betty, or do we have to visit Barbara?
(either)
13. Can Allan take the written test first, or must he do the
oral? (either)
14. Would you like the blue car, or would you prefer the
red one? (not-either)
15. Can we buy the electric typewriter, or must we have the
standard model? (either)

NEGATIVE OPENINGS

132 INTERMEDIATE/ADVANCED

Compare sentences A with sentences B.

A
- **Everyone** (**everybody**) knows John.
- **Many** people enjoy driving.
- **All** (of) these books are mine.
- **One** of these records is Peter's.
- **Someone** (**somebody**) loves Susan.
- **Something** has happened to Mary.
- **Both** (of) these girls are pretty.

B
- **Not everyone** knows me.
- **Not many** (people) enjoy hunting.
- **Not all** of them are novels.
- **None** of them is Richard's.
- **No one** (**nobody**) loves Betty.
- **Nothing** has happened to Sue.
- **Neither** (of them) is rich.

Notes:
Much may be used in this pattern, but is not so common as the above.

EXAMPLES:
Much of what you've said is important.

Not much of what he told us was easy to understand.

Neither is the subject of a singular verb, but it is sometimes used in apposition to the plural subject of a verb in plural form.

EXAMPLES:
Neither of the boys **goes** fishing.

They neither of them **go** fishing.

None is the subject of a singular or a plural verb according to the sense.

EXAMPLES:
None of these boats **is** Chichester's 'Gipsy Moth'.

None of these boats **are** privately owned.

If in doubt, use a plural verb for **none** when speaking informally.

To practise negative openings, respond as shown:

Did either of the girls want to go?
No. Neither of them did.

Does everyone here like cheese?
No. Not everyone here does.

Are any of you from Poland?
No. None of us are/is. (See the notes.)

Did anybody knock at the door just now?
No. Nobody did.

1. Do any of you take drugs?
2. Is everybody you meet reliable?
3. Has anything happened to Sally?
4. Do all of you have a big breakfast?
5. Do many people sleep during the day?
6. Do any of you know English very well?
7. Do all of you work during the evening?
8. Are any of you from the United States?
9. Did either of the boys pass his exams?
10. Are both those shops closed on Saturdays?
11. Can either of you help me with my work?
12. Are any of these exercises very difficult?
13. Were any of you living in Geneva last year?
14. Does everyone in Canada speak good English?
15. Do both of them take an interest in sport?
16. Do any of you go to Bermuda for your holidays?
17. Are all your sentences in English correct?
18. Would any of you like to take next Monday off?
19. Is any of that article suitable for publication?
20. Does everyone here take an interest in economics?
21. Are any of the rooms in that hotel very comfortable?
22. Does anybody want to dance with Sally Jones tonight?
23. Did anything happen to Susan when she was on holiday?
24. Would anyone here like to spend the winter in Scotland?
25. Do all of the national daily papers give information about share prices?

You'd better go now, **or else** you'll be late.
Sue had better stop,   **or else** Jim'll be angry.

Note:
Or else is similar in meaning to **or, otherwise** or **if not**.

To practise or else, *respond as shown:*

If she doesn't study, she won't learn English.
She'd better study, or else she won't learn English.

If he doesn't leave now, he'll miss his plane.
He'd better leave now, or else he'll miss his plane.

If they don't stop smoking, they may get lung cancer.
They'd better stop smoking, or else they may get lung cancer.

1. If you don't work hard, you'll fail your exam.
2. If Gordon doesn't write, his wife will be upset.
3. If Jim doesn't ask Bob, he won't know what to do.
4. If Tom doesn't learn English, he won't get the job.
5. If I don't buy a ticket, I shan't be able to travel.
6. If the street isn't widened, there'll be an accident.
7. If Joe doesn't make a reservation, he won't get a seat.
8. If Paul doesn't get a job, Mary won't see him any more.
9. If Allan doesn't answer the letter, there'll be trouble.
10. If Sheila doesn't relax, she'll have a nervous breakdown.
11. If John doesn't go now, his train will leave without him.
12. If Tom doesn't ask for a rise in salary, he won't get one.
13. If Paul doesn't read that report, he won't know how to act.
14. If you don't go to the shops, we shan't have anything to eat.
15. If we don't have our TV set repaired, we'll have to watch Bob's.

I didn't take the car.	**Someone (somebody) else** did.
Bob's at the office.	Is **anyone (anybody) else** there?
Allan can do the job.	**No one (nobody) else** can.
I stayed at the party.	**Everyone (everybody) else** left.
The plate didn't break.	**Something else** did.
The beer's finished.	Is there **anything else?**
Why are you studying?	There's **nothing else** to do.
You can wash the dishes.	**Everything else** has been done.
Your watch isn't here.	It must be **somewhere else.**
The money must be here.	It can't be **anywhere else.**
Has he looked everywhere?	Yes, there's **nowhere else.**
Sheila must be at home.	I've looked **everywhere else.**

Notes:

(i) The above compounds represent:

some		person
no	other	thing
any		place
every		

(ii) Example of the possessive form:
It wasn't our Morris. It was somebody else's car.
/it wəz ˈsʌmbədi ˈelsiz ˌkɑː/

(iii) Compare: A: John took two people to the dance: Mary, and
someone else. (An additional person.)
B: Peter didn't take Susan to the dance; he took
someone else. (A different person.)

To practise someone else, nobody else, *etc., respond as shown:*

She wanted Philip to come. (no one)
No one else did.

Jim won't be going to Canada. (somewhere)
He'll be going somewhere else.

Harry didn't want to see *Sheila*. (someone)
He wanted to see someone else.

I'll have to do the work myself. (anyone)
There isn't anyone else to do it.

Richard took his own car. (anybody)
He didn't take anybody else's.

1. Bill wants John's help. (anybody)
2. Peter didn't take the pen. (someone)
3. Betty hasn't met *Mr Brown*. (everyone)
4. Harry refuses to eat at home. (somewhere)
5. Only Mary's essay was good enough. (nobody)
6. Jane will go to bed early tonight. (nothing)
7. Betty doesn't like the new house. (everyone)
8. Mary didn't have steak for dinner. (something)
9. Gordon didn't look in the bedroom. (everywhere)
10. We've searched every room in the house. (nowhere)
11. George wants to take Sally out to lunch. (anyone)
12. Peter will have to watch TV tonight. (anything)
13. Mr Hammond hasn't seen *Elizabeth* today. (everyone)
14. Richard spends his holidays in Sardinia. (anywhere)
15. Sheila's still got the shopping to do. (everything)

---

135 ELSE with Interrogatives   **IA**

Where else did John see Sandra?
What   else could Mary do for John?
Who   else came to see Elizabeth?

How   else should I have travelled?
When   else do you visit Richard?
Why   else would he have come here?

Notes:
 (i) The above forms represent 'what other place, thing, person, manner, time and reason'.

EXAMPLE:
'John went to the hospital to see Elizabeth.'

'Who else went to see her?'
/'huː `els ˌwent tə ˌsiː hə/

(ii) **Else** is more commonly found with **where**, **what** and **who(m)** than with **how**, **when** and **why**.

(iii) An obvious statement such as 'I took *my wife* to the party' may produce the remark 'Who else would you have taken?' meaning that your taking anyone else would have been unlikely.

To practise the above patterns, respond as shown:

John and Mary came to the party late. (who—nobody)
STUDENT A: **Who else came to the party late?**
STUDENT B: **Nobody else did.**

Mary will go to Australia. (where—New Zealand)
STUDENT C: **Where else will she go?**
STUDENT D: **She'll go to New Zealand.**

Paul did some work with the computer last night. (what—report)
STUDENT E: **What else did he do?**
STUDENT F: **He did some work on his report.**

John took Mary out last night. (who/would—Sally)
STUDENT G: **Who else would he have taken out?**
STUDENT H: **He might have taken Sally out.**

1. I can come on Monday. (when—Tuesday)
2. Jim likes to travel by bus. (how—train)
3. Paul saw Mary in the bar. (who—Susan)
4. Bob told me about his hobbies. (what—work)
5. Henry met Peter at the banquet. (who—Sandra)
6. Bill did his homework last night. (what—TV)
7. Don has been to New York. (where—San Francisco)
8. Bob goes to Madrid every summer. (when—Christmas)
9. Richard bought three magazines. (what—a newspaper)
10. Peter couldn't have taken the car. (who/could—David)
11. George went to America to see Mary. (why/would—Helen)
12. Mary might have gone to the bank. (where/might—grocer's)
13. You shouldn't have spoken to John like that. (how/should—politely)

14. Susan bought a car to get to work. (why/would—not have to travel by bus)
15. John got Paul's address by looking it up in the phone book. (how/could—ask)

It

Introductory notes:

(i) **It** is used as the subject of an impersonal verb, especially in expressions of time, weather, distance, etc.

EXAMPLES:

It's 12 o'clock.

It was fine yesterday.

It isn't far to the nearest town.

(ii) **It** may refer to a person in such sentences as:

Who is **it**? (the person knocking)
It's me. (Grammatically incorrect but usual in speech.)
If **it**'s the baker (at the door), we don't want any.

(iii) **It** is used as a subject anticipating the real subject, which may be a clause or phrase. (The real or virtual subject is in italics in the examples.)

EXAMPLES:
It's good *to be home*.

It was necessary *for you to see John*.

It seems wrong *not to invite Mary*.

(iv) **It** may be a formal object in patterns related to those in (iii) above.

EXAMPLES:
He found **it** hard to believe *that she was a thief*.

The professor thought **it** undignified *to run for a bus*.

(v) There is never sentence stress on **it** in any of the uses mentioned above.

136 ELEMENTARY/INTERMEDIATE

To practise simple question and answer with it, *respond as shown:*

Is it nice out?
Yes, it is. It's nice out.

Is it six o'clock yet?
No, it isn't. It's not six o'clock yet.

Did it rain yesterday?
Yes, it did. It rained yesterday.

Was it Jill on the phone? (Helen)
No, it wasn't. It was Helen on the phone.

1. Is it warm out?
2. Is it time to go?
3. Has it rained recently?
4. Was it cloudy yesterday?
5. Has it been cold recently?
6. Will it get warmer next week?
7. Was it Paul on the phone? (Bob)
8. Was it silly of Peter to come? (yes)
9. Was it warm enough to swim last week?
10. Does it cost a lot to go to New York?
11. Is it John I can see over there? (Jim)
12. Was it easy for Bob to get a taxi? (no)
13. Is it necessary to wear an overcoat today?
14. Was it John who was speaking just now? (Jim)
15. Was it expensive for Jim to come by sea? (no)
16. Is it possible for me to buy a newspaper now?
17. Is it important to have a good pronunciation?
18. Will it be necessary to repeat this exercise?
19. Is it difficult for you to understand English?
20. Is it far from here to Bermuda? (quite a long way)

---

137 Anticipatory **It**   **I**

A very common pattern: IT + adj. (+*for* + (pro)noun)
+ *to*-infinitive

See also Ex. 116b.

(a) *To practise* it + *adj.* + to-*infinitive, respond as shown:*

It's bad to study every day, isn't it?
No. It's good to study every day.

It was easy to get up early, wasn't it?
No. It was difficult to get up early.

It's honest to take people's money, isn't it?
No. It's dishonest to take people's money.

1. It was necessary to buy that book, wasn't it?
2. It's advisable to drink cheap whisky, isn't it?
3. It was easy to understand what he said, wasn't it?
4. It was boring to look around the museum, wasn't it?
5. It was nice to hear that foreign accent, wasn't it?
6. It's unusual to see girls in mini-dresses, isn't it?
7. It will be cheap to fly to the United States, won't it?
8. It's possible to work twenty-four hours a day, isn't it?
9. It will be necessary to repeat this practice, won't it?
10. It was interesting to see John's collection, wasn't it?
11. It's horrible to spend the day learning English, isn't it?
12. It's important to know who signed the agreement, isn't it?
13. It was possible to stop the fire from spreading, wasn't it?
14. It would be pleasant to live in a one-room flat, wouldn't it?
15. It was difficult to arrange an interview with Bob, wasn't it?

(b) *To practise* it + *adj.* + for + (*pro*)*noun* + to-*infinitive*, respond as shown:

It's not necessary to study.

It may not be necessary for *you* **to study, but it** *is* **necessary for** *us*.

It was easy to do that exercise.

It may have been easy for *you* **to do that exercise, but it** *wasn't* **easy for** *me*.

1. It's not hard to study all day.
2. It's cheap to fly to Washington.
3. It wasn't necessary to go by bus.
4. It was interesting to speak to Jim.
5. It's easy to understand English.
6. It was funny to see you fall down.
7. It wasn't easy to find a taxi quickly.
8. It's too cold to go into the water.
9. It was impossible to write that report.
10. It was boring to see the same film again.
11. It's not difficult to speak English well.
12. It will be necessary to look that word up.
13. It's possible to drive there in two hours.
14. It wasn't difficult to get some cigarettes.
15. It will be nice to live in the town centre.

Another **it** pattern: **it** + adj. + *of* + (pro)noun + *to*-infinitive.
See also Ex. 117.

To practise this pattern, respond as shown:

Should John have helped Mary with her work? (considerate)
If he did, it was considerate of him.
/if hi ˅did it wəz kən`sidərit ɔv him/
Should Richard have driven without a licence? (silly)

If he did, it was silly of him.
Should Mary have told Sally not to come to her house?
(unkind)
If she did, it was unkind of her.

1. Should Betty have lied to Jim? (stupid)
2. Should David have offered to help? (good)
3. Should Peter have given up his job? (wrong)
4. Should John have told Paul to shut up? (rude)
5. Should David have fought that intruder? (brave)
6. Should Betty have asked that question? (sensible)
7. Should Susan have stopped before finishing? (lazy)
8. Should Mary have left the door unlocked? (careless)
9. Should Peter have opened the door for Mary? (polite)
10. Should John have stayed on at university? (sensible)
11. Should Mary have telephoned Susan's husband?
    (naughty)
12. Should Henry have removed the TV set? (inconsiderate)
13. Should Jim have called on Lucy at 11 p.m.? (thoughtless)
14. Should Jim have picked Mary up at the office?
    (thoughtful)
15. Should Sally have agreed to look after the children?
    (kind)

It is necessary	to work hard to succeed.
It was stupid of him	**not** to drive more carefully.
It is important	to listen to good English.
It will be better for him	**not** to drink so much.

Notes:
 (i) The **not** in the above examples refers to the infinitive phrase.

(ii) The perfect infinitive can replace the present infinitive in the second example above:

    It was stupid of him **not to have driven** more carefully.

To practise this, choose between the affirmative and the negative:

What's a good idea? (overwork)
It's a good idea not to overwork.

What was necessary? (buy a computer)
It was necessary to buy a computer.

What was considerate of Bob? (call too early)
It was considerate of him not to call too early.

  1. What's wrong? (write home)
  2. What's stupid? (drive carefully)
  3. What's nice? (have to work on Sundays)
  4. What was unwise? (rely on that young girl)
  5. What's difficult? (speak English correctly)
  6. What's advisable? (keep in with the manager)
  7. What would be better? (read that stupid book)
  8. What was clever of Robert? (reveal his identity)
  9. What's silly? (see London while you're in England)
10. What's bad for the health? (stay up late every night)
11. What was thoughtful of Peter? (phone early last night)
12. What would be ridiculous? (spend all your time studying)
13. What's dangerous? (keep your eyes on the road while driving)
14. What's impolite of a man? (give his seat to a lady on a train)
15. What would be more convenient? (have the meeting after dinner)

---

140 Anticipatory **It**   A

Note:

It may be used when the subject is a clause.

It is amusing **that Bob caught the wrong bus**.

It was a mystery **how John managed to win**.

It is obvious **why Peter went to the bank**.

This pattern often takes *should*.

It is strange **that he should not have known**.

It is unbelievable **that Mary should have forgotten**.

To practise the pattern: It + be *(seems, etc.) complement (noun or adj.)* + *clause, respond as shown:*

John made that mistake. It's a mystery.
Yes, it's a mystery how John made that mistake.

The match had to be called off. It's unfortunate.
Yes, it's unfortunate that the match had to be called off.

Mary didn't tell you. It seems unbelievable.
Yes, it does seem unbelievable that Mary should not have told me.

1. Peter knew we were coming. It's surprising.
2. David forgot his appointment. It's incredible.
3. John came very late. It's unfortunate. (use *so*)
4. Bob didn't see what was going on. It's remarkable.
5. John has been selected for the job. It's fortunate.
6. Mary was expected to go out to work. It's unbelievable.
7. Jim didn't know about the accident. It's extraordinary.
8. Bob had to resign from his job last month. It's obvious.
9. David has decided not to take up medicine. It seems a pity.
10. Jane wore old-fashioned clothes. It's ridiculous. (use *such*)
11. Very few people were in the train. It's remarkable. (use *so*)
12. Susan brought up six children all by herself. It's a mystery.
13. Henry lost his way in the town last night. It's unbelievable.
14. Brian wasn't told about the new play. It seemed surprising.
15. The workers went on strike without giving any warning. It's extraordinary.

Too and **Enough**

These shoes are	small.		
These shoes are **too** small.			
These shoes are **too** small		**for** Mary.	
These shoes are **too** small		**for** Mary **to** wear.	

Those shoes are	big.		
Those shoes are	big	**enough.**	
Those shoes are	big	**enough for** John.	
Those shoes are	big	**enough for** John **to** wear.	

Note:
Other very common patterns are:

too + many/few (+ plural noun):
John has **too many shoes**, but Mary hasn't got **too many**.

too + much/little (+ uncountable noun):
Mary uses **too much make-up**; nice girls don't use **too much**.

enough (+ plural or uncountable noun):
Mary hasn't got **enough shoes**.
Have you got **enough butter**?—Well, I've got nearly **enough**.

To practise the following two patterns:
      be + too + *adj.*
and   be + *adj.* + enough

Respond as shown:

I can't see the ship.	**It's too far away.**
(far away)	**It isn't near enough.**
John can't wear that shirt.	**It's too big.**
(big)	**It isn't small enough.**
Bob can't do these exercises.	**They're too hard.**
(hard)	**They aren't easy enough.**

  1. Bob can't eat those apples. (sour)
  2. Sally can't use that glass. (dirty)

3. Susan can't go to the theatre. (far)
4. George can't run in the race. (slow)
5. David can't speak to strangers. (shy)
6. Peter can't sleep in that bed. (hard)
7. Bill can't wear those trousers. (long)
8. George can't wear those shoes. (small)
9. Philip can't join the youth club. (old)
10. Mary can't read those reports. (boring)
11. Jane can't swim in the sea today. (cold)
12. Jim can't buy that furniture. (expensive)
13. John can't go to the cinema alone. (young)
14. Paul can't understand that book. (difficult)
15. Anne can't concentrate on her work. (excited)

142 **Too** and **Enough** I

See the note to the previous exercise.

Other patterns with **too** are:
(a) verb + *too* + adverb
EXAMPLES:
Peter speaks **too quickly.**

Anne applied the brakes **too sharply.**

(b) verb + *too* + adjective or adverb + *to*-infinitive
EXAMPLES:
She is **too thin to wear** that dress.

He was driving **too fast to stop** in time.

(c) verb + *too* + adjective or adverb + *for* + (pro)noun
EXAMPLES:
Jean was **too clever for John.**

You speak **too indistinctly for them.**

(d) verb + *too* + adjective or adverb + *for* + (pro)noun + *to*-infinitive
EXAMPLES:
Bob walks **too quickly for Mary to keep up.**

Peter is **too self-centred for Helen to fall** in love with him.

To practise the various patterns with too, *respond as shown:*
John eats a lot. He's fat.
John eats too much.

Jim speaks quickly. I can't understand him.
Jim speaks too quickly for you to understand.

Jane's a big girl. She can't get into that dress.
Jane's too big to get into that dress. (or: . . . **big for** . . .)

1. Jim's tired. He refuses to get up.
2. Mr Brown's old. He won't get the job.
3. Allan arrived late. The party was over.
4. The water's rough. The ship can't sail.
5. David arrived early. Betty wasn't ready.
6. Don's unhappy. He won't go to the dance.
7. John was laughing hard. He couldn't stop.
8. The river's deep. The men can't cross it.
9. The walk was long. Susan got tired quickly.
10. Sheila's busy. She can't watch TV tonight.
11. The suit was large. George couldn't wear it.
12. The suitcase was heavy. Jean couldn't lift it.
13. Paul speaks quickly. You don't understand him.
14. George is comfortable. He doesn't want to move.
15. Harry drives fast. John can't keep up with him.
16. The street was narrow. I couldn't overtake Peter.
17. The wall was high. Gordon couldn't climb over it.
18. Elizabeth's lazy. She never does any work in class.
19. The taxi ride was uncomfortable. David couldn't relax.
20. Mary invited a lot of people. Not everybody got a drink.

---

143 Too and Enough   I

See the notes to Exercises 141 and 142.
Other patterns with **enough** are:

(a) verb + adverb + *enough*
    EXAMPLES:
    Mary never eats **fast enough.**

    Gordon doesn't speak **slowly enough.**

(b) verb + adjective or adverb + *enough* + *to*-infinitive
    EXAMPLES:
    She was **polite enough to apologise.**

    He sang **well enough to make a living.**

(c) verb + adjective or adverb + *enough* + *for* + (pro)noun

EXAMPLES:
John isn't **clever enough for Helen.**

He didn't speak **clearly enough for Bob.**

(d) verb + adjective or adverb + *enough* + *for* + (pro)noun
+ *to*-infinitive
EXAMPLES:
Paul will never be **rich enough for Sue to marry.**

Susan danced **well enough for the film producer to offer**
her a contract.

To practise the various patterns with enough, *respond as shown:*

Joe's driving fast. He'll arrive in time.
Joe's driving fast enough to arrive in time.

This exercise is easy. I can do it without help.
This exercise is easy enough for me to do without help.

The suitcase is big. It will take all my things.
The suitcase is big enough to take all my things.
   (or: . . . **enough for** . . .)

1. Elizabeth ran fast. She caught the bus.
2. The watch was cheap. I was able to buy it.
3. George spoke well. He won the speech prize.
4. The suitcase was light. Susan could lift it.
5. Mary drove well. She passed her driving test.
6. Philip was hungry. He asked for another cake.
7. Richard's intelligent. He will know what to do.
8. Alice isn't attractive. Nobody wants to marry her.
9. Paul was clever. He made a fortune selling used cars.
10. The doctor says that Gordon's well now. He can get up.
11. Henry was considerate. He gave his seat to an old lady.
12. Mr Brown's wealthy. He can retire and live in Trinidad.
13. John knows English well now. He can stop going to class.
14. Barbara got to the theatre early. She saw the first act.
15. Richard's work wasn't good. His manager wasn't satisfied.
16. George has lived here for a long time. He knows everybody.
17. Betty's very interested. She will ask for further details.
18. Sally didn't drink her tea fast. Her friends wouldn't wait.

19. Helen was angry. She called the police and made a complaint.
20. John got home early. He watched his favourite TV programme.

INTERROGATIVES

Introductory notes:
  (i) Questions are of two types:
      (a) with an interrogative word (Wh— questions).

          EXAMPLES:
          Where have you been?

          What did you say?

          How do you pronounce your name?

          Who was at the party?

      Wh— questions usually end with a falling intonation:

      /ˈhuː wəz ət ðə ˋpɑːti/

      (b) with an auxiliary (Yes/No questions).

          EXAMPLES:
          Will Sue have a holiday?

          Didn't John arrive late?

          Does Bill like coffee?

          Don't you like coffee?

      Yes/No questions usually end with a rising intonation:

      /ˈdəunt ju ˈlaik ˏkɔfi/

 (ii) Question phrases, sometimes called 'tags', may be attached to statements.

      EXAMPLES:
      You're English, **aren't** you?

      He's gone, **hasn't** he?

      Jim went yesterday, **didn't** he?

      (See Exs. 294–298)

(iii) Prepositions governing interrogatives come at the end of spoken questions.

176

EXAMPLES:

Who do you wish to speak **to**?

What was Mary looking **at**?

Where has John just come **from**?

(iv) Certain interrogative words may be used with **ever** (See Ex. 159) and **else** (See Ex. 135).

EXAMPLES:

Why ever did Mary see John?

How ever will she get here by 7 p.m.?

Where else can John find a room?

What else could I have done?

(v) Care must be taken to distinguish a question from a noun clause.

Question: **What happened last night** at the club?
Noun clause: **What happened last night** worried Jim.

Since intensive practice with Yes/No questions (those with auxiliaries) is given throughout this book (especially concentrated in the exercises on the tenses and anomalous finites) the emphasis in the exercises to follow is on Wh— questions (those with interrogative words).

---

144 Interrogatives   E

QUESTION			ANSWER		
Who	's	that?	It	's	**Peter.**
Who	is	it?	It	's	**me.**
Who	's	he?	He	's	**Harry.**
Who	are those people?		They're **Mr and Mrs Brown.**		
Who	are they?		They're **Mr and Mrs Smith.**		
Who	are you?		I	'm	**John.**
What	are you?		I	'm	**a student.**
What	are they?		They're **teachers.**		
What	's	Peter?	He	's	**an engineer.**
What	's	Mary?	She	's	**a secretary.**
What	are those people?		They're **production assistants.**		
What	are they?		They're **computer programmers.**		

Note:
Who is used only for **people**, **NEVER** for things.

Who's that? (Mary)
It's Mary.

Is that Jane? (Mary)
No, it isn't Jane. It's Mary.

Are you John Brown?
No, I'm Peter Brown.

Who are they? (Mr and Mrs Simpson)
They're Mr and Mrs Simpson.

Are those students? (teachers)
No, they're teachers.

What are those people? (workers)
They're workers.

Is that Harry?
Yes, it's me.

1. Are you John Brown?
2. Who's that? (Anne)
3. Is that Peter? (John)
4. Who are they? (Bob and Joe)
5. Are they Harry and Bill? (Harry and Bill)
6. What is he? (doctor)
7. What are they? (clerks)
8. Are they scientists? (engineers)
9. Is he a technician? (technician)
10. Who's this? (Paul)
11. Isn't Mary a housewife? (secretary)
12. What are you?
13. What's John? (salesman)
14. Is Paul a salesman? (buyer)
15. Who's that? (Susan)
16. What is she? (air hostess)
17. Isn't she a journalist?
18. What are those people? (businessmen)
19. Aren't they government officials?
20. Are you a student?

Further practice with who *and* what.

letter—news
 STUDENT A: **What's in the letter?**
 STUDENT B: **There's some news in the letter.**

chair—Betty
 STUDENT C: **Who's in the chair?**
 STUDENT D: **Betty's in the chair.**

corner—chair
 STUDENT E: **What's in the corner?**
 STUDENT F: **There's a chair in the corner.**

1. bedroom—Paula
2. parcel—book
3. bottle—wine
4. bathroom—John
5. cup—tea
6. pocket—money
7. case—documents
8. message—information
9. wardrobe—nothing
10. lounge—nobody
11. suitcase—clothes
12. bed—Mary
13. glass—water
14. bank—Peter
15. sandwich—cheese
16. post office—Bob
17. garage—cars
18. tin—soup
19. bar—Sally
20. boot—luggage
21. box—radio
22. flat—Bill
23. garden—Mary
24. studio—equipment

Here are examples of three question patterns:

(a) question word + auxiliary + (pro)noun + verb

What time	does	Mary	get up?
Who(m)	is	Tom	looking at?
How	can	Bob	learn English?
What	has	John	got that dog **for**?

(b) question word + auxiliary + (pro)noun + verb + *to*-infinitive

Where	do	you	have	to go?
Why	have	they	got	to pay?
Whose pen	are	you	going	to use?
When	might	Bob	want	to come?

(c) question word (+ auxiliary) + verb

Who	is	staying here?
What		disappeared?
Which car	will	be here first?

NOTE:

How compounds are: How many/much/long/soon/far/often, etc.

To practise pattern (a) *above with* who(m) *and* what, *respond as shown:*

I saw someone.	**Who did you see?**
	I saw Peter.
Bob heard somebody.	**Who did he hear?**
	He heard John.
Alice wrote something.	**What did she write?**
	She wrote a letter.

1. I read something.
2. Mary found somebody.
3. John broke something.
4. Bill began something.
5. Peter brought someone.
6. Mary built something.
7. Sally lost something.
8. Henry bought something.
9. Susan chose somebody.
10. David caught something.
11. Bob met someone.
12. Henry did something.
13. James drove something.
14. Bob forgot someone.
15. Betty had something.
16. Peter spoke to someone.
17. Don got something.
18. I heard somebody.
19. John kept something.
20. Mary learnt something.
21. George made something.

22. I paid someone.
23. Jim read something.
24. Peter said something.
25. James saw somebody.
26. Don sold something.
27. George took something.
28. David upset somebody.
29. Sally wrote to someone.
30. Mary woke someone up.

---

147 Interrogatives EI

Making a choice. Practice with which.

coffee or tea
   STUDENT A: **Which do you prefer, coffee or tea?**
   STUDENT B: **I prefer coffee. Which do you prefer?**
   STUDENT A: **I prefer tea.**
the radio or TV
   STUDENT C: **Which do you prefer, the radio or TV?**
   STUDENT D: **I prefer the radio. Which do you prefer?**
   STUDENT C: **I prefer the radio too.**

1. opera or ballet
2. work or leisure
3. the cinema or the theatre
4. the Sunday papers or the daily papers
5. rock or jazz
6. English people or American people
7. living in a hotel or living at home
8. a double bed or a single bed
9. a trouser suit or a skirt
10. classical music or pop music
11. whisky or rum
12. Chinese food or Indian food
13. watching TV or reading
14. travelling by air or by sea
15. driving on the left or on the right
16. Shakespeare or Dante
17. English pronunciation or American pronunciation
18. women with make-up or women without make-up
19. dinner out or dinner at home
20. living in a flat or in a house

181

(a) *To practise the pattern 'question word + auxiliary + (pro)-noun + verb', ask questions as shown. (The teacher or another student may supply the answers if required.)*

Paul went to New York.

why	STUDENT A:	**Why did Paul go to New York?**
when	STUDENT B:	**When did Paul go to New York?**
who with	STUDENT C:	**Who did Paul go to New York with?**

Mary comes to class.

why	STUDENT D:	**Why does Mary come to class?**
how often	STUDENT E:	**How often does Mary come to class?**
what time	STUDENT F:	**What time does Mary come to class?**

1. Bob helped Mary. (how—why—when)
2. Susan's gone. (where—why—how far)
3. I'll be in town. (how long—when—where)
4. Tom got married. (how long ago—why—where)
5. Bob's taking the exam. (why—when—where)
6. Jane took the book. (when—why—where from)
7. Gordon got a taxi. (how—how long ago—why)
8. Jim will find a flat. (how—where—how soon)
9. John plays golf. (where—how often—who with)
10. Dick was watching TV. (what time—where—why)
11. Sheila went swimming. (where—how long ago—why)
12. George will be in London. (when—how long—where)
13. Don uses his typewriter. (where—when—how often)
14. Allan has been working. (how long—why—who with)
15. Jim will be on holiday. (how soon—where—how long)
16. Bob borrowed the book. (why—who from—how long ago)
17. Elizabeth speaks English. (how well—how often—when)
18. John went to Edinburgh. (why—how long ago—who with)
19. Bob and Jim are looking. (what for—what at—who for)
20. Richard's opening the tin. (what with—who for—why)

(b) *To practise the pattern 'question word + auxiliary + (pro)noun + verb + to-infinitive', ask questions about the final word in the statement.*

I had to do it.   **What did you have to do?**

I have to meet him.   **Who do you have to meet?**
I've got to be there.   **Where have you got to be?**

1. I'm going to see him.
2. I've got to know it.
3. I want to do it.
4. I have to hear her.
5. I'm going to buy it.
6. I've got to stay there.
7. I'll have to go then.
8. I had to use it.
9. I mean to see him.
10. I'm going to eat it.
11. I've got to have it.
12. I'll have to be there.
13. I'm going to speak to him.
14. I have to come then.
15. I've got to get it.
16. I had to write to her.
17. I intend to meet him.
18. I have to leave then.
19. I'll have to help them.
20. I'm going to sell it.

(c) *To practise the pattern 'question word (+ auxiliary) +
    verb', ask questions about the first word in the statements.*

Someone has it.
Who has it?

Something happened.
What happened?

One of them is going.
Which one of them is going?

Some of it arrived late.
How much of it arrived late?

Some of them made mistakes.
How many of them made mistakes?

1. Somebody took it.
2. Something fell on them.
3. One of them is coming.

183

4. Some of them knew it all.
5. Some of it tasted bad.
6. Someone has borrowed it.
7. Something broke it.
8. One of them spoke to me.
9. Some of them will be here.
10. Somebody has checked it.
11. Something will happen.
12. Somebody is reading it.
13. One of them had a meal.
14. Some of them got out.
15. Some of it helped him.
16. Somebody was looking for it.
17. Something happened to it.
18. One of them didn't come.
19. Some of them have played it.
20. Some of it has been stolen.

---

149 Interrogatives I

Note:
How questions are often answered with **by** + noun or gerund.

EXAMPLES:
How did you get here?
I came here **by** air/sea/train/car/taxi/bus. (but **on** foot)

How will you know when to come?
By asking Mary. (Cf. I'll ask Mary.)

To practise using **by** *when answering questions with* how, *respond as shown:*

How did John get to the United States? (air)
By air.

How will Bob know what time to come? (contact Paul)
By contacting Paul.

How can Jim improve his spoken English? (do oral drills)
By doing oral drills.

How does Mary manage to keep her car looking so nice?
   (use it in bad weather)
By not using it in bad weather.

1. How can Mary lose weight? (eat so much)
2. How can I improve my golf? (watch the experts)
3. How can I make sure John will come? (invite Mary)
4. How will you manage to finish early? (start early)
5. How did Joe annoy Jean? (ring her up after midnight)
6. How did Jim manage to wreck his car? (drive carefully)
7. How can I find out what's on at the cinema? (ask Peter)
8. How can I get to the city centre quickly? (underground)
9. How did you manage to get there on time? (get a move on)
10. How can Mary make herself more popular? (be more polite)
11. How can Sally get an invitation to the party? (see Susan)
12. How did you manage to get away so early? (make an excuse)
13. How can Paul avoid being late for class? (get up earlier)
14. How did John please Mary? (promise not to see Anne again)
15. How did Tom manage to pass his exam? (let up for a moment)
16. How will you dispose of your car? (put an ad in the paper)
17. How did John irritate Jane? (offer to give her a lift home)
18. How can I find out what's on TV? (have a look in the paper)
19. How can we get hold of a newspaper? (call at the newsagent's)
20. How can Jim improve his pronunciation? (use the sounds of his own language when he speaks English)

---

150 Interrogatives   **I**

To practise why, *respond as shown.* (*See also Exs.* 216–218.)

Why are you waiting inside? (rain)
Because it's raining.

Why did Peter come here? (Jill)
Because Jill wanted him to.

Why do you watch TV? (English)
Because it's good for my English.

1. Why is David in bed? (ill)
2. Why mustn't Tom smoke? (health)
3. Why didn't Jane phone you? (forget)
4. Why doesn't Jim go to church? (sleep)
5. Why was John wearing his coat? (cold)
6. Why did you buy those records? (cheap)
7. Why did you go to bed so late? (party)
8. Why couldn't you buy the book? (stock)
9. Why didn't you do your homework? (time)
10. Why can't Bob go on holiday now? (work)
11. Why doesn't Paul learn to swim? (afraid)
12. Why did you open the window? (fresh air)
13. Why weren't you at the meeting? (boring)
14. Why didn't you go to the cinema? (tired)
15. Why didn't anybody answer the door? (out)
16. Why don't you get married? (right person)
17. Why are you learning English? (need—job)
18. Why aren't there any buses today? (strike)
19. Why didn't you watch the programme? (before)
20. Why don't you stay here a bit longer? (home)

---

151 Interrogatives   I

To practise forming Wh— *questions, respond as shown:*

Ask me what I did last night.   **What did you do last night?**
I watched TV.

Ask me who I shall go with.   **Who will you go with?**
I shall go with Mary.

Ask me where I have been.   **Where have you been?**
I've been to my room.

1. Ask me where I was born.
2. Ask me how big my room is.
3. Ask me what I did that for.
4. Ask me who sold me that car.
5. Ask me when the train leaves.
6. Ask me which newspaper I take.

186

7. Ask me what kind of music I like.
8. Ask me whose dictionary that is.
9. Ask me how much my typewriter cost.
10. Ask me how often I go to the cinema.
11. Ask me how many times I've been there.
12. Ask me why I was so late getting to bed.
13. Ask me how many teachers there are here.
14. Ask me how far away New York is from here.
15. Ask me who I saw at the club last night.
16. Ask me what time I had breakfast this morning.
17. Ask me how far it is from here to the station.
18. Ask me how important it is to have a good accent.
19. Ask me how much time you will need for the homework.
20. Ask me how soon there will be a flight to San Francisco.

---

152 Interrogatives   I

To practise forming Yes/No *questions, respond as shown:*

Ask me if John went away for the weekend.
Did John go away for the weekend?
Yes, he did.

Ask me whether Bob will take Mary out tonight.
Will Bob take Mary out tonight?
No, he won't.

Ask me if Susan has caught up with Helen yet.
Has Susan caught up with Helen yet?
Yes, she has.

1. Ask me whether Harry is moving in.
2. Ask me if John is trying on the coat.
3. Ask me if you can give me some help.
4. Ask me if Richard will take on that job.
5. Ask me if Don intends to give up smoking.
6. Ask me whether George gets on with Sheila.
7. Ask me if Betty has got rid of her cold yet.
8. Ask me if Michael often overtakes dangerously.
9. Ask me if Sandra can put Philip up for a week.
10. Ask me whether John's plane took off at 4 p.m.
11. Ask me if teaching takes up a lot of Bob's time.
12. Ask me whether the dishes have been washed up yet.

13. Ask me if the corner shop had sold out of newspapers.
14. Ask me whether Robert has thought about the problem yet.
15. Ask me whether David will pick Sally up at the station now.

---

153 Interrogatives   I

Ask about the word(s) in italics. When doing this exercise with students' books closed either put emphasis on the italicised word or replace it by the word 'blank' (e.g. 'I took blank's car by mistake.')

I took *John's* car by mistake.
Whose car did you take by mistake?
John's.

I see *Brian* every day.
Who do you see every day?
Brian.

Paul went to London *last week*.
When did Paul go to London?
Last week.

1. I go to New York *every year*.
2. Betty puts sugar in *her tea*.
3. Paul *watched TV* last night.
4. Peter will buy the *blue* shirt.
5. Mary went to Australia *by air*.
6. Sally has to share *her kitchen*.
7. Bob *read a good play* last night.
8. We made a *birthday* cake for her.
9. Richard got here *by car* last week.
10. Mary got up *at 10 a.m.* yesterday.
11. Harry goes *to the station* by taxi.
12. Harry smokes *forty* cigarettes a day.
13. David's in England *to learn English*.
14. She caught him *stealing her handbag*.
15. Marion taught French *three months ago*.
16. Betty visited Canada when she was *five*.

17. David married Jill *because he loved her.*
18. I sold the *old* camera to a friend of mine.
19. Mr Smith took a taxi *so as not to be late.*
20. Mary gets *a new dress* from John every week.
21. I put on my sweater *as soon as I felt cold.*
22. *Bob* learnt how to swim when he was thirteen.
23. Jill brought *her friend Sue* to class with her.
24. Sally phoned *so that she could speak to Betty.*
25. John didn't tell Mary *that she didn't speak well.*

---

154 Interrogatives   IA

Ask for information about the words someone (somebody), something, somewhere, *etc.*

Peter took someone to the theatre last night.
Who did he take to the theatre last night?

Peter and Sally have spent some time in Austria.
How much time have they spent there?

Somebody went with Bill when he visited his family.
Who went with him when he visited his family?

1. John got to Canada somehow.
2. Sheila had something to eat.
3. Somebody's taken my dictionary.
4. Betty asked someone to help her.
5. Somebody helped Jim with his work.
6. Some things are better left unsaid.
7. Peter sometimes goes to the theatre.
8. Someone woke me up early this morning.
9. Something's happened to the hotel lift.
10. Elizabeth's left something at the hotel.
11. Someone's left his car in front of my house.
12. Joe spent some time in Paris earlier this year.
13. I saw someone's luggage being taken into the room.
14. Richard expects to find peace and quiet somewhere.
15. Somehow Sandra will have to change Jim's opinion of
    her. (use: be able to)

Ask questions about the word(s) in brackets, as shown:

I normally work during the week. (weekends)
What do you normally do at weekends?
I relax.

Barbara wants to buy the green blouse. (skirt)
Which skirt does she want to buy?
The blue one.

John visited London last year. (the year before)
Where did he go the year before?
He went to New York.

1. Susan's been here for six years now. (Barbara)
2. Jim usually calls for Mary at 6 p.m. (Elizabeth)
3. Bob rang Tom up for some urgent information. (Jim)
4. Joe went to Bermuda five times last year. (Trinidad)
5. I've already had three cups of tea. (pieces of toast)
6. I shall visit Richard on Saturday morning. (afternoon)
7. Peter had steak and chips for lunch yesterday. (dinner)
8. I think James Mason is the best British actor. (actress)
9. David went to London to see Buckingham Palace. (New York)
10. There were 200 people at the concert on Friday. (Saturday)
11. Tom bought a woollen jumper a few days ago. (his grey suit)
12. It takes Jim five minutes to get here in the morning. (home)
13. I read an interesting article in today's paper. (yesterday's)
14. Tom had to spend nine hours at the office on Monday. (Friday)
15. George has to attend lectures twice a week. (use the language laboratory)

Ask questions to elicit further information about the sentences below, then make a short summary of what has been said.

EXAMPLE:
An old friend came to see me.

When did he come?
He came last night.

What did he want?
He wanted to borrow something.

Did he want to borrow money?
Yes, he did.

What for?
To pay an urgent bill.

Did you lend him anything?
No, I didn't.

What did I tell you?
> **You told us that an old friend came to see you last night wanting to borrow money in order to pay an urgent bill, but you didn't lend him anything.**

1. Tom's written a book.
2. I went to the theatre.
3. I've got rid of my car.
4. Sheila's getting married.
5. David saw a road accident.
6. I've bought a tape-recorder.
7. John had a wonderful weekend.
8. Gordon jumped into the river.
9. I saw a good programme on TV.
10. Rosemary had a really good meal.
11. Peter will take Jane to New York.
12. Carol spent six weeks in hospital.
13. Gordon showed me some photographs.
14. Bob saw a picture in his newspaper.
‡   John found some money in the street.
16. Harry's been dismissed from his job.

17. Gordon took a girl to the night-club.
18. Tom's been living in the United States.
19. Philip's decided to abandon his studies.
20. Steve only finished his homework at 2 a.m.

'Ever' Compounds

157 INTERMEDIATE/ADVANCED

I can live	**wherever**	I like.
Ask	**whoever**	you see.
He came	**whenever**	he wanted.
Choose	**whichever**	(one) you like.
You can travel	**however**	you wish.
Do	**whatever**	you want.

Notes:
  (i) The general meaning of these compounds is: 'any place, person, time, one, manner, thing'.

  (ii) Sentence stress falls on the first syllable of **ever**.

   EXAMPLE:
   /ai kn ˈliv wɛərˈevər ai ˋlaik/

  (iii) You will occasionally hear **whatsoever** /wɔtsəuˈevə/. This may be used for emphasis, and is placed at the end of the sentence.

   EXAMPLES:
   I have no money **whatsoever**.

   We have no time **whatsoever**.

   Other compounds including **so** in this way: **who(m)soever**, **whichsoever**, etc. are very seldom heard nowadays.

To practise the above pattern. Respond as shown:

Who shall I ask? (like)
Ask whoever you like.

Where shall I go? (please)
Go wherever you please.

How often did he come? (could)
He came whenever he could.

192

1. What shall I do? (want)
2. When does she come? (can)
3. Who did she speak to? (meet)
4. Which one shall I take? (prefer)
5. What will Peter do to help? (can)
6. How often did you see Mary? (come)
7. How do you suggest I travel? (like)
8. Where does she go on holiday? (want)
9. Who shall we ask to the party? (like)
10. How often does she make mistakes? (tired)
11. What will John have for dinner? (there is)
12. Which TV channel shall we watch? (prefer)
13. Where does Peter usually have dinner? (cheap)
14. Which book is Barbara going to buy? (recommend)
15. How often do you go to the cinema? (good film on)

---

158 **Ever** Compounds   A

Whoever	it is, we shan't answer the door.
However	hard she tries, she won't succeed.
Whatever	they do, there'll still be trouble.
Wherever	you go, you'll find bad weather.
Whenever	the bus comes, I'll be ready for it.
Whichever	car he chooses, he won't be satisfied.

Notes:
  (i) The general meaning of **ever** in the above compounds is 'it makes no difference', 'it doesn't matter', or 'no matter'. These expressions may be used instead of the **ever** compounds.

  EXAMPLES:
  It makes no difference who it is, . . .

  It doesn't matter where you go, . . .

  No matter how hard she tries, . . .

 (ii) **May** is often used in this pattern.

  EXAMPLES:
  Wherever he **may** go, bad luck will follow. (**Wherever** he goes, . . .)

> **Whatever** he **may** have done, he doesn't deserve to be hanged. (**Whatever** he did, ...)

(iii) **Whenever** may mean 'on whatever occasion' or 'at whatever time'.

To practise the above pattern, answer the following questions by choosing suitable ever *compounds:*

Does John always take Mary with him? (. . . he goes)
Yes. Wherever he goes, John always takes Mary with him.

Did Bill have to see the representative? (. . . he called)
Yes. Whenever the representative called, Bill had to see him.

Will they have to finish the job? (. . . difficult it may be)
Yes. However difficult it may be, they'll have to finish the job.

1. Does the car have to be insured? (. . . uses it)
2. Would you lend that woman any money? (. . . she is)
3. Does Jim always do everything badly? (. . . he does)
4. Will that firm try to compete? (. . . small it may be)
5. Do you still like Richard? (. . . you may say about him)
6. Is Sue always waiting up for Tom? (. . . he may come in)
7. Shall we have to invite them in for drinks? (. . . calls)
8. Is Gordon always bored with TV? (. . . programme he watches)
9. Will Elizabeth have to be told? (. . . unpleasant the news is)
10. Will John marry Mary? (. . . reaction he gets from his parents)
11. Is Sheila always dissatisfied? (. . . well her students respond)
12. Is Sue still interested in Bob? (. . . he may have done last night)
13. Will you still have to pay the bill? (. . . much I complain about it)
14. Will Bob always speak with that accent? (. . . hard he tries to overcome it)
15. Does Jean still prefer her own country? (. . . often she visits the United States)

Where ever did that boy come from?
Why ever did Elizabeth say that?
When ever did I promise to do that?
What ever will Richard say next?
What ever did Sally ask Susan **for**?
How ever did Jim wake up in time?
Who ever is he trying to imitate?

Notes:

(i) The use of **ever** with interrogatives indicates surprise, annoyance, indignation, etc.

(ii) The general meaning of **ever** here is 'What possible . . . ?'. ('What possible place . . . ?', 'What possible person . . . ?' etc.)

(iii) Perfect infinitives may be used.

EXAMPLES:
A: Peter went shoplifting yesterday.
B: **Why ever** should he have done that?
(Cf. **Why ever** did he do that?)

A: Someone's broken the window.
B: **Who ever** could have done that?
(Cf. **Who ever** has done that?)

(iv) The expression 'on earth' may be used as an alternative to the above use of **ever**. It is even more colloquial.

EXAMPLES:
Where on earth did that boy come from?

Why on earth did Elizabeth say that?

To practise the above pattern, respond as shown:

John's been to Russia. (when)
When ever did he go there?

Jim asked Mary to leave him alone. (why)
Why ever should he have done that?

Sally will have to be back by 4 p.m. (how)
How ever will she manage to be back by then?

John saw a stranger in the room. (who)
Who ever could it have been?

1. Gordon's not here. (where)
2. Bill caught his train. (how)
3. Peter has been to Miami. (when)
4. Here's the ring you lost. (where)
5. Someone rang me up at 2 a.m. (who)
6. Peter's been given a kitten. (what)
7. Mary arrived before midnight. (how)
8. Paul missed his rail connection. (how)
9. Jean has bought herself a bicycle. (why)
10. Mary has decided to write a book. (when)
11. I saw a strange woman in the garden. (who)
12. Susan sold her typewriter last week. (why)
13. Mary refused to dance with David. (what for)
14. Jim has decided to emigrate to Canada. (when)
15. The chairman visited the canteen yesterday. (why)

ANOMALOUS FINITES—'SPECIAL' VERBS

Introductory note:
Anomalous finites can be classified into two functions:

(a) as structural words to form:
  (i) negatives   She **does** not want to go.
  (ii) interrogatives   **Did** she want to go?
  (iii) the emphatic   I **do** want to go!
  (iv) short answers   Yes, I **shall**.
  (v) question 'tags'   You will go, **won't** you?

(b) as modal verbs to express concepts such as:
  (i) permission   You **may** go now.
  (ii) possibility   She **might** go tomorrow.
  (iii) ability   He **can** go.
  (iv) obligation   I **must** go.

A high proportion of English sentences contain examples of the structural use of the anomalous finites, and exercises practising these can be found throughout this book.

196

Note the two distinctly different verb patterns:

A		B	
I can come.		**I am able** *to* come.	
I must come.		**I have** *to* come.	
I should come.		**I ought** *to* come.	
I needn't come.	but:	**I need** *to* come.	
I daren't come.		**I dare** *to* come.	
I shall come.		**I am going** *to* come.	
I will come.		**I used** *to* come.	
I may come.			
I might come.			
I could come.			
I would come.			

Can (Ability)

160 ELEMENTARY

STATEMENT	QUESTION	SHORT ANSWER
I can swim.	**Can** you swim?	Yes, **I can.**
I can't play tennis.	**Can't** you play tennis?	No, **I can't.**

Notes:

(i) In affirmative statements **can** is usually unstressed.

> EXAMPLE:
> Bob can swim.
> /'bɔb kn `swim/

(ii) In questions **can** may be stressed or unstressed. Where rhythm is the only consideration many native speakers use the strong form /kæn/ with sentence stress if the next syllable is unstressed, without sentence stress if the next syllable is stressed.

> EXAMPLES:
> Can you swim?
> /'kæn ju ‚swim/
>
> Can Bob swim?
> /kæn 'bɔb ‚swim/

(iii) **Can't** /kɑːnt/ usually has sentence stress. It is **cannot** in formal written English.

(a) *To practise* can *in statements, respond as shown:*

John (drive)
John can drive.
He's a very good driver.

Mary (play golf)
Mary can play golf.
She's a very good golfer.

Bob (swim)
Bob can swim.
He's a very good swimmer.

1. Sheila (dance)
2. Gordon (drive)
3. Don (swim)
4. Susan (bowl)
5. Patrick (ski)
6. Betty (ride)
7. Jean (play cards)
8. Jim (play tennis)
9. Elizabeth (run)
10. Harry (teach)
11. Bill (play golf)
12. Paul (play table-tennis)

(b) *To practise forming questions with* can.

speak English
Can you speak English?
Yes, I can.

dance
Can you dance?
No, I can't.

understand English
Can you understand English?
Yes, I can.

1. play tennis
2. drive a car
3. swim
4. type
5. ride a horse
6. play chess
7. bowl
8. speak Spanish
9. understand French
10. speak German
11. ski
12. understand me
13. play golf
14. water-ski
15. play bridge
16. speak Italian
17. understand Russian
18. play table-tennis
19. come to my party
20. speak French
21. lend me some money

198

(c) *To contrast affirmative and negative forms.*

Can John speak German and French?
He can speak German, but he can't speak French.

Can Mary swim and ski?
She can swim, but she can't ski.

1. Can Paul bowl and ski?
2. Can David play tennis and golf?
3. Can Susan play bridge and poker?
4. Can Gordon understand you and me?
5. Can Philip play chess and tennis?
6. Can you speak English and Chinese?
7. Can Paul speak Russian and French?
8. Can Mary understand German and English?
9. Can Harry understand Michael and Peter?
10. Can Richard drive a car and a tractor?
11. Can Jimmy do this exercise and that one?
12. Can Sheila ride a horse and a motorbike?
13. Can John understand German and Spanish?
14. Can Sally make a sandwich and boil an egg?
15. Can Bill use a tape-recorder and a computer?

Going to

161 ELEMENTARY

The train is **going to** arrive in a minute.
I'm **not** **going to** see Mary this afternoon.
The men are **going to** do the work now.

Note:
Going to indicates **intention** or **certainty**. It is often used to express simple futurity but it is not always safe to use it for that purpose, e.g. 'It's going to be my birthday on Saturday' might sound quaint.
In careful speech it may be better not to use the verb **go** with **going to**, e.g. 'I'm **going to** go to New York tomorrow' may be better expressed: 'I **intend to** go to New York tomorrow' or 'I'm going to New York tomorrow.'

199

(a) *To practise simple statements with* going to.

watch TV tonight	**I'm going to watch TV tonight.**
speak only English	**I'm going to speak only English.**
have a coffee	**I'm going to have a coffee.**

1. have a rest
2. see John later
3. listen to the radio
4. have another drink
5. type some letters
6. do my homework
7. have a cup of coffee
8. meet John in the town
9. write some letters
10. find out the answer
11. buy a notebook
12. get some stamps
13. make a phone call
14. have a walk
15. call a taxi
16. do some work
17. visit New York
18. speak to my friend
19. answer the phone
20. turn on the light

(b) *Further practice with* going to.

watch TV/look through today's lesson
STUDENT A: **Are you going to watch TV?**
STUDENT B: **No, I'm not.**
STUDENT A: **What are you going to do?**
STUDENT B: **I'm going to look through today's lesson.**

have a swim later/have a bath
STUDENT C: **Are you going to have a swim later?**
STUDENT D: **No, I'm not.**
STUDENT C: **What are you going to do?**
STUDENT D: **I'm going to have a bath.**

1. take the car/take a taxi
2. do your homework/read a book
3. have a walk later/have a rest
4. listen to the radio/watch TV
5. play golf tomorrow/visit the town
6. have a cup of tea/do some shopping
7. pack your suitcases now/buy my ticket
8. play tennis tomorrow/have a game of chess
9. do some reading tonight/write some letters
10. visit the night-club tonight/do some reading
11. ask Sheila for help/try and manage by myself
12. have a holiday soon/continue to learn English
13. have something to drink/have something to eat
14. stay in bed tomorrow/get up and do some work
15. change your job/ask for an increase in salary

May (Permission)

You **may** go now if you wish.
Sue **may** come home when she likes.
May I leave now?

Notes:
(i) Students may hear a weak form of **may** but they need not practise it. **May** in this sense is often unstressed in the affirmative.

/'suː mei kʌm 'həum wen ʃi ˋlaiks/

but it is likely to have sentence stress in the questions formed in
the exercise below.

/'mei wi ˏsməuk/

(ii) **Can** may also indicate 'permission'.

To practise may *with the meaning of 'permission', respond as
shown:*

Do you want to smoke?
May we smoke?
Yes, you may.

Do you want to go now?
May I go now?
Yes, you may.

Do you want to help me?
May I help you?
Yes, you may.

1. Do you want to sit here?
2. Do you want to open the window?
3. Do you want to put on the fire?
4. Do you want to do your work later?
5. Do you want to write to me?
6. Do you want to come to my party?
7. Do you want to borrow my book?
8. Do you want to join us?
9. Do you want to look at my paper?

10. Do you want to speak to me?
11. Do you want to ask me a question?
12. Do you want to buy me a drink?
13. Do you want to offer me a cigarette?
14. Do you want to lend me your pen?
15. Do you want to use my car?

May and Might (Possibility)

John **may** come. (It's possible that he'll come.)

Mary **might** come. (It's possible, but more uncertain, that she'll come.)

Mary said, 'John **may** know the answer.' (Direct Speech)

Mary said that John **might** know the answer. (Reported Speech)

Notes:
(i) There is some emphasis on **may** and **might** in Exercise 163.

Do you think John will come?—He may come.
/hi ˋmei ˈkʌm/

Are you going for a walk?—I might go for a walk.
/ai ˋmait ˌgəu fər ə ˌwɔːk/

(ii) Possibility may be expressed with 'maybe' and 'perhaps'.

EXAMPLES
Perhaps John will come.

Maybe Mary will come.

163a ELEMENTARY

To practise may, *respond as shown:*

Do you think John will come?
He may come.

Do you think Mary will be late?
She may be late.

Do you think Tom's English will improve?
It may improve.

202

1. Do you think Sally will need help?
2. Do you think Susan will be on time?
3. Do you think Paul will buy a new car?
4. Do you think Gordon will take a taxi?
5. Do you think Betty will pass her exam?
6. Do you think Paul will know the answer?
7. Do you think Jim will have dinner early?
8. Do you think Sue will have to go by air?
9. Do you think Bob will be able to tell me?
10. Do you think Harry will work this evening?
11. Do you think Elizabeth will go out tonight?
12. Do you think Alice will have her hair done?
13. Do you think Peter will have a holiday soon?
14. Do you think Tom will come to class tomorrow?
15. Do you think Bob will be in time for the train?

163b INTERMEDIATE

To practise might, *respond as shown:*

Are you going for a walk later? (the weather)
I might go for a walk later. It depends on the weather.

Is Joe going to watch TV tonight? (there's anything good on)
He might watch TV tonight. It depends if there's anything good on. (colloquial)

Are you going to the party tonight? (I receive an invitation)
I might go to the party tonight. It depends on whether I receive an invitation.

1. Is Peter going to see Mary tonight? (her mother)
2. Is John going to the bank later? (he needs any cash)
3. Is Philip going to have a holiday soon? (his manager)
4. Are you going to visit the United States one day? (my job)
5. Are you going to the cinema tonight? (Anne will come too)
6. Is Bob going to buy a new car? (the condition of his old one)
7. Are you going to spend the weekend here? (an excursion has been arranged)
8. Is Paul going to help Susan with her homework tonight? (she asks him to)

9. Is David going to take part in the discussion this evening? (the subject)
10. Are John and Mary going by hovercraft? (the service is still operating)
11. Is Sally going to stay up late tonight? (there's anything worth watching on TV)
12. Is Sheila going to buy any clothes while she's here? (she sees anything she fancies)
13. Is Henry going to join the local golf club? (he'll be able to find the time to play)
14. Is Harry going to be able to play cards tonight? (there's anything else he has to do)
15. Is Tom going to continue learning English after leaving here? (he can find a good teacher)

Must—Have to—Have got to

EXPRESSING OBLIGATION	EXPRESSING NON-NECESSITY
I've got to ⎱	**I haven't got to** ⎱
I have to ⎬ go home now.	**I don't have to** ⎬ go home now.
I must ⎰	**I needn't** ⎰

Notes:
(i) **Have to** usually forms its interrogative and negative forms with *do*, *does* and *did*, etc. It is not anomalous and is included here for contrast with **have got to** and **must**.

(ii) In expressions of obligation **have to** is often pronounced /ˈhæftu/ or /ˈhæftə/, with a corresponding /ˈhæstu/ or /ˈhæstə/ for **has to**.

See Ex. 165 for notes on **have**.
See Ex. 169 for practice with **needn't** only.

164a ELEMENTARY

To practise must, *in its strong form with sentence stress, respond as shown:*

Do you want to go now?
I must go now.
/ai ˈmʌst ˌgəu ˌnau/

204

Does Bob need to speak English?
He must speak English.

Do they want to buy that book?
They must buy that book.

1. Do we need to hurry?
2. Does Tom want to go now?
3. Does Mary need to fly home?
4. Do you need to take a taxi?
5. Do you want (to have) a rest?
6. Does John need to buy a car?
7. Do they need to find a flat?
8. Does Sally want to leave soon?
9. Do you want to get some records?
10. Does Henry want to stop smoking?
11. Does Paul need to take the exam?
12. Does David need to order a paper?
13. Does Jill want (to have) some help?
14. Does John need to borrow some money?
15. Do you want (to have) something to eat?

To practise must *in its unstressed weak form, repeat the exercise, changing the form of the answers to:*

Yes. I must certainly go now.
/'jes ai məst (*or*: məs) 'səːtnli ˌgəu ˌnau/

Yes. He must certainly speak English.
Yes. They must certainly buy that book.

164b Must—Have to—Have got to   EI

To practise 'obligation' and 'non-necessity' patterns, give the negative form as shown:

John's got to go home by air.
Mary hasn't got to go home by air.

John has to take the bus.
Mary doesn't have to take the bus.

John must pack his things now.
Mary needn't pack her things now.

1. John must go home by sea.
2. John has to walk to school.
3. John's got to work late.
4. John has to go shopping.
5. John must hire a car.
6. John's got to have a rest.
7. John must work very hard.
8. John has to make his bed.
9. John's got to buy a watch.
10. John must visit Japan.
11. John has to get up early.
12. John's got to take a taxi.
13. John must learn Russian.
14. John's got to see Sally.
15. John must have a car.
16. John's got to get a paper.
17. John must type his letters.
18. John's got to buy a radio.
19. John has to take Anne out.
20. John must do his work now.
21. John's got to wear a suit.
22. John has to be home early.
23. John's got to write an essay.
24. John must go to New York.
25. John has to pick David up.
26. John's got to see the doctor.

164c **Must—Have to—Have got to**   I

Further practice.

John must go to Canada soon. (an appointment to take up there)
   STUDENT A: **Why must he go to Canada soon?**
   STUDENT B: **Because he has an appointment to take up there.**

Mary's got to go shopping now. (a new dress)
   STUDENT C: **Why's she got to go shopping now?**
   STUDENT D: **Because she needs a new dress.**

Pat has to study this afternoon. (an exam to prepare for)
STUDENT E: **Why does she have to study this afternoon?**
STUDENT F: **Because she has an exam to prepare for.**

1. Richard must get a new car. (a write-off)
2. You've got to study tonight. (do you good)
3. Bob must read more. (very small vocabulary)
4. Jim's got to learn how to swim. (go sailing)
5. Susan's got to get a job. (husband out of work)
6. Tom has to work harder. (not make much progress)
7. I have to walk to the station. (car out of order)
8. Richard must go into hospital now. (an operation)
9. Joe must get himself a new suit. (go to a wedding)
10. Sandra has to use the computer. (problems to solve)
11. Barbara's got to put the money in the bank. (stolen)
12. Peter's got to change his job. (not make enough money)
13. Jill must learn English. (able to speak to her clients)
14. Jim's got to get up earlier in the morning. (always late)
15. Paul must speak more slowly. (difficult to understand him)
16. Allan must borrow a typewriter. (business letters to write)
17. I have to visit the library tomorrow. (book on pronunciation)
18. Bob has to go to Sydney. (important negotiations to attend to)
19. Betty has to pass her driving test. (able to drive in her new job)
20. Susan's got to be back before 11 p.m. (not have permission to stay out any longer)

Have

---

165 INTERMEDIATE

Notes:
(i) **Have** is anomalous in the following:

I **haven't** (got) a camera.
(Cf. I **don't have** a camera.—regular)

They've **got to** leave early.
(Cf. They **have to** leave early.—regular)

Mary **has** never had a cold.
John said he **had** been there before.

(ii) **Have** is not anomalous when it means 'eat', 'drink', 'take', 'receive', or 'experience'.

EXAMPLES:

John **had** a sandwich and a glass of beer.

Mary will **have** a shower after the game.

June hasn't **had** a present from Sheila.

(iii) Compare the following:

    A. I **don't have** headaches.   (habit)
    B. I **haven't got** a headache.   (a particular occasion)

Some people use **don't have** with B, but nobody uses **haven't got** with A.

To practise and contrast the anomalous and regular forms of have, *make the following negative:*

I have a car.
I don't have a car. (I haven't a car.)

I've got to sell my car.
I haven't got to sell my car.

I've had a car.
I haven't had a car.

I'll have to buy a car.
I won't (shan't) have to buy a car.

I had a car.
I didn't have a car.

I have to use a car.
I don't have to use a car.

I had my car serviced.
I didn't have my car serviced.

I'm having trouble with my car.
I'm not having trouble with my car.

1. He has a job.
2. He's got to have a job.
3. He's had a job.
4. He'll have to get a job.
5. He had a job.
6. He has to get a job.

7. He had the job done.
8. She has some money.
9. She's got to get some money.
10. She's had some money.
11. She'll have to get some money.
12. She had some money.
13. She had to get some money.
14. She had her money stolen.
15. She's having her money invested for her.
16. They've got a flat.
17. They've got to get a flat.
18. They've had a flat.
19. They'll have to rent a flat.
20. They had a flat.
21. They have to get a flat.
22. They were having their flat done up.
23. They had Jim do up the flat.
24. I have a newspaper.
25. I've got to have a newspaper.
26. I've had a newspaper.
27. I have to read a newspaper.
28. I'll have to read a newspaper.
29. I had a newspaper delivered.
30. I'll be having a newspaper delivered.

Daren't

166 ELEMENTARY/INTERMEDIATE

Notes:
(i) **Dare** is anomalous in the following:
   I **daren't** ask Betty that question.
   Dare you jump from that high wall?
   How **dare** you take my car without asking me?
   I **dare** say you're right.

(ii) **Dare** is not anomalous in the following:
   Bob didn't **dare** (to) come in late.
   I **dare** you to swim across that river!

(iii) **Daren't** may be employed for future, present and past time.

To practise daren't, *respond as shown:*

Do the students miss class?
No. They daren't miss class.

Does Bob speak to Susan?
No. He daren't speak to Susan.

Will Paul fly in this weather?
No. He daren't fly in this weather.

1. Will you be late?
2. Will Bob risk it?
3. Does Sue go there alone?
4. Will John fight that bull?
5. Does Tom make Bill angry?
6. Do you drink and drive?
7. Does Mary make mistakes?
8. Does Jim speak to Anne?
9. Will Don write to Sally?
10. Will Mary see John again?
11. Does Susan wear that dress?
12. Will you leave the money here?
13. Will Mary miss the interview?
14. Does Jim drive that old car?
15. Will Tom break his promise?
16. Does Barry let his dog out?
17. Does Paul go into the water?
18. Will Mary leave the baby alone?
19. Does Tom argue with his wife?
20. Does Mary stay out late?

Used to

Peter **used to** speak French, but he doesn't **any more.**
Betty **used to** swim well,   but she can't   **any more.**
Did David **use** to play golf?
*He **didn't use** to play tennis.

Notes:

(i) **Used to** indicates a past habit. It is pronounced /'juːstə/.

210

Compare the above with the following:

> I'm not **used to** /'juːst tə/ making my own bed. (I'm not **accustomed to** making . . .)
> I shall have to get **used to** /'juːst tə/ making it, if no one will do it for me. (I shall have to become **accustomed to** making . . .)
> Making my own bed will take getting **used to**! /'juːst tu/
> Bob said he wasn't **used to** travelling in a non-smoking compartment.
> Tom says he **used** [juːzd] Mary's car, but he didn't **use** [juːz] it for long.

It is probable that only advanced students will hear the difference between /'juːstə/ (**used to** for a past habit) and /'juːst tə/ (= accustomed to—the /t/ of /juːst/ formed but not exploded).

(*ii) The form **used not to** /'juːsnt tu/ is sometimes employed for the negative.

167a Used to

EI

To practise the affirmative and negative forms of used to, *respond as shown:*

Peter—teach Spanish
Peter used to teach Spanish, but he doesn't any more.

Mary—not write to me
Mary didn't use to write to me, but she does now.
/'didnt 'juːstə/

Harry—be a good swimmer.
Harry used to be a good swimmer, but he isn't any more.

1. Betty—drink a lot
2. Jane—not watch TV
3. Richard—stay out late
4. Helen—be in love
5. Mary—not have a pet
6. David—not have a car
7. Jean—go to the theatre
8. Paul—read a lot
9. Bill—live in New Zealand
10. George—not be interested in girls

11. Robert—work hard
12. Don—not smoke
13. Harry—be married
14. John—play chess
15. Tom—not use a typewriter
16. Peter—be interested in economics
17. Don—visit Anne
18. Philip—not like Helen
19. Bob—read short stories
20. John—write to Mary

167b Used to   IA

Rephrase the following sentences, using used to *or* didn't use to:

There was no language laboratory in that school until two
    years ago.
**There didn't use to be a language laboratory in that school, but
    there is one now.**
I had no phone in my house until the Post Office put one in.
I used to have to make my calls from a public phone box.

He had been an actor before he became a businessman.
He didn't use to be a businessman—he used to be an actor.

1. Cigarettes are much more expensive than they were.
2. Jim spoke German at school, but he has now forgotten
   it.
3. No one could read my letters until I began to type them.
4. Tom admired John until he found out that he was
   dishonest.
5. I didn't like Mary until I got to know her better at a
   party.
6. Susan was a nurse before she got married and raised a
   family.
7. My bank manager was very kind and polite to me until
   last week.
8. Mary has told John that he may not go to the night-club
   any more.
9. Sally played tennis when abroad, but she prefers swimming now she's at home.
10. Until last year I shopped at supermarkets. Now I buy
    from small retailers.

212

11. David couldn't play golf last year, but he has had some lessons since then.
12. That newsagent's didn't sell 'The Times' until there was a strong demand for it.
13. I got fed up having to watch TV in the noisy hotel lounge. I have now bought my own set.
14. The theatre was used only for plays. Now it is used for wrestling and gambling.
15. Television programmes were once worth watching. Now they are full of violence and sex.

Could and Was Able

168a INTERMEDIATE

I	**could**	play tennis when I was twelve years old. (I knew how to)
I	**was able to**	play tennis yesterday afternoon. (because it wasn't raining)
Mary **could**		swim at the age of six. (she knew how to)
Mary **was able to**		swim last week. (because the pool was open)

Notes:
 (i) In the above examples, **could** is used to express knowledge or ability in the past; **was/were able to** indicates that an objective was attained. (**Was/were able to** may replace **could**)

 (ii) **Could** is frequently used with verbs of perception (and certain other verbs).

   EXAMPLES:
   I **could** imagine what she was thinking.

   She **could** see that he wasn't interested.

   We **could** understand his attitude.

   They **could** hear the music clearly.

   I **could** taste the vinegar on the salad.

   Everybody **could** smell the burning meat.

(iii) **Could** in the past may also indicate **permission**.

Mary said I **could** take her to the cinema.

I **could** go out whenever I wanted.

To practise and contrast could *and* was able, *answer the following in the affirmative:*

Peter understood the question, didn't he?
Yes, he could understand the question.

David finished the book in an hour, didn't he?
Yes, he was able to finish it in an hour.

Jim knew how to ride a horse when he was ten, didn't he?
Yes, he could ride a horse at the age of ten.

1. Jim smelt the toast burning, didn't he?
2. Henry took the exam last year, didn't he?
3. Sally tasted the onion in the soup, didn't she?
4. Mary had the afternoon off yesterday, didn't she?
5. Richard picked Helen up at the station, didn't he?
6. Mary did her homework in under an hour, didn't she?
7. George saw Betty through his binoculars, didn't he?
8. Susan bought the coat before meeting John, didn't she?
9. David heard Sally in spite of the bad line, didn't he?
10. John did his shopping during the afternoon, didn't he?
11. Susan saw Mr Green before she went to dinner, didn't she?
12. David finished the decorating before going out, didn't he?
13. You understood some English before coming here, didn't you?
14. Mrs Brown finished making the beds before lunch, didn't she?
15. Peter knew how to ride a horse at the age of ten, didn't he?
16. Allan watched his favourite TV show last night, didn't he?
17. Jane typed and posted the letters before 4 p.m., didn't she?
18. Peter knew how to swim when he was six years old, didn't he?

19. Paul read the letter before it was put into the envelope, didn't he?
20. Sheila knew how to type before she took the secretarial course, didn't she?

Couldn't

168b INTERMEDIATE

Could Mary go out last night?
No. Mary **couldn't** go out (because her mother wanted her to stay in).
Could John go out last night?
No. John **couldn't** go out (because it was raining and he had no raincoat).

Note:
In the above examples, Mary did not have permission to go out, while John was prevented from going out by his not having a raincoat to keep off the rain.

To practise couldn't, *respond as shown:*

Peter wanted to have the day off. (manager wanted him)
Peter couldn't have the day off because his manager wanted him at the office.

Gordon wanted to buy the record. (not in stock)
Gordon couldn't buy the record because it wasn't in stock.

1. Paul wanted to go to bed. (early)
2. Gordon wanted to have a swim. (cold)
3. Susan wanted to play tennis. (locked)
4. Bob wanted to take a holiday. (office)
5. I wanted to have some ice-cream. (Jane)
6. I wanted to buy a newspaper. (sold out)
7. I wanted to use the telephone. (not in use)
8. The team wanted to drink beer. (captain)
9. The children wanted to stay up. (naughty)
10. Susan wanted to understand Peter. (accent)
11. Sally wanted to learn French. (no patience)
12. Bill wanted to buy the picture. (expensive)

13. The pilot wanted to take off. (control tower)
14. Mary wanted to get into her room. (key inside)
15. Don wanted to understand 'Hamlet'. (difficult)
16. Susan wanted to use Bob's pen. (use it himself)
17. Bill wanted to take Sheila out. (go out with Jim)
18. The manager wanted to dismiss Bob. (indispensable)
19. Mary wanted to go out last night. (husband not let her)
20. Jim wanted to speak to the hotel manager. (another guest)

Needn't

Need/Must Philip work so hard?
Yes, he **must.** (It is necessary.)

Need/Must John wear that suit?
No, he **needn't.** (It is not necessary.)

Needn't Susan go now?
No, she **needn't.**

Note:
The following alternative question form may be used:

Does John **need** to go home so early? (No, he **doesn't.**)
Do they **need** to come to class today? (No, they **don't.**)

To practise needn't, *respond as shown:*

Need John do his work now? (later)
No, he needn't. He can do it later.

Must you go to town today? (tomorrow)
No, I needn't. I can go tomorrow.

Need Susan work tomorrow? (day off)
No, she needn't. She can have the day off.

1. Must I buy the book? (library)
2. Need Peter go home so soon? (stay)
3. Must I walk to the station? (taxi)

216

4. Need Sue stay in every evening? (go out)
5. Must we repeat this exercise? (the next)
6. Need I pay cash for this purchase? (cheque)
7. Must Sarah take her holiday now? (next month)
8. Need Sally see John right away? (after class)
9. Must Allan write home every day? (once a week)
10. Need I explain every new word to you? (look up)
11. Must I dial to get the number I want? (operator)
12. Need Peter attend class every day? (twice a week)
13. Must David go to the post office himself? (Betty)
14. Need Harry give Mary an expensive present? (cheap)
15. Must we carry this parcel to the cleaners? (collect)
16. Need we always eat at the same place? (another place)
17. Must Paul go to a language school in America? (Europe)
18. Need I visit the newsagent's to get my paper? (deliver)
19. Must John spend every holiday with his family? (by himself)
20. Need Jim do everything his wife tells him? (have his own way)

Mustn't

---

170 INTERMEDIATE

You	**mustn't** try to learn everything at once. (It is inadvisable.)
You	**mustn't** park in that street. (It is not permitted.)
	Mustn't I park there?
No, you **mustn't**.	

Notes:
(i) **Mustn't** /ˈmʌsnt/ usually has sentence stress.

You **mustn't** park in that street.
/ju ˈmʌsnt ˈpɑːk in ˌðæt ˌstriːt/

Mustn't I park there?
/ˈmʌsnt ai ˈpɑːk ˌðɛə/

(ii) **Can't** and **may not** also indicate that something is not permitted.

217

To practise mustn't, *respond as shown:*

Jim's got a fever. Can he get up?
He mustn't get up if he's got a fever.

It's not allowed to park there. Can I park there?
You mustn't park there if it's not allowed.

They're supposed to leave at 2 p.m. May they leave at 3 p.m.?
They mustn't leave at 3 p.m. if they're supposed to leave at 2 p.m.

1. It isn't permitted to speak Spanish. May I speak Spanish?
2. Mr Hammond has a splitting headache. Can he go to work today?
3. Hospital visiting hours are from five to six p.m. Can I go at seven p.m.?
4. Fishing in that part of the river is not permitted. Can Jim fish in it?
5. Sheila promised to go to the cinema with Bill. Can she now refuse to go with him?
6. Foreign students are not allowed to work in this country. Paul is a student. May he take a job?
7. Tom has been disqualified from driving. Can he take Mary to the station in his car?
8. Mr Brown has been advised to take it easy from now on. May he continue his job as a film stunt man?
9. A coffee bar isn't allowed to sell alcoholic beverages. Mary runs a coffee bar. May she sell whisky?
10. The speed limit on the motorways is a hundred kilometres an hour. Can I drive at one hundred and twenty kilometres an hour?
11. It's not allowed to remove books from the reference room at the library. May Bob take out one of the encyclopedias?
12. Jill's passport isn't up-to-date. Can she travel in foreign countries?
13. Sally is supposed to write an essay this evening. May she go to John's twenty-first birthday party?
14. Susan knows that Peter is a heavy gambler and has no sense of responsibility. Can she safely marry him?
15. Jim wants to spend the weekend in the country. He's promised to take Alice to the city on Saturday. May he spend Saturday in the country?

218

Should

Anne	**should (ought to)** drive more carefully.
	(It's advisable, desirable.)
Paul	**should (ought to)** write home more often.
	(It's his duty.)
	Should I stop smoking?
Yes, you **should**.	

Notes:
(i) Students will hear weak forms for **should** /ʃəd, ʃd/ but they need not practise them. In the exercise **shouldn't** is stressed (as the —**n't** forms of the anomalous finites usually are); **should** does not bear sentence stress.

You **shouldn't** be lazy. You **should** work hard.
/juː ˈʃudnt bi ˌleizi—juː ʃud ˈwəːk ˈhaːd/

(ii) **Should** is perhaps used more frequently than **ought to**, and is preferred in interrogative structures.

To practise should *and* shouldn't, *respond as shown:*

I'm lazy. (work hard)
You shouldn't be lazy. You should work hard.

Bob stays in bed in the morning. (get up early)
He shouldn't stay in bed. He should get up early.

Mary's looking out of the window. (pay attention)
She shouldn't look out of the window. She should pay attention.

1. Henry stays at home a lot. (travel)
2. Sally reads trash. (read good books)
3. We waste time in the morning. (work hard)
4. Mary's late every day. (come to class early)
5. Susan goes around in old clothes. (dress well)
6. I leave my books behind. (bring them to class)
7. I spend my time gambling. (learn more English)
8. Gordon works all the time. (go to a few parties)

9. Paul leaves his bills unpaid. (pay them promptly)
10. Bill is uncooperative. (let his teacher help him)
11. The children stay in all the time. (go for walks)
12. Tom and Bob go out every evening. (do their homework)
13. Jim looks at the girls on the pavements. (drive carefully)
14. Betty tries to learn everything from books. (use the language lab)
15. Tom says the first thing that comes into his head. (think before he speaks)

171b Should   I

A common use of *should* (with 1st person *I* only) is to express advice.

EXAMPLES:

I *should* watch the traffic if I were you.
I *should* wear a sweater today if I were you.

To practise this use of should, *respond as shown:*

about this broken TV set (have—repair)
  STUDENT A: **What shall I do about this broken TV set?**
  STUDENT B: **I should have it repaired if I were you.**
     or **I should throw it away if I were you.**

with this old furniture (replace)
  STUDENT C: **What should I do with this old furniture?**
  STUDENT D: **I should replace it if I were you.**
     or **I should burn it if I were you.**

1. about this mess (clean up)
2. with that letter (tear up)
3. about the accident (report)
4. about this telegram (answer)
5. with the car (leave—car-park)
6. with all this money (put—bank)
7. with this table (put—next room)
8. with these wet clothes (take off)
9. with that painting (have—frame)
10. about that leaking tap (have—fix)
11. about all this luggage (get a porter)
12. with that rusty lawn-mower (get rid of)

13. with this overdue library book (take back)
14. with those filthy trousers (send—cleaners)
15. about this pile of old magazines (try to sell)

171c Should   A

Certain uses of *should* are less common than those practised elsewhere in this book (the Index gives references) and here are examples of these:

(a) A: "Will Tom be here tonight?" B: "How *should* I know?" (it is impossible for me to know) /ˈhau ʃud ˠai͵ nəu/
(b) Tom was walking in London, when who *should* he see but Joe! (an unexpected event) /wen ˈhuː ʃudi ˈsiː bət ˠdʒeu/
(c) Why *should* some people starve while others have too much? (the speaker sees no justification or reason for this)
(d) Richard made a request that I should help him.*
(*should* may be found in dependent clauses following expressions of request, desire, command, will and determination)
(e) I was surprised that Gordon *should* have failed his test. (*should* may be used after expressions of surprise, disbelief, annoyance, etc.)
(f) There is nothing I should like better than that we *should* leave.
(*should* follows *than that* in a comparison clause)
(g) I put the letter away safely so that no one *should* read it. (*should* may follow *so that* in a clause of purpose)
(h) I am not a servant that you *should* expect me to wait on you. (*should* may be found in a clause indicating reason)

*Note:
Instead of using words such as *desire* or *request* a simpler pattern may be preferred.

 EXAMPLES:
 John wanted me to help him. (desire)
 John asked me to help him. (request)

In this exercise, certain ideas will be presented which you should re-express or respond to by using the pattern indicated.

 I want Mary to get fit again. I want nothing more. (f)
 I want nothing more than that Mary should get fit again.

Some children have a good start in life. Others have a poor one. (c)

Why should some children have a good start in life while others have a poor one?

1. Is Sally fond of John? (a)
2. Paul came out of his room. He saw Judy. (b)
3. Am I a baby? Do you expect me to drink milk? (h)
4. John did not know the answer. It was strange. (e)
5. Mary did not notice Harry. It is unbelievable. (e)
6. Some workers get a high salary. Others do not. (c)
7. John was very annoyed. Mary went out with George. (e)
8. Peter took out insurance. He wanted to be covered. (g)
9. Philip gave orders. No one would be allowed to leave. (d)
10. David got a place at university. We weren't surprised. (e)
11. Tom came out of one betting shop. He went into the next one. (b)
12. I am not a clown. Do you expect me to make you laugh all the time? (h)
13. Paul put his name on the door. He wanted everybody to know where he lived. (g)
14. I like a child to be beautiful. It is more important that she is healthy. (f)
15. I published all the facts. I did not wish to be accused of hiding anything. (g)
16. I am quite willing. You may own a certain number of shares in the company. (d)
17. I would rather deliver the parcel myself. Mary is not to be relied upon. (f)
18. Jimmy came out of prison. He immediately went back to shoplifting. (b)
19. George is determined. He wants his friends to make a contribution towards Bill's retirement present. (d)
20. Some people live in grand houses and own beautiful cars. I have to put up with a one-roomed flat and a bicycle. (c)

---

172 Would A

The common uses of *would* are dealt with in other exercises (consult the Index for these). Here are examples of useful, but perhaps less common, functions:

(a) A: "Someone was singing at 3 a.m." B: "That *would** be Tom."
    (it was certainly Tom who was singing)
(b) John *would* not drive when he knew he was incapable.
    (he refused to drive)
(c) Paul *would* often appear at breakfast dressed in pyjamas.
    (it was his habit to do this)
(d) Betty *would** not leave her bed unmade.
    (an assumption based on a knowledge of Betty's character)
(e) You *would* think that Mary would be tired of John by now.
    (a reasonable expectation from known facts)
(f) David *would* have me believe that he never makes mistakes.
    (this is his wish)
(g) George *would* wear dirty shoes in the kitchen. /ˈdʒɔːdʒ
    ˈwud ˌwɛə . . ./
    (it is characteristic of him to do such a thing)
(h) It *would* appear/seem that the safe has been forced open.
    (the speaker is uncertain of the facts)

*Note:
To make it quite clear that it is a *past* action which is being considered, the perfect infinitive may be preferred.

EXAMPLES:

(a) "That *would have been* Tom."

(d) Betty *would not have left* her bed unmade.

Re-express or respond to the following. Model your sentences on the examples given above, as shown:

Peter has locked himself out of his room. (g)
He would (lock himself out of his room)!

I cannot understand why Paul is not a director yet. (e)
You would think that Paul would be a director by now.

1. Richard missed the train. (g)
2. Sally often took an early morning swim. (c)
3. To all appearances the lift is not working. (h)
4. Bob wants everybody to be a vegetarian. (f)
5. Somebody called to see you about overdue rent. (a)
6. Dick refused to let the children stay up late. (d)
7. Tom frequently used to go for walks in the woods. (c)
8. Mary was not on speaking terms with Joe on Friday. (b)
9. It is not in Susan's nature to want to upset Anne. (d)

223

10. Allan wants us to invite him to dinner every night. (f)
11. It was John's habit to have a short nap after lunch. (c)
12. A man phoned to say that you could have tomorrow off. (a)
13. I get the impression that Bob does not like studying. (h)
14. Bill forgot to turn off the TV set before going to bed. (g)
15. The students did not agree to take the oral examination. (b)
16. We cannot understand why Joe has not made his mind up yet. (e)
17. I am sure that it was not Sally who left the room in a mess. (d)
18. I think the Government intends to introduce new legislation. (h)
19. I cannot understand why Sheila has not sold her old car yet. (e)
20. I know Henry well enough to be certain that he did not take the money. (d)

Should—Must—Will (Drawing a conclusion)

173 INTERMEDIATE/ADVANCED

Harry **must** be very embarrassed.
(His face is red.)
George **should** be at the office by now.
(He left home early.)
Susan **will** know the answer.
(She is very clever.)

Notes:
(i) Of the three forms shown above **must** is the strongest way to indicate the conclusion being drawn. In this use ('logical inference') the strong form /mʌst/ is usual, and the word is likely to have sentence stress.

(ii) Negatives are: **can't, shouldn't** and **won't**.

EXAMPLES:
He **can't** be ill.
(Look at him working!)

224

John **shouldn't** have any difficulty in finding a job.
(He is fully qualified.)

Peter **won't** have any petrol in his tank.
(He never buys more than a gallon.)

(iii) **Ought to** may be used instead of **should**.

(iv) See Exs. 265, 268 and 269 for the **must/couldn't/can't have**
patterns.

To practise and contrast must, should *and* will (*and negatives*)
in the above patterns, respond as shown:

I can see the doctor going into John's room. (well)
He can't be well.

The club I belong to admits only important people.
(important)
You must be an important person.

Jim's been studying English for three years. (know it well
by now)
He should know it well by now.

1. Allan's only gone out to get a sandwich. (long)
2. Harry's had thirty driving lessons. (pass his test)
3. Jim's just received a very large bill. (very pleased)
4. There's someone at the door. I'm expecting Paul. (Paul)
5. I can't get any answer from my telephone. (out of order)
6. You'll never find Bob in a library or bookshop. (a
student)
7. The factory workers are all out on strike. (want more
money)
8. Tom's been in the manager's office for two hours. (out
soon)
9. Peter's been at university for only two years. (leaving
yet)
10. Jim carries a large briefcase everywhere he goes.
(important)
11. There's someone asking to speak to you on the phone.
(Gordon)
12. Tom's train left on time for once. (late getting to the
office)
13. Sheila went upstairs to change at least an hour ago.
(ready yet)

14. Richard's trying to learn English without a teacher. (finding it difficult)
15. Joe's looking for a parking place on the outskirts of the city. (find one there)
16. I saw Rosemary looking inside the back of her TV set just now. (working properly)
17. Tom's never read anything by Shakespeare. (know much about 'King Lear')
18. John's given himself only one hour to drive from Calais to Paris. (mad)
19. Alice is having dinner out and then going on to the theatre. (back before midnight)
20. Bob's fully qualified for the job he's applied for. (have no difficulty in getting it)

Had/Would Rather

174 INTERMEDIATE/ADVANCED

A
| I'd | **rather** | **go** to town tomorrow. |
| I'd | **rather not go** to town this afternoon. |

B
| She'**d** **rather** | you **didn't go** tomorrow. |
| She'**d** **rather** | you **went** this afternoon. |

Notes:
(i) In 'A' above the infinitive (**go**) denotes action by the subject of **'d rather**. The negative adverb (**not**) goes between **rather** and the infinitive. In 'B' the —**n't** form follows the subject of the clause.

(ii) The **'d** represents either **had** or **would**, but the question form 'Had you rather . . . ?' is now old-fashioned. Say:

Would you **rather** I shut the window?
You'd rather I shut it, **wouldn't** you?

(iii) **'d rather** may be followed by the past perfect tense.

226

He**'d rather** you**'d** told him the truth.

I**'d rather** you **hadn't** bought that car.
(Cf. I wish you hadn't bought that car.)

To practise had/would rather, *respond as shown:*

Shall we go to bed at 11 p.m., or at midnight?
I'd rather not go to bed at 11 p.m.; I'd rather go at midnight.

Do you want me to turn on the fire, or leave it off?
I'd rather you didn't turn on the fire; I'd rather you left it off.

Would you like a game of tennis, or a game of golf?
I'd rather not have a game of tennis; I'd rather play golf.

1. Would you like a glass of beer, or a sherry?
2. Would you like to visit Sheila, or Elizabeth?
3. Would you like to study Esperanto, or English?
4. Would you prefer to have dinner out, or here?
5. Shall I show you my holiday snaps, or my books?
6. Shall we ask for help, or have another go at it?
7. Would you prefer Mary to stay in, or to go out?
8. Would you like to watch TV, or go to the cinema?
9. Do you want Jim to pick Mary up, or John to do it?
10. Do you want to see that old film, or something else?
11. Shall we visit the local library, or the art gallery?
12. Would you like John to stay for a month, or for a week?
13. Shall we have the party on Sunday, or on Saturday night?
14. Do you want Jim to get married, or to remain a bachelor?
15. Shall we do a dictation, or shall we do more oral drills?
16. Shall we read a popular newspaper, or a more serious one?
17. Would you like to listen to some opera, or some pop music?
18. Do you want Peter to spend the day in bed, or at the office?
19. Would you like me to take my holiday now, or to take it later?
20. Do you want to hear about Bob's operation, or about his holiday?

175 INTERMEDIATE/ADVANCED

She	**'d better**	buy a dictionary.	(advice)
He	**'d better**	be polite in future.	(warning)
We	**'d better not**	have dinner yet.	(advice)
You	**'d better not**	be late.	(warning)

Compare: A. You**'d better go** *now*.
B. It **would be better** if you **went** *now*.

The 'A' sentence has no past form. The past form for 'B' is
'It **would have been better** if you **had gone** (yesterday).'

To practise the above patterns, respond as shown:

Will Bob go to Susan's party, or will he stay away?
He'd better go to her party; he'd better not stay away.

Will everything go smoothly, or will there be trouble?
**Everything had better go smoothly; there'd better not be
trouble.**

Shall I look for a hotel now, or shall I leave it till later?
**You'd better look for one now; you'd better not leave it till
later.**

1. Shall I ask Jim to do it, or shall I ask Bob?
2. Will the car go, or will it break down again?
3. Shall we eat now, or shall we wait until later?
4. Will you work this evening, or will you go out?
5. Shall I shut the door, or shall I leave it open?
6. Will John take his coat, or will he go without it?
7. Shall I send that camera back, or shall I keep it?
8. Shall I lay the table, or shall I help in the kitchen?
9. Shall I ring Susan up, or shall I go round and see her?
10. Shall I tell Jim to hire a car, or shall I lend him mine?
11. Will there be somebody there, or will the house be
empty?
12. Will John rewrite the article, or will he send it in again?
13. Will Paul tell the truth, or will he try and hide the facts?

14. Shall I get the map, or shall we try and manage without one?
15. Will Peter see the doctor, or will he ignore his chest pains?
16. Will Jim be able to keep his appointment, or will he be late?
17. Will the firm appoint a new manager, or will they keep Jim on?
18. Will the men accept the pay increase, or will there be a strike?
19. Will Mary take the children with her, or will she leave them here?
20. Will the arrangements be all right, or will they have to be changed?

---

176 Revision of Negative Forms I

The anomalous finites **is, are, was, were, have, has, had, do, does, did, shall, should, will, would, can, could, might, must, need, dare, ought** can be joined to the contracted form of **not**.

EXAMPLES:
They **weren't** here last night.

John **daren't** go to class late.

EXAMPLES OF VERBS FOLLOWED BY **not**:

I **may not** go.	I **am not** to go.
I'**d rather not** go.	I **used*** not to go.
I'**d better not** go.	I'**d prefer not** to go.
I'**d sooner not** go.	I'**d just as soon not** go.

EXAMPLES OF VERBS PRECEDED BY **not**:

I don'**t have** to see Mary.
I don'**t need** to see Mary.
I did**n't use*** to see Mary. (more common)
I'm **not able** to see Mary.
I'm **not going** to see Mary.

See also Ex. 292.

To practise and contrast different positions of not, *make the following negative. Speak about John:*

Mary must be French.
John can't be French.

Mary'd better visit Robert.
John had better not visit Robert.

Mary has to book her seats now.
John doesn't have to book his seats now.

1. Mary's car might be ready.
2. Mary used to play golf.
3. Mary should leave now.
4. Mary must park her car here.
5. Mary has to wear a suit.
6. Mary must be in danger.
7. Mary may have the day off.
8. Mary had to wait an hour.
9. Mary's got to go to class.
10. Mary'd rather have tea.
11. Mary'd prefer to wait here.
12. Mary's had to take an exam.
13. Mary had been there before.
14. Mary'll have to work late.
15. Mary could see Richard.
16. Mary dared to open the box.
17. Mary ought to go to Canada.
18. Mary may be able to see Jim.
19. Mary'd better stay away.
20. Mary has to be able to swim.
21. Mary'll be able to find out.
22. Mary would like to help Tom.
23. Mary'd rather stay at home.
24. That'll be Mary at the door.

THE COMPARATIVE AND THE SUPERLATIVE

Introductory notes:
(i) When we make a simple comparison (the comparison of equals)
we use the **as** . . .**as** construction.

EXAMPLES:
You are **as** big **as** me.
/ˈjuər əz ˈbig əz ˈmiː/

She is **as** intelligent **as** Peter.
This book is **as** expensive **as** that one.

(ii) The comparative and superlative of single-syllable adjectives is formed by adding the sounds /ə/ (spelt **er**) and /ist/ (spelt **est**) to the positive.

	Positive	Comparative	Superlative
	tall /tɔːl/	taller /'tɔːlə/	tallest /'tɔːlist/
(g—gg)	big /big/	bigger /'bigə/	biggest /'bigist/
(—e)	wise /waiz/	wiser /'waizə/	wisest /'waizist/
(y—i)	dry /drai/	drier /'draiə/	driest /'draiist/

long, strong, young are exceptions, adding /gə/, /gist/:
  long /lɔŋ/   longer /'lɔŋgə/   longest /'lɔŋgist/

(iii) The comparative and the superlative of adjectives with three or more syllables are formed by using **more** and **most** before the positive.

   comfortable   more comfortable   most comfortable

Notice that **most** can sometimes mean 'very'.

EXAMPLES:
She is **most** beautiful.

You are **most** kind.

(iv) Two-syllable adjectives do not follow 'rules' like those above. It is generally true that the following add /ə/, /ist/:
(a) 2 syllables with the second stressed:

   polite /pə'lait/ —er /pə'laitə/ —ist /pə'laitist/

But adjectives beginning *a—* (*afraid, alone, aware* etc.) are exceptions: **more** aware, **most** afraid.
(b) 2 syllables ending with unstressed /ə/, /i/, /əu/ and syllabic /l/:

clever /'klevə/	cleverer /'klevərə/	cleverest /'klevərist/
pretty /'priti/	prettier /'pritiə/	prettiest /'pritiist/
narrow /'nærəu/	narrower /'nærəuə/	narrowest /'nærəuist/
noble /'nəubl/	nobler /'nəublə/	noblest /'nəublist/

(v) The following are irregular:

good/better/best	far/farther/farthest
bad/worse/worst	far/further/furthest
late/later/last	old/elder/eldest

The station is **further/farther** than the hotel.

I need a **further** ten minutes to finish the job.

Paul was the **last** to arrive. (the final person)
  (Cf. Bob's **latest** book is about History.)

Jane is the **elder** of the two sisters.

John is the **eldest** son.
  (Cf. Jane is **older** than John. Ben is the **oldest** student here.)

---

177 The Comparative and the Superlative   E

My	car's		fast.			It can do 140 k.p.h.
My	car's	**as**	fast	**as**	yours.	It can also do 140 k.p.h.
My	car's		faster	**than**	Bob's.	Bob's car can do
Bob's	car's not	**as/so**	fast	**as**	mine.	130 k.p.h.
Tom's	car's	**the**	fast**est**.			It can do 150 k.p.h.

To practise the as . . . as *form.*
  My car's fast.
  My car's not as fast as yours.

  My books were cheap.
  My books were as cheap as yours.

  My house is big.
  My house is not as big as yours.

  My bed was comfortable.
  My bed was as comfortable as yours.

  1. My work's important.
  2. My typewriter's new.
  3. My health's good.
  4. My job's interesting.
  5. My country's modern.
  6. My suitcases were full.
  7. My intonation's good.
  8. My watch was accurate.
  9. My sweaters are well-made.
  10. My chair's comfortable.

11. My eyesight's good.
12. My writing's legible.
13. My hobby's useful.
14. My friends were generous.
15. My newspaper was informative.
16. My house is attractive.
17. My work's satisfying.
18. My TV set's dependable.
19. My room's tidy.
20. My pronunciation's good.

178 The Comparative and the Superlative   E

When we make a comparison of two persons or things that
are unequal we use the comparative with **than**.

Note:
The words **much** and **even** add emphasis.

EXAMPLES:
Betty is **even taller than** Susan.

Sally is **much more intelligent than** Bill.

To practise the comparative, respond as shown:

My car is fast. (John's)
I agree that your car is fast, but John's is faster than yours.

Jim's tennis was bad. (Don's)
**I agree that Jim's tennis was bad, but Don's was worse than
Jim's.**

English food is good. (French)
**I agree that English food is good, but French food is better
than English.**

1. Mary is young. (Sally)
2. Paris is big. (Tokyo)
3. Gordon is happy. (Mary)
4. My driving was bad. (Jim's)
5. Philip is lucky. (John)
6. Mary is beautiful. (Anne)
7. The moon is far away. (Mars)
8. David will be late. (Allan)

9. My English is good. (Bob's)
10. Don's Spanish is bad. (Jim's)
11. John's car is slow. (Mary's)
12. Lucy is very nice. (Sue)
13. This camera is small. (that)
14. My case was heavy. (Paul's)
15. Joe's suit is dark. (Jim's)
16. This beer's bitter. (that)
17. These chairs are comfortable. (those)
18. Cigarettes are expensive. (cigars)
19. The water here is very shallow. (over there)
20. Exporting watches is profitable. (cars)

---

179 The Comparative and the Superlative   I

To practise the superlative, respond as shown:

film—good (see)
  STUDENT A: **Can you tell me something about the film?**
  STUDENT B: **It's the best film (that) I've ever seen.**

John—nice (meet)
  STUDENT C: **Can you tell me something about John?**
  STUDENT D: **He's the nicest person (that) I've ever met.**

exercise—difficult (do)
  STUDENT E: **Can you tell me something about the exercise?**
  STUDENT F: **It's the most difficult exercise (that) I've ever done.**

1. sweater—big (put on)
2. actor—brilliant (see)
3. car—cheap (buy)
4. picture—beautiful (see)
5. runner—fast (see)
6. job—easy (do)
7. programme—good (watch)
8. story—amusing (hear)
9. man—intelligent (speak to)
10. girl—tall (see)
11. drink—sweet (taste)

234

12. party—nice (be to)
13. book—interesting (read)
14. flat—small (live in)
15. bed—uncomfortable (sleep in)
16. watch—accurate (have)
17. John—friendly person (meet)
18. new car—bad (drive)
19. Jill—happy person (meet)
20. city—modern (visit)

---

180 The Comparative and the Superlative I

Note:
 (i) The patterns used for the comparison of adjectives are also
    used for the comparison of adverbs.

> EXAMPLES:
> He drives **as** safely **as** John.
> We speak **better than** them.
> I ran **the fastest**.

(ii) The comparative and the superlative forms of adverbs:
    (a) Single-syllable adverbs, and sometimes *early* and *often*,
        add /ə/ and /ist/.
    (b) All other adverbs use **more** and **most**.

To practise the comparison of adverbs, speak about Paul, John,
Mary *and* Peter.

Paul plays well.
   STUDENT A: **John plays as well as Paul.**
   STUDENT B: **Mary plays better than Paul.**
   STUDENT C: **Peter plays the best.**

Paul drives fast.
   STUDENT D: **John drives as fast as Paul.**
   STUDENT E: **Mary drives faster than Paul.**
   STUDENT F: **Peter drives the fastest.**

 1. Paul runs fast.
 2. Paul began late.
 3. Paul sings well.
 4. Paul works hard.

5. Paul speaks English well.
6. Paul listens attentively.
7. Paul started early.
8. Paul talks a lot. (more)
9. Paul smokes a little. (less)
10. Paul drove a short distance. (far)

COMPARISON AND CONTRAST

181 INTERMEDIATE

George's job is **the same as**	John's.	They are both teachers.
George's job is **different from**	Harry's.	Harry is a doctor.
Harry's job is **similar to**	Peter's.	Peter is a dentist.
Jane's dress is **like**	Susan's.	Both dresses are black and have a high neck-line.
Mary looks **like**	her mother.	
John drinks **like**	a fish.	

Use the correct phrase or word to connect each pair of sentences:

John works a lot. A horse works a lot.
John works like a horse.

This computer is a model 360. That one is a 240.
This computer is different from that one.

Paul's nationality is French. Jean is French too.
Paul's nationality is the same as Jean's.

My Ford car is ten years old. Yours is nine years old.
My car is similar to yours.

1. David runs fast. The wind is fast.
2. This material is wool. That is nylon.
3. My coat is black. Sheila's is yellow.
4. George swims well. A fish swims well.
5. My information is about Jim. Yours is about Bob.

236

6. This dictionary is comprehensive. That one is too.
7. My present was a camera. Yours was a film-projector.
8. The programme I saw was 'Peyton Place'. You saw it too.
9. This electric fire has two bars. That one has only one.
10. These flowers are natural. Those flowers are artificial.
11. The play I watched was 'Othello'. You watched it as well.
12. My newspaper is 'The Times'. Yours is 'The Daily Telegraph'.
13. Mary has brown eyes and blonde hair. Her mother has the same.
14. The doctor who examined me was Dr Brown. He also saw Barbara.
15. Jim is tall, dark and handsome. Bob is tall, dark and handsome.
16. Jill's room is small and uncomfortable. Jean's is the opposite.
17. Bob's idea is to open a coffee-bar. Don's is to open a tea-shop.
18. The road I took went through Zurich. Betty also took this road.
19. My book was called 'Spoken English'. John's was 'Oral English'.
20. Henry's friends are always 'broke'. John's friends are wealthy.

---

182 Comparison and Contrast   IA

The expressions **the same as, different from, similar to** and **like** were practised in the previous exercise. Use these expressions, also bringing in the positive (**as . . . as**) and comparative (**larger, more interesting,** etc.) to compare and contrast the following:

EXAMPLE:
Scotland/England

> STUDENT A: **England is geographically larger than Scotland, and has a larger population.**

STUDENT B: **The English are very similar to the Scottish in character.**

STUDENT C: **Scotland has a colder winter than the South of England, and has more rain.**

STUDENT D: **Scotland is different from England in many respects. In my opinion, one of the biggest differences is that Scotsmen wear kilts. These are seldom seen south of the border.**

STUDENT E: **Scotland is like England in many ways: take government for instance; both countries have the same Parliament, at Westminster.**

STUDENT F: **Scotland is the same as England in that the people of both countries speak English.**

1. a city/a town
2. Germany/Japan
3. a novel/a short story
4. a private school/a state school
5. Africa/South America
6. the United States/Britain
7. the Russian Premier/the President of the United States
8. Canada/Australia
9. China/India
10. classical music/modern music
11. a hotel/your own home
12. a library/a bookshop
13. classical art/modern art
14. a theatre play/a TV play

---

183 Comparison and Contrast   A

To assist you in doing the following exercise some useful expressions are given below. You will also find useful certain of the conjunctions and phrases listed in Appendix A.

There is a (slight/great, etc.) **difference in** . . .

There is (a/no/little, etc.) **difference/similarity between** . . . **and** . . .

There is a/are (further/(an)other, etc.) **difference(s)/similarity(ies) in that** . . .

. . . **resembles/differs from** . . . **in that** . . .

There is (no/little, etc.) **connection between** . . . **and** . . .

Note:
The English used in the example is formal, as if uttered by one student as an address. It is also possible to do the exercise as a discussion, in which case the language will be less formal.

Compare and contrast the following:

EXAMPLE:
The school John attends is in Switzerland. It has three hundred students of mixed nationality, most of whom are boarders. The school was built in 1866 and stands in its own grounds consisting of four acres of well-kept gardens.

The school Mary goes to is in Germany. It has two hundred and eighty students, all girls, who live in the school. It is completely modern, and stands in about five acres of land.

There is a considerable difference between the two schools. While John's was built in the last century, Mary's is completely modern and no doubt incorporates the latest developments in educational architecture. Although both schools have roughly the same number of students, in the case of the boy's school not all of the students live in, whereas all the girls are boarders. There is a slight difference in the size of grounds— the girl's school is larger by about one acre. However, the main difference lies in the fact that the two schools are to be found in different parts of Europe, one being in Switzerland and the other in Germany.

1. John's car is a 1934 Ford convertible. It suffers from wobbly steering, brake-fade, bald tyres and it often slips out of gear.
   Mary's is the latest Ford saloon with power-assisted steering and brakes, and is fully automatic. She will, however, soon need new tyres.
2. John lives in somewhat austere surroundings, with a single bed, one armchair with the stuffing coming out, and a table. He keeps his clothes in his suitcase under the bed, but spreads his other belongings all over the room.
   Mary's bedroom suite comprises a double divan bed, twin wardrobes, dressing-table and seat. She has numerous perfumes and make-up aids on the table, and the room generally is quite untidy since she rarely puts things away.

3. John's favourite holiday resort is Miami. He likes to lie on the beach and soak up the sun. If it rains, he stays in and watches TV or reads. He is not interested in doing anything else while on holiday. He has three weeks off every year.

Mary prefers to go to Italy for her annual three-week holiday. She loves wandering around the capital looking at museums and art galleries. She likes to paint, and spends a lot of her time trying to put what she sees on to canvas.

4. John likes good music. He prefers Beethoven and Mozart, but does not mind listening to Brahms or Wagner. He is not the slightest bit interested in jazz or pop music and despises those people who go to festivals or special concerts to hear this type of music.

Mary likes classical music, has a preference for Chopin and Bach, but enjoys Beethoven and Mozart nearly as well. She avoids listening to jazz and pop music, but tolerates those people who take an interest in them and is prepared to discuss them with enthusiasts.

5. John went to university. He studied psychology and French for the first year, and then decided to change to English. He ended up by taking an honours degree in English. While at university he took an active interest in many of the students' societies, especially the drama group. He had visions of becoming a successful actor after finishing his studies.

Mary went to a college of education. She wanted to become a teacher because her father had been one, and because she liked looking after children. Her main subject was English, but she had taken Advanced-level French at school and so she continued her study of this language. While at College she thought about joining the drama group, but decided against it, preferring instead to join the debating society, of which she became president. She received her teacher's certificate one year after leaving the college, having completed her teaching practice satisfactorily.

6. Sir Hugh Peterson is 65 years of age, and is chairman and managing director of a large engineering company in Bedfordshire. Educated at Eton and Oxford, he joined Thompson Brown Engineering Ltd in 1921, became a

director in 1929 and managing director in 1932. He founded his present engineering company in 1935 and formed the Peterson Corporation in 1951. He produces gears, machine tools, tractors and cars. He farms 150 acres in Bedfordshire, and his recreations are hunting, polo and yachting.

Lord Hunt (Life Peer created 1962) is aged 52 and is chairman of the National Coal Board, the largest single employer of manpower in the nationalised industries and the largest industrial organisation in the whole of Western Europe. He attended a local secondary school, and was very active in trade union affairs until he became chairman of the T.U.C.* in 1963, when he concentrated on administration and reorganisation. He was an M.P.† for many years, being Postmaster General during Attlee's post-war Labour Government. His recreations are gardening and stamp-collecting.

---

184 Comparison and Contrast   A

Compare and contrast the following. It will be found useful to define the words first, and follow this by giving contexts.

1. an accident
   an incident

2. a statesman
   a politician

3. murder
   manslaughter

4. publicity
   propaganda
   advertising

5. friend
   acquaintance
   colleague

6. liberty
   freedom
   independence

7. habit
   custom
   tradition

8. revolution
   riot
   civil disobedience

9. sympathy
   pity
   understanding

10. envy
    jealousy

11. sin
    crime

12. socialism
    communism

* Trades Union Congress
† Member of Parliament

ADVERBS AND ADVERBIALS

Introductory notes:

(i) Many adverbs are formed from adjectives by adding the syllable /li/ (spelt **ly**).

EXAMPLES:

clever**ly**   clear**ly**   persistent**ly**

quick**ly**   sad**ly**   beautiful**ly**

This suffix never affects stress.

(ii) Adverbial phrases are used, *a.* where no adverb can be formed from the adjective, *b.* where it may be considered more natural, or *c.* where adding **ly** to the adjective would change its meaning.

EXAMPLES:

(a) She did the exercise **with difficulty**.

(b) He addressed the crowd **in a broken voice**.

(c) She spoke **in a high voice**.
(Cf. She spoke **highly** of him.)

(iii) Generally speaking, adverbs and adverbials go into a sentence in the order **manner**, **place** and **time**.

EXAMPLES:

Bob did **well in the competition last June**.

Sue spoke **politely at the meeting on Thursday**.

Betty sang **beautifully on TV last night**.

The car ran **smoothly on the way to the office yesterday**.

When a verb indicates movement **to** a place, the 'place' usually comes immediately after the verb.

EXAMPLES:

Jim drove **to the station in a hurry on Monday**.

Jill went **to New York by air this morning**.

Certain adverbials indicating frequency are usually preceded by 'place' and 'direction' adverbials. (Cf. pre-verb frequency adverbs—Ex. 185)

EXAMPLES:

Bob taught **at the university twice a week in 1970**.

Mary went **to the United States three times last year**.

---

185 Frequency Adverbs   E

| I | **never** | get up early. |
| She | **rarely** | knows the answer. |

It	**seldom**	rains there.
He	**hardly ever**	comes to class.
She	**scarcely ever**	does any cooking.
They	**occasionally**	miss dinner.
I	**sometimes**	go to the cinema.
We	**frequently**	travel by train.
She	**often**	writes home.
They	**generally**	understand him.
We	**usually**	arrive before her.
He	**always**	has tea at 4 p.m.
Do you **ever**		make mistakes?

Notes:

(i) **Never, rarely, seldom, hardly ever** and **scarcely ever** are **negative** adverbs. We use **often, always**, etc. with anomalous finites in the negative, e.g. 'I **don't always** go to class' etc., but we do not use the negative adverbs in this way.

(ii) Frequency adverbs usually follow anomalous finites.

EXAMPLES:
Mary is **occasionally** a little nervous.
John can **often** visit the library.
Paul may **never** smoke at home.

But to provide emphasis the adverb may come before the anomalous finite. In this case both adverb and anomalous finite carry sentence stress.

EXAMPLES:
He **often** *is* wrong.
/hi ˈɔfn ˋiz ˌrɔŋ/

She **sometimes** *can* drive well.
/ʃi ˈsʌmtaimz ˋkæn ˌdraiv ˌwel/

Bob **generally** *does* help Richard.
/ˈbɔb ˈdʒenərəli ˋdʌz ˌhelp ˌritʃəd/

(iii) **Ever** is compounded with **hardly** and **scarcely** to mean **rarely**. Although used mainly in questions ('Do you **ever** . . . ?', 'Has she **ever** . . . ?', etc.) **ever** is sometimes placed with **not** to mean **never** in statements, in this way providing emphasis.

EXAMPLES:
I don't **ever** want to see you again!
  (Cf. I don't want to see you **ever** again!)

I won't **ever** know the reason for her action.

243

In your answers to the following give the adverbs that apply to you personally. (Be careful with Nos. 6 and 13.)

get up
> STUDENT A: **What time do you get up?**
> STUDENT B: **I usually get up at 8 o'clock.**
> STUDENT A: **Do you ever get up at 10 o'clock?**
> STUDENT B: **I hardly ever get up at 10 o'clock.**

get to class
> STUDENT C: **What time do you get to class?**
> STUDENT D: **I usually get to class at about 9 a.m.**
> STUDENT C: **Do you ever get to class at 9.30 a.m.?**
> STUDENT D: **No, I never get to class at 9.30 a.m.**

1. have breakfast
2. have your morning break
3. finish your morning break
4. go to lunch
5. come back from lunch
6. classes finish for the day
7. have tea
8. do your homework
9. have dinner
10. finish dinner
11. watch TV
12. go to the bar
13. the bar close
14. go to bed (turn in)
15. turn out the light
16. go to sleep (drop off)

---

186 Frequency Adverbs   E

In the following sentences insert the frequency adverbs that suit your own personal habits, e.g. one will say of the first example 'I often watch TV.' while another will say 'I seldom watch TV.'

I watch TV.	**I often watch TV.**
I read in the evening.	**I usually read in the evening.**
I come to class late.	**I occasionally come to class late.**

1. I drive.
2. I sleep well.

3. I arrive early.
4. I cook for myself.
5. I watch TV.
6. I go to the cinema.
7. I listen to the radio.
8. I have lunch at 2 p.m.
9. I go to the theatre.
10. It rains in my country.
11. I wake up before 6 a.m.
12. I write letters home.
13. I have a beer before dinner.
14. I need help with my work.
15. I go shopping on Sundays.
16. I go to bed before 11 p.m.
17. I make mistakes in my work.
18. I pay attention in class.
19. I feel better after a holiday.
20. I have a cigarette before breakfast.

---

187 Frequency Adverbs   E

Answer the following questions as shown:

Do you ever feel depressed?	**I seldom feel depressed.**
Are you ever late for class?	**I'm never late for class.**
Do you ever go to bed late?	**I sometimes go to bed late.**

1. Am I ever wrong?
2. Are you ever homesick?
3. Do you ever get angry?
4. Do you ever eat too much?
5. Are you ever early for class?
6. Do you ever cook for yourself?
7. Do you ever go out to dinner?
8. Do you ever think about the past?
9. Do you ever feel tired after class?
10. Do you ever have too much to drink?
11. Are you ever very late going to bed?
12. Do you ever spend your holidays abroad?
13. Are you ever at home during the weekend?
14. Do the other students ever smoke in class?
15. Do you ever have difficulty in getting to sleep?

Note:
Most non-frequency adverbs go after the main verb, or after the object if there is one.

EXAMPLES:
They are learning   **slowly**.
They are learning English **slowly**.

Elizabeth speaks   **fast**.
Elizabeth speaks English **fast**.

Compare the adjective and adverb patterns below:

ADJECTIVE		ADVERB
Peter's a **slow**	driver.	He drives **slowly**.
Harry's a **careful**	driver.	He drives **carefully**.
Allan's a **dangerous**	driver.	He drives **dangerously**.
Susan's a **hard**	worker.	She works **hard**.
Helen's a **fast**	walker.	She walks **fast**.
Betty's a **good**	swimmer.	She swims **well**.

Use an adverb in your response, as shown:

Don's a slow worker.	**Yes, he works slowly.**
Lucy's a good teacher.	**Yes, she teaches well.**
Peter's a careful driver.	**Yes, he drives carefully.**

1. John's a hard worker.
2. Peter's a good driver.
3. Harry's a fast runner.
4. Helen's a bad driver.
5. Joe's a good teacher.
6. Mary's a fast typist.
7. Jean's a slow worker.
8. Henry's a good swimmer.
9. Peter's a noisy eater.
10. David's a fast talker.
11. Jim's a careless driver.
12. Jane's a careful typist.
13. Jim's a good dancer.

14. Bill's a fluent speaker.
15. Sally's a fast swimmer.
16. Joe's a slow reader.
17. Jim's a bad actor.
18. Susan's a good actress.
19. Gordon's a fast driver.
20. Anne's an efficient worker.

---

189 Adverts I

Give the opposite for Mary:

John did well in his exam.
Mary did badly in her exam.

John behaved properly.
Mary behaved improperly.

John holds his fork correctly.
Mary holds her fork incorrectly.

1. John drives safely.
2. John walked hurriedly.
3. John spoke respectfully.
4. John went out quickly.
5. John taught Bob carefully.
6. John washed the dishes well.
7. John behaved intelligently.
8. John plays enthusiastically.
9. John argues logically.
10. John behaved pleasantly.
11. John waited calmly.
12. John arrived punctually.
13. John behaves honestly.
14. John speaks politely.
15. John acted responsibly.
16. John behaves normally.
17. John spoke aggressively.
18. John hit Bob accidentally.
19. John goes to class regularly.
20. John spoke optimistically.

Change the adjective in brackets into an adverb and use in your response, as shown:

John drives. (careful)
John drives carefully.

It rained. (continuous)
It rained continuously.

Mary speaks English. (fluent)
Mary speaks English fluently.

(a) 1. John swims. (good)
    2. Richard fell. (heavy)
    3. Susan types. (perfect)
    4. Mary dresses. (elegant)
    5. Steve appeared. (sudden)
    6. I did the job. (thorough)
    7. Jim listened. (attentive)
    8. The sun shone. (brilliant)
    9. Philip acted. (impulsive)
    10. Mary came here. (special)
    11. John goes to school. (reluctant)
    12. Tom signed the paper. (willing)
    13. Bob waited for Susan. (anxious)
    14. Paul took the exam. (successful)
    15. Jim phoned Mary. (optimistic)
    16. Paul agreed with me. (complete)
    17. John made the call. (immediate)
    18. Mary slammed the door. (violent)
    19. Jim speaks English. (effortless)
    20. John looked at Peter. (serious)

(b) As (a) above (further practice).

    1. Paul speaks. (persuasive)
    2. Bob works. (conscientious)
    3. Paul came in. (unexpected)
    4. Jim spoke to Bill. (angry)
    5. John reacted. (surprising)
    6. I opened the box. (eager)
    7. Bob does his work. (proper)

8. Tom was educated. (private)
9. I gripped the rope. (tight)
10. Joe looked at Sue. (tender)
11. Bob kicked the ball. (vicious)
12. Peter commented. (favourable)
13. Tom judged the race. (impartial)
14. Jim searched the room. (frantic)
15. John took the drug. (unwitting)
16. The job was done. (scientific)
17. Mary opened the door. (hesitant)
18. I examined the ring. (suspicious)
19. Jill looked at Peter. (inviting)
20. Allan read the report. (nervous)

---

191 Adverbial Phrases   IA

See note ii above Ex. 185. The noun in the adverbial phrase
may be modified:

I did the work with **considerable** difficulty.
Peter dismissed Robert with **a great deal of** reluctance.
Betty treated Harry without **much** consideration.

'Manner' may also be expressed in the following ways:

John behaved **in an irresponsible manner**.
Richard swims **in an unusual fashion**.
Elizabeth dressed **in a special way**.

*Choose from the above patterns when responding to the follow-
ing. Indicate where a simple adverb* may be used instead of an
adverbial phrase.*

How did Sally look at Sheila? (admiring)
She looked at her in admiration. (. . . admiringly)*

How does John treat Mary? (indifferent)
He treats her with considerable indifference.

How did Peter tackle the job? (determined)
**He tackled it in a very determined manner. (. . . with deter-
mination)**

1. How does Elizabeth speak? (persuasive)
2. How did Rosemary dress? (careful)

3. How does David use persuasion? (subtle)
4. How did Peter look at Mary? (interested)
5. How did Harry start the car? (difficult)
6. How does Sandra treat John? (considerate)
7. How did Paul pose the question? (certain)
8. How did John tackle the problem? (cautious)
9. How will Mary have her hair done? (different)
10. How did Gordon treat the visitors? (courteous)
11. How did Mary deal with the situation? (tactful)
12. How did Sheila speak to Richard? (confidential)
13. How did Philip behave at the party? (outrageous)
14. How does Richard treat his employer? (respectful)
15. How did Sally behave towards her sister? (selfish)
16. How did Richard approach the problem? (methodical)
17. How did Betty react to your suggestion? (favourable)
18. How did Elizabeth accept the verdict? (philosophical)
19. How did Rosemary look at Richard? (astonishing)
20. How does Peter treat his colleagues at work? (friendly)

---

192 Adverbs   IA

Notes:
  (i) Certain adverbs (of 'degree') are usually placed between the subject and the main verb of the sentence, or after the anomalous finite.

   EXAMPLES:
   John **greatly** admires his father.

   I'm **strongly** opposed to hard work.

   I **thoroughly** enjoy a cup of coffee.

 (ii) Certain adverbs may be placed before the subject of the sentence.

   EXAMPLES:
   Normally, Mary would have been here.

   Generally, we know what to do in advance.

   Fortunately, I knew what was to happen.

(iii) Here are some examples of variable-position adverbs:

   Actually, you're quite right.
   You are, **in fact**, quite right.
   You're quite right, **of course**.

The following three exercises (a, b and c) practise placing adverbs into sentences. Choose a good position (there may be more than one) for the adverb in brackets, as shown:

Do you like John? (rather)
I rather like John.

Did you catch the train? (only just)
I only just caught the train.

Do you still make mistakes? (naturally)
Naturally, I still make mistakes.

(a)   1. Do you like Sheila? (quite)
     2. Did you speak to Steve? (only)
     3. Did you see Susan? (personally)
     4. Will it rain later? (very likely)
     5. Have you been to the doctor's? (just)
     6. Are you opposed to apartheid? (strongly)
     7. Do you know everybody here? (practically)
     8. Do you think I've made a mistake? (rather)
     9. Do you always take the short cut? (nearly)
   10. Didn't Richard get the job? (unfortunately)
   11. Did Harry make it to the station? (only just)
   12. Does Steve want to see that film? (definitely)
   13. Had you finished when Tom came in? (just about)
   14. Did you remember to bring the tickets? (luckily)
   15. Did you suggest to Jim that he should come earlier? (merely)

(b) As (a) above (further practice).
     1. Did the sun come out? (all at once)
     2. Did you forget about Mary? (completely)
     3. Did the dentist examine your teeth? (just)
     4. Were you aware of what Tom was doing? (fully)
     5. Is there going to be any trouble? (evidently)
     6. Do you remember the first act? (particularly)
     7. Did the painting belong to Gordon? (originally)
     8. Do you refuse to lend John your car? (absolutely)
     9. Are you sure that David wants to go alone? (quite)
   10. Was Betty confused about the situation? (thoroughly)
   11. Are you interested in buying some shares? (definitely)
   12. Did Paul come when he knew you needed him? (immediately)

13. Are you worried about what Sandra intends to do? (rather)
14. Did you know what was going on in the house? (fortunately)
15. Can't you tell me the name of the sales manager? (actually)

(c) As (a) above (further practice).
1. Has John gone to bed? (very likely)
2. Are you worried about Betty? (really)
3. Shall I be invited as well? (no doubt)
4. Are you sure how far it is? (of course)
5. Will Anne hear from Jim again? (perhaps)
6. Was Bob chosen to do the job? (specially)
7. Are you confident that you'll win? (fairly)
8. Is Tom involved in the conspiracy? (deeply)
9. Did you have time to tell Richard? (scarcely)
10. Weren't you anxious about the results? (at all)
11. Was Allan responsible for the accident? (partly)
12. Is Henry right about the increased costs? (quite)
13. Did you feel it was the right time to call? (hardly)
14. Did Bob manage to reach his destination? (eventually)
15. Did you dismiss Jim from his job? (rightly or wrongly)

ADVERBS WITH INVERSION

193 ADVANCED

Certain adverbs and adverb phrases are followed by inversion of the subject and verb when they are used at the beginning of the sentence. They can also be used in other parts of the sentence without inversion:

Jim had **hardly** sat down when the phone rang.

The 'front position' with inversion construction is emphatic or rhetorical; in most cases it is not ordinary conversational English.

EXAMPLES:
Hardly had Richard left the house when the letter came.
Jim doesn't even like Mary; **still less** does he love her.
No sooner had Tom turned on the TV than the fuse went.

252

To practise the above pattern, respond as shown:

Have you ever met such a charming person? (seldom)
Seldom have I met such a charming person.

Did the phone ring as soon as Jim had sat down? (hardly)
Hardly had Jim sat down when the phone rang.

Did Mary complain to the head waiter and the manager?
  (not only)
Not only did Mary complain to the head waiter, but also to the
  manager.

1. Did Bob realise how serious Tom was? (little)
2. Will Steve call on Mary, or ring her up? (nor)
3. Did Lucy's request interest Peter? (so unusual)
4. Does John like Mary and her sister? (still less)
5. Is Jim ridiculous and impolite as well? (not only)
6. Will Mary really understand John's motives? (never)
7. Did Tom stay for tea and also for dinner? (not only)
8. Can I go with you if I promise not to chatter? (only)
9. Do you remember what happened on that occasion?
   (well)
10. Shall I see such architecture anywhere else? (nowhere)
11. Can I see Mary without making an appointment? (only
    by)
12. Have you ever seen Peter looking so happy? (never
    before)
13. Will you visit that seaside town again? (never again)
14. Did Jim get a reminder after he'd paid the bill? (no
    sooner)
15. Can Bob get into university without passing the exam?
    (only)
16. Will Sandra be allowed to see Allan? (under no circum-
    stances)
17. Was Peter dismissed as soon as he'd been promoted? (no
    sooner)
18. Did Tom have to start work immediately he'd come in?
    (scarcely)
19. Did John have to go out again as soon as he'd got home?
    (hardly)
20. Have you ever witnessed such a courageous action?
    (never before)

ADVERBIALS OF TIME, FREQUENCY and DURATION

Introductory note:
   Adverbials of time answer the question **when**? and certain other 'time' question words (see Ex. 194a, b and c).

   EXAMPLES:
   Harry went to school **last month**.

   Susan got up **at 8 o'clock**.

   Paul had a drink **10 minutes ago**.

Adverbials of frequency answer the question **how often**? (see Ex. 195a)

   EXAMPLES:
   I come here **twice a month**.

   Sheila has a rest **every afternoon**.

   They go to Bermuda **once a year**.

Adverbials of duration answer the question **how long**? (see Ex. 195b)

   EXAMPLES:
   Susan stayed here **for two weeks**.

   Peter has been in Mexico **since Saturday**.

   Mary was living there **from March to June**.

---

194 Adverbials of Time   EI

Note:
In (a) and (b) below, the cue given in brackets is the same as the conversational short answer; in conversation the question 'When did Peter come?' could be answered with:

Early this morning.
/ˈəːli ðis ˈmɔːniŋ/

But for the sake of the drill the student should answer as shown. Separate practice using the short answer might be added.

(a) *To practise some very common adverbials.*

   When did Peter come? (early this morning)
   He came early this morning.

254

When will George be here? (later this month)
He'll be here later this month.

When did Philip leave? (last month)
He left last month.

1. When is the play? (tonight)
2. When will Jim come? (tomorrow)
3. When did Henry go? (last night)
4. When was the party? (yesterday)
5. When is the film on? (all this week)
6. When shall I see Peter? (tomorrow evening)
7. When will Paul be here? (tomorrow morning)
8. When did Susan ring up? (yesterday morning)
9. When was the accident? (yesterday afternoon)
10. When does the next course begin? (next month)
11. When did Bob leave? (the day before yesterday)
12. When will Jim be on holiday? (later this year)
13. When is the next concert? (one day next week)
14. When is Alice coming to dinner? (tomorrow night)
15. When shall we meet Mr Brown? (tomorrow afternoon)
16. When will Sally be going? (the day after tomorrow)
17. When did Pat first meet Sally? (this time last year)
18. When did George first come here? (the year before last)
19. When is Allan starting his holiday? (early next week)
20. When can we have seats for the show? (the week after next)

(b) *To practise adverbials of time with prepositions* (*see also Exs.* 299 *and* 305).

When did Bob arrive? (on Saturday)
He arrived on Saturday.

When will Anne be here? (after dinner)
She'll be here after dinner.

What time did the plane take off? (at 10 o'clock)
It took off at 10 o'clock.

How early were you at the airport? (before 9 o'clock)
I was there before 9 o'clock.

1. When is the conference? (in April)
2. Which day is the party? (on Saturday)
3. When will you be free? (by 8 o'clock)

4. When will Bob leave here? (before lunch)
5. Which month did Philip come here? (in May)
6. When does the film start? (after the news)
7. What time does Peter have dinner? (at 7 p.m.)
8. What time did the train go? (at about 11 a.m.)
9. How soon can John see Barbara? (after the lesson)
10. What time did you get up this morning? (at 8 a.m.)
11. What time did David have his interview? (at 9 a.m.)
12. What time must you meet your friend? (at lunch-time)
13. When does Peter have his holidays? (during the summer)
14. How soon is the coffee break? (in half an hour's time)
15. How soon can Bob go to a more advanced class? (on showing more improvement)

(c) *To practise adverbials of time with* ago.

How long ago did you come here? (a week)
I came here a week ago.

When did Paul arrive? (three months)
He arrived three months ago.

How long ago were the last Olympic games? (—years)
They were — years ago.

1. How long ago did you come here?
2. When was the accident? (six months)
3. When was the present government elected?
4. When did Susan have her interview? (a month)
5. When did that parcel arrive? (a few moments)
6. How long ago did Betty come in? (five minutes)
7. When did Gordon leave for New York? (not long)
8. How long ago did Paul get married? (three years)
9. How long ago was that book published? (two weeks)
10. How long ago was the computer installed? (three years)
11. When did Mary get back from the shops? (a short while)
12. How long ago was that photograph taken? (a long time)
13. How long ago did the programme start? (a few minutes)
14. When did the suit come back from the cleaners? (two days)
15. How long ago did Sue pass her driving test? (nine months)

(a) *To practise adverbials of frequency—end or (sometimes) front position (see also the frequency adverbs in Ex. 185).*

How often must John take that medicine? (every two hours)
He must take it every two hours.

How often does Harry go to class? (several times a day)
He goes to class several times a day.

How often does John see Mary? (every now and again)
He sees her every now and again.

1. How often did Paul go swimming? (every day)
2. How often did Mary write to John? (twice a week)
3. How often did John write to Mary? (once a year)
4. How often is Peter late for class? (every so often)
5. How often did the phone ring? (every few minutes)
6. How often does Bob call on Sue? (three times a week)
7. How often does that magazine come out? (twice a month)
8. How often does Don take Sally out? (every other week)
9. How often did Ken stop for a rest? (every now and again)
10. How often does Anne change her job? (every now and then)
11. How often did the navigator check his position? (every hour)
12. How often does Paul buy himself a new car? (every two years)
13. How often does John go to New York? (once every six months)
14. How often will David attend evening classes? (every other day)
15. How often does Susan have to answer the door? (several times a day)

Note:
The cue given in brackets for Ex. 195a is the same as the conversational short answer.

(b) *To practise adverbials of duration introduced by* for, since, until *and* from—to/until/till.

How long have you been here now? (for . . .)
I've been here (for) a week.

How long was Peter in Canada? (. . . 1965 to 1970)
He was there from 1965 to 1970.

How long will you be at the school? (until . . .)
I'll be here until I know English well.

How long has Betty been studying English? (. . . she changed her job)
She's been studying it since she changed her job.

1. How long can you stay here? (until . . .)
2. How long have you been here? (since . . .)
3. How long was John here? (. . . a fortnight)
4. How long did Sally stay? (. . . she'd finished)
5. How long will Sheila wait? (. . . the rain stops)
6. How long would you like to stay here? (for . . .)
7. How long have you been learning English? (for . . .)
8. How long has Jim been waiting? (. . . the office closed)
9. How long was John in hospital? (. . . just over a month)
10. How long did Bob remain in Rome? (. . . his money ran out)
11. How long have Jim and Don been here now? (. . . two weeks)
12. How long has Paul been living in London? (. . . last March)
13. How long has Gordon been in the classroom? (. . . breakfast)
14. How long did Betty have to study English? (. . . a long time)
15. How long will Jim be in the examination room? (. . . an hour)
16. How long did Bob stay away? (. . . April till June last year)

17. How long will John watch TV? (. . . the end of the programme)

18. How long will Bob be here? (. . . today until the twenty-first)

19. How long has Peter been living in New York? (. . . he left here)

20. How long did Jim watch the beauty contest? (. . . his wife made him switch off)

ADVERBIAL CLAUSES AND PHRASES OF TIME

Introductory note:

In the examples below, **when** and **while** introduce adverbial clauses; **during** introduces adverbial phrases.

While means 'during the time that'

EXAMPLES:

I spoke to her **while** she was drinking.

He was singing **while** they were dancing.

When means (1) 'every time' or 'on every occasion' (**whenever**)

(2) 'at the same time as'

(3) 'immediately'

EXAMPLES:

(1) Paul gets up **when** Mary comes in.

(2) Paul was getting up **when Mary** came in.

(3) Paul got up **when** Mary came in.

When may also introduce a surprise, or sudden action.

EXAMPLES:

Paul was getting up, **when** Mary came in!

(or: . . . , **when** who should come in but Mary!)

We were having a walk, **when** the cliff gave way!

During indicates 'in the course of'

EXAMPLES:

He was living in Canada **during** the war.

I did a lot of swimming **during** my holiday.

259

ADVERBIAL CLAUSES AND PHRASES OF TIME

196 INTERMEDIATE

To practise and contrast when, while *and* during, *respond as shown:*

When did you get that suntan? (. . . my last holiday)
I got it during my last holiday.
/ai 'gɔt it djuəriŋ mai 'lɑːst ˋhɔlədi/

When do you read your newspaper? (. . . I'm having breakfast)
I read it while (or **when**) **I'm having breakfast.**
/ai 'riːd it wail aim 'hæviŋ ˋbrekfəst/

When did Robert buy that radio? (. . . he'd found out the price)
He bought it when he'd found out the price.

1. When was the crime committed? (. . . the night)
2. When will Bob use the computer? (. . . it's free)
3. When did the phone ring? (. . . I was in my bath)
4. When did you watch TV? (. . . my friends had gone)
5. When will John have his hair cut? (. . . the lunch-hour)
6. When did Paul propose to Susan? (. . . he first saw her)
7. When did Harry get seasick? (. . . the channel crossing)
8. When will Jimmy arrive? (. . . all the work has been done)
9. When did Gordon leave the office? (. . . the Board meeting)
10. When did Peter get off the train? (. . . it was still moving)
11. When does Bob have his first cup of coffee? (. . . breakfast)
12. When will John buy the theatre programme? (. . . the interval)
13. When did Jim start seeing Mary? (. . . they were at university)
14. When does Susan come home? (. . . everybody else has gone to bed)
15. When was the washing-up done? (. . . the rooms were being cleaned)
16. When did Richard meet Sally for the first time? (. . . the summer)

17. When did you wake up this morning? (. . . the alarm clock went off)
18. When did Mary start crying? (. . . the hero in the film was killed)
19. When did the other students do their homework? (. . . the afternoon)
20. When did Betty hear about the accident? (. . . she got a phone call from Bob)

Practise also the conversational short answer.

When did you get that suntan? (. . . my last holiday)
During my last holiday.
/'djuəriŋ mai 'lɑːst `hɔlədi/

When do you read your newspaper? (. . . I'm having break-fast)
While I'm having breakfast.
/'wail aim 'hæviŋ `brekfəst/

---

197 Adverbial Clauses and Phrases of Time   IA

See Ex. 196 for practice with **when**, **while** and **during**. Ex. 195b practises **since**, **for**, **until** and **from . . . to/till/until**.

Other words to introduce 'time' are **as soon as**, **as long as**, **once**, **(not) long after**, **before**, **by the time**, **now (that)**.

EXAMPLES:
Anne spoke to me **after** she had eaten, not **before**.
Betty arrived at the station **long after** Susan did.
I can stay in this country **as long as** I want to.
I suggest you join the club **as soon as** you can.
Bob will understand **by the time** we've finished.
Richard will like Mary **once** he gets to know her.
I can put in the answer **now that** I know what it is.

To practise the above, and to give further practice with other 'time' conjunctions and phrases.

How long has Sally been working? (since . . .)
She's been working since she left university.

How soon will Jim be able to come? (as soon as . . .)
He'll be able to come as soon as he's finished his work.

When did Jane put the baby to bed? (while . . .)
She put the baby to bed while Henry was putting the car away.

1. How long did Jim stay? (for . . .)
2. When did David go out? (when . . .)
3. When's Jill coming? (not until . . .)
4. When did Jim visit France? (while . . .)
5. When will Bob be here? (by the time . . .)
6. How long was Susan helping John? (for . . .)
7. How long has Mary been teaching? (since . . .)
8. When did John go to the next class? (once . . .)
9. How soon will Jane be dressed? (before . . .)
10. How long will the party go on? (as long as . . .)
11. When did the concert take place? (as soon as . . .)
12. How soon will Mary be ready to go out? (once . . .)
13. When can I borrow your typewriter? (while . . .)
14. How soon do you plan to leave here? (as soon as . . .)
15. How early will you be able to come? (immediately . . .)
16. How long will Bob be staying at the hotel? (until . . .)
17. How soon does the main film start? (not long after . . .)
18. How long has Jim been learning English? (ever since . . .)
19. When did Bob finish studying last night? (long after . . .)
20. When was Richard living in the United States? (during . . .)

Practise also the conversational short answers.

EXAMPLE:
How long has Sally been working? (since . . .)
Since she left university.

How soon will Jim be able to come? (as soon as . . .)
As soon as he's finished his work.

So and Such

198 INTERMEDIATE

Peter's very	busy.		He	can't	see you.
Peter's too	busy		to		see you.
Peter's **so**	busy	(that)	he	can't	see you.
Peter's **such** a busy man	(that)		he	can't	see you.

Further examples:

John speaks	**so**	quickly	(that)	I can't understand him.
Jill has	**so**	many friends	(that)	she can't count them.
Mary had	**such**	a lot of money	(that)	she didn't know what to do with it.
Jim plays with	**such**	skill	(that)	he beats every one at tennis.

Note:

The conjunction **that** is often omitted after **so** . . . , and less frequently after **such a**. . . . Sometimes **that** must be included for clarity or rhythm, and it is never 'wrong' to include it. Students are advised to utter it in all cases. The conjunction **that** never bears sentence stress, and it is usually pronounced /ðət/.

Peter's so busy that he can't see you.
/ˈpiːtəz ˈsəu ˌbizi ðət hi ˈkɑːnt ˈsiː juː/

To practise so . . . (*that*) . . . , *respond as shown:*

The coffee's hot. I can't drink it.
The coffee's so hot (that) you can't drink it.

Many people came. Many didn't get into the hall.
So many people came that many didn't get into the hall.

The car went slowly. People behind were trying to overtake.
The car went so slowly that people behind were trying to overtake.

1. This saucepan's clean. You can see your face in it.
2. The chair was comfortable. Bob went off to sleep in it.
3. The walk was very long. George and Susan soon got tired.
4. The play was good. The audience clapped for ten minutes.
5. The building was old. The Council wanted to pull it down.
6. Richard's keen on golf. He plays nearly every afternoon.
7. The house was large. Bob decided to convert it into flats.

8. The students had little homework to do. They became bored.
9. The water was cold. Peter came out after only two minutes.
10. The plate was hot. Mary dropped it on the kitchen floor.
11. The lesson was boring. Allan spent the time looking at Mary.
12. John's worried about the future. He's taken out insurance.
13. Paul has few friends. He spends most of his time by himself.
14. The exercise was easy. Don asked for something more difficult.
15. John's speech was short. Everybody thought he hadn't finished.
16. The director was impressed with Jim. He decided to promote him.
17. Bob's driving was bad. The examiner failed him after one minute.
18. The dress was very short. Sue's father wouldn't let her wear it.
19. The exam was difficult. Harry didn't bother to finish the paper.
20. John was fascinated by Helen. He couldn't take his eyes off her.

---

199 So and Such
I

To practise such . . . (*that*) . . . , *respond as shown:*

Peter had a lot of trouble with his car. He sold it.
Peter had such a lot of trouble with his car that he sold it.

You were a long time making the tea. Jim lost his temper.
I was such a long time making the tea that Jim lost his temper.

Bob was having a wonderful holiday. He didn't want to come home.
Bob was having such a wonderful holiday that he didn't want to come home.

1. Harry spoke good English. Everyone remarked on it.
2. Mary has a comfortable bed. She very often oversleeps.

264

3. Patrick knows a lot. Everybody comes to him for advice.
4. John buys cheap clothes. He always looks badly dressed.
5. Jean has a well-designed flat. Her friends are envious.
6. It was an inexpensive magazine. Everyone could afford it.
7. Tom gave a dull lecture. His students complained about it.
8. Helen has a small room. She can't hold any meetings there.
9. Richard's an early riser. He always sees the sun come up.
10. Peter's a brilliant businessman. He's already a millionaire.
11. Betty showed an interest in John's work. He was flattered.
12. A lot of people have cars these days. The roads are crowded.
13. This is a nice place to live. We shall probably retire here.
14. George has known Sheila for a long time. He's got used to her.
15. The salesman had a lot to do. He had to give up his day off.
16. Michael's been smoking very strong tobacco. It's made him ill.
17. They've had cold weather recently. The rivers have frozen over.
18. It was a very difficult course. Richard couldn't complete it.
19. Anne spends a lot on food. She can't afford to buy any clothes.
20. The police used effective methods. My money was soon recovered.

---

200 So and Such   A

To contrast so *and* such, *respond as shown:*

I have a lot of money. I don't know what to spend it on.
You have such a lot of money (that) you don't know what to spend it on.
You have so much money (that) you don't know what to spend it on.

Jim explained the lesson well. Even Bob understood it.

Jim gave such a good explanation that even Bob understood the lesson.

Jim explained the lesson so well that even Bob understood it.

1. Many people came. There wasn't room to sit down.
2. The meeting was important. Nobody dared miss it.
3. John had a lot to drink. He had to be driven home.
4. John's work was promising. He got a rise in salary.
5. The TV programme was very good. We all enjoyed it.
6. The letter interested Peter. He read it seven times.
7. Mary's a good dancer. She's been offered a film part.
8. The necklace is valuable. It has to be kept locked up.
9. Sally has been gone a long time. I'm worried about her.
10. Betty opened the parcel carefully. Nothing dropped out.
11. David showed intelligence. His parents were proud of him.
12. Peter tells funny jokes. It's a pleasure to listen to him.
13. The news caused confusion. Few people knew what was going on.
14. John had a strong foreign accent. Nobody could understand him.
15. Bob plays the piano very well. He's always in demand at parties.
16. Sheila has a fear of spiders. She screams whenever she sees one.
17. The plane was heavily loaded. I thought it would never take off.
18. The boys came in late. Their parents were already in bed. (use: a late hour)
19. Paul drove very fast. The police car couldn't catch up with him. (use: speed)
20. My house is a long way from here. We'll need four hours to reach it. (use: far)

Still and **Any more**

---

201 Still   I

John	**still** goes to the nearest seaside resort whenever he has a holiday.
He	**still** hasn't been abroad.
Mary is **still** hoping that he will take her to Bermuda.	

To practise still, *respond as shown:*

David hasn't begun to study yet. (holiday)
He still hasn't begun to study.
He's still on holiday.

Susan hasn't visited Paris yet. (hope to go)
She still hasn't visited Paris.
She's still hoping to go.

Jim hasn't lent Bob the book yet. (read)
He still hasn't lent him the book.
He's still reading it.

1. Pat hasn't come home yet. (cinema)
2. John hasn't got married yet. (think)
3. Angela hasn't made the beds yet. (unmade)
4. Peter hasn't had a haircut yet. (too long)
5. Paul hasn't learnt to swim yet. (afraid)
6. Tom hasn't finished his essay yet. (write)
7. Gordon hasn't returned the record yet. (use)
8. I haven't turned the TV set on yet. (read)
9. Bill hasn't finished eating yet. (restaurant)
10. Arthur hasn't posted the letters yet. (stamps)
11. Sue hasn't stopped making mistakes yet. (learn)
12. Mrs Brown hasn't done the shopping yet. (coffee)
13. I haven't found a place to park my car yet. (look)
14. Paul hasn't taken Sally out yet. (take Sheila out)
15. The army hasn't ordered the new weapon yet. (test)

202 **Still** and **Any More**   I

Bob used to live in Mexico.
Last year he moved to Texas.
He doesn't live in Mexico   **any more**.
When I last saw him he was   **still**   in Texas.

Notes:
 (i) **Any more** (like 'yet') is used in negative and interrogative
     sentences.

(ii) **Still** indicates that the situation has not changed; **any more** indicates that a change has taken place and the former situation no longer exists.

(iii) There is a considerable difference between the implications of these questions.

> John **still** doesn't smoke cigarettes, does he?
> (He never started.)

> John doesn't **still** smoke cigarettes, does he?
> (He hasn't stopped yet.)

To contrast any more *and* still.

> John had a cold last week. He has a cold now.
> **John still has a cold.**

> Mary used to swim a lot. She plays tennis instead now.
> **Mary doesn't swim any more.**

> John didn't use to go to the cinema. John doesn't go to the cinema.
> **John still doesn't go to the cinema.**

1. Don had an accent. Don has an accent now.
2. Peter had a job. Now he doesn't have a job.
3. Anne used to eat too much. Anne eats too much.
4. Gordon wasn't married. Gordon isn't married now.
5. Bill couldn't type last year. He can't type now.
6. Ben used to have a car. He doesn't have a car now.
7. John used to watch TV. John doesn't watch TV now.
8. The exercise was difficult. The exercise is difficult.
9. Harry went sailing last year. He goes sailing this year.
10. George drove a car all last year. He doesn't drive now.
11. John used to visit Russia. He doesn't go to Russia now.
12. Peter used to enjoy walking. Peter never goes walking now.
13. Bob didn't use a dictionary. Bob doesn't use a dictionary.
14. I used to read a daily newspaper. I read a daily newspaper.
15. John didn't use to catch colds. He doesn't catch colds now.
16. Bill worked for that company last year. He works for it now.

17. Jim didn't know how to speak English. He can't speak English.
18. Paul used to like Mary very much. Paul doesn't like Mary now.
19. Mary used to read books in French. She reads books in French.
20. I wasn't interested in Jane. I'm not interested in Jane now.

So do I, Neither/Nor do I, etc.

Short Responses

203 ELEMENTARY

STATEMENT	RESPONSE			
I like coffee.	**So**	**do**	I.	(I like coffee **too**.)
Jim likes coffee.	**So**	**does** Tom.		(Tom likes coffee **too**.)
I don't like tea.	**Neither do**	I.		(I don't like tea **either**.)
Jim doesn't like tea.	**Nor**	**does** Tom.		(Tom doesn't like tea **either**.)

Note:
Neither and **nor** have the same meaning in this pattern.

To practise so *and* neither/nor *with the simple present tense, respond as shown:*

Mary goes to class. (I)	**So do I.**
John sleeps well. (Peter)	**So does Peter.**
I don't play golf. (Gordon)	**Neither does Gordon**
He doesn't speak German. (I)	**Nor do I.**

1. I don't know the way. (I)
2. Bob doesn't drink. (Tom)
3. John works hard. (we)
4. Joe likes Mary. (John)
5. Mary never laughs. (Jim)
6. I have a car. (Gordon)

7. I don't understand. (I)
8. We enjoy studying. (Lucy)
9. Betty goes to class. (I)
10. David reads a lot. (Tom)
11. Joe doesn't sleep well. (Mary)
12. Tom swims like a fish. (John)
13. The trousers don't fit. (coat)
14. Bob speaks English well. (you)
15. Jim doesn't have a car. (John)
16. Trains arrive late. (buses)
17. I don't know Peter. (we)
18. Jack has a typewriter. (Peter)
19. Jim doesn't take drugs. (I)
20. I use the language lab. (we)

---

204 So do I, Neither do I, etc.

To practise more of the 'special' verbs, respond as shown:

I must go now. (John)	**So must John.**
Gordon can't swim. (Bob)	**Neither can Bob.**
Harry wasn't at home. (Jim)	**Neither was Jim.**
Robert went to New York. (Jean)	**So did Jean.**

1. I got a letter. (Peter)
2. Paul had a swim. (Betty)
3. John was here. (Sally)
4. Bob shouldn't worry. (Jim)
5. Betty saw the film. (Susan)
6. Jim can't stand Anne. (Don)
7. Paul hasn't been away. (I)
8. I must stay for a week. (Don)
9. Harry bought a car. (Richard)
10. Helen came early. (my friend)
11. I shall be late. (John)
12. Bob didn't understand. (Jim)
13. I have to go to bed. (Sally)
14. Mary had a party. (David)
15. I haven't had any tea. (Jim)
16. Sue hadn't been before. (Bob)
17. Sally might be there. (Helen)

18. I wanted to go by air. (Jill)
19. John mustn't smoke. (Richard)
20. John has caught a cold. (Bob)

The Conjunctions
Both . . . And, Neither . . . Nor, . . . Too, So, . . . Either

205 ELEMENTARY/INTERMEDIATE

| James can swim.
Betty can swim. | **Both** James **and** Betty can swim.
James can swim **and** Betty can **too**.
James can swim **and so** can Betty. |

| Bob can't swim.
Jim can't swim. | **Neither** Bob **nor** Jim can swim.
Bob can't swim **and** Jim can't **either**.
Bob can't swim **and neither/nor** can Jim. |

| James can swim.
Bob can't swim. | James can swim, but Bob can't. |

To practise the above patterns, respond as shown:

Paul must go to class.   Jean must go to class.

> STUDENT A: **Both Paul and Jean must go to class.**
> STUDENT B: **Paul must go to class and Jean must too.**
> STUDENT C: **Paul must go to class and so must Jean.**

Paul doesn't drive well.   Jean doesn't drive well.

> STUDENT D: **Neither Paul nor Jean drives well.**
> STUDENT E: **Paul doesn't drive well and Jean doesn't either.**
> STUDENT F: **Paul doesn't drive well and neither/nor does Jean.**

Paul went home yesterday.   Jean didn't go home yesterday.

> STUDENT G: **Paul went home yesterday, but Jean didn't.**

1. Paul speaks English. Jean speaks English.
2. Paul hasn't left yet. Jean hasn't left yet.
3. Paul didn't stay long. Jean didn't stay long.

4. Paul has been to Spain. Jean has been to Spain.
5. Paul recognised the man. Jean recognised the man.
6. Paul didn't disturb John. Jean didn't disturb John.
7. Paul should pay attention. Jean should pay attention.
8. Paul has a two-car garage. Jean has a two-car garage.
9. Paul won't know the answer. Jean won't know the answer.
10. Paul had too much to drink. Jean had too much to drink.
11. Paul upset George yesterday. Jean upset George yesterday.
12. Paul doesn't have to go yet. Jean doesn't have to go yet.
13. Paul must get another book. Jean needn't get another book.
14. Paul didn't have any trouble. Jean didn't have any trouble.
15. Paul's house is very central. Jean's house is very central.
16. Paul doesn't like that hotel. Jean doesn't like that hotel.
17. Paul parked in a side street. Jean parked in a side street.
18. Paul spoke to the manager. Jean didn't speak to the manager.
19. Paul didn't ask any questions. Jean didn't ask any questions.
20. Paul doesn't enjoy going to the cinema. Jean doesn't enjoy going to the cinema.

Either . . . Or

You may **either** do the work today,	**or** do it tomorrow.
Either have tea now,	**or** have it later.
You can **either** work in Paris,	**or** work in London.
Either be quiet,	**or** go away.

Note:
The conjunction **either** . . . **or** indicates that of two available actions **one** or **the other** is possible (but **not both**).

272

To practise either . . . or, *respond as shown:*

Shall I see Peter now, or shall I see him later?
You can either see him now, or see him later.

Shall I go to the cinema, or shall I watch TV?
You can either go to the cinema, or watch TV.

Shall I turn on the radio, or shall I turn on the TV?
You can either turn on the radio, or turn on the TV.

1. Shall I go by air, or shall I go by sea?
2. Shall I work tonight, or shall I go out?
3. Shall I take a taxi, or shall I go by bus?
4. Shall I have a swim, or shall I go for a walk?
5. Shall I have meat for dinner, or shall I have fish?
6. Shall I read a book, or shall I write some letters?
7. Shall I do that exercise now, or shall I do it later?
8. Shall I have a whisky, or shall I have something else?
9. Shall I have a haircut now, or shall I have one later?
10. Shall I ring John up, or shall I go round to his house?
11. Shall I spend my holiday in Rome, or shall I spend it in Paris?
12. Shall I dial direct, or shall I ask the operator to put me through?
13. Shall I ask for a rise in salary now, or shall I leave it until next year?
14. Shall I dress up for dinner tonight, or shall I wear something comfortable?
15. Shall I get in touch with John by cable, or shall I try to get him on the phone?

Practise also omitting unnecessary repetition. In the examples the first response can be:

You can see him either now or later.

(*It is best for the word or group of words after* either *to be of the same grammatical kind as the word or group after* or.)
In the rest of the exercise six responses can be shortened. Which are they?

CONJUNCTIONS

But, So, However, Therefore, Because, If, Unless, etc.

Some very common conjunctions and phrases:

If	**But**	**So**	**Because**
Unless	**However**	**Therefore**	**Because of**
Whether or not	**Although**		
	In spite of		

Examples of how these words are used:

I shall come to the party **if** you come too.
I shan't come **unless** you come.
Peter will go **whether** you go **or not**.

John will be able to go the party, **but** Anne will not.
Anne can't go. **However**, she will be able to go to the next one.
Although Anne can't go, she doesn't feel too badly about it.
Anne is smiling **in spite of the fact** that she can't go.

Harry can go to the party, **so** he has gone to get dressed.
He's taking Susan with him; **therefore** he can't take Mary.

Jill can't go, **because** nobody will baby-sit for her.
Now the party has been called off **because of** a flu epidemic!

To contrast but *and* so, *respond as shown:*

I like coffee. I don't like tea.
You like coffee, but you don't like tea.

Susan hasn't been to France. She can't speak French.
Susan hasn't been to France, so she can't speak French.

1. The fur coat suited Mary. She didn't buy it.
2. The restaurant was crowded. John and Mary went in.
3. Bill loves Betty. He is interested in what she does.
4. John said he wasn't lying. Susan didn't believe him.
5. The policeman spoke to me. He didn't speak to Peter.

274

6. I don't have any transport. I can't go to the shops.
7. Anne hadn't had any lessons. She couldn't drive a car.
8. Bob was curious to know what had happened. I told him.
9. The doctor gave me some good advice. I didn't follow it.
10. Bill didn't turn up outside the cinema. Susan went home.
11. The couple wanted a hotel. They couldn't find a good one.
12. Bob has known Jim for many years. He has confidence in him.
13. The driver tried to control the car. It crashed into a tree.
14. John likes watching TV. He doesn't like going to the cinema.
15. The managing director made many mistakes. The firm collapsed.

---

208 Conjunctions—**If/Unless**   **I**

Note:
The dictionaries usually give 'if not' as the meaning of **unless**, but the two are not always interchangeable. In particular, **unless** is not used in 'impossible' conditions (type C on page 345):

I wouldn't have heard him **if** he had**n't** shouted.

and even in 'possible' conditions (type A) there is often a difference, e.g. in

You will hurt yourself **if** you are **not** careful.
(A moment's carelessness may result in injury.)

You will hurt yourself **unless** you are careful.
(Constant care may prevent injury, which is otherwise certain.)

To contrast if *and* unless, *give both responses as shown:*

I shall read the book. (long)
I shall read the book if it is not long.
I shall read the book unless it is long.

John will be late. (taxi)
John will be late if he doesn't take a taxi.
John will be late unless he takes a taxi.

Nobody can read John's letters. (type)
Nobody can read John's letters if he doesn't type them.
Nobody can read John's letters unless he types them.

1. George smokes. (wife watching)
2. You will feel better. (overdo it)
3. I shan't pay that bill. (correct)
4. Peter won't finish the job. (help)
5. Gordon will catch a cold. (sweater)
6. Richard is amusing. (drink too much)
7. Sheila doesn't get angry. (irritated)
8. Jane will buy that camera. (expensive)
9. John will go by hovercraft. (sea rough)
10. The plane should land at 5 p.m. (delay)
11. You won't understand. (listen carefully)
12. I can pay for my holiday. (buy a new suit)
13. I will carry your suitcase for you. (heavy)
14. Jim makes mistakes. (pay attention in class)
15. I shall stay at the hotel. (outside the town)

---

209 Conjunctions   I

To practise whether or not, *respond as shown:*

Will you take the boat out if it's windy?
I shall take the boat out whether it's windy or not.

Will you watch TV tonight if there's anything good on?
I shall watch TV tonight whether there's anything good on or not.

Will John go to the cinema if the programme finishes early?
John will go to the cinema whether the programme finishes early or not.

1. Will John buy a car if he gets a rise in salary?
2. Will the firm install a computer if they need one?
3. Will Sheila stay out late if her mother permits it?
4. Will Peter work tonight if he has an exam tomorrow?
5. Will the pilot take off if there's snow on the runway?
6. Will you go by train if you can get a fast connection?
7. Will John eat at that restaurant if the prices are high?
8. Will David give up smoking if his doctor advises him to?
9. Will Mary continue to see John if he goes out with Susan?
10. Will George buy that book if it's by a well-known author?

11. Will the airport be built if the local residents complain?
12. Will the film be shown if press reviews are satisfactory?
13. Will Jane emigrate to the United States if Peter goes with her?
14. Will Jill have that extra ice-cream if it's bad for her figure?
15. Will the road be completed next week if the men work overtime?

---

210 Conjunctions   I

To contrast although *and* because, *respond as shown:*

The stain wouldn't come out. Mary washed the shirt twice.
The stain wouldn't come out although Mary washed the shirt twice.

The meeting went on for two hours. Everybody was interested.
The meeting went on for two hours because everybody was interested.

1. Mary didn't have any lunch. She wanted to lose weight.
2. Gordon didn't earn much last year. He worked very hard.
3. Anne entertained Bob. She would rather it had been Jim.
4. Don is happy with his car. He thinks he's got a bargain.
5. Jim won the competition. He'd had no previous experience.
6. Richard was upset yesterday. He'd had a row with his wife.
7. Harry enjoyed the party very much. He had to leave early.
8. Jane took a course in typing. She wanted a better-paid job.
9. Peter took on another secretary. He didn't really need one.
10. Sheila put up all the sails. Light winds had been forecast.
11. The firm set up a factory. There were few workers available.
12. Bob found that his watch was still going. He had dropped it.

13. Allan didn't have lunch with Betty. He was annoyed with her.
14. John thinks he's failed the exam. He didn't do much studying.
15. Sue is learning how to cook. She doesn't intend to get married.

---

211 Conjunctions I

Note:

Therefore and **however** are both rather formal. They are useful for serious discussion, lecturing etc. but in informal conversation the student is safer with **so** and **but**, which could be used in these sentences even in quite formal discussion.

To contrast therefore *and* however, *respond as shown:*

John doesn't know Anne's last name. He knows her address.
John doesn't know Anne's last name; however, he knows her address.

I expected Jane to get in late. I left the door unlocked.
I expected Jane to get in late; therefore I left the door unlocked.

1. The ship began to break up. The crew abandoned her.
2. I was sent a form to fill in. I have not read it yet.
3. Gordon caused the accident. Sheila took him to court.
4. Jim is a notorious liar. Jane believes every word he says.
5. The hikers were exhausted by their walk. They had a rest.
6. Bob has an excessive liking for whisky. He is seldom sober.
7. Jim hopes the weather will clear up. I do not think it will.
8. The doctor examined Peter. He found nothing wrong with him.
9. Don was unable to work. Richard had twice as much to do.
10. David has a quantity of radio equipment. He seldom uses it.
11. Bob has done some deep-sea diving. He must be a good swimmer.
12. Richard was not trained as a teacher. He will teach this term.

13. Jim loved his wife very much. He was completely faithful to her.
14. The scientist mislaid the formula. He still had it in his head.
15. The firm had to close. The shareholders did not lose their money.

---

212 In spite of/Because of   IA

To contrast **in spite of** and **because of**, respond as shown. In each case the expression is followed by a combination of the kind studied in Ex. 102. (**Despite** may replace **in spite of**.)

Sam lost his job. He had a good record of attendance.
Sam lost his job in spite of (despite) his good attendance record.

The boats in the harbour all stayed put. There was a warning of a gale.
The boats in the harbour all stayed put because of a gale warning.

1. The police were alerted. There was a raid on a bank.
2. I was angry. I'd read an article in the newspaper.
3. I got to my office. There was a strike on the railway.
4. John had to pull up. The lights controlling the traffic were red.
5. People are still coming to this country. There's an epidemic of flu.
6. The land's valueless. There's been erosion of the soil.
7. Nobody moved out of the block of flats. There was a leak of gas.
8. You'd expect people to drive more slowly. There are many hazards on this road.
9. They pass you at 160 in the fast lane. There's a limit on speed on the motorway.
10. Jim had to work throughout July. He'd made arrangements for a holiday in the summer.
11. John was laid up yesterday. He'd received an injury while playing football.
12. All aircraft have been grounded. There's a shortage of fuel.

There are, of course, many more conjunctions than the ones already practised. In this free-completion exercise you should add to the sentence given a clause or phrase beginning with the conjunction or phrase shown.

Mary likes John.

but   STUDENT A: **Mary likes John, but she isn't in love with him.**

and   STUDENT B: **Mary likes John and she goes out with him a lot.**

so   STUDENT C: **Mary likes John, so she doesn't go out with Bob.**

1. Anne's always late for class.
   and so
   however
   besides

2. Peter had an accident.
   although
   and as a result
   because

3. Philip stayed at home.
   even though
   whereas
   therefore

4. Tom plays tennis on Fridays.
   although
   if
   unless

5. Sally's bought a washing-machine.
   so that
   and also
   and that's why

6. Mary wears a mini-skirt.
   in spite of
   consequently
   because

7. John went to Paris.
   nevertheless
   for
   in order to

8. Jane teaches English.
   therefore
   instead of
   whenever

9. Bob must learn English.
   otherwise
   because of
   however

10. Jim will attend the conference.
    whether or not
    despite
    and in addition

Owing to, Due to and Because of

214 ADVANCED

Note:
There are still teachers, editors and examiners who say that because
due is an adjective it must be linked to a noun. They allow:

Bob's **ignorance** is **due** to a lack of education.

but they do not recognise:

Due to a lack of education Bob is ignorant.

It is now necessary to recognise the fact that **due to** has become a
compound preposition which, like **owing to** and **because of**, may
introduce an adverbial:

Due to
Owing to } the need for engineers in Caracas, Tom is going there
Because of next year.

John hesitated { **owing to**
due to } a feeling of uncertainty.
because of

Use **due to** after (pro)noun + be:

John's hesitation was **due to** a feeling of uncertainty.
Tom's departure is **due to** a need for engineers in Caracas.

The committee considered the strike to be **due to** general dissatisfaction.
The men's constant striking has been **due to** general dissatisfaction.

In this free-completion exercise, add owing to, due to, *or* because of *and complete the phrase in any suitable way. If more than one of these expressions is possible, say so.*

I decided that my failure to pass the driving test—
I decided that my failure to pass the driving test must have been due to indigestion—the tester's.

It was decided that—the whole committee should resign.
It was decided that owing to/due to/because of the angry scenes at the annual general meeting the whole committee should resign.

1. We lost a lot of time on the journey—
2. —the journey was a very uncomfortable one.
3. The extreme discomfort of the journey was—
4. Mary decided to look for another flat—
5. Her choice of her present flat was probably—
6. —she isn't at all pleased with her present flat.
7. They thought the failure of the company must have been—
8. The company failing must, they thought, have been—
9. —the company had failed.
10. —it won't do the 160 kilometres an hour it is supposed to do.
11. It will only do a rather noisy 90—
12. The garage said its failing to reach 160 was entirely—
13. —I'm ashamed to take Betty or Angela on the motorway in it.
14. The whole show will have to take place in the Scouts' hut—
15. It seems that—it wasn't possible to have the show in the open.

LINKING

To create a piece of continuous speaking or writing it is vital to use correct linking. Use conjunctions, participles, relative pronouns, etc. to join the following. Make one or two sentences.

Paul sat down. A pretty waitress came up to him. He asked for a kiss. He received for his pains a slapped face. He also received a glass of beer over his head.

Paul had no sooner sat down than a pretty waitress came up to him. Asking for a kiss he received for his pains a slapped face and a glass of beer over his head.

1. Peter hadn't seen the film. He couldn't recommend it to Mary. She decided to see it anyway.
2. Alice made the beds. She then did the washing-up. This had been waiting to be done since the night before.
3. Barry bought a paper. He didn't have time to read it. He put it into his cupboard. It stayed there untouched for a week.
4. Harry went to the bar. He had been there the night before. He spoke to the manager. He asked if his wallet had been found.
5. Paul met a girl. She asked him to a party. This was to be held that evening. He told her he couldn't go. He had some work to do.
6. John saw a suit. He wanted it. He went into the shop and asked the price. He found that it was too expensive for him. He decided to buy a pair of shoes instead.
7. Betty turned on the TV. She didn't see anything worth watching. She went next door. She wanted to see Mary. She knew Mary would like to have a chat.
8. Robert had a look at the computer. It had just been installed. He'd had quite a lot of experience with the model. He demonstrated it to Jim.
9. A man asked John the way to the station. John had never seen him before. John told him that he was a stranger himself in the town. As a result of this he couldn't help him.

10. The chairman of the Board spoke. He informed the directors that their presence would be required. This would be the following morning. A decision would then have to be reached. This decision would be whether the firm was to go into liquidation or not.

11. She knew a man. This man would be able to get her out of the trouble she was in. She went round to his house. She intended to speak to him. He was not at home. She went into a coffee-bar. She had a cup of tea.

12. Every member of the club had failed. They could not beat Jones at poker. Mr Smith decided to have one last try. He went into the bar. He found the gentleman concerned. He was drinking his victim's health. Mr Smith challenged him to a game.

13. The wardrobe had been filled with Mary's clothes. He was able to carry it into the next room. He did this by first emptying it. He wedged it into the corner. This was near the fireplace. He did this in a certain way. It could only have been moved again with the greatest difficulty.

14. The ship left the harbour. It dropped the pilot. The captain went below. He wrote letters to his wife and son. He would not be seeing them for the next eighteen months. This was unless the company brought him home earlier.

15. John saw a very pretty girl. She was sitting behind the reception desk. He did not have anything else to do. He went into the shop. He introduced himself. He said that he was an agent for a film producer. This film producer was to make a film on location in that city. She would probably meet this film producer. This would be if she agreed to have dinner with John that evening.

PURPOSE AND REASON

216 Purpose

I

| I have come here | | to learn English. |
| I have come here | in order | to learn English. |

284

Jim arrived at 8.45 a.m. **in order not to** be late for class.
Sue studied Spanish **so as** **to** be able to speak to Juan.
Bob switched on early **so as not to** miss the news.
I went to New York **for** a holiday.

Notes:
(i) **For** is generally used with nouns in the expression of purpose.

EXAMPLES:
She went to the shop **for** some cakes.
(She went to the shop **to buy** some cakes.)

He comes here **for** lessons.
(He comes here **to have** lessons.)

(ii) The pattern 'for + gerund' may be used.

EXAMPLES:
That's used **for** opening tins. (. . . used **to open** . . .)

This is used **for** hanging things on. (. . . used **to hang** . . .)

Cf. She was sent to prison **for** shoplifting.
(because she had been convicted of shoplifting)

(a) *To practise the Infinitive of Purpose, respond as shown:*

Why did you come here? (learn English)
I came here to learn English.

Why is Sally working hard? (pass her exam)
She's working hard to pass her exam.

Why does Mary phone John? (give him her news)
She phones him to give him her news.

1. Why did Mary come here? (take an exam)
2. Why has Peter gone to Canada? (see Mary)
3. Why did Sally stop? (buy some cigarettes)
4. Why will Jim call on Jane? (see how she is)
5. Why has Bob left the room? (answer the phone)
6. Why did John take a walk? (get some fresh air)
7. Why will Paul visit the U.S.A.? (see his parents)
8. Why is Jim staying in bed? (get over his illness)
9. Why will Helen go to the doctor? (have a check-up)
10. Why does Betty come to class? (please her husband)
11. Why do Mary and John take drugs? (calm their nerves)
12. Why did Jane go to the party with Bob? (infuriate Jim)

13. Why did Mary go into the town yesterday? (do some shopping)
14. Why is Paul looking in the paper? (find out what's going on)
15. Why did Jill wear that awful dress? (make Tom buy her another one)

(b) *To practise* to . . . , in order to . . . , so as to . . . , for . . .

Why has Sally bought those records? (English)
She's bought those records to learn English.

Why did Mary run down the street? (miss the bus)
She ran down the street so as not to miss the bus.

Why is Mrs Brown going into the supermarket? (eggs)
She's going into the supermarket for some eggs.

1. Why has Susan gone to Canada? (a holiday)
2. Why is Bob going to university? (chemistry)
3. Why did Betty take up judo? (protect herself)
4. Why did John go to the station? (meet Barbara)
5. Why did John visit Sally yesterday? (a present)
6. Why did Bob leave the party so early? (last bus)
7. Why has Tom gone into the tobacconist's? (matches)
8. Why did John buy that suit? (his interview tomorrow)
9. Why is Sandra going out? (clothes to the launderette)
10. Why has Betty gone to the seaside? (change of scenery)
11. Why did Jean hurry over her breakfast? (late for class)
12. Why did Sheila look out of the window? (Mary was coming)
13. Why did Gordon bend down just now? (money he had dropped)
14. Why has Peter turned on the TV now? (the set's working)
15. Why did Angela weigh herself? (if she's putting on weight)
16. Why does Bob go to the bank on Fridays? (pay in his salary)
17. Why did you look in the newspaper just now? (what's on TV)
18. Why did Richard see the play? (able to discuss it with Anne)

19. Why has Paul bought a dictionary? (replace the one he's lost)
20. Why has John gone to the library? (a book on English history)

Practise also, in both (a) and (b), the short conversational response:

(a) Why did you come here?
   To learn English.
   /tə ˈləːn ˋiŋgliʃ/

   Why is Sally working hard?
   To pass her exam.
   /tə ˈpɑːs hər igˋzæm/

(b) Why did Mary run down the street?
   So as not to miss the bus.
   /səuəz ˈnɔt tə ˈmis ðə ˋbʌs/

   Why is Mrs Brown going into the supermarket?
   For some eggs.
   /fə səm ˋegz/

---

217 Purpose   I

So that (In order that)

I'll get a taxi **so that** you won't get your feet wet.
He learnt English **so that** he could work in the U.S.A.
She will come early **so that** we can show her the house.

Notes:
 (i) Compare the use of **because** (Ex. 150) and **in order to** (Ex. 216).

   I took a taxi **because** I didn't want to be late.

   I took a taxi **in order not to** be late.

 (ii) Compare the following:

   Sue went to Japan **so that** she could be with Bob. (Purpose)

   I worked **so** hard **that** I had a nervous breakdown. (Result)

(iii) The **so that** construction is particularly useful when there is a different subject in the purpose clause—when it is not possible to use **in order to**.

To practise so that (in order that), *answer the following questions:*

Why did you visit the museum? (tell my friends about it)
I visited the museum so that I could tell my friends about it.

Why have you bought that piano? (Mary . . . learn how to play)
I've bought that piano so that Mary can learn how to play.

Why is Paul having his holiday now? (his partner can go next month)
He's having his holiday now so that his partner can go next month.

1. Why did Mr Brown sell his shop? (retire)
2. Why did John make his own bed? (be angry)
3. Why did Sally look at her watch? (be late)
4. Why has Jim taken off his jacket? (the label)
5. Why did Tom put on his best suit? (proud of him)
6. Why has John lent Bob his car? (take Richard home)
7. Why does Susan take extra lessons? (faster progress)
8. Why is Bob going to buy a camera? (take some pictures)
9. Why is Paul staying in Yokohama? (near his girl-friend)
10. Why did Jim buy a large car? (all his family on holiday)
11. Why did Anne wear that hat at the airport? (recognise her)
12. Why has John borrowed those shoes? (play tennis with Jimmy)
13. Why was Bill waiting outside the school? (buy Mary a coffee)
14. Why did Paul go to the dance with Mary? (have to go with Sue)
15. Why is Harry taking his car to the station? (pick up his wife)
16. Why did Paul help Alice with her work? (able to go out with him)
17. Why is Betty having a phone installed? (Richard . . . ring her up)
18. Why did Susan ignore Richard? (concentrate on the TV programme)
19. Why did Mrs Hammond run to the telephone? (children . . . get there first)
20. Why did Peter write to Elizabeth? (she . . . have to write to him)

Practise also the short conversational answers:

Why have you bought that piano?
So that Mary can learn how to play.
/səu ðət ˈmɛəri kn ˈləːn hau tə ˈplei/

Why is Paul having his holiday now?
So that his partner can go next month.
/səu ðət hiz ˈpɑːtnə kn ˈgəu ˈnekst ˈmʌnθ/

---

218 Purpose and Reason   IA

See the structures and notes to Exs. 216 and 217.

Notes:
 (i) Two common conjunctions used to introduce **reason** clauses are
     because and **as**.

> EXAMPLES:
> I visited Australia **because I had heard such a lot about the
> country**.
>
> **As I was feeling very hot** I took off my coat.

(ii) The following prepositional phrases indicate **cause**:

> The parcel was late **on account of the strike**.
>
> The delay was **due to a stoppage at the docks**.
>
> There was an accident **because of the narrow bridge**.

For practice with **because** see Exs. 150 and 164 (c); to contrast
because/although see Ex. 210; to contrast **because of/in spite of**
see Ex. 212; for **due to/owing to/because of** see Ex. 214.

See Appendix A at the back of the book for a more complete selection of **purpose** and **reason** clauses. Compare these with **result**
clauses.

To contrast purpose *and* reason/cause, *connect the following
by choosing suitable conjunctions and prepositions:*

Why did Paul come over last night (. . . dinner)
He came over for dinner.

Why did Mary bring in the washing? (. . . it wouldn't get
   wet)
She brought it in so that it wouldn't get wet.

Why will Pat call on Sue before the wedding? (... congratulate her)
She'll call (on her) to congratulate her.

1. Why did Bill leave in such a hurry? (... be late)
2. Why are you doing up the house? (... I want to sell it)
3. Why are you going to ring up Bob? (... see if he's free)
4. Why has Richard got to take a taxi? (... catch his train)
5. Why did you get that tape-recorder? (... record some music)
6. Why did John resign from the company? (... personal reasons)
7. Why do you want to speak to Mary? (... I can ask her opinion)
8. Why did you go to the meeting so early? (... get a good seat)
9. Why does Anne go out with Harry? (... get to know him better)
10. Why didn't Mary have her usual walk last night? (... the rain)
11. Why did Henry give up taking drugs? (... the sake of his health)
12. Why are the organisers postponing the concert? (... the bad weather)
13. Why did Paul learn how to use a computer? (... he would be promoted)
14. Why hasn't Don got used to living here yet? (... he still misses his family)
15. Why has David bought that hi-fi equipment? (... play his stereo records)
16. Why didn't Peter overtake the bus? (... the danger of exceeding the speed limit)
17. Why did you want to find out where Richard lives? (... I could write to him)
18. Why did Sally pick Susan up at the office? (... they were going out that evening)
19. Why is Paul cutting down that tree? (... get more light in his sitting-room)
20. Why did John want to be dropped off at the bank? (... he could draw out some money)

Practise also the conversational short answers:

Why did Paul come over last night?
For dinner.
/fə `dinə/

Why did Mary bring in the washing?
So that it wouldn't get wet.
/səu ðət it 'wudnt 'get `wet/

---

219 Purpose and Reason   A

See the examples and notes to Exs. 216–218.

For further practice with words introducing purpose *and* reason *invent answers to the following questions:*

Why has George come here?

STUDENT A: **To learn English.**
STUDENT B: **In order not to forget the English he's already learnt. (or so as not to . . .)**
STUDENT C: **For a holiday.**
STUDENT D: **So that he can renew old acquaintances.**
STUDENT E: **Because he likes the school.**

1. Why did Jim buy that picture?
2. Why did Bob telephone Susan?
3. Why has Sally hired a cook?
4. Why does Bill have two jobs?
5. Why is Jane getting married?
6. Why did Harry buy a house?
7. Why did Henry go by taxi?
8. Why has Mary bought a dog?
9. Why did Jim write that book?
10. Why was Mary on a diet?
11. Why did Joe buy a typewriter?
12. Why did Bob run to the phone?
13. Why has Tom gone to Mexico?
14. Why is John learning Russian?

Another—Other(s)—The Other(s)

These books are mine.	**The others**	are yours.	(pro.)
	The other ones	are yours.	(adj.)
Some books are good.	**Others**	are bad.	(pro.)
	Other books	are bad.	(adj.)
One student is reading.	**Another**	is talking.	(pro.)
	Another student	is talking.	(adj.)

To practise another.

There is a hotel in the High Street. (Queen Street)
And there's another (one) in Queen Street.

There's a double bed in the corner. (the window)
And there's another (one) by the window.

There's been an accident at the station. (the garage)
And there's been another (one) at the garage.

1. There's a train at 9 a.m. (10 a.m.)
2. There's a party at the club. (Bob's flat)
3. There's a newspaper on that shelf. (chair)
4. There's been a conference in Rome. (Paris)
5. There's a girl sitting in the bar. (lounge)
6. There's a light on in the classroom. (hall)
7. There's a library in this town. (next town)
8. There'll be a discussion tonight. (next week)
9. There'll be a meeting tomorrow. (the day after)
10. There's a TV set in that room. (reading-room)
11. There's a very good film on this week. (next week)
12. There was a mistake at the top of the page. (bottom)
13. There's a grocer's shop on the corner. (up the street)
14. There's a group of people outside the cinema. (theatre)
15. There's a towel hanging in the bathroom. (on that hook)

Note:
Other(s) may contrast with **some** (stressed and in its strong form /sʌm/). It is also possible to use **some** . . . **(and) some** . . . to convey the same idea:

In America, some girls are beautiful; others are homely.
/in əˇ'merikə 'sʌm 'gəːlz ə `bjuːtəfl 'ʌðəz ə `həumli/

In England, some girls are beautiful—and some aren't.
/in ˇ'iŋglənd 'sʌm 'gəːlz ə ˌbjuːtəfl ən 'sʌm `ɑːnt/

To practise others.

Some cars are fast.	**Others are slow.** or **Other cars are slow.**
Some children are good.	**Others are naughty.** or **Other children are naughty.**
Some people drive with care.	**Others drive dangerously.** or **Other people drive dangerously.**

1. Some exercises are easy.
2. Some roads are dangerous.
3. Some rooms are large.
4. Some students speak badly.
5. Some people are always right.
6. Some cigarettes are strong.
7. Some people are generous.
8. Some shops are old fashioned.
9. Some drinks are sweet.
10. Some students are bright.
11. Some things are cheap.
12. Some streets are wide.
13. Some hotels are new.
14. Some people speak rudely.
15. Some ideas are simple.
16. Some people are young.

To practise the other.

I've got two close friends.	**One's my doctor, and the other's my partner.**
John has two drinks here.	**One's a lager, and the other's a whisky.**
Bill's had two holidays.	**One was in Spain, and the other was in France.**

1. Harry has two cars.
2. John had two visitors.
3. Mary has two children.
4. Barry has two hobbies.
5. That man has two houses.
6. Bob knows two politicians.
7. Paul received two presents.
8. Peter will visit two shops.
9. Helen met two women.
10. Henry had two accidents.
11. Susan saw two paintings.
12. The cottage had two rooms.
13. Bill's been to two cities.
14. John goes in for two sports.
15. Mary's written two books.
16. Tom's just read two magazines.

223 INTERMEDIATE

To practise the others.

Some of the ideas were practicable.
The others were impracticable.

Some of the children were obedient.
The others were disobedient.

Some of the books were replaceable.
The others were irreplaceable.

1. Some of the men were observant.
2. Some of the people were patient.

3. Some of the drugs were effective.
4. Some of the people were literate.
5. Some of the guests were grateful.
6. Some of the cars were repairable.
7. Some of the rules were convenient.
8. Some of the women were prejudiced.
9. Some of the diseases were curable.
10. Some of the comments were relevant.
11. Some of the measurements were exact.
12. Some of the paintings were suitable.
13. Some of the speakers were articulate.
14. Some of the ideas were comprehensible.
15. Some of the instructions were reasonable.

SUGGESTIONS

224 ELEMENTARY

Shall I call a taxi?	Yes, please do.
Shall we go now?	Yes. I'm ready.
Shall I open the window?	No, please don't.
Shall we visit John?	That's a good idea!

Note:
(i) **Shall** in questions such as the above indicates that the speaker is making a suggestion. Do not confuse this pattern with the simple future.

Compare: $\begin{cases} \textbf{Shall I pass the exam?} & \text{(future)} \\ \textbf{Shall I turn on the light?} & \text{(suggestion)} \end{cases}$

(ii) Students will hear **shall I/we** . . . ? offers and suggestions with and without stressed **shall** and sometimes with the unstressed weak form /ʃl/. Perhaps they would be wise to practise with a stressed /ʃæl/, which may sound more solicitous, or more interested in the wishes of the person spoken to:

/ˈʃæl ai ˈkɔːl ə ˌtæksi/
/ˈʃæl wi ˌgəu ˈnau/

To practise making suggestions with shall I/we, *respond as shown:*

My feet are killing me. (rest) That's a good idea.	**Shall we have a rest?**
The room's cold. (fire) Thank you very much.	**Shall I put on the fire?**
The taxi hasn't come yet. (wait) We shall have to.	**Shall we wait a little longer?**

1. I've no money on me. (lend)
2. There's a bar over there. (in)
3. This case is very heavy. (carry)
4. The letters haven't gone yet. (post)
5. It's rather draughty in here. (window)
6. I can't do the homework by myself. (help)
7. This chair isn't very comfortable. (another)
8. I've got nothing to do after dinner. (cinema)
9. There's something wrong with the car. (garage)
10. The post office is a long way from here. (bus)
11. I don't want to watch TV tonight. (night-club)
12. I don't feel like walking to the station. (taxi)
13. I've been to that restaurant before. (different)
14. I have no idea what to do this evening. (theatre)
15. There's someone knocking at the front door. (see)

---

225 Suggestions I

Let's	go for a walk.
Let's not argue.	
Let's	have a drink, **shall we**?

Note:
Let's (let us) indicates that the speaker is making a suggestion that includes himself and all the people he is addressing. You may hear **don't let's** instead of **let's not**.

To practise let's *and* let's not, *respond as shown:*

Shall we listen to the radio? (TV)
Let's not listen to the radio. Let's watch TV, shall we?

Shall we discuss politics? (economics)
Let's not discuss politics. Let's discuss economics, shall we?

Shall we eat here tonight? (somewhere else)
Let's not eat here tonight. Let's eat somewhere else, shall we?

1. Shall we go by air? (sea)
2. Shall we get a taxi? (walk)
3. Shall we ask George? (Susan)
4. Shall we ring Jim up? (call on)
5. Shall we have a game now? (later)
6. Shall we go out tonight? (stay in)
7. Shall we visit Trinidad? (Bermuda)
8. Shall we see that film? (different)
9. Shall we pack now? (in an hour's time)
10. Shall we speak to Bob about it? (Susan)
11. Shall we invite Richard over? (Rosemary)
12. Shall we do the shopping now? (cup of tea)
13. Shall we have something to drink? (go back)
14. Shall we see over the castle? (have a rest)
15. Shall we work on Saturday morning? (tennis)

Practise also the short responses common between friends:

Let's go to the cinema—
No. Let's not. /ˈnəu ˈlets ˈnɔt/
Yes, let's. /ˈjes ˈlets/
No. Don't let's. /ˈnəu ˈdəunt ˌlets/

---

226 Suggestions   IA

Here are some ways to introduce suggestions:

Let's . . . (see Ex. 225)	Couldn't we . . . ?
Why not . . . ?	Why don't you . . . ?
How/What about . . . ?	My suggestion is . . .
I suggest . . .	I should like to suggest . . .
May I suggest . . . ?	I have a suggestion to make: . . .

Make suggestions that suit the following situations:

What shall I do this evening?

STUDENT A: **Why not go dancing?**
STUDENT B: **Why don't you catch up with your reading?**

STUDENT C: **I suggest you watch TV; there's a good film on.**

etc.

1. Where shall I go on my holiday?
2. What kind of house shall I buy?
3. How far shall we go on our walk?
4. How can I get in touch with John?
5. Where shall we hold the conference?
6. How can I improve my pronunciation?
7. Who shall we invite to the party?
8. How can I avoid being late for class?
9. How shall we spend tomorrow afternoon?
10. How shall we have the consignment sent?
11. How can we get the strikers back to work?
12. What can we do to increase export orders?
13. What books shall I get out of the library?
14. What shall I do with this unwanted present?
15. How can I get hold of a good second-hand car?

REQUESTS AND INVITATIONS

Simple requests can be made by using the imperative (usually preceded by 'please'). Compare the following:

INDICATIVE MOOD		IMPERATIVE MOOD	
I	have lunch.	**Have** lunch.	
I	speak English.	**Speak** English.	
I	drive fast.	**Drive** fast.	
I don't have lunch.		**Don't have** lunch.	
I don't speak Spanish.		**Don't speak** Spanish.	
I don't drive fast.		**Don't drive** fast.	

There are a number of ways in which we can express a request, and the choice of form used depends on the situation and also our relationship with the person concerned.

In the spoken language the following polite request forms are the ones most commonly employed:

> Please **open the door**.
>   **Open the door**, will you?
>   Could you **open the door**?
>   Would you **open the door**?
>   Will you **open the door**?
>   Can you **open the door**?

Note:
Students must realise that it is possible for the most elaborate request form to sound brusque and discourteous and for the briefest imperative to sound charming. Stress and intonation make the difference (if smile and gesture cannot be seen). It is not possible to suggest particular stress-tone patterns out of the very many in use; imitation of good models is the answer.

---

227 Requests   E

(a) *Make a simple request with 'please' as shown:*

Do you want a glass of water? (give me)
Yes. Please give me a glass of water.

Do you want some cigarettes? (let me have)
Yes. Please let me have some cigarettes.

Do you want to get to the station? (show me the way)
Yes. Please show me the way to the station.

1. Do you want a taxi? (call)
2. Do you want any help? (give me)
3. Do you want a ticket? (let me have)
4. Do you want to watch TV? (turn on)
5. Do you want any stamps? (let me have)
6. Do you want a piece of cake? (hand me)
7. Do you want a cup of tea? (pour me out)
8. Do you want a good book to read? (recommend)
9. Do you want to buy a good dictionary? (show me)
10. Do you want to make a telephone call? (show me how)
11. Do you want to go to the cinema? (tell me what's on)
12. Do you want the post office? (tell me where I can find)

13. Do you want something to drink? (show me where I can get)
14. Do you want to go to the laundry? (show me how to get to)
15. Do you want to see the director? (make an appointment for me)

(b) *To practise the negative request pattern, respond as shown:*

May I speak Danish?	**Please don't speak Danish.**
May we smoke?	**Please don't smoke.**
Shall I open the window?	**Please don't open the window.**

1. May I go?
2. May we come late?
3. Shall I use your car?
4. May we sit here?
5. Shall I ring him up?
6. May I take the book?
7. Shall I shut the window?
8. May we stay out late?
9. Shall I call you?
10. May I be late?
11. Shall I get up?
12. May we look up the answers?
13. Shall we get you a ticket?
14. May I use your typewriter?
15. Shall I leave?
16. Shall we wait for you?

---

228 Requests   EI

To practise the spoken request patterns with would, could, can *and* will, *respond as shown:*

turn on the TV (would)

STUDENT A: **You want me to turn on the TV.**
STUDENT B: **Would you turn on the TV, please?**

pay attention (could)

STUDENT C: **You want me to pay attention.**
STUDENT D: **Could you pay attention, please?**

1. turn on the light (will)
2. sit down (would)
3. open the door (could)
4. turn off the fire (can)
5. pull the curtains (will)
6. lend you my pen (could)
7. come early (could)
8. wake you up early (would)
9. remind you to go (will)
10. call a taxi (could)
11. ring Mary up for you (would)
12. carry your suitcases (will)
13. tell you the right time (could)
14. be a little quieter (can)
15. lend you my paper (will)
16. help you with your work (would)
17. see who's at the door (will)
18. get on with my work (could)
19. call you at 6 a.m. (would)
20. start again at No. 1 (will)

---

229 Requests   I

This is a substitution exercise to practise request patterns.

Could you tell me the time?	**Could you tell me the time?**
please	**Please tell me the time.**
open the window	**Please open the window.**
would you be kind enough	**Would you be kind enough to open the window?**
would you be so kind	**Would you be so kind as to open the window?**

1. could you
2. tell me the way to the station
3. please
4. can you
5. would you please
6. carry my suitcases for me
7. I should appreciate your
8. I should appreciate it
9. will you
10. help me with my homework
11. please
12. can you
13. drive me to the station
14. would you be kind enough

301

15. would you be so kind
    as to
16. please
17. call a taxi
18. would you
19. I should appreciate it
20. I would appreciate your
21. will you
22. answer the door
23. would you be so kind
24. I should be obliged
25. please
26. turn on the TV
27. would you
28. I should appreciate your
29. would you be kind
    enough
30. let us finish this
    exercise now

---

230 ELEMENTARY/INTERMEDIATE

(a) The common patterns for invitations are:

> would you like + *to*-infinitive, etc.
> would you like + noun

EXAMPLES:

Would you like **to come** to my party?

Would you like **a cup of tea**?

Cf. $\begin{cases} \text{Would you come to my party?—Request} \\ \text{What about coming to my party?—Suggestion} \end{cases}$

Note

*The response to an invitation varies greatly, especially in the case of acceptance. In the exercise students might choose from the following acceptance responses:

Thank you. /ˈθæŋk ju/ (But with the appropriate intonation and gesture this can also be a refusal.)
   Yes. Thank you. /ˈjes ˈθæŋk ju/
   Yes, please. /ˈes ˈpliːz/, /ˈjes ˌpliːz/ etc.
   Yes, I would. /ˈjes ai ˈwud/
   That's very kind of you. /ˈðæts ˈveri ˌkaind əv juː/
   Oh, yes! /ˈəu ˈjes/

It is unwise to imitate some people's supposedly amusing answers like 'I don't mind if I do', 'Try and stop me', etc.

To practise giving spoken invitations, respond as shown:

sit here   STUDENT A: **Would you like to sit here?**
              STUDENT B: **(Yes. Thank you.)***

302

a cigarette   STUDENT C: **Would you like a cigarette?**
                STUDENT D: **No, thank you.**

1. borrow my pen	11. an ice-cream
2. a drink	12. write to me
3. come to the party	13. a dance
4. an apple	14. go to the cinema
5. go swimming	15. a beer
6. a cup of tea	16. come out with me
7. go to the concert	17. something to eat
8. some help	18. read this book
9. hear my records	19. a sandwich
10. go for a walk	20. come for a drive

(b) The statement pattern 'I should (I'd) like . . .' is common.
To practise this, respond as shown:

go home

      STUDENT A: **I'd like to go home. What about you?**
      STUDENT B: **I'd also like to go home.**

a swim

      STUDENT C: **I'd like a swim. How about you?**
      STUDENT D: **I'd like a swim too.**

1. a rest	11. something to drink
2. go out this evening	12. have a day off
3. a walk	13. some time off
4. see that film	14. talk to Mary
5. a game of cards	15. a game of tennis
6. read that magazine	16. go to the party
7. a new suit	17. a higher salary
8. hear that record	18. buy that coat
9. some help	19. a coffee
10. visit that town	20. meet Mr Brown

REFLEXIVE AND EMPHASISING PRONOUNS

Introductory notes:
  (i) The reflexive pronouns indicate that the subject and the object
     are the same.

Paul shot **himself**. /'pɔːl `ʃɔt himself/

I saw **myself** in the mirror.

Mary asked **herself** the same question.

(ii) If a preposition is involved, the reflexive pronoun follows it.

He's always speaking **to himself**. /hiːz 'ɔːweiz 'spiːkiŋ tu him`self/

She's always looking **at herself**.

Gordon has to depend **on himself**.

If an adverbial is involved, the reflexive pronoun comes between the verb and its particle.

Mary **let herself out**. /'mɛəri 'let həself `aut/

The bank robber **gave himself up**.

The students didn't **put themselves out**.

(iii) Reflexive pronouns do not normally have sentence stress. The exception occurs in certain cases when the pronoun follows a preposition, as seen in the example:

'He's always speaking to himself.'

(iv) Emphasising pronouns reinforce the subject or object of a sentence.

I took Mary to the airport **myself**.
  (or:* I **myself** took Mary to the airport.)

You had a similar experience **yourself**.
  (or:* You **yourself** had a similar experience.)

The forms marked (*) are rather formal as a general rule, but they may preclude ambiguity. In speech there should, however, be no ambiguity in:

He spoke to the chairman himself.
/hi 'spəuk tə ðe `tʃɛəmən him`self/
  (not to anybody else)

/hi 'spəuk tə ðə `tʃɛəmən him`self/
(he didn't send somebody else)

Emphasising pronouns are always stressed.

I can make	a sandwich.	
I can make **myself**	a sandwich.	(Reflexive)
I can make	a sandwich **myself.**	(Emphatic)
I can make	a sandwich **for myself.**	(for me to eat)
I can make	a sandwich **by myself.**	(without any help, alone)

---

231 Emphasising Pronouns   E

To practise relating person to pronoun, respond as shown:

(Practice both /ai 'did it mai `self/ and /ˆai ˌdid it mai ˇself/.)

I	**I did it myself.**
she	**She did it herself.**
they	**They did it themselves.**

1. she	9. she	17. we	25. we
2. we	10. he	18. she	26. they
3. you (s.)	11. I	19. he	27. she
4. they	12. she	20. we	28. I
5. he	13. they	21. they	29. he
6. you (pl.)	14. he	22. you (s.)	30. you (pl.)
7. we	15. you (pl.)	23. she	
8. they	16. I	24. I	

---

232 Reflexive and Emphasising Pronouns   EI

(a) *This is a substitution exercise to give further practice in relating person to pronoun.*

She wanted to do it herself.	**She wanted to do it herself.**
he	**He wanted to do it himself.**

305

I	I wanted to do it myself.
wanted to work by myself	I wanted to work by myself.
she	She wanted to work by herself.
we	We wanted to work by ourselves.

1. I
2. got myself a flat
3. he
4. we
5. they
6. made it themselves
7. she
8. I
9. you (s.)
10. we
11. must decide for ourselves
12. they
13. she
14. you (pl.)
15. should correct yourselves
16. he
17. they
18. you (s.)
19. needn't do it yourself
20. she
21. I
22. he
23. she
24. can drive herself to the station
25. I
26. they
27. we
28. saw the manager himself
29. she

(b) *Complete the following by inserting the correct pronoun* (*and preposition if necessary*):

he likes a lot	He likes himself a lot.
she bought a car	She bought herself a car.
	or: She bought a car herself.
Mary's sitting	Mary's sitting by herself.

1. I'm looking
2. the car stopped
3. they're listening
4. I walked to the station
5. she wanted him to do it
6. I prefer tea
7. he must wake up
8. you can do it
9. I don't know her
10. she made a cake
11. we watched TV
12. she came to class
13. they had dinner
14. we prefer to work
15. Mary likes to walk
16. do it
17. help
18. he paid for it
19. you think too much
20. I drove to the station
21. he wrote the letter
22. the fire went out

23. he punished
24. I put in his shoes
25. she has to play golf
26. they got a drink
27. we did the job
28. I often speak
29. she saw the director
30. we turned the set on

---

233 Reflexive and Emphasising Pronouns I

Use the pronouns in brackets in your response to the following:

Who repaired the TV set? (myself)
I did it myself.

Did Anne make the omelette for you? (herself)
No. She made it for herself.

Who did Jim come to school with this morning? (himself)
No one. He came by himself.

1. How did Richard learn English? (himself)
2. Does Sally like anyone very much? (herself)
3. Did Mr Brown pay for Sheila's car? (herself)
4. Did anyone help you to the potatoes? (myself)
5. Did Allan let the cat out last night? (itself)
6. Who helped Helen to write that letter? (herself)
7. Did anyone wake Gordon up this morning? (himself)
8. How did Peter manage to stop the engine? (itself)
9. Did Sheila go out with anyone last night? (herself)
10. Is that the car you bought for your friend? (myself)
11. Did Joe and Bob sit with Mary and Susan? (themselves)
12. Does Mary talk to anyone when she's at home? (herself)
13. What did Mary cook for your dinner last night? (myself)
14. What did Philip do with that knife I gave him? (himself)
15. Who did you go to the cinema with last night? (myself)
16. Did they hear anything on the tape-recorder? (themselves)
17. Did Jane need any help in translating that book? (herself)
18. Did you see the manager on behalf of Mr Hammond? (himself)

19. Did you send John to buy your tickets for you?
    (ourselves)
20. Did Jane ask Jim to get the library book for her?
    (herself)
21. Was it you who telephoned John on behalf of Sally?
    (herself)
22. Why was Jim angry when you bought that old cottage?
    (himself)
23. What happened to that drink Peter bought for Richard?
    (myself)
24. Did you have any help with your homework yesterday?
    (ourselves)
25. Do Bob and Sue work hard when they are with Gordon?
    (themselves)

THE PASSIVE

Active:	I	**shall**	**send**	the parcel tomorrow.
Passive:	The parcel	**will be**	**sent**	tomorrow.
Active:	We		**answer**	questions in class.
Passive:	Questions	**are**	**answered**	in class.
Active:	Someone	**has**	**taken**	my book.
Passive:	My book	**has been**	**taken**.	
Active:	Mary		**bought**	John some books.
Passive:	John	**was**	**bought**	some books.
Active:	George told me that	the Station Master **had**	**cancelled**	the train.
Passive:	George told me that	the train **had been**	**cancelled.**	

Introductory notes:
The passive voice is used if we are more interested in what is done than in who or what performed the action. It is also used for the sake of convenience and if the doer of an action is unknown.

(i) Sometimes an **agent** is required.

EXAMPLES:
Active: John bought the typewriter.
Passive: The typewriter **was bought by John**.
    (not by Mary)

Active: John will use the car.
Passive: The car **will be used by John**.
    (not by Peter)

An agent is not required if it is clear who performed the action:

John **was arrested**. (It must have been **by the police**.)

(ii) If a verb has two objects (direct and indirect) the **person** is usually the subject in a passive sentence.

EXAMPLE:
Active: Somebody handed **me** a leaflet.
Passive: **I was handed** a leaflet.

This is not ordinarily the case where the personal object could be replaced by *for* + (pro)noun (see p. 319). We do not say 'The latecomers were cooked for a meal' but:

A meal **was cooked** for the latecomers.

(iii) The continuous is formed with **being**.

EXAMPLE:
Active: Someone is looking after your children.
Passive: Your children **are being looked after**.

(Only the present and past continuous forms are common.)

(iv) The Infinitive: She wants **to be invited** to the party.
The Perfect Infinitive: She was **to have been invited**, but we decided not to hold the party.

(v) The following verbs take the *-ing* form as an alternative to the passive infinitive:

The furniture **needs** polishing.
The car   **wants** washing.
The room   **requires** cleaning.

(vi) An adverb of **manner** usually precedes the main verb in the passive.

EXAMPLES:
The door **was** *quietly* **opened**.
The lock **had been** *secretly* **oiled**.

(vii) There is no passive voice of verbs which are normally intransitive.

To practise forming the passive, respond as shown:

They took the car.	**The car was taken.**
They do homework.	**Homework is done.**
They will buy the house.	**The house will be bought.**

1. They wrote the letter.
2. They've made mistakes.
3. They blew the whistle.
4. They've brought the book.
5. They will build the house.
6. They bought the carpet.
7. They've taken the chair.
8. They will use English.
9. They chose the present.
10. They've cut the cake.
11. They dealt the cards.
12. They did the work.
13. They will sell the car.
14. They've found the ring.
15. They ate the sandwich.
16. They promoted Mr Brown.
17. They've hidden the watch.
18. They lost the books.
19. They've paid the bill.
20. They rang the bell.
21. They will wear suits.
22. They heard Richard.
23. They woke Mary up.
24. They held up traffic.
25. They will need help.
26. They received a letter.
27. They've thanked Sally.
28. They follow instructions.
29. They will remember Jane.
30. They will ask questions.

To practise and contrast affirmative and negative forms, respond as shown:

Was the exercise done? (correct)
Yes. It was done, but it wasn't corrected.

Has the typewriter been repaired? (return)
Yes. It's been repaired, but it hasn't been returned.

Will John be prosecuted? (convict)
Yes. He'll be prosecuted, but he won't be convicted.

1. Was Peter seen? (hear)
2. Was the food prepared? (eat)
3. Will Bob be promoted? (pay more)
4. Were the dishes dried? (put away)
5. Were any questions asked? (answer)
6. Have the letters been typed? (post)
7. Will John be reprimanded? (dismiss)
8. Has the car been paid for? (deliver)
9. Has the book been written? (publish)
10. Have the goods been unpacked? (check)
11. Have the flats been erected? (furnish)
12. Have the carpets been bought? (put down)
13. Were the applicants interviewed? (take on)
14. Has the computer been switched on? (programme)
15. Has the car been taken to the garage? (service)

---

236 The Passive I

The passive continuous is used with the present and past tenses.

EXAMPLES:
I'm being interviewed tomorrow.
Jim **was being interviewed** yesterday afternoon.

To practise the passive continuous, respond as shown:

at the car showrooms (new models—demonstrate)
(cars—sell)

What's happening at the car showrooms?
New models are being demonstrated and cars are being sold.

at the TV studio (programmes—produce)
(recordings—make)

What was happening at the TV studio?
Programmes were being produced and recordings were being made.

1. at the races   (bets—make) (money—lose)
2. in Parliament   (debates—hold) (laws—pass)
3. at the post office (letters—post) (mail—sort)
4. at the school   (lessons—give) (exercises—do)
5. at the shop   (people—serve) (goods—display)
6. at the restaurant (meals—serve) (bills—make out)
7. at the cinema   (a film—show) (people—entertain)
8. at the airport   (tickets—sell) (passengers—call)
9. at the bank   (money—pay in)
                   (cheques—make out)
10. at the church   (a service—hold) (a couple—marry)
11. at the office   (phone calls—make) (letters—sign)
12. at the port   (baggage—examine)
                   (passports—check)
13. at the hotel   (reservations—make)
                   (rooms—prepare)
14. at the laboratory (research—do)
                   (experiments—carry out)
15. at the doctor's (appointments—make)
                   (patients—examine)

---

237 The Passive   I

To practise modal verbs and infinitives, respond as shown:

You can't take drinks out of the bar.
No. Drinks can't be taken out of the bar.

They may have to replace that TV set.
Yes. That TV set may have to be replaced.

They must've asked Jim to work overtime.
Yes. Jim must've been asked to work overtime.

1. No one can use that milk.
2. They couldn't see the ship.
3. They might have caught Richard.

4. People mustn't park cars here.
5. They would have asked her by now.
6. They could do the work tomorrow.
7. They're not going to persuade you.
8. You should invite George to come.
9. They shouldn't have dismissed Jim.
10. They should have checked the results.
11. They needn't take the pictures now.
12. Nobody will expect you until 2 p.m.
13. They ought to take Jane to hospital.
14. You may not take books into the exam.
15. They had to answer all the questions.
16. They may give you several alternatives.
17. They used to pick Mary up at the office.
18. The writer has to make the article longer.
19. They will have to discuss the arrangements.
20. They are to make maximum use of the computer.

This is a substitution exercise to practise and contrast different tenses in the passive:

The letter was posted at 3 p.m.	**The letter was posted at 3 p.m.**
now	**The letter is being posted now.**
not	**The letter isn't being posted now.**
typed	**The letter isn't being typed now.**
tomorrow	**The letter won't be typed tomorrow.**

1. no work will be done
2. now
3. yesterday
4. since yesterday
5. the men haven't been paid
6. have been
7. tomorrow
8. yesterday
9. now
10. John
11. sent to New York
12. yesterday
13. tomorrow
14. met at the airport
15. now
16. last night

17. the goods were delivered
18. no goods
19. since Friday
20. tomorrow
21. the car
22. now
23. repaired

24. not
25. when I saw it
26. by tomorrow
27. serviced
28. now
29. the typewriter
30. since last year

---

239 The Passive   A

Notes:
 (i) **It** may be used with certain verbs in the passive to introduce *that*-
     clauses.

> EXAMPLES:
> **It** is **felt** that the matter is very serious.
> (Cf. The matter is felt to be very serious.)
>
> **It** was **thought** that you wouldn't appreciate it.

The structure is rather formal. It is intended to suggest that the
statement is the result of objective consideration.

(ii) The passive perfect infinitive may be used (see Note iv on
     page 309).

> EXAMPLES:
> Mary was **to have been allowed** to go out, but her mother had
> second thoughts.
>
> The men were **to have been dismissed**, but the manager decided
> to give them a second chance.

*To practise the above two patterns, respond as shown. Where
possible, change any other active verbs into the passive.*

They were to have given the club members the information,
    but they eventually decided against this.
**The club members were to have been given the information,
    but this was eventually decided against.**

People say that pride comes before a fall.
It is said that pride comes before a fall.

They were to have re-covered the chair with a special material, but no one could find any in the shops.

The chair was to have been re-covered with a special material, but none could be found in the shops.

1. People thought that designers would replace the miniskirt with something more modest.
2. People believe Mary to be an undesirable influence on John.
3. They were to have informed him of the decision by post, but they never sent the letter.
4. The group were to have discussed company policy, but the organisers cancelled the meeting.
5. People hope that Jim's manager will give him something worth having on his retirement.
6. The lecturer was to have told the audience about Antarctica, but a traffic jam held him up.
7. People know that the local authority may have to close the public library owing to lack of funds.
8. Mary Baker was to have read the news, but the TV director thought that a man would do the job better.
9. Experts consider it wrong for teachers to encourage students to spend too much time preparing for examinations.
10. John was to have paid the money back by last Thursday, but he has now promised to let me have it next Friday.
11. They were to have built George's garage yesterday, but the construction firm employing the workmen had given the men another job to do.
12. One of the directors was to have addressed the meeting, but the Board felt that they should ask the chairman to speak.
13. Many people feel that the managing director should have requested John Smith to resign from the company. (It is generally . . .)
14. People think that the university administrators should allow students greater autonomy in the running of their own affairs.
15. The engineers anticipated that the new motorway would prevent future traffic congestion, but their computer proved them wrong.

THE EMPHATIC AND EXCLAMATIONS

Preliminary notes:

Emphasis may be given by:

(i) placing an anomalous finite between the subject and main verb, and stressing this in speech.

EXAMPLES:

She **does** look beautiful!

/ʃi ˈdʌz ˌluk ˌbjuːtəfl/

He **did** take my pen!

I **do** know the answer!

(ii) stressing the anomalous finite already present. This can be indicated in written English by the use of italic printing or by underlining.

EXAMPLES:

He _is_ making a noise!

/hiː ˈiz ˌmeikiŋ ə ˌnɔiz/

You _have_ got brown!

They _will_ get wet!

Other words may be emphasised in written English in the same way.

EXAMPLES:

She gave the book to _me_.

/ʃi ˈgeiv ðə ˈbuk tə ˈmiː/

_I_ sent the letter.

(iii) isolating the negative adverb **not**.

EXAMPLES:

They will not see me again! (normal: won't)

/ðei wil ˈnɔt ˌsiː miː əˌgen/

She does not love Peter! (normal: doesn't)

(iv) using the emphasising pronouns (see Note iv, page 304).

(v) Making an exclamation.

EXAMPLES:

How generous she is!

/hau ˌdʒenərəs ʃi iz/

What a good meal that was!

/ˈwɔt ə ˈgud ˌmiːl ðæt wɔz/

How happy I am!

What nice friends she has!

316

Use do, does *and* did *in your response to the following, as shown:*

Paul came late.	**Yes. He did come late, didn't he?**
I like coffee.	**Yes. You do like coffee, don't you?**
Mary drinks a lot.	**Yes. She does drink a lot, doesn't she?**

1. I make mistakes.
2. Lucy has many friends.
3. They work hard.
4. I spent a lot.
5. Mary comes late.
6. You speak well.
7. Paul did well in the exam.
8. Philip looks angry.
9. Jane went to bed late.
10. Paul smokes a lot.
11. Sally wants to go.
12. They made a lot of noise.
13. You promised to do it.
14. Betty does her work badly.
15. Gordon behaved stupidly.
16. They do it often.
17. Peter had a lot of trouble.
18. Mary has a lot of money.
19. Elizabeth had to hurry.
20. You need to work harder.

240b Exclamations   I

To practise making exclamations, respond as shown:

He has a bad cough.	**What a bad cough he has**!
This is a boring film.	**How boring this film is**!
	or **What a boring film this is**!
John typed that letter quickly.	**How quickly John typed that letter**!

1. There's a lot of news.
2. That fire's very hot.
3. This is an interesting picture.

4. They get a lot of rain here.
5. Mary seems very tired.
6. This is a difficult job.
7. I've got a lot of books.
8. Peter drives dangerously.
9. This is a fascinating programme.
10. That camera's expensive.
11. It's a pity Jane's away.
12. Henry looks very funny in that hat.
13. It seems a long way.
14. There are a lot of people here.
15. Betty's hair is very long.

240c Emphasis   IA

To practise placing emphasis on certain words in a sentence.
Choose which word(s) you wish to emphasise in the following.
Make any necessary changes and add a short sentence to
indicate the implication of your emphasis.

EXAMPLE: I speak English well.

I speak English well. Those other students don't.
/ˈai ˌspiːk ˌiŋgliʃ ˌwel/

I *do* speak English well. You're wrong if you think I don't.
/ai ˈduː ˌspiːk ˌiŋgliʃ ˌwel/

I *speak* English well. I don't write it well.
/ai ˈspiːk ˌiŋgliʃ ˌwel/

I speak *English* well. I don't speak German well.
/ai spiːk ˈiŋgliʃ ˌwel/

I speak English *well*. I don't speak it badly.
/ai 'spiːk 'iŋgliʃ ˈwel/

1. Harry's car goes well.
2. Tom understands German.
3. Susan opened the telegram.
4. Rosemary came out at 4 p.m.
5. Paul has a sister in Mexico.
6. I listened to the news on TV.
7. David has visited South America.
8. Mary did her housework before lunch.

9. Richard will close the back door now.
10. Joe doesn't want to read about Scotland.
11. John didn't ask to go to a private school.
12. Jane never allows Tom to kiss her in public.
13. My newspaper showed a picture of the actress.
14. Mr Brown expects the new students to work hard.
15. Betty thought that she had failed the oral test.

VERBS WITH TWO OBJECTS

Note:
A common structure is that where a verb has **two** objects. The first one after the verb is the **indirect** object, the second is the **direct** object. If the objects are named in a different order a preposition is used.

Indirect + direct object
with NO preposition   *with the preposition TO*
I gave **Gordon a present**.   or I gave **a present to Gordon**.
I tell **people the truth**.   or I tell **the truth to people**.
I sold **him   a car**.   or I sold **a car   to him**.

                                         with the preposition FOR
I cashed **Betty a cheque**.   or I cashed **a cheque for Betty**.
I cooked **Helen a meal**.   or I cooked **a meal   for Helen**.
I made   **Peter a cake**.   or I made **a cake   for Peter**.

          only with the preposition TO
          I speak   **English   to Mary**.
          I explained **the answers to Paul**.
          I said   **'goodbye' to them**.

Notes:
 (i) I asked **her a question**. (Do not use **to** with the verb *ask*.)

(ii) As a general rule the main stress is on the noun naming the **direct** object.

        I gave Gordon a present.
        /ai ˈgeiv ˈgɔːdn ə ˋpreznt/

        I sold him a car.
        /ai ˈsəuld him ə ˋkɑː/

(iii) The pattern subject + verb + indirect object + direct object is not used when the direct object is shorter than the indirect object. We do not say 'I gave Gordon's brother it' but:

I gave **it to Gordon's brother**.
/ai ˈgeiv it tə ˈgɔːdnz ˋbrʌðə/

---

241 Two Objects EI

To practise the 'indirect + direct' object pattern, respond as shown:

What did you give Mary? (a present)
I gave her a present.

What's Bob sold to John? (his old car)
He's sold him his old car.

What will you tell Peter? (what to do)
I'll tell him what to do.

1. What does Mr Brown teach Jill? (French)
2. What did you send your friend? (a letter)
3. What have you just passed to David? (a note)
4. What did you take John just now? (his keys)
5. What did you ask John just now? (a question)
6. What did Sheila give her parents? (a holiday)
7. What did Peter pass Sally just now? (the salt)
8. What's the salesman sold to Gordon? (a typewriter)
9. What did John lend Bob just now? (his dictionary)
10. What will Mary teach her students now? (some idioms)
11. What did John send Mary for her birthday? (a postcard)
12. What have you just told your friend? (what you told me)
13. What will the guide show the visitors? (the new factory)
14. What did Sally take Paul this morning? (breakfast in bed)
15. What did the sales manager bring to the chairman? (a message)

---

242 Two Objects I

To practise the two-object pattern with to, *respond as shown:*

Who did you explain the mistake to? (Anne)
I explained the mistake to Anne.

What will you say to Jim before he leaves? ('Goodbye')
I'll say 'goodbye' to him.

What language do you speak to the people you meet here?
  (English)
I speak English to them.

1. What did Jill say to Peter? ('Hello')
2. What did you explain to Philip? (the job)
3. Who did you introduce to Peter? (John)
4. What will you say to Richard? ('Good luck')
5. Who has John been describing to Paul? (Jim)
6. What language does Mary speak to John? (English)
7. What did Elizabeth mention to Paul? (John's name)
8. Who did you say 'Goodbye' to when you left home?
9. Who have you explained the situation to? (Gordon)
10. What language does Bob speak to his friends? (French)
11. What did Mary describe to the group? (the new exhibits)
12. What did George explain to the workers? (the wage-freeze)
13. Who will Richard introduce to the students? (Mrs Brown)
14. What did the announcer describe to the listeners? (the scene)
15. What must the director explain to the staff? (cuts in salary)

---

243 Two Objects   I

To practise the two-object pattern with for, *respond as shown:*

Who ordered the steak for me?
I ordered it for you.

What have you got there for Jim? (a special gift)
I've got a special gift here for him.

What can I do for you? (a lot)
You can do a lot for me.

1. Who did Peter cash the cheque for? (Sheila)
2. What's Sally going to cook for David? (some ham)
3. Who did John open the door for just now? (Mary)
4. What did the clerk post for the firm? (some parcels)

5. What kind of seats has Bob booked for us? (front row)
6. What did Sheila get for her husband? (some cigarettes)
7. Who will Mrs Jones order a new suit for? (her husband)
8. What are you going to buy for the children? (some sweets)
9. What have the builders done for John? (constructed a shed)
10. What have the police investigated for Sally? (the robbery)
11. What will the doctor prescribe for Gordon? (an antibiotic)
12. What did Mary repeat for the new student? (a difficult word)
13. What's the bank changed for Mrs Hammond? (a ten-dollar note)
14. Who did you ask to carry the suitcases for you? (a friend)
15. What does Jim buy for the family every Sunday? (the newspapers)

---

244 Two Objects   IA

Note:
When the direct object is long it is normally preceded by the preposition and indirect object. This may also avoid ambiguity or confusion.

Short direct object: He explained **the matter** to Mary.
Long direct object: He explained to Mary **the reason for his late return**.

Cf. $\begin{cases} \text{I described} \\ \text{I told} \end{cases}$ **to** her what had happened.
her what had happened.

(a) *To practise and contrast long and short direct objects, respond as shown. This is a substitution exercise.*

I explained the situation to John.	**I explained the situation to John.**
why I was late	**I explained to John why I was late.**
told	**I told John why I was late.**
mentioned	**I mentioned to John why I was late.**
the matter	**I mentioned the matter to John.**

1. to her
2. the problem
3. described
4. what had happened to Sally
5. told
6. explained
7. the situation
8. the subject
9. we
10. introduced
11. the person who was to speak
12. the guests
13. to him
14. described
15. what we wanted him to do
16. they
17. told
18. mentioned
19. explained
20. the facts
21. how it was to be done
22. told
23. the workers
24. I
25. mentioned
26. the plans
27. explained
28. the instructions
29. who they were to contact
30. told

(b) *For further practice with long and short direct objects, respond as shown:*

What did Peter explain to John? (his action) (the reason for his being late)
Peter explained his action to John.
Peter explained to John the reason for his being late.

What must you describe to Mary? (the arrangements we've made for the party) (the party)
I must describe to Mary the arrangements we've made for the party.
I must describe the party to Mary.

1. What did she mention to Mary? (the fact that she hadn't been kind) (the difficulty)
2. What does she give to her friends at Christmas? (well-chosen presents) (those presents that she knows will be most appreciated)
3. What will Jim describe to the students? (the city) (those places where he has spent the past six months)
4. What did you say to John? (exactly what I had said to Peter) (nothing)
5. What did Jim mention to Paul? (the matter) (the number of people who were taking the business management course)

323

6. What has John been reading to his sister? (all those letters that she has not as yet had a chance to look at) (Mary's letters)
7. What did the speaker announce to the audience? (the debate) (the subject that the team was to spend the evening discussing)
8. What did the messenger hand to the secretary? (a message) (an important communication to be given direct to the chairman)
9. What will she take with her to class? (her books) (the notes that she has been taking throughout the course)
10. What has the man just announced to the spectators? (the reason for the withdrawal of two members of the team) (the results)
11. What has the lawyer just explained to his clerk? (the contract) (the terms that will have to be included in the contract)
12. What must Mr Brown leave to his assistants? (the negotiations) (the task of getting in touch with the widow of the deceased)
13. What has Anne mentioned to Peter? (her misfortunes) (the fact that she had already been three times married, but had never found happiness)
14. What did the doctor describe to the medical students? (details of how the growth had penetrated and destroyed vital cells and tissues) (the disease)
15. What did the guard explain to the passengers? (the delay) (the reason for their having to spend the night in the small, cold station waiting-room)

Say and **Tell**

---

245 INTERMEDIATE

John **said**,	'It's going to rain.'
John **said**	(that) it was going to rain.
Mary **said**	nothing.

324

John **told** **me** (that) it was going to rain.
John **told** **me** to get my umbrella.
John **told** **(me)** the truth.

(a) *To practise and contrast the patterns with* say *and* tell, *respond as shown. This is a substitution exercise.*

I said (that) he was wrong.	**I said (that) he was wrong.**
told	**I told him (that) he was wrong.**
her	**I told her (that) she was wrong.**
to go	**I told her to go.**
we	**We told her to go.**

1. come
2. that she was late
3. said
4. could leave
5. told
6. not to be early
7. Peter was coming
8. I
9. said
10. I was sorry
11. he could use the car
12. told
13. not to use
14. what to do
15. they
16. he would have to go
17. he was told
18. John told him
19. said
20. nothing
21. to me
22. told
23. the truth
24. what he'd been doing
25. that he'd been ill
26. said
27. Mary
28. 'Hello'
29. we would be late
30. told

(b) *To practise and contrast* say *and* tell *in questions and answers, respond as shown:*

the new student ('Hello')

STUDENT A: **What did the new student say?**
STUDENT B: **He said 'hello'.**

John—the visitor (where to go)

STUDENT C: **What did John tell the visitor?** (or . . . say to . . .)
STUDENT D: **He told him where to go.**

325

the operator—the caller (to hold the line)

STUDENT E: **What did the operator tell the caller?** (or
 . . . say to . . .)
STUDENT F: **She told him to hold the line.**

1. the waiter (he was busy)
2. the policeman ('Don't park there.')
3. the receptionist ('Can I help you?')
4. the teacher—Peter (to pay attention)
5. the bus-conductor ('Tickets, please.')
6. the typist ('Do you want another copy?')
7. the bank manager (I could borrow the money)
8. the passenger—the driver (not to go so fast)
9. the doctor (she would have to go into hospital)
10. the housewife—milkman (to leave three bottles)
11. the air-hostess ('Please fasten your seatbelts.')
12. the postman ('There aren't any letters for you.')
13. the customer—the assistant (to show him some shirts)
14. the lawyer—his client (how much the case would cost)
15. the lady in the shop—you (the book was out of stock)
16. the motorist—the mechanic (to have a look at his car)
17. the computer operator (the terminals weren't operating)
18. the dentist—the patient (two fillings were necessary)
19. the office manager—the secretary (to answer the phone)
20. the hotel manager—the guest (he hoped she would return)

THE 'ACCUSATIVE AND INFINITIVE'

Mary wants **John**.
Mary wants **to know.**
Mary wants **John to know.**
Mary wants **to know Paul.**
Mary wants **John to know Paul.**

To practise want, *respond as shown:*

Who do you want? (Susan)
I want Susan.

Where does Peter want to go? (New York)
He wants to go to New York.

What do the tourists want to see? (the museum)
They want to see the museum.

When does Paul want Anne to meet John? (tomorrow)
He wants her to meet him tomorrow.

1. What do you want to do? (TV)
2. What do you want Jim to do? (help me)
3. Where does Sally want to go? (her hotel)
4. Where does Sally want John to go? (away)
5. Who wants to come? (Susan)
6. Who wants Susan to come? (nobody)
7. Who does Helen want? (Peter)
8. Who does Helen want to marry? (Peter)
9. Who does Helen want Peter to marry? (her)
10. Why does Helen want Peter to marry her? (in love)
11. Why do you want to meet Jim? (interesting)
12. Why do you want Mary to meet Jim? (a lot in common)
13. How does Paul want to travel? (car)
14. How does Paul want Alice to travel? (sea)
15. What time do you want to leave? (9 p.m.)
16. What time do you want John to leave? (10 p.m.)
17. What time do you want Mary to bring David? (1 p.m.)
18. Which car do you want? (blue)
19. Which car do you want to buy? (blue)
20. Which car do you want John to buy? (red)
21. Which car do you want John to buy Mary? (green)
22. When does Mary want to come? (tomorrow)
23. When does Mary want Bob to come? (next week)
24. When does Mary want to see Bob? (next week)
25. When does Mary want Susan to see Bob? (tonight)

Note:

Other verbs that take this pattern are: *wish, help, like, expect, ask, mean, prefer, choose, hate, love, invite, can't bear; should/would love, hate, like, prefer.*

This is a substitution exercise to practise want *and certain other verbs taking this pattern.*

I want John.	**I want John.**
to go	**I want John to go.**
him	**I want him to go.**
asked	**I asked him to go.**
to help me	**I asked him to help me.**
to leave early	**I asked him to leave early.**

1. they
2. wanted
3. us
4. to stay
5. me
6. she wants
7. to have a party
8. him
9. she asked
10. to speak
11. they
12. intended
13. like

14. wanted
15. her
16. preferred
17. to come
18. expected
19. us
20. to go
21. him
22. to teach
23. she
24. them
25. to come
26. invited

27. he
28. wanted
29. to meet Mary
30. asked
31. to speak to
32. wanted to speak to
33. she wants
34. to see
35. a holiday
36. to have
37. we
38. to stop
39. you

Further practice with verbs that take this pattern.

John will help you. What do you want?
I want John to help me.

Paul will give you a ring. Who will you remind?
I shall remind Paul to give me a ring.

Betty didn't lend Richard your car. What did you ask her?
I asked Betty not to lend Richard my car.

1. Peter's here on time. What do you like?
2. Mary comes home late. What do you allow?
3. Paul told you the story. What did you get?
4. I shall wear a suit. What do you recommend?
5. Mary made less noise. What did you request?
6. Susan will see a doctor. What do you advise?
7. Bob will represent us. Who can we choose?
8. Sally reads your letters. What do you permit?
9. Harry watched the match. What did you expect?
10. Peter came to the party. Who did you invite?
11. Jim will call a taxi for you. What do you want?
12. Sue didn't see Bob again. What did you warn her?
13. Robert got back at 9 p.m. What did you tell him?
14. The children went to bed. What did Richard order?
15. John told you what he'd done. What did you ask him?
16. Betty let you use her flat. Who did you persuade?
17. Tom didn't know where you were. What did you prefer?
18. Alice is using a typewriter. Who are you teaching?
19. Richard sent Bob the message. Who did you instruct?
20. Henry will look Paul up in Canada. What would you like?

So and Not

Do you think it will rain?	I	expect so.
Will Peter be at the party?	I	think so.
Have you done well in the exam?	I	hope so.
Will Mary be able to come?	I don't	expect so.
Has Philip arrived yet?	I don't	think so.
Has there been an accident?	I	hope *not*.
Did you remember to ring him up?	I'm	afraid *not*.

Notes:
(i) **So**, representing a *that*-clause, follows the verbs **expect**, **think**, **hope**, etc. to avoid repetition.

(ii) Negative clauses may be represented by **not**.
Hope and **be afraid** (regret) *are* followed by **not**, but **suppose** and **expect** (and some other verbs) have both forms:

She's not coming, is she?   No. I **don't** expect **so**.
                or No. I   expect **not**.

He won't phone, will he?   No. I **don't** suppose **so**.
                or No. I   suppose **not**.

There is often a difference of emphasis:

/ˋnəu ai ˈdəunt iks ˋpekt ˏsəu/

/ˋnəu ai iksˈpekt ˋnɒt/

(iii) Certain of the verbs in this pattern are preceded by **should**.

EXAMPLES:
Is he grateful to her?   I **should** imagine so.
Will the train be late?   I **shouldn't** think so.

The use of **should** may indicate indignant agreement.

EXAMPLES:
He didn't marry her.   I **should** hope not!
            /ai ʃud ˮhəup ˋnɒt/

I refused to see him.   I **should** think so
            /ai ʃud ˏθiŋk ˎsəu/ or /ai ʃud ˎθiŋk ˏsəu/

(iv) The uses of **so** considered above should not be confused with two other uses:

(a) **so** is used as the object of **do** when **do** is substituted for a verb already used.

EXAMPLE:
I haven't cleaned my teeth yet, but I'll **do so** after breakfast.

(b) **So** is used as a pronoun representing a preceding statement in the pattern: **so** + subject + verb.

EXAMPLES:
It's a Boeing 747.—**So** I see. /ˈsəu ai ˎsiː/

You can see the French coast from here.—**So** you can.
/ˏsəu ju ˎkæn/

He's dead.—**So** the policeman said. /ˏˈsəu ðə pəˎliːsmən ˏsed/

This structure is common when a word following the **so** is emphasised.

To practise so *and* not, *respond as shown:*

Is that building on fire? (hope)
I hope not.

Hasn't John been to Canada? (think)
I don't think so.

Will you be working tonight? (imagine)
I imagine so.

Did you phone Paul as I asked? (afraid)
I'm afraid not.

Has Peter done his homework yet? (believe)
I believe so.

1. Is Bob a heavy drinker? (hope)
2. Have you got the time? (afraid)
3. Did Gordon use his car? (imagine)
4. Hasn't John seen that film? (think)
5. Will Mary see John tonight? (suppose)
6. Will Elizabeth be leaving soon? (hope)
7. Will David get rid of his car? (expect)
8. Can't you afford that sweater? (afraid)
9. Is the library open now? (should imagine)
10. Is John going away for the weekend? (think)
11. Did John call for Mary last night? (presume)
12. Aren't you going to see Sally again? (afraid)
13. Is there anything good on TV tonight? (hope)
14. Was it Rosemary who took the book away? (think)
15. Is Gordon having trouble with his car? (believe)
16. Won't Sheila be going out this evening? (suppose)
17. Won't David be going home by train? (should think)
18. Will the firm have to go into liquidation? (afraid)
19. Will you have to work hard all next week? (suppose)
20. Will there be another war in the near future? (hope)

To practise so *as the object of* do, *respond as shown:*

Have you checked the oil? (before we start)
No. But I'll do so before we start.

Have you fastened your seatbelt? (after posting the letters)
No. But I'll do so after posting the letters.

1. Have you rung Mary up? (straight away)
2. Have you looked the word up? (right now)
3. Have you put the kettle on? (in a moment)
4. Have you taken the books back? (later today)
5. Have you told John what to do? (now he's here)
6. Have you phoned Peter? (as soon as I have time)
7. Have you got rid of the rubbish? (before dinner)
8. Have you had your car serviced? (early next week)
9. Have you asked Peter to come over? (without delay)
10. Have you booked the seats? (at the first opportunity)
11. Have you spoken to Tom about it? (immediately I see him)
12. Have you invited Mary to the party? (when I next see her)
13. Have you had the room decorated? (now that I can afford it)
14. Have you called a taxi? (when Bob's finished with the phone)
15. Have you woken Paul up? (as soon as we've finished this exercise)

249c INTERMEDIATE/ADVANCED

To practise the pattern: so + *subject* + *verb. Place a strong falling stress on the verb, as shown:*

Mary's got a new hat. (see)
So I see. /'səu ai ˅siː/

Paul passed his exam. (hear)
So I heard. /'səu ai˅həːd/

You'll have to take a later train. (tell)
So I've been told. /'səu aiv biːn ˅təuld/

1. John's had his hair cut. (see)
2. Paul's got a new girl-friend. (hear)
3. Mary won't be coming tomorrow. (gather)
4. The grass hasn't been cut for ages. (notice)
5. There's to be an election soon. (understand)
6. There are no flights until next week. (gather)
7. Tom had an accident in his car yesterday. (hear)
8. The club's putting up its subscription rate. (believe)
9. Jim's looking for a publisher for his book. (understand)
10. The visit to the cathedral has had to be called off. (tell)

Continue the exercise, but this time place a rising stress on 'so'.

It's raining.	**So it is!**	/ˌsəu it ˑiz/
Mary's done the test.	**So she has!**	/ˌsəu ʃi ˑhæz/
I've done the exercise.	**So you have!**	/ˌsəu ju ˑhæv/

11. John came first.
12. I can touch the ceiling.
13. There's some mail for you.
14. Mary's wearing a new dress.
15. Susan's brought Jean with her.
16. Someone's left a suitcase here.
17. Sheila's wearing a wedding ring.
18. The TV set has been on all night.
19. Bob's got your paper under his arm.
20. The chairs have all been taken away.
21. John's forgotten to put his socks on.
22. Jill told you she wouldn't be coming.
23. There's a wheel missing from your car.
24. Sandra's doing some work for a change.
25. We had all the cakes for tea yesterday.

NON-CONCLUSIVE VERBS

250 INTERMEDIATE/ADVANCED

There are certain verbs that are not often found in the progressive tenses. Mental states or feelings usually do not change, have no end, and are therefore expressed in non-progressive tenses. It is when we consider the idea of 'incompletion' that we need to use the progressive tenses: to indicate an 'in progress' activity. When a non-conclusive verb is used in the progressive we usually find that there is a change of meaning.

I **think** you are wrong.
   (Cf. I'm **thinking** of leaving tomorrow.)

I **see** what you mean.
   (Cf. Bob is **seeing** Tom at his flat now.)

(a) *To practise using verbs that are not generally found in the progressive, respond as shown:*

Are you intentionally rude? (mean)
No. I don't mean to be.

Can you follow what you hear on TV? (understand)
I don't understand everything I hear.

Don't you think John owes Mary an apology? (agree)
Yes. I agree (that) he should apologise to her.

1. Is that your car? (belong)
2. Is Jim very sensible? (possess)
3. Is John very fond of Mary? (love)
4. Isn't it much colder today? (seem)
5. Shouldn't I get a reward? (deserve)
6. Will Tom ever find his watch? (doubt)
7. Aren't the two houses the same? (differ)
8. Do you know who that man is? (recognise)
9. Don't you want to speak English well? (wish)
10. Are there clothes in that suitcase? (contain)
11. Are you anxious that John should come? (want)
12. Does that flat have only two rooms? (consist)
13. Does Susan make her parents happy? (displease)
14. Don't you think John looks like Bob? (resemble)
15. Can you see the improvements I've made? (notice)
16. Is it important who comes to the party? (matter)
17. Do you think there will be another strike? (foresee)
18. Can't you tell me who was driving the car? (remember)
19. Is Sue usually of the same opinion as Mary? (disagree)
20. Do you like the theatre better than the cinema? (prefer)

(b) *Non-conclusive verbs are often followed by a* that-*clause, which functions as object to the verb. Consider the following situation:*

John and Mary have been going out together for the past six months.

Some possible comments:

I know	(that) they have been going out together.
I believe	(that) they are in love.
I think	(that) they are just right for each other.
I imagine	(that) they will get married soon.
I hope	(that) nothing will happen to prevent the marriage.
I suppose	(that) my wife will make me attend the wedding.
I expect	(that) the couple will go abroad for their honeymoon.
I feel	(that) they will be happy living together.
I fear*	(that) there will be the usual domestic upsets.
I assume*	(that) they wish to raise a family.
I hear	(that) John's mother is buying a house for them.
I suspect	(that) she intends to live with them.
I presume*	(that) Mary will object to this.

Note:
(i) Certain of the verbs in this pattern have a second meaning. Compare A with B below:

A	B
I hear (that) you've been promoted.	I can **hear** some music.
I understand* (that) Philip's away.	I can **understand** French.
I feel (that) the horse should win.	The doctor **felt** my pulse.
I suppose (that) Mary's at home.	I'm **supposed** to be at home.

(ii) This structure with the verbs marked (*) is rather formal.

To practise the pattern: verb + that-clause, use a selection of the above verbs as in the following example. (Advanced students may make suitable comments without question prompts.)

Situation: Peter had an accident in his car yesterday.

What do you know?	**I know (that) he had an accident.**
What do you suspect?	**I suspect (that) he wasn't looking where he was going.**
What do you hope?	**I hope (that) nobody was hurt.**
What do you expect?	**I expect (that) he will have his licence endorsed.**

335

Continue with the following situations:

1. Gordon gave a party last night.
2. Anne was at the doctor's yesterday.
3. Sheila didn't go to class yesterday.
4. David has just come back from Mexico.
5. Tom keeps on making the same mistakes.
6. Peter worked until 4 a.m. this morning.
7. Susan refuses to speak to Bob any more.
8. Patrick doesn't like to travel in lifts.
9. Allan has bought a very fast sports car.
10. Betty was an hour late for the interview.
11. Richard paid a lot of money for his house.
12. Jim didn't finish the book he was reading.
13. Susan enjoyed herself very much in New York.
14. I saw David going into the restaurant just now.
15. Peter was looking at travel brochures yesterday.

(c) *To practise using verbs found in both the progressive* and *non-progressive forms, respond as shown:*

I think . . .	. . . of sending Tom to Canada.
I'm thinking . . .	. . . you are wrong.

I think you are wrong.
I'm thinking of sending Tom to Canada.

Tom's appearing . . .	. . . to have made a mistake.
Tom appears . . .	. . . on stage tonight.

Tom's appearing on stage tonight.
Tom appears to have made a mistake. (also . . . appears on stage . . .)

1. I think . . .	. . . I'm ready.
I'm thinking . . .	. . . about food.
2. I expect . . .	. . . a letter.
I'm expecting . . .	. . . you're right.
3. The doctor feels . . .	. . . Mary's pulse.
The doctor's feeling . . .	. . . he's made a mistake.
4. I can see . . .	. . . you're angry.
I'm seeing . . .	. . . the manager tomorrow.
5. I enjoy . . .	. . . myself.
I'm enjoying . . .	. . . looking at paintings.
6. I imagine . . .	. . . her car's broken down.
I'm imagining . . .	. . . things.

336

7. I wasn't minding . . .	. . . my own business.
I didn't mind . . .	. . . what Bob said about me.
8. I couldn't help . . .	. . . Mary when John came in.
I was helping . . .	. . . seeing you at the party.
9. I'm finding . . .	. . . there's no case to answer.
I find . . .	. . . the problem difficult.
10. I'm hearing . . .	. . . from the firm next week.
I hear . . .	. . . you've been successful.
11. It depends . . .	. . . on what the weather's like.
I'm depending . . .	. . . on you to help me.
12. I'm hoping . . .	. . . you don't mind sitting here.
I hope . . .	. . . to go to New York next year.

VERBS WITH DIRECT OBJECT AND PREDICATIVE ADJUNCT

251 INTERMEDIATE

John	calls	**his dog**	**'Roger'.**
The chairman's wife	named	**the ship**	**'Seaswift'.**
The people	made	**Mr Jones**	**their leader.**
We	selected	**Bill**	as **our representative.**
They	chose	**Jim**	as **their adviser.**
The club members	appointed	**John**	(as) **treasurer.**
The workers	elected	**Jim Smith**	(as) **spokesman.**
The party	nominated	**Bob Jones**	(as) **their candidate.**

(a) *To practise the above patterns, respond as shown:*

What does Mr White call his son? ('Bill')
He calls him 'Bill'.

Who did they elect as their leader? (George)
They elected George as their leader.

What did the chairman's wife name the ship? ('Free Trader')
She named the ship 'Free Trader'.

1. What do we call this country?
2. What was Robert called at school? ('Bob')
3. Who will they appoint as chairman? (Jim)
4. What does Mr Smith call his daughter? ('Sal')
5. Who would you have chosen as leader of your country?
6. What did the director's wife name the ship? ('Anna Maria')
7. Who has the chairman appointed as treasurer? (Mr Brown)
8. Who did they elect as leader of their country? (Mr Smith)
9. Who has the group appointed as economic adviser? (Mr Jones)
10. Who did the staff elect as their representative? (Bob)
11. Who have the players chosen as their captain? (George)
12. Who did the governors select as headmaster? (Mr Black)
13. Who would you make spokesman (or spokeswoman) of the class?
14. Who did the workers appoint as their representative? (a trades union official)
15. Who have the party nominated as their candidate? (a well known businessman)

(b) *This is a substitution exercise for further practice.*

We elected Jim as our leader.	**We elected Jim as our leader.**
chose	**We chose Jim as our leader.**
made	**We made Jim our leader.**
didn't	**We didn't make Jim our leader.**
select	**We didn't select Jim as our leader.**

1. appoint
2. economic adviser
3. they made
4. made Peter
5. chose
6. will
7. select
8. the new manager

9. have made	20. selected
10. their candidate	21. calls
11. nominated	22. Robert 'Bob'
12. elected	23. the baby
13. appointed Robert	24. named
14. Robert treasurer	25. the ship 'Maria'
15. chosen	26. called
16. he	27. Tom his partner
17. made	28. has chosen
18. captain	29. made
19. appointed	30. a director

CAUSATIVE USE OF 'have' AND 'get'

252 INTERMEDIATE

George	had	**his trousers**	**lengthened.**
Peter	got	**the wardrobe**	**repaired.**
Harry	has	**his clothes**	**dry-cleaned.**
Roger	gets	**his hair**	**cut** regularly.

Note:
Have, in this use, is usually stressed. The strong forms /hæv/, /hæz/, /hæd/ are used.

To practise have *in the above pattern, respond as shown:*

you—broken watch (repair)
  STUDENT A: **What are you going to do about that broken watch?**
  STUDENT B: **I'm going to have it repaired.**

Richard—long hair (cut)
  STUDENT C: **What's Richard going to do about his long hair?**
  STUDENT D: **He's going to get it cut.**

Susan—dirty clothes (wash)
  STUDENT E: **What's Susan going to do about those dirty clothes?**
  STUDENT F: **She's going to have them washed.**

1. Jim—dirty suit (clean)
2. David—bad wall (repair)
3. Alice—unmade bed (make)
4. Tom—new book (publish)
5. Bob—noisy engine (look at)
6. Mary—dirty dishes (wash)
7. Peter—socks (mend)
8. Tom—house (do up)
9. David—cases (load)
10. Jim—dirty shoes (clean)
11. Betty—worn carpet (replace)
12. Jean—rubbish (take away)
13. Anne—old chair (throw out)
14. Jill—long skirts (shorten)
15. Bob—painful back (see to)
16. Helen—long grass (cut)
17. John—awful piano (tune)
18. Paul—spectacles (adjust)
19. John—contract (draw up)
20. Jim—leaflets (distribute)

---

253 INTERMEDIATE/ADVANCED

I'll have **Peter** get the car.*
Jane had **Henry** give a talk.*
John got **Harry to** buy some milk.
Jill gets **Susan to** read to her.

Note:
More and more English people are using the pattern marked (*) but it is not yet so common in Britain as in the United States. It would be wise for students to practise the pattern with **get** for their own use.

To practise the above pattern with get, *respond as shown:*

John had his car repaired, didn't he? (garage)
Yes. He got the garage to repair his car.

Mary is having a meal prepared, isn't she? (Susan)
Yes. She's getting Susan to prepare a meal.

Jim will get the flat redecorated, won't he? (Peter)
Yes. He'll get Peter to redecorate the flat.

1. Bob got the radio repaired, didn't he? (Tom)
2. Jim had his socks mended, didn't he? (Sheila)
3. Richard got his hair cut, didn't he? (assistant)
4. Bob's having his knee looked at, isn't he? (doctor)
5. John's getting his car serviced, isn't he? (mechanic)
6. Susan got her homework corrected, didn't she? (teacher)
7. Mary had the chair re-covered, didn't she? (upholsterer)
8. Elizabeth will have the furniture moved, won't she? (Jim)
9. Bob finally got his room cleaned, didn't he? (chambermaid)
10. John will have the trunk sent on to him, won't he? (agents)
11. Jim had the man dismissed from his job, didn't he? (foreman)
12. The pilot will get his position checked, won't he? (navigator)
13. The librarian's having the books restored, isn't she? (experts)
14. Peter will have Sarah picked up at the station, won't he? (wife)
15. Susan got the floors scrubbed and the furniture polished, didn't she? (husband)

VERBS WITH (PRO)NOUN AND ADJECTIVE

254 INTERMEDIATE

David **has**	**his hair**	long.	
Peter **likes**	**his coffee**	white.	
Susan **found the lesson**		interesting.	
Harry **wants his car**		well polished.	

Note:
The emphasis is usually on the adjective:
/ˈpiːtə ˈlaiks his ˈkɔfiː ˎwait/
/ˈsuːzn ˈfaund ðə ˈlesn ˎintristiŋ/

To practise the above pattern, respond as shown:

How does Jim like his coffee? (black)
He likes it black.

How do you find the climate here? (mild)
I find it mild.

How did Peter want his eggs? (soft boiled)
He wanted them soft boiled.

1. How did Tom want his tea? (weak)
2. How does Jim have his hair? (short)
3. How does Sue like her eggs? (poached)
4. How does Jill want her skirts? (short)
5. How does Sally like her dresses? (long)
6. How did you find the shops there? (busy)
7. How do you find the people here? (polite)
8. How does Tom prefer his toast? (well done)
9. How did you find the lesson? (interesting)
10. How do you like your coffee? (black—white)
11. How do you find the road manners here? (good)
12. How did Mary want her steak? (medium to rare)
13. How does Jim like his meals? (promptly served)
14. How does Michael prefer his fish? (well fried)
15. How did Allan find the weather? (sunny and warm)

INCHOATIVE VERBS

Changes in condition or state may be indicated by the use of the verbs: *become**, *get**, *grow**, *turn*, *go*, *come*, *fall*, *wear* and *run*.

EXAMPLES:

John's *got* thin.

I'm *becoming* bored.

Tom's face *turned* purple.

Here are further examples of how these words may be used:

Tom wants to *become* a doctor. (+ noun)

I *got* to know Mary at a party. (+ *to*-infinitive)

Bob's *getting* better at golf. (+ comparative of adjective)

The toy *came* to pieces in my hands. (+ prepositional phrase)

Cf. { When shall I *get* a large beefsteak?
{ When shall I *become* rich enough to buy a large beefsteak?

*These verbs are more common than the others.

To practise getting + *adj., respond as shown:*

Is John rich?	**He's getting rich.**
Is Mary better?	**She's getting better.**
Are good teachers scarce?	**They're getting scarce.**

1. Is it late?
2. Is your car old?
3. Is Peter angry?
4. Is it complicated?
5. Is John tired?
6. Is the water hot?
7. Is it dark?
8. Are air fares cheaper?
9. Is David homesick?
10. Is Tom irritated?
11. Is Jimmy drunk?
12. Is the wind strong?
13. Is the weather cold?
14. Is food more expensive?
15. Is the procession near?
16. Is Patrick impatient?
17. Are Paul's shoes dirty?
18. Is John worried?
19. Are the exercises difficult?
20. Is Mary's hair long?

255b Inchoative Verbs   I

Give your response in the present perfect tense, as shown:

Are the leaves brown? (turn)
Yes. They've turned brown.

Are we out of petrol? (run)
Yes. We've run out of petrol.

Are you accustomed to the weather here? (grow)
Yes. I've grown accustomed to it.

1. Is Mary mad? (go)
2. Is John fat? (get)

3. Is Paul ill? (fall)
4. Is the milk sour? (go)
5. Is Sally married? (get)
6. Is Sally asleep? (fall)
7. Is the zip undone? (come)
8. Is the bread mouldy? (go)
9. Is the handle loose? (come)
10. Is the liquid green? (turn)
11. Are the steps smooth? (wear)
12. Is Paul a director? (become)
13. Are you short of money? (run)
14. Is the weather colder? (turn)
15. Is the line (phone) dead? (go)
16. Is George the manager? (become)
17. Is Richard out of favour? (fall)
18. Is Mary interested in Bob? (become)
19. Are you used to getting up early? (get)
20. Are you accustomed to being away from home? (become)

CONDITIONAL SENTENCES

AFFIRMATIVE
A. Bob **will** **learn** English if he **goes** to class.
B. Bob **would** **learn** English if he **went** to class.
C. Bob **would have learnt** English if he **had gone** to class.

NEGATIVE
A. Bob **will not** **learn** English if he **does not go** to class.

B. Bob **would not** **learn** English if he **did not go** to class.

C. Bob **would not have learnt** English if he **had not gone** to class.

Notes:
  (i) The *if*-clause in pattern A above contains a condition that may or may not be fulfilled. The pattern is:

  future tense + *if* + present tense

  Other tenses may be used, and also modal verbs.

Examples of clauses of open condition:

John **will go** home next week if he **has finished** his course.
If you **speak** Spanish in class, how **can** you **expect** to learn English?
Take him to the police station if you **think** he is drunk.
You **must take** a test if you **wish** to drive on the roads.
If you **know** London you **(must) know** Piccadilly Circus.
Should he **refuse** to leave, **telephone** me.*
If you **should have to call** me, **don't leave** it until the last minute.

(ii) The *if*-clause in patterns B and C above introduces a theoretical condition. The patterns are:

should/would/etc. + stem + *if* + simple past tense
should/would/etc. + *have* + past participle + *if* + past perfect tense

As in pattern A, modal verbs and other tenses may be used.

Examples of clauses of theoretical condition:

Pattern B. (Improbable conditions)

You **could learn** Russian if you **attended** evening classes.
She **might get** to France quicker if she **went** by hovercraft.
He **would be able to go** to China if he **could get** a visa.
I **should study** psychology if **I thought I could get** a degree.
I **might be able to follow** your argument better if you **would explain** your point of view.

Pattern C. (Impossible conditions)

I **could have written** that book if I **had been able to find** the right ideas.
She **might have become** a teacher if she **had gone** to university.
He **would have been able to see** me if I **had come** earlier.
I **should have spoken** to him if he **had visited** the office.
Had I read the paper yesterday, I **should have known** about it.*
If I **had come** here last year you **would** now **be** complimenting me on my English.

(iii) **Were** (the subjunctive form) will be heard instead of **was** in imaginary suppositions, especially in the example 'If I **were** you'.

Examples of the subjunctive **were**:

If she **were** prettier I should take her out.
If he **were** here he could assist us.
If he **were to arrive** now he would see her.
(Cf. If he **arrived** . . .)

(iv) The patterns marked (*), with inversion of subject and verb in the condition clause, are becoming much less common. Students are advised not to use them in conversation.

(v) Although **if** is the most common introduction to conditional clauses, the following may also be used:

> I shall not come **unless** you do. (**if not**—but see note for Ex. 208)
> I don't care **even if** she does refuse to see me.
> **Provided** you leave now, you will see the show. (**providing**)
> **Suppose** she makes a mistake . . . (**supposing, what if**)
> She will go out with John **on (the) condition** that he brings her home before midnight.
> You will be admitted **so/as long as** you arrive before 10 p.m.

(vi) Notice the exceptional use of **will** and **would** after **if** in the following:

> A. If you **will/would** come, I **shall/should** be very glad.
>
> B. If Jim **will/would** see Mary, what **can/could** I do?

In 'A' the verbs **will** and **would** are unstressed and have the meaning of 'agree to'.

In 'B' they are stressed and have the meaning of 'insist on'.

Won't may mean 'refuse to':

> If Jim **won't** do the job, I'll have to do it myself.

---

256 Conditional Sentences   EI

To practise forming sentences containing conditions that may or may not be fulfilled.

You won't forget me. I shan't forget you.
If you don't forget me, I shan't forget you.

Peter may go to New York next week. He will go by air.
If Peter goes to New York next week, he will go by air.

Henry may buy a car. He can take Sally out.
If Henry buys a car, he can (will be able to) take Sally out.

Bob may wish to attend university. He must apply for a place.
If Bob wishes to attend university, he must (will have to) apply for a place.

(Continue with the following:)

1. Mary may come early. She can help us.
2. Bob may turn on the radio. Jim will wake up.
3. You must imitate me. You can speak English well.
4. Mary may go away again. Steve will be very upset.
5. Dick may get fat. Jane will make him go on a diet.
6. Sheila may go upstairs again. She can get my books.
7. Gordon may buy a TV set. We can all watch together.
8. Susan may write to Jim soon. She can tell him the news.
9. David may decide to take the exam. He will take it here.
10. Peter won't drive carefully. The car may go off the road.
11. The weather forecast may be correct. It may rain tomorrow.
12. David may continue to turn up late. You must speak to him.
13. Paul may meet Alice at the station. She won't have to walk.
14. John must help Susan with her work. He can take her dancing.
15. Bob should start looking now. He may be able to find a flat.
16. Jane won't be here in time. Elizabeth must leave without her.
17. Bob may want Jill to visit him. He must tell her his address.
18. Jim may want to get that job. He must take a computer course.
19. Tom will be able to sit next to Sue. He will work much harder.
20. John will have to do this exercise again. He will throw the book out of the window.

---

257 Conditional Sentences I

To practise forming sentences containing a theoretical condition (the pattern: should/would/etc. *+ stem +* if *+ simple past tense).*

Brian may go to the theatre if Mary goes with him.
Brian might go to the theatre if Mary went with him.

I shall have a holiday in Canada if I can get the time off.
I should have a holiday in Canada if I could get the time off.

Bill will have to go to New York if his director asks him to.
Bill would have to go to New York if his director asked him to.

1. I shall do my shopping if it isn't raining.
2. Don will wake up early if he uses an alarm-clock.
3. Sally will listen to her husband if he talks sense.
4. Bob must go to the party if he receives an invitation.
5. Jim can speak well if he thinks about what he's saying.
6. David won't be able to go if his wife doesn't permit it.
7. George will sleep better if he doesn't drink so much beer.
8. Joe may go to the races if he can get away from the office.
9. Jim will eat at the Chinese restaurant if it's cheap there.
10. Bob will be able to concentrate if Helen doesn't bother him.
11. Alice may make fewer mistakes if she listens to her teacher.
12. Richard can use my car if he promises to drive it carefully.
13. Peter must ring Mary up if he wants to speak to her urgently.
14. John will have to buy the suite of furniture if Anne wants it.
15. Jim will be able to call on Sue if she tells him where she lives.

Further practice with the pattern: should/would/*etc.* + *stem* + if + *simple past tense.*

I like Mary. She isn't selfish.
I shouldn't like Mary if she was (or: were) selfish.

Jim won't wear that shirt. It doesn't suit him.
Jim would wear that shirt if it suited him.

John can't speak English. He doesn't go to classes.
John could speak English if he went to classes.

1. Richard isn't happy. He's married.
2. Bill makes a lot of money. He works hard.
3. Paul's going to the bank. He needs a loan.
4. John's interested in Mary. She dresses well.
5. Susan can't go to the next town. There's no bus.
6. Bob doesn't use a computer. He doesn't know how to.
7. I shan't finish the book. It isn't very interesting.
8. Richard will go by train. His car is being serviced.
9. Jim has to make his own bed. Sue won't do it for him.
10. John can't catch up. His scooter isn't very powerful.
11. Mary can't teach the game. She can't play it herself.
12. Joe will have to fly. He has to be in Canada tomorrow.
13. George doesn't feel well. He eats all the wrong foods.
14. David isn't learning anything. He doesn't attend class.
15. Peter can't take a holiday. He has too much work to do.
16. I can't ring Don up. I don't know his telephone number.
17. Jill always makes the same mistakes. She isn't corrected.
18. Bob isn't hurrying. He doesn't have to be home before Mary.
19. Anne will visit the United States. She can speak English well.
20. Gordon can't buy that coat. He doesn't have enough cash on him.

---

259 Conditional Sentences   IA

To practise the pattern: should/would/*etc.* + have + *past participle* + if + *past perfect tense.*

Bob didn't work in London, because his firm didn't want him to.
Bob would have worked in London if his firm had wanted him to.

Mary didn't go to the club, because she couldn't find a baby-sitter.
Mary might have gone to the club if she'd been able to find a baby-sitter.

Jim was able to buy a new suit because his wife didn't want a new dress.
Jim couldn't have bought a new suit if his wife had wanted a new dress.

1. John drove because he didn't know that he was incapable.
2. Mary didn't write her letters, because she had to go to class.
3. Jim didn't play chess, because he was obliged to do some work.
4. Barbara walked to the station because she couldn't get a taxi.
5. Jane didn't run after the bus, because it wasn't the last one.
6. Gordon had to get back early because Mary was waiting for him.
7. Jim didn't enjoy going to the cinema, because he had to go alone.
8. Brian had to wear glasses because he couldn't read without them.
9. Tom wasn't able to learn Russian, because he didn't go to Moscow.
10. I didn't enrol for another course, because I didn't have the time.
11. You didn't forget all those words, because you practised using them.
12. Class didn't begin at the right time, because the students were late.
13. Jim lent Joe his car because he didn't know what Joe wanted it for.
14. Sue wasn't a good cook, because Bob wouldn't stay out of the kitchen.
15. John didn't borrow money from Bob, because he didn't really need it.
16. I couldn't repair the TV set, because I couldn't locate the fault.
17. Bob didn't really understand the play, because he hadn't read it first.
18. The boys didn't hire a car, because they couldn't find one locally.
19. I couldn't stay with Anne, because I hadn't written to say I was coming.
20. The man charged too much because he thought he could get away with it.

Note:
As a general rule the auxiliary verbs in a conditional sentence (as in most other sentences) carry sentence stress only in their negative form.

Bob would have died if you hadn't saved him.
/'bɔb wudəv 'daid if juː ˌhædnt ˌseivd him/

He wouldn't have gone if he'd known.
/hi 'wudntəv 'gɔn if hiːd ˌnəun/

Further practice with the pattern: should/would/etc. + have + *past participle* + if + *past perfect tense.*

Bob couldn't go to the party. He wasn't invited.
Bob could have gone to the party if he'd been invited.

Joe didn't sign the contract. He didn't agree the terms.
Joe would have signed the contract if he'd agreed the terms.

Bill woke up in time for breakfast. Mary banged on his door.
Bill mightn't have woken up in time for breakfast if Mary hadn't banged on his door.

1. Bill wasn't late. He looked at his watch.
2. Sally spoke to David. He apologised to her.
3. Bob got good marks in the exam. He worked hard.
4. Richard couldn't have the room. It was occupied.
5. George turned up on time. He ran to catch the bus.
6. Don shouted. He caught his finger in the car door.
7. Jane couldn't come to class yesterday. She was ill.
8. John stopped smoking. He listened to Mary's advice.
9. The man escaped. The detective lost him in a crowd.
10. Susan saw Paul on the corner. She was out shopping.
11. Anne didn't know the answer. She didn't ask Richard.
12. Joe got over his cold very quickly. He stayed in bed.
13. Paul was annoyed. Jill didn't show him much affection.
14. Bob was able to write the book. His wife inspired him.
15. David couldn't go on holiday. He didn't save any money.
16. Harry didn't spend the day out of doors. It was cloudy.
17. Bill watched the programme on TV. He saw it advertised.

18. Jimmy got a letter from Susan. He wrote to her last week.
19. John was able to meet me. I didn't have to go to Bermuda.
20. Jim failed the test. He didn't keep his eyes on the road.
21. Paul and Anne were able to play tennis. It wasn't raining.
22. John had to get dressed quickly. He was late for the office.
23. Bob wasn't able to see Jim. He didn't come to work that day.
24. Gordon couldn't understand. George spoke too quickly for him.
25. Jim didn't have to stay in after class. He did his work well.

---

261 Conditional Sentences   A

(a) *To contrast the three main types, respond as shown:*

if you miss your train (have to wait for the next one)
STUDENT A: **What will you do if you miss your train?**
STUDENT B: **If I miss my train I'll have to wait for the next one.**

if someone stole your car (report the theft to the police)
STUDENT C: **What would you do if someone stole your car?**
STUDENT D: **If someone stole my car I'd report the theft to the police.**

if Mary hadn't been able to come (invite Jane)
STUDENT E: **What would you have done if Mary hadn't been able to come?**
STUDENT F: **If Mary hadn't been able to come I'd have invited Jane.**

1. if John didn't offer to help (do it alone)
2. if there's a general strike (stay at home)
3. if you wanted to earn more (get another job)
4. if the flight's postponed (extend my holiday)
5. if you come into a lot of money (stop working)
6. if you lost your books (have to look for them)

7. if the hotel's fully booked (try somewhere else)
8. if Tom hadn't been able to go (send Mary instead)
9. if all the lights had fused (call an electrician)
10. if the car had got out of control (jump for my life)
11. if the suit's too expensive (find something cheaper)
12. if you were the teacher (give everybody the day off)
13. if the maid didn't clean your room (make a complaint)
14. if the trains hadn't been running (have to go by bus)
15. if someone broke into your house (hide under the bed)
16. if there'd been no newspapers (watch the news on TV)
17. if the flat's too small (have to find something larger)
18. if all the shops had been closed (go to town the next day)
19. if the cleaners don't return your laundry (submit a claim)
20. if the exercise had been too difficult (do something else)

(b) *Further conditional practice* (*with modal verbs*). *This is a substitution exercise.*

She'll learn a lot if she studies.
> **She'll learn a lot if she studies.**

would   **She would learn a lot if she studied.**

would have   **She would have learnt a lot if she'd studied.**

could have   **She could have learnt a lot if she'd studied.**

1. gone to class
2. would have
3. might
4. may
5. make progress
6. John
7. could have
8. will
9. pays attention
10. please his teacher
11. would
12. would have
13. done his homework
14. will
15. Mary
16. wouldn't have been told off
17. mightn't have
18. been quiet
19. sent out of the room
20. needn't be
21. wouldn't
22. did what she was told
23. would get on better
24. studied harder
25. I
26. shall
27. have more practice
28. speak English better
29. be able to
30. might
31. could have
32. would

Wish

I	can't speak	English well.
I **wish** (that) I	**could** speak	English better.
Anne	will speak	Spanish in class.
I wish (that) she	**would** speak	English in class.
I	don't know	England very well.
I **wish** (that) I	**knew**	England better.
I	should like	to be at home now
I **wish** (that) I	**was** (or **were**)	at home now.

Notes:

(i) The examples above show **wish** expressing an idea in present time. This pattern may also express future time, e.g. 'I wish I could see Mary **tomorrow**.' See Ex. 263 for **wish** with past time.

(ii) The word 'will' in the sentence 'Anne will speak . . .' means 'insists on'—'B' in Note vi on page 346. It is not the future 'will'.

(iii) Compare the following:

> I wish the post **came** earlier.
> I wish the postman **would come** earlier.

In the first example we are dealing with an inanimate object (the post). It is only with people that we use **would** in this pattern, unless we are personifying the object (e.g. 'I wish this door **would** close.').

(iv) The subjunctive **were** in this pattern (Cf. Note iii on page 345) indicates that the wish cannot be realised. But **was** is now common.

(v) Other patterns with **wish**:

> You couldn't **wish for** a better husband.
> Jim doesn't **wish to** discuss the matter.
> John won't **wish** me **to** go to that party.
> Mary wants to **wish** you a Happy New Year.

---

262 **Wish**   I

(a) *To practise the past tense pattern in the affirmative, answer the questions as shown:*

Won't Anne write to you again?
No, she won't. I wish she would write to me again.
/ai 'wiʃ ʃi ˮwud ˌrait tə mi ə ˌgen/

Would you like Mary to be here now?
Yes, I would. I wish she was here now.
/ai 'wiʃ ʃi ˮwɔz hiə ˌnau/

Don't you have enough time to learn English really well?
No, I don't. I wish I did have time to learn English really well.

Can't you go to Bermuda for your holiday?
No, I can't. I wish I could go to Bermuda for my holiday.

1. Has your friend got a car?
2. Will Jim be able to help you?
3. Would you like Joe to eat less?
4. Won't Betty turn down the radio?
5. Would you like to keep that book?
6. Would you like to be at home now?
7. Do you want me to speak more slowly?
8. Is there anything Jim can do to help?
9. Doesn't your bed have enough blankets?
10. Doesn't the post come early every day?
11. Do you want me to change the TV channel?
12. Won't the hotel manager give you another room?
13. Would you like me to come and see you some time?
14. Can't you read that book without a dictionary?
15. Doesn't your bedroom get the sun in the morning?

(b) *To practise the past tense pattern in the negative, respond as shown:*

I must go home now.
I wish you didn't have to go home now.

Gordon's always late for class.
I wish he wasn't always late for class.

Children make a lot of noise.
I wish children didn't make so much noise.

John always leaves the windows open.
I wish he wouldn't always leave the windows open.

1. Food costs a lot.
2. Trains arrive late.
3. Mary smokes too much.
4. Bill has to go home now.
5. That car is too expensive.
6. The club must close at 11 p.m.
7. Mary has to be in bed by 10 p.m.
8. This train stops at every station.
9. Bob has a very strong Irish accent.
10. David always gets his answers wrong.
11. The cost of living is very high now.
12. Sandra's taking a holiday next month.
13. John will have to spend a week in bed.
14. Jim's taking Susan out instead of Anne.
15. Tom turns up at the office late every day.

---

263 Wish   I

I wish (that) John		spent less on drink	
I **wish** (that) John	**had**	**spent** less on drink	**last night.**
I wish (that) Anne could	see	me	now.
I **wish** (that) Anne	**could have seen**	me at the party	**last night.**

Notes:

(i) The past perfect tense forms (or the perfect infinitive with **could**) indicate **past** time. The past tense form after **wish** indicates **present** or **future** time.

(ii) The alternative to **could have seen** is **had been able to see**. (I wish that Anne **had been able to see** me . . .)

(iii) In the exercise students respond to a statement in such a way that the stress pattern of the response is not a neutral one.

> Peter wasn't there at the time.—**I wish he had been there**.
> (ai ˈwiʃ hiː ˈhæd biːn ˌðɛə/

Compare:

> Were you all alone?—**Yes. I wish Peter had been there.**
> /ai ˈwiʃ ˈpiːtə həd biːn ˌðɛə/

356

To practise the use of wish *relating to past time.*

Peter wasn't at home yesterday.
I wish he had been at home yesterday.

You missed a good play on TV last night.
I wish I hadn't missed the play.

Susan couldn't come to the dance last night.
I wish she could've come to the dance.
(or: . . . she had been able to come . . .)

1. Jim's had his hair cut short.
2. The bar was out of beer last night.
3. Bob didn't tell you what was wrong.
4. You couldn't buy the car you wanted.
5. John didn't study English last year.
6. Jim wasn't up when you called on him.
7. Mary got rid of your favourite chair.
8. Peter had to go home early last night.
9. Richard couldn't catch up in the race.
10. Sheila's decided to live somewhere else.
11. George wasn't able to pay the money back.
12. John didn't learn very much at university.
13. Bob threw all the important documents away.
14. Jim couldn't get through the traffic in time.
15. You couldn't go to New York for your holiday.
16. I couldn't tell you I was going to be delayed.
17. I'm sorry I couldn't find the time to see you.
18. Patrick made a rude remark about Betty's dress.
19. Sheila had to take the early train to the city.
20. Richard didn't let me know that he was leaving.

---

264 Wish   A

To practise combining wish *with conditions.*

Peter wasn't at home yesterday.
I wish he had been at home, because if he had, I would've been
able to ask him what he'd done with my car.

You missed a good play on TV last night.
I wish I hadn't missed the play, because if I hadn't, I could've
discussed it with you, couldn't I?

357

Susan couldn't come to the dance last night.

I wish she had been able to come to the dance, because if she had, she'd have heard the new pop group that was playing.
Continue with sentences 1–20 in Ex. 263 as a free-completion exercise.

THE PERFECT INFINITIVE (1)

The examples in this section illustrate the use of the perfect infinitive with modal verbs in the situations described.

265 INTERMEDIATE

Situation
Unknown to her parents, Sheila was at a party at a friend's house last night. She didn't come home until 3 a.m. There was a telephone in the house.

She	**should have** come home earlier.	
She	**might have** forgotten what time it was.	
She	**could have** telephoned to say that she was going to be late.	
Her mother **must**	**have** been worried about her.	

Notes:
 (i) In the above pattern **ought to** is sometimes used instead of **should**, and **could** instead of **might**.

(ii) Pay particular attention to the pronunciation of the following:
    should have,   might have,   could have,   must have.
    /'ʃudəv/   /'maitəv/   /'kudəv/   /'mʌstəv/

To practise should have (ought to have).

   Jim didn't do his homework last night.
   He should have done his homework last night.

   John didn't give Mary a lift home.
   He should have given her a lift home.

1. Mary didn't ring John up.
2. Betty didn't get a present.
3. George didn't go to bed early.
4. Tom didn't knock before going in.
5. Bob didn't stop after the accident.
6. David didn't ask the girl her name.
7. John didn't have breakfast this morning.
8. Jim didn't watch the play on TV last night.
9. Peter didn't take Helen to the theatre yesterday.
10. Gordon didn't try to get on with the new manager.
11. Harry didn't look at the contract before signing it.
12. Richard didn't put on his raincoat before going out.
13. Philip didn't buy his wife anything for her birthday.
14. Sandra didn't take the medicine the doctor prescribed.
15. Bob didn't examine the camera properly before buying it.

---

266 The Perfect Infinitive I

To practise might have (could have).

Do you think Peter had an accident with his car?
He might have had an accident with his car.

Do you think Sally went to the club last night?
She might have gone to the club last night.

1. Do you think Sally spoke to Peter?
2. Do you think John was ill yesterday?
3. Do you think the train arrived late?
4. Do you think David gave Jim the money?
5. Do you think Bob passed his examinations?
6. Do you think Henry saw Susan at the office?
7. Do you think David had his holiday in Canada?
8. Do you think John was able to finish his work?
9. Do you think there was trouble at that factory?
10. Do you think Philip went for a walk last night?
11. Do you think it was necessary for Anne to see Bob?
12. Do you think Sandra took your newspaper by mistake?
13. Do you think David did everything he was told to do?
14. Do you think Susan knew what was wrong with her car?
15. Do you think Tom managed to persuade Jim to help him?

To practise must have.

I'm sure the plane took off at 1 p.m.
Yes. It must have taken off at 1 p.m.

I'm certain John was held up in the traffic.
Yes. He must have been held up in the traffic.

1. I'm sure Anne's got the job.
2. I'm certain Paul turned up late.
3. I'm positive Don's car broke down.
4. I'm sure Jim had a look at the book.
5. I'm positive Betty let Richard down.
6. I'm certain Henry got the time wrong.
7. I'm sure Michael's got over his cold.
8. I'm certain Susan stayed out very late.
9. I'm positive John got in touch with Bob.
10. I feel sure it was John who put Sally up.
11. I'm positive Mary was fed up with her job.
12. I'm sure the cheque was made out to George.
13. I feel sure John sent away for the spare part.
14. I'm positive Pat's got rid of the guests by now.
15. I'm sure Steve had to put up with a lot from Jill.

Situation:
A police officer in a patrol car overtook Bob while he was out driving yesterday and forced him to stop. He told him that he was arresting him for exceeding the speed limit.

Bob	**shouldn't have**	exceeded the speed limit.
Bob	**couldn't have**	stopped quickly at the speed he was travelling.
Bob	**couldn't have**	seen the patrol car, or he would have slowed down.
Bob	**mightn't have**	noticed he was going so fast.
The officer **needn't**	**have**	arrested Bob.

Note:
(i) 'He **couldn't have** stopped quickly . . . ' means '**it would have been impossible** for him to stop quickly . . . '
'He **couldn't have** seen the patrol car, . . . ' indicates that a conclusion is being drawn.
(Cf. 'He **couldn't** see the patrol car, because he had no rear-view mirror.')

(ii) Remember the important difference:

We **needn't have** driven fast. We arrived with time to spare.— But we *did* drive fast.
We **didn't need to** drive fast. We arrived with time to spare.— And we *didn't* drive fast.

(a) *To practise* should, could, might, need + not + have.

I'm sure that Harry didn't see the patrol car coming up behind him.
Harry couldn't have seen the patrol car coming up behind him.

Perhaps Mary didn't finish her homework before dinner.
Mary mightn't have finished her homework before dinner.

Peter met Mary at the station yesterday. It wasn't necessary.
Peter needn't have met Mary at the station yesterday.

George drove straight across a red traffic light.
George shouldn't have driven across a red traffic light.

Henry needed his wife's help to write the book.
Henry couldn't have written the book without his wife's help.

1. Paul needed Peter's help to start his car last Saturday.
2. The clerk at the hotel reception gave Jim the wrong key.
3. I don't think Tom locked the car doors before coming in.
4. I helped Sheila unpack. She didn't really need my help.
5. Jim's had his hair cut very short. It doesn't suit him.
6. I'm not certain if Jimmy asked Sandra to go out with him.
7. I'm positive that Peter didn't write that letter to Mary.
8. It was wrong of the manager to misinform the shareholders.
9. I'm not sure if Richard and Sally got on the right train.
10. The clerk needed help to obtain the necessary information.

11. I'm not sure if Tom and Jim went to the cinema yesterday.
12. John took his secretary out to dinner instead of his wife.
13. Richard possibly wasn't at the office yesterday afternoon.
14. I'm absolutely positive that Joe wasn't taken to hospital.
15. Bill went to the window to open it. It was already open.
16. John spoke at the meeting although he wasn't feeling well.
17. It's possible that Jane didn't follow the doctor's advice.
18. Jim bought himself a watch. Mary bought him one as well.
19. It's possible that Anne didn't read the book Jim gave her.
20. I was sure that the computer hadn't given the right answer.
21. Tom forgot his dental appointment the day before yesterday.
22. I don't know if John and Bob were with Sheila at the dance.
23. I cannot believe that Rosemary passed all her examinations.
24. Mary visited John in hospital. Sally had just been there.
25. I'm not certain that all the books were paid for by cheque.

(b) *To contrast* needn't have + *past participle and* didn't need + to-*infinitive.*

Tom ran all the way. It wasn't necessary.
Tom needn't have run all the way.

Tom didn't run. He had plenty of time.
Tom didn't need to run.

1. John took the exam. It wasn't necessary.
2. Paul told a lie. It was an unnecessary one.
3. Sally didn't wait for John. He came on time.
4. I waited two hours for Mary. She didn't come.
5. We didn't go to the bank. We had enough money.
6. Mary didn't take the exam. It wasn't necessary.
7. The men worked late. It wasn't really essential.
8. Joe didn't apply for the job. He already had one.
9. Mary gave me all these sweets. I only wanted a few.

10. Tom walked to the chemist's. He could have gone by bus.
11. Jim didn't go to the station. Jane offered to pick Bob up.
12. Paul didn't borrow Jim's car. Paul's car was going all right.
13. I bought expensive petrol for my car. It runs on cheap petrol.
14. We took the TV set to the shop. There was nothing wrong with it.
15. Tom didn't go to the doctor. There wasn't anything wrong with him.

---

269 The Perfect Infinitive   I

Situation:
John hasn't come to work today. I know he was ill yesterday.

He **may**   **have** decided to spend the day in bed.
He **may not have** felt well enough to work today.
He **can't**   **have** told anybody, because his manager doesn't
                 know where he is.

Notes:
(i) **May have**, **may not have** and **can't have** are often used with adverbs of time such as **today**, **this morning**, **recently**, etc. You will sometimes hear **might have**, **might not have** and **couldn't have** used instead.

Notice the usual pronunciation of:

may have,   **may not have**
/'meiəv/   /'mei nɔtəv/ or sometimes: /'meintəv/

can't have
/'kɑːntəv/

To practise the above pattern, respond as shown:

Perhaps Mary hasn't got up yet.
Mary may not have got up yet.

I think John has gone to the chemist's.
John may have gone to the chemist's.

I'm sure that Peter hasn't seen Sally yet.
Peter can't have seen Sally yet.

1. Perhaps John has been held up.
2. I think David hasn't eaten yet.
3. Maybe there's been an accident.
4. I'm positive he's not been here.
5. Perhaps Mary has taken up tennis.
6. I don't think Jane has seen Peter.
7. I'm sure that Sally hasn't finished.
8. I think that we've run out of petrol.
9. I think the man has taken the wrong car.
10. Perhaps John has already paid the money in.
11. I'm sure that Paul hasn't forgotten to come.
12. I don't think that Richard has gone home yet.
13. I'm sure that David hasn't sold his house yet.
14. I'm positive Pat hasn't signed the letters yet.
15. I think Jill has already been on the hovercraft.
16. Maybe the television set hasn't been switched off.
17. I don't think Sandra has booked a room for us yet.
18. I'm sure that Sally hasn't bought a dictionary yet.
19. I think Richard has made up that story about Betty.
20. I don't think George has got rid of his bad cold yet.

The Continuous Form

Situation:
   Susan was watching TV while David was doing the washing-up.

   She **should   have been**   doing the washing-up.
   She **shouldn't have been** watching TV.

Situation:
   I'm sure that David was staying at the Ritz Hotel last week.

   He **must   have been**   staying at the Ritz Hotel.
   He **couldn't   have been**   staying at the Royal Hotel.

364

Situation:
I'm not sure what Jim was doing in his room yesterday.

He **might   have been**   work**ing** in his room.
He **might not have been**   work**ing** in his room.

To practise the above forms, respond as shown:

Tim's engaged to Sue. He was thinking about Mary.
He should have been thinking about Sue.

I'm not sure if it was Peter I saw driving the car.
Peter might have been driving the car.
or **It might have been Peter driving the car.**

I'm quite sure that John wasn't living in Canada last
   year.
He couldn't have been living in Canada last year.

I heard music and laughter coming from Bob's flat.
He must have been having a party.

1. Barry was chewing gum during the oral practice.
2. I saw Susan in the gift shop on Jack's birthday.
3. I think Peter was taking Mary home at eleven p.m.
4. I'm sure that Tom wasn't paying attention in class.
5. I'm not sure what Sally was doing in the night-club.
6. I saw Bob going into town. He was carrying his suit.
7. John was looking at Pat while the teacher was speaking.
8. I saw Lucy helping Richard with his homework last
   night.
9. I'm not sure whether Anne was expecting Paul to call
   her.
10. Peter was driving home at 10 p.m. He'd had ten
    whiskies.
11. I saw Mr Smith running after a bus. He has a weak
    heart.
12. Bob was studying the 'situations vacant' columns last
    week.
13. Paul saw a pretty girl on the pavement. His car hit a bus.

14. I saw Don speaking to Maria, but I know she speaks no English.
15. I saw John talking to Jim after dinner. I know he's short of money.

---

271 The Perfect Infinitive

Bob didn't go on the training course,	but he **could have**.
Peter had too much to drink last night,	but he **shouldn't have**.
George said that he had seen New York,	but he **couldn't have**.
I didn't think Paul had done the work,	but he **must have**.
Harry went to the station to meet Anne,	but he **needn't have**.
Joe didn't kiss his wife this morning,	but he **should have**.
Sue didn't think Harry wanted to relax,	but he **might have**.
Tom thought Paul wanted to see his car,	but he **might not have**.

Note:
The use of the short form (*but he . . .*) avoids repetition of the preceding sentence.

There are two complete intonation patterns (two tunes) in each of these utterances.

Bob didn't go on the training course, but he could have.
/'bɒb 'didnt 'gəu ɒn ðə ˋtreiniŋ ˏkɔːs—bət hi ˇkudəv/

Peter had too much to drink last night, but he shouldn't have.
/'piːtə hæd 'tuː mʌtʃ tə ˋdriŋk ˏlaːst ˏnait—bət hi ˇʃudntəv/

To practise the above, respond as shown:

Harry didn't ask anybody to lend him a hand.
Harry didn't ask anybody to lend him a hand, but he could have.

George used floor polish on his car.
George used floor polish on his car, but he shouldn't have.

Peter gave the walls of his room four coats of paint.
Peter gave the walls of his room four coats of paint, but he needn't have.

1. John told Harry to shut up.
2. The record didn't appeal to Jim.
3. Richard didn't use his car in Paris.
4. Bob took his camera with him on holiday.
5. I didn't think that Mr Brown wanted the job.
6. Sally and Sheila had their skirts shortened.
7. George didn't take his driving test last week.
8. Mr Smith repeated the sentence twice for Mary.
9. I thought the waiter had understood what I said.
10. Bob didn't pay all the money back to his parents.
11. I thought John had agreed to come to the meeting.
12. Mrs Hammond laid the table an hour before dinner.
13. Sheila didn't go to the play with her boy-friend.
14. Many shops have increased the price of cigarettes.
15. I thought John hadn't intended to have a haircut.
16. Paul said that he'd turned in before three o'clock.
17. Mrs Jackson sent her daughters to a boarding school.
18. Bill didn't change before going on the tennis court.
19. Mary didn't upset David when she went out with John.
20. Brian didn't learn much Italian while he was in Rome.

---

272 The Perfect Infinitive   A

To practise forming questions with should, could, needn't, *etc., respond as shown:*

Henry did the job. (needn't)
Needn't he have done it?

Paul didn't repair his car. (could)
Could he have repaired it?

Elizabeth was at the party. (shouldn't)
Shouldn't she have been at the party?

1. Susan turned up early. (needn't)
2. Paul was at the dance. (shouldn't)
3. Tom hasn't given up drinking. (should)
4. Jim didn't attend the meeting. (could)

5. Sally stayed away from school. (should)
6. Patrick didn't have the day off. (could)
7. Mary's lost a lot of weight. (shouldn't)
8. I wasn't given a rise in salary. (should)
9. Bob's read every page in the book. (need)
10. My shoes wore out after a month. (should)
11. John used a lot of hot water. (shouldn't)
12. We didn't take part in the match. (could)
13. Paul wasn't granted an interview. (should)
14. The luggage has all been sent. (shouldn't)
15. Sally was at the office on Saturday. (need)
16. Sarah didn't take the car with her. (could)
17. Gordon's bought Mary a present. (shouldn't)
18. Sheila took care of all the children. (need)
19. Bob didn't make much money last year. (could)
20. I helped Elizabeth with her work. (shouldn't)

THE PERFECT INFINITIVE (2)

Introductory structure and notes.

The structure below indicates the use of the perfect infinitive
preceded by **to**:

A. I **was to have gone** to Bolivia yesterday.

(but I didn't go)

They **were to have come** here last week.

(but they didn't come)

B. I **should like** **to have been** there. (but I wasn't)

Mary **would like** John **to have seen** the film.

(but he didn't)

Notes:

(i) In pattern 'A' you will often hear *supposed* + *to*-infinitive
instead of the perfect infinitive:

I **was supposed to go** . . .
They **were supposed to come** . . .

In negative sentences the *supposed* + *to*-infinitive form is
preferred.

368

(ii) Native speakers of English are frequently confused over pattern 'B'. Perhaps we should distinguish:

He **would like** + **to have done** it.
(He is sorry *now* that he did not do it.)

He **would have liked** + **to do** it.
(He was sorry *at the time* that he couldn't do it.)

But not many people are clear-headed about the distinction (as Fowler's *Modern English Usage* suggests in the article *perfect infinitive* 2). Students should try to avoid such excesses as: 'He would have liked + to have done it', but if they fall into the trap they will be in good company.

(iii) The negative form for 'B':

I   **shouldn't like**   **to have been** there.
Mary **wouldn't like** John **to have seen** the film.
(Cf. She **would prefer** him **not to have seen** the film.)

---

273   The Perfect Infinitive   I

To practise was/were to have + *past participle, respond as shown:*

Did you speak to Peter yesterday? (turn up)
No. I was to have spoken to him, but he failed to turn up.

Did Jim and Bob spend their holiday in the U.S.A.? (change)
No. They were to have spent it there, but they changed their minds and went to Canada instead.

1. Did Tom give you the book? (forget)
2. Did Bob and Sally meet at 1 p.m.? (traffic)
3. Did Susan visit the museum last week? (close)
4. Did Peter attend the conference? (his manager)
5. Did Jimmy borrow the money from Robert? (find)
6. Did the workmen do the job yesterday? (strike)
7. Did the orchestra play at the Town Hall? (fire)
8. Did Sheila drive John into the town? (accident)
9. Did Jim and Bob work all day yesterday? (tired)
10. Did Harry take his wife out to lunch? (business)
11. Did David go bowling yesterday afternoon? (golf)
12. Did Michael drop in for a drink last night? (ill)
13. Did Bob take a computer programmers' course? (busy)
14. Did the firm build a block of flats there? (Council)
15. Did you visit the hairdresser's last week? (no time)

(a) *To practise the pattern 'should/would like + perfect infinitive', respond as shown:*

Peter spent the day in bed. (I)
I should like to have spent the day in bed too.

John's read that book. (Elizabeth)
Elizabeth would like to have read that book as well.

Richard went on holiday last week. (we)
We should also like to have gone on holiday last week.

1. Jane rang Jim up. (Mary)
2. John's seen that film. (Tom)
3. Steve had some more to eat. (I)
4. Jim's emigrated to Canada. (Paul)
5. I watched TV last night. (Harry)
6. I was able to have the day off. (I)
7. Betty avoided meeting Philip. (Mary)
8. Paul studied English last year. (Jim)
9. Jill had some help with her work. (I)
10. Tom worked in America last year. (Bob)
11. Lucy sat next to Tom in class. (Sally)
12. Steve went to Mexico last week. (Betty)
13. Patricia gave up smoking for good. (Bob)
14. Allan bought himself a new car. (Richard)
15. Peter called on Paul last Tuesday. (Lucy)

(b) *To practise the pattern 'should/would like (+(pro)noun) + perfect infinitive'. This is a substitution exercise.*

I should like to have gone.
        I should like to have gone.

he   **He would like to have gone.**

like me   **He would like me to have gone.**

met Bob   **He would like me to have met Bob.**

like to have **He would like to have met Bob.**

we   **We should like to have met Bob.**

seen John **We should like to have seen John.**

370

1. like you
2. like to have
3. they
4. wouldn't
5. like David
6. she
7. caught the wrong train
8. I
9. like to have
10. done that job
11. he
12. would
13. like Tom
14. I
15. been here
16. she
17. like to have
18. taken the exam earlier
19. like Mary
20. we
21. shouldn't
22. she
23. like to have
24. her holiday then
25. I
26. should
27. prevented the accident
28. he
29. been promoted
30. like John

REPORTED SPEECH (Indirect Speech)

A.	I know England.	He said he **knew** England.
	I don't know Canada.	He said he **didn't know** Canada.
B.	Speak English!	He told me **to speak** English.
	Don't speak Spanish!	He told me **not to speak** Spanish.
C.	Are you studying?	He asked me **if I was studying.**
	Why are you studying?	He asked me **why I was studying.**
D.	Shall I call a taxi?	He asked me **if he should call** a taxi.
	Shall I ever speak English well?	He asked me **if he would** ever **speak** English well.

Notes:
(i) When the reporting verb (tell, say, ask, etc.) is in the present, present perfect or future tense no change is made in the tense of the verb in the following clause.

When the reporting verb is in the past tense a change is usually made in the tense of the verb in the following clause.

EXAMPLES:

NO CHANGE

I watch TV.   She   **tells** us that she **watches** TV.
                She **has told** us that she **watches** TV.
                She **will tell** us that she **watches** TV.

CHANGE

I **shall watch** TV.	She **said** that she **would watch** TV.
I **watch** TV.	She **said** that she **watched** TV.
I **have watched** TV.	She **said** that she **had watched** TV.
I **watched** TV.	She **said** that she **had watched** TV.

If the fact reported is still true there may be no change:

> I **watch** TV every evening. She **said** that she **watches** TV every evening.

But this is not a 'rule'. Very often the tenses change by convention, and we may get:

> She **said** a moment ago that she **watched** TV every evening and that she **wasn't** going to miss it tonight.

(ii) It is necessary to distinguish between a **suggestion** and a **question** about the **future**.

> 'Shall I call a taxi?' is a suggestion.
> 'Shall I ever speak English well?' asks about the future.

See 'D' above for the way in which to report these two sentences.

(iii) In 'C' and 'D' above, **whether** may be used instead of **if**.

(iv) Certain time words may change in reported speech. The most important of these are: today (that day), yesterday (the previous day, the day before), tomorrow (the following day, the next day). But much will depend on the time of reporting.

(v) Compare the following sentences to see how **must** and **needn't** are reported:

> direct: I **must** go to Miami **tomorrow**.   (shall have to)
> reported: Jim said he **would have to** go to Miami **the next day**.

> direct: I **needn't** go to Miami **tomorrow**.   (shan't have to)
> reported: Jim said he **wouldn't have to** go to Miami **the next day**.

> direct: I **must** go to Miami **now**.   (have to)
> reported: Jim said he **had to** go to Miami **immediately**.

> direct: I **needn't** go to Miami **now**.   (don't have to)
> reported: Jim said he **didn't have to** go to Miami **immediately**.

372

To practise reported present tense statements, respond as shown. (With reporting verbs marked (*) it is better not to omit the conjunctive that.)

I'm having a party. What did John say?
He said (that) he was having a party.

John doesn't go away very often. What did Sue mention?
She mentioned that John didn't go away very often.

David's in London on business. What did Richard tell you?
He told me (that) David was in London on business.

1. I must go to New York. What did I say?
2. Tom has to get a car. What did Bob say?
3. You needn't go. What did Henry tell Bob?
4. David can't swim. What did John tell you?
5. Sally's got to leave. What did Peter say?
6. Bob should be at home. What did Susan say?
7. Jill's not working. What did the teacher say?
8. Mary may be at the meeting. What did Tom say?
9. John has many friends. What did Jane tell you?
10. Joe's having a lot of fun. What did Jim mention?*
11. You're quite fit. What did the doctor assure you?
12. Jim doesn't watch football. What did Joe tell you?
13. Tom doesn't do his homework. What did Bob tell you?
14. Smoking's bad for you. What did the doctor warn* Jim?
15. We keep mail for guests. What did the girl tell you?
16. Bob must have an operation. What did the surgeon say?
17. The blue car's the best. What did the salesman state?*
18. There's a political crisis. What did the man announce?*
19. The pump's not working. What did the mechanic explain?*
20. Tom's to be made captain. What did the newspaper report?*

To practise changes in statements with tenses other than the present tense, respond as shown. (* = It is better not to omit that.)

I shall watch TV. What did John say?
He said (that) he would watch TV.

Mary has been in Canada. What did Sally mention?
She mentioned* that Mary had been in Canada.

Helen handed the envelope to Jim. What did John assure you?
He assured me (that) Helen had handed the envelope to Jim.

1. I shan't be late. What did Jim promise?
2. Tom hurt himself. What did Bob tell you?
3. I'll have some salad. What did Peter say?
4. I'll have to see Sally. What did Paul say?
5. Tom's always been early. What did Jane say?
6. Joe ordered a beer. What did John tell Mary?
7. We tried to rescue the boy. What did Bob say?
8. Bob's going to hire a car. What did Betty say?
9. The car was stolen. What did the policeman say?
10. I've bought a new suit. What did John tell Dick?
11. I'll take my holiday soon. What did Jane promise?
12. Bob's had his interview. What did John tell Peter?
13. Paul hesitated before going in. What did Susan say?
14. Joe will be coming tomorrow. What did Bob point out?*
15. We'll win next time. What did the politician promise?
16. I'll be able to see Tom later. What did John tell Bob?
17. Paul hasn't taken out any insurance. What did Jack say?
18. Dick made me walk home. What did Mary tell David?
19. The cost of living's gone up. What did the paper report?*
20. I'll have enough money for a house. What did Bill mention?*

---

277 Reported Speech   I

To practise reported imperatives respond as shown:

Shut the window. What did Richard ask Sheila?
He asked her to shut the window.

Don't come home late again. What did Bob warn Jane?
He warned her not to come home late again.

374

Speak English all the time. What did Jim advise you?
He advised me to speak English all the time.

Don't make so much noise. What did the nurse tell you?
She told me not to make so much noise.

1. Do me a favour. What did Helen ask David?
2. Turn on the lights. What did Jim ask Paul?
3. Make up your mind. What did Mary tell John?
4. Fly to Bermuda. What did Paul advise Susan?
5. Don't run so fast. What did Betty ask Paul?
6. Fix the door. What did Jim tell the workmen?
7. Don't be late. What did Gordon advise Peter?
8. Have lunch early. What did Dick remind John?
9. Don't forget me. What did Marion ask Gordon?
10. Help me with my work. What did Tom ask Peter?
11. Don't sit there. What did Mr Green tell Paul?
12. Get rid of it. What did Mrs Smith tell George?
13. Stand up. What did the officer order Jim to do?
14. Come and see me. What did Bob invite Tom to do?
15. Don't work so hard. What did Sheila beg Robert?
16. Introduce me to Jane. What did John ask Sandra?
17. Open your mouth. What did the dentist tell Paul?
18. Don't wear a bikini. What did Allan tell Angela?
19. Have another one. What did Tom invite Jim to do?
20. Don't give up hope yet. What did Joe advise Bob?

---

278 Reported Speech   IA

To practise reported questions, respond as shown:

What time does the bus leave? Paul asked Joe —
Paul asked Joe what time the bus left.

Are you coming to the meeting? Tom asked me —
Tom asked me if/whether I was going to the meeting.

How many cigarettes do you have a day? John asked me —
John asked me how many cigarettes I had a day.

Will Bob be in class tomorrow? Mary asked Jim —
Mary asked Jim if/whether Bob would be in class the next day.

1. Must you go now? Bill asked Mary —
2. Is there a bar here? I asked John —

3. What's Jane really like? Tom asked us —
4. Does Bob know what time it is? I asked Joe —
5. Must Paul leave tomorrow? Peter asked Sally —
6. Will you be coming tomorrow? Jim asked Peter —
7. When did you lose your key? Jane asked Philip —
8. Why did you get such low marks? Bob asked Jim —
9. Has there been a message for me? Tom asked Joe —
10. Will you give me some help? The boy asked Jane —
11. Do I have to do all the work now? Paul asked me —
12. Have you used this camera before? John asked Tom —
13. How can I get to the station? The girl asked Mary —
14. Whose car is that outside? The policeman asked us —
15. Does it have to be so untidy here? Jane asked Paul —
16. Did you do any studying yesterday? David asked John —
17. Have I to return the books tomorrow? Joan asked Paul —
18. How many children have you got? The inspector asked me —
19. Who was the last owner of the car? I asked the salesman —
20. How much can I draw out now? Joe asked his bank manager —

---

279 Reported Speech   IA

To contrast reported suggestions and questions about the future, respond as shown:

Shall I open the window? Sally asked — (suggestion)
Sally asked if she should open the window.

Shall I have an answer soon? Peter wanted to know — (future)
Peter wanted to know if he would have an answer soon.

Shall I switch off the light? Jim wanted to know — (suggestion)
Jim wanted to know if he should switch off the light.

Shall we be able to use this tape-recorder tomorrow? Paul asked the electrician — (future)
Paul asked the electrician if they would be able to use the tape-recorder the following day.

1. Shall I call a taxi? Henry asked —
2. Shall I answer the door? Sally asked —
3. Shall we have the window open? Pat asked —
4. Shall I ever see you again? Jane asked Bob —
5. Shall I get a letter tomorrow? Betty wondered —
6. Shall we make the beds now? Pat wanted to know —
7. Shall I read that book? Mary asked her teacher —
8. Shall we hear from Bob soon? Sheila asked Sally —
9. Shall I come tomorrow as usual? Richard wondered —
10. Shall we get the TV set back soon? Sheila asked —
11. Shall I switch on the fire? Gordon wanted to know —
12. Shall I ever know English perfectly? Jim wondered —
13. Shall I see you tomorrow? Elizabeth asked Richard —
14. Shall I pull the curtains? Patricia wanted to know —
15. Shall we get any more phone calls this evening? Jim asked Mary —

THE GERUND

Introductory notes:
The gerund is a verbal noun. Compare the following:

I'm **swimming**.
I like **swimming**.

The first **swimming** is a present participle. The second is a gerund, the object of the verb **like**.

(i) The gerund after certain verbs:

EXAMPLES:
I **enjoy dancing**.
/ai in'dʒɔi `dɑːnsiŋ/

She **hates playing** tennis.
/ʃi 'heits 'pleiiŋ `tenis/

They **remember doing** the work.

(ii) The gerund after prepositions:

EXAMPLES:
I'm interested **in learning** English.
/aim 'intristid in 'ləːniŋ `iŋgliʃ/

She's used **to being** married.

She's tired **of** always **doing** the same thing.

(iii) The gerund as subject of a sentence:

EXAMPLES:
Having breakfast at 12 noon is a bad habit.
(Cf. It is a bad habit **to have** breakfast at 12 noon.)

Going to class late annoys the teacher.
(Cf. It annoys the teacher **if/when** you **go** to class late.)

(iv) The perfect gerund:

EXAMPLES:
He remembers **having been** to Japan when he was very young.

He forgets **having posted** the letters.

(v) The passive gerund:

EXAMPLES:
She tries to avoid **being seen** by her ex-husband.

She likes **being taken** out to dinner.

He resents not **having been invited** to the party.

(vi) The gerund as a modifier (adjective):

EXAMPLES:
This car has no **starting** handle.
/ðis 'kɑː hæz 'nəu ˋstɑːtiŋ hændl/

She has reached **breaking** point.

He likes to sit in a **rocking** chair.

(When we use a gerund attributively we place a primary stress on it. A present participle used in this way may have less stress than the following noun. See Note Aiib on page 388.)

(vii) The gerund preceded by the accusative personal pronoun:

EXAMPLES:
John hit Bob yesterday.

I can't understand **him wanting** to do that.

I tried to stop **him hitting** Bob.
(Cf. I tried to stop **his hitting** Bob. (also **John's hitting**).)

The possessive form is rather formal and is not often found in colloquial English.

---

280 The Gerund   EI

(a) *Give complete 'yes' or 'no' answers to the following:*
Do you enjoy learning English?
Yes. I enjoy learning English.

Do you like travelling to foreign countries?
Yes. I like travelling to foreign countries.

Can you remember doing this exercise before?
No. I can't remember doing (having done) this exercise before.

1. Do you like dancing?
2. Do you enjoy swimming?
3. Could you give up smoking?
4. Will you start working hard?
5. Can you avoid making mistakes?
6. Do you want to stop wasting time?
7. Do you fancy going out this evening?
8. Do you enjoy being taken out to dinner?
9. Do you avoid speaking to English people?
10. Do you keep on making the same mistakes?
11. Do you remember locking your door last night?
12. Do you fancy watching television this evening?
13. Did you finish dressing before 9 this morning?
14. Can you resist eating things that are bad for you?
15. Is it any use expecting to learn English in a month?

(b) *For further practice in using the gerund after certain verbs, respond as shown:*

What does John dislike? (work)
He dislikes working.

What do you remember? (see Mary)
I remember seeing Mary.

What did Mary enjoy? (be taken out)
She enjoyed being taken out.

1. What don't you mind? (wait)
2. What does Peter enjoy? (skate)
3. What did Paul stop doing? (drink)
4. What can't Bob resist? (tell jokes)
5. What did Henry deny? (take the books)
6. What can't Jim stand? (be interrupted)
7. What did you finish doing? (take notes)
8. What can't you help doing? (make mistakes)
9. What can't you imagine? (John come on time)
10. What does Sally detest? (people ask her age)

11. What do you appreciate? (you want to help me)
12. What don't you remember? (see that film before)
13. What will you try to avoid? (be late in future)
14. What won't Peter tolerate? (Bob use bad language)
15. What did Tom want to postpone? (sign the contract)
16. What can you understand? (Jane not want to see Bob)
17. What does Philip dislike? (Sheila wear a mini-skirt)
18. What does Tim regret? (ask Mary to the party)
19. What did John admit? (take my car without permission)
20. What do you fancy doing tonight? (go out for a drink)

---

281 The Gerund   I

Use the gerund to connect the following:

You went to the club with Mary. I can't understand it.
You can't understand me/my going to the club with Mary.

Peter took Anne to the theatre last night. He enjoyed it.
Peter enjoyed taking Anne to the theatre last night.

(a) 1. You want to help me. I appreciate it.
     2. Brian has to stay in bed. He detests it.
     3. Peter's sometimes late. He can't help it.
     4. Gordon has to get up early. He dislikes it.
     5. Paul asked Mary to come home. He remembers it.
     6. Bob has an interview tomorrow. He mentioned it.
     7. Sheila's trying to get the car going. It's no use.
     8. The police say that John saw the girl. He denies it.
     9. Jill occasionally speaks Spanish. She can't avoid it.
    10. Richard took the books home with him. He admitted it.
    11. Jim didn't take his holiday until May. He delayed it.
    12. Mr Chips drives a sports car? I can't imagine it.
    13. Jim was speaking French when Bob came in. He
        stopped.
    14. Don doesn't think he's met Sue. He can't remember it.
    15. John doesn't want to be stared at. He can't stand it.

(b) *As (a) above (further practice)*

     1. Something was creeping up behind me. I sensed it.
     2. Jim wanted to see the race. He didn't want to miss it.
     3. I shall have to do that exercise again. I can't face it.

4. We shall have to spend the night there. Just imagine it.
5. Peter calls on Mary at about tea time. He can't resist it.
6. Bob would like to spend the evening with Sue. He fancies it.
7. I had lunch with an Italian film star. I'll never forget it.
8. John didn't take Mary out last night. I can't understand it.
9. You may have an accident if you drive that car. You risk it.
10. David wasn't told that he was to be dismissed. He resents it.
11. Mary wanted to have dinner at a restaurant. She suggested it.
12. Don't ask Richard to lend you his tape-recorder. It's no use.
13. You should speak English all the time. You should practise it.
14. Bob doesn't want to make a big profit. I can't understand it.
15. Students demonstrate in the town. The authorities won't tolerate it.

282 The Gerund   IA

Peter is	interested in		learning English.
John is	tired	of	having to listen to Mary.
David is **not** used		to	seeing Anne in a mini-skirt.
Bill was	ashamed	of	having made mistakes.
Paul is	angry	about not being	invited to the party.

Notes:
(i) The gerund is used in the above sentences because of the preceding preposition. The preposition is not stressed:

Mary's afraid of catching cold.
/ˈmɛəriz əˈfreid əv ˈkætʃiŋ ˈkəuld/

(ii) The gerund may also follow adverbial particles.

EXAMPLES:
We put **off going** until the last moment.

She went **on speaking** for an hour.

Bob's going to give **up smoking**.
/ˈbɔbz gəuiŋ tə ˈgiv ˈʌp ˈsməukiŋ/

To practise using the gerund after prepositions, respond as shown:

David's studying. He's bored —
David's bored with studying.

Pat lives in a small hotel. She's accustomed —
Pat's accustomed to living in a small hotel.

Richard doesn't speak English well. He has difficulty —
Richard has difficulty in speaking English well.

(a) 1. Bob's often laughed at. He's used —
    2. Jim came home early. I was surprised —
    3. Harry has lunch late. He's accustomed —
    4. Sheila breaks dishes. She has the habit —
    5. Paul passed his exams. He was successful —
    6. Gordon likes to watch football. He's keen —
    7. Michael tells Susan he loves her. He's fond —
    8. Peter wants to learn English. He's interested —
    9. Susan made a 'scene' in public. She's ashamed —
   10. Betty can't do the homework. She's not capable —
   11. George wants to be promoted. He has little hope —
   12. Jim went out when I came in. He was on the point —
   13. Sheila keeps her own room tidy. She's responsible —
   14. Richard wasn't sent an invitation. He was furious —
   15. Jim hoped to see Lucy yesterday. He was optimistic —

(b) *As* (a) *above (further practice).*

    1. John has to get up early. He's used —
    2. Richard may not win. He's apprehensive —
    3. Sally will visit her aunt. She's excited —
    4. Allan has to do all the cooking. He's not happy —
    5. Susan will meet Gordon. She's looking forward —
    6. Joe audits the firm's accounts. He's responsible —
    7. Paul doesn't want to be misunderstood. He's afraid —
    8. Mary's gone off on her own. Her friends are anxious —
    9. Pat doesn't know how to speak English. She's worried —
   10. Jane has to do the housework by herself. She's tired —
   11. Richard's not been given a rise in salary. He's angry —
   12. Alice is often let down by her boy-friend. She's used —
   13. John wants to keep his promise. He may have difficulty —

14. George won't be able to see Patricia. There's no chance —
15. I'll have to tell Jim the bad news. I'm not enthusiastic —

---

283 The Gerund IA

To practise the gerund as subject of the sentence, respond as shown:

I shall have a swim. It will cool me down.
Yes. Having a swim will cool you down.

Tom doesn't have a car. It's frustrating for him.
Yes. Not having a car is frustrating for Tom.

You speak English well. It requires a lot of practice.
Yes. Speaking English well requires a lot of practice.

1. Jim watches TV. It's his favourite occupation.
2. Jim gave up smoking. It was very difficult for him.
3. John listens to English records. It helps him a lot.
4. Bob reads in a bad light. It's very bad for the eyes.
5. Jim's had a book published. It's made him big-headed.
6. You want to build a house here. It would be a mistake.
7. Tom has to wear a suit. It makes him feel overdressed.
8. Anne does some exercises every day. It keeps her young.
9. Betty didn't know if she'd passed. It made her nervous.
10. Sheila gives presents. It's her way of saying 'thanks'.
11. John got Jill to clean the house. It required patience.
12. Let's go out today. It will give us a much-needed break.
13. I shall type the letter. It will make it easier to read.
14. John has to write home every week. It bores him to tears.
15. You should read a newspaper. It will keep you up to date.
16. Bob had the day off. It meant that he could visit Sandra.
17. Richard does Sally's homework for her. It keeps him busy.
18. Bill likes to water-ski. It keeps him fit during the summer.
19. Anne looks after five children. It keeps her fully occupied.
20. Mary gets letters from Jim. It makes her feel less home-sick.

Note:
Certain verbs in English may be followed by the gerund **or** the infinitive. Compare the following:

I **prefer watching** TV to going to the cinema.
I **prefer to watch** TV tonight if you don't mind.

I **hate seeing** women in trousers.
I should **hate to see** my wife in trousers.

The manager doesn't **allow dancing** in the bar.
The manager doesn't **allow** anyone **to dance** in the bar.

I don't actually **remember locking** the back door last night.
I know I **remembered to lock** the back door on Tuesday night.

Richard will never **forget driving** all night in that storm.
Americans sometimes **forget to drive** on the left in England.

Sue **tried giving** her husband Chinese food, but he hated it.
Patrick **tried to give** Mary a kiss and she slapped his face.

The economic situation **meant** everybody **having** to work hard.
John **meant to have** a walk yesterday, but he felt too tired.

Choose between the gerund and the infinitive when linking the following (*in some cases either may be used*):

I didn't make that phone call. I forgot —
I forgot to make that phone call.

Jim doesn't think he's met Bob before. He doesn't remember —
Jim doesn't remember meeting Bob before.
(or: . . . **having met** . . .)

Mary wants to make plans for the weekend. She would like —
Mary would like to make plans for the weekend.

    1. George learnt English at the age of ten. He began —
    2. Mary will stay with a family. Being 'Au pair' means —
    3. Gordon couldn't get the top off the bottle. He tried —

4. I must speak to Henry before he leaves. I must remember —
5. Mary wanted to do her shopping before 11 a.m. She meant —
6. David wants Anne to have dinner with him. She would love —
7. Jim often has to see animals in captivity. He can't bear —
8. I want to go to the play with you tonight. I should like —
9. The builder wants to erect a block of flats. He proposes —
10. Have a good look at the house first. The agent advised us —
11. Peter has to make his own bed and tidy his room. He hates —
12. The chairman spoke in spite of interruptions. He continued —
13. Nobody may smoke in that room. The regulations don't allow —
14. I have to tell you that there's been an accident. I regret —
15. You could open that bottle by heating the neck. Why not try —
16. The secretary didn't take the documents with her. She forgot —
17. It's dangerous for you to go there alone. I shouldn't advise —
18. Betty saw Richard driving in the race. She will never forget —
19. Mr Smith wants to set up a new factory here. He's considering —
20. Patrick has chosen to go on holiday in January. He will regret —
21. Sheila has her friends round on Saturday afternoons. She loves —
22. Bob didn't tell me he'd had an accident with my car. He forgot —
23. I opened the door, went in and turned on the light. I remember —
24. Peter couldn't spend the weekend in London. Betty didn't allow —
25. Jim wanted to search the flat for the lost papers. He suggested —

GERUNDS (AND PARTICIPLES) AS ADJECTIVES

Introductory notes:

(i) We can distinguish between gerunds and present participles used attributively (before nouns) by asking what the person or thing is doing. For example, of the expression 'shopping basket' (gerund) we cannot ask 'What is the basket doing?' because the answer 'shopping' is nonsense. But of the expression 'boiling water' (participle) we can ask 'What is the water doing?' because 'boiling' makes sense. Now ask the question 'What is the basket for?' The answer 'shopping' makes sense.

(ii) In speech, we usually place a primary stress on the noun when a present participle is used attributively, and a primary stress on the gerund when this is used attributively. The present participle may have a primary or secondary stress.

285a Gerunds as Adjectives　　　　　　　　　　　　　　　　　E

Answer the following questions, as shown:

What are those boats used for? (sail)
They're for sailing; they're sailing boats. / ˈseiliŋbəuts/

What's that mirror used for? (drive)
It's used for driving; it's a driving-mirror. / ˈdraiviŋmirə/

What's that basket used for? (shop)
It's used for shopping; it's a shopping basket. / ˈʃɔpiŋbɑːskit/

1. boat (row)
2. list (shop)
3. machine (sew)
4. place (meet)
5. tablets (sleep)
6. needle (knit)
7. costume (swim)
8. room (change)
9. utensil (cook)
10. paper (write)
11. gloves (drive)
12. pool (swim)
13. room (sit)
14. implement (garden)
15. device (record)
16. short (run)
17. iron (solder)
18. needle (darn)
19. room (read)
20. fluid (clean)
21. cupboard (air)
22. machine (teach)
23. tool (cut)
24. can (water)
25. machine (wash)
26. office (book)
27. stick (walk)
28. machine (weigh)
29. well (wish)
30. board (iron)

Rephrase the following, as shown:

The year that's coming.

The coming year. /ðə ˈkʌmiŋ ˈjəː/

A woman who's sleeping.

A sleeping woman. /ə ˈsliːpiŋ ˋwumən/

Weather that's freezing.

Freezing weather. /ˈfriːziŋ ˋwəðə/

1. A child who's running.
2. A house that's burning.
3. A play that excites.
4. A flower that's dying.
5. A boy who's growing.
6. A remark that insults.
7. The week that's coming.
8. A person who charms.
9. A film that thrills.
10. A woman who fascinates.
11. An inquiry that searches.
12. A time that was amusing.
13. A woman who was crying.
14. A child who's laughing.
15. An experience that terrified.
16. A programme that entertains.
17. A story that interests.
18. A look that seems to inquire.
19. A proposition that will pay me.
20. A proposition that will make money.

THE PARTICIPLES

Introductory notes:

Participial patterns:

A. (i) As part of the continuous form of the verb.

> EXAMPLES:
>
> John is **thinking** about Mary just now.
>
> Paul was **living** in Spain last year.
>
> Peter has been **teaching** English.

(ii) Adjectivally.

EXAMPLES:
(a) The man **sitting** on the sofa was a doctor.
The woman **driving** the car was Sheila.
The people **attending** the conference are here.

(b) It was a **thrilling** programme.
He has a **fighting** chance.

I've just heard a **disturbing** rumour.
/aiv 'dʒʌst 'hɜːd ə dis'tɜːbiŋ 'ruːmə/

(iii) After verbs of perception.

EXAMPLES:
I heard him **singing**.

She saw Susan **leaving**.

Mary watched Peter **drinking**.

(iv) To replace an adverbial clause of cause (not very common in informal conversation).

Events in parallel: **Being** ill, she stayed in bed.
(As she was ill, she stayed in bed.)

Events in sequence: **Having been** ill, she took it easy for a few days. (As she had been ill, ...)

(v) In adverbial clauses of time (not very common in informal conversation).

EXAMPLE:
(While) **running** down the road he bumped into Jim.
(Cf. He bumped into Jim **running** down the road.)

(vi) To replace the present perfect or past perfect tense (not common in conversation).

EXAMPLES:
Having typed the letter, Mary gave it to Peter to sign.
(When she *had* typed the letter ...)

Having typed the letter, Mary *will* give it to Peter to sign.
(When she *has* typed the letter ...)

B. The past participle is used:
(i) To form certain tenses, the passive voice and the perfect infinitives.

EXAMPLES:
I have **been** to India.

He has **travelled** a long way.

388

She was **asked** to leave.

They should have **come** to class.

He ought to have **known** the answer.

(ii) Adjectivally ('b' is not common in informal conversation).

EXAMPLES:
(a) The book **borrowed** from the library was the wrong one.
The man **dismissed** from his job had refused to do any work.

(b) **Discarded** by its owner, the old suitcase lay in the gutter.
Given only six months to live, John decided to use up his savings on a world cruise.

(c) She made a **pointed** remark.
He looked for a **hidden** meaning.
They hunted for the **lost** gold.
She has an **upset** stomach.

---

286 The Participles I

Notes:
(i) The patterns practised in this exercise are useful in formal speaking. For informal occasions most people use a clause rather than a participle structure.

(ii) Modern English avoids using a non-defining participle structure between subject and verb as is common in a number of other languages. We do not say: 'Jim, seeing his chance, accelerated hard', but:

(Formal narrative)	**Seeing his chance**, Jim accelerated hard.
(Informally)	Jim saw his chance and accelerated hard.

This does not apply to a defining structure:

(Formal narrative)	The policeman **directing the traffic** looked tired.
(Informally)	The policeman who was directing the traffic looked tired.

To practise related participles. Decide which noun the participle relates to before giving your response.

The typist looked at the woman. She was dictating the letter.

The typist looked at the woman dictating the letter.

389

Jim thought about his teacher. He was preparing for his exam.

(While) preparing for his exam, Jim thought about his teacher.

The man wanted to see the doctor. He was sitting in the waiting-room.

The man sitting in the waiting-room wanted to see the doctor.

1. The actress opened the magazine. She was lying in bed.
2. The driver watched the mechanic. He was repairing his car.
3. The dentist examined the patient. He was holding his drill.
4. The watchman noticed an intruder. He was hiding near a shed.
5. Sheila went up to the lady. She was standing by the counter.
6. Peter saw the pilot come in. He was chatting to a passenger.
7. The manager interviewed the man. He was applying for the job.
8. Sally spoke sharply to the woman. She was using her telephone.
9. The surgeon operated on the man. He was suffering from a cold.
10. The men addressed the crowd. They were standing on a platform.
11. Bob spoke to the cinema manager. He was waiting to see the film.
12. The doctor looked at the patient. He was sitting behind his desk.
13. The man saw the director. He was coming out of the board meeting.
14. The engineer saw the customer. He was repairing a television set.
15. The author approached the publisher. He was hoping to have his book accepted.

---

287 The Participles   IA

To contrast events in sequence and events in parallel, respond as shown:

390

I was in New York. I was able to attend the exhibition.
Being in New York, I was able to attend the exhibition.
I saw New York. I was able to tell everyone at home all
    about it.
**Having seen New York, I was able to tell everyone at home
all about it.**

1. Anne was frightened. She ran.
2. I had breakfast. I was not hungry.
3. Mary was downstairs. She heard the bell.
4. Tom was given a map. He knew where to go.
5. Jean was at the counter. She was able to serve Bob.
6. I connected the radio to the mains. I switched it on.
7. Philip saw the film. He was able to tell Jim about it.
8. Joe is not a teacher. He cannot answer those questions.
9. Sheila finished making the dress. She showed it to Barry.
10. George was in love. He decided to ask Rosemary to
    marry him.
11. I did not have any matches. I was not able to light the
    fire.
12. Patricia has just woken up. She is in no mood for Tom's
    jokes.
13. Peter has not been given the facts. He cannot make a
    decision.
14. Gordon is a doctor. He is very often called out late at
    night.
15. John has not met David. He would not be able to
    recognise him.

---

288 The Participles   **IA**

---

*Further practice in contrasting the present participle with the
pattern:* having + *past participle.*

I did not see the letter. I did not know what it was about.
Not having seen the letter, I did not know what it was about.
Jim looked quickly through the book. He noticed that there
    were a number of illustrations in it.
**(While) looking quickly through the book, Jim noticed that
there were a number of illustrations in it.**

1. Bob heard the bad news. He rang up Mary.
2. John went to bed. He did not want to be disturbed.

391

3. Andrew drove around London last week. He got lost.
4. Jim walked down the street yesterday. He met Sally.
5. Tom did not have anything to drink. He drove home safely.
6. Allan did not have a wink of sleep. He felt very irritable.
7. Richard washed the dishes. He dried them and put them away.
8. Peter found both computers fully occupied. He took a break.
9. John went to Canada by sea last week. He fell overboard and was drowned.
10. Jim listened to the rain. He remembered that sunny weather had been forecast.
11. Mrs Smith finished preparing the meal. She called the family in from the garden.
12. The mechanic did not service the car. He could not tell the owner it was ready.
13. Paul made up his mind what to do. He rolled up his sleeves and set to work.
14. Mary watched the procession. She saw a woman faint in the crowd opposite her.
15. Richard typed the manuscript. He wondered how the critics would view the play.
16. Henry did not order a newspaper. He should not have expected one to be delivered.
17. I read the Stock Exchange page in my newspaper. I noticed that prices had fallen.
18. Bob studied his course book. He realised that he had little hope of passing the exam.
19. Anne did her shopping in the morning. She was able to put her feet up for most of the afternoon.
20. Sally was talked into buying an expensive encyclopedia. She decided to read it from cover to cover.

---

289 The Participles   A

The pattern: having + *past participle is practised in Exs. 287 and 288. In this exercise this pattern is again practised, but is restricted to the participial construction replacing an adverbial clause of cause (e.g. 'As Jill had been away, . . .' = 'Jill having been away, . . .') and is contrasted with the present participle pattern (e.g. 'As Jim was in the house, . . .' = 'Jim being in the house, . . .'). It should be noted that these participial patterns are mostly found in written English.*

Note:
It and **there** may be used in subject position in this pattern.

EXAMPLES:
It having rained heavily during the night, there was no racing the following day.

There being nobody at home, Jim decided to go out.

It was cold. No one went out.
It being cold, no one went out.

John was ill. Peter had to do two men's work.
John being ill, Peter had to do two men's work.

You know John. You can tell me something about him.
Knowing John (as you do), you can tell me something about him.

There was no demand for the product. The firm had to close down.
There being no demand for the product, the firm had to close down.

1. All the work was done. The men went home.
2. Jim had nothing better to do. He mowed the lawn.
3. It was sunny. Jill decided to sit out on the grass.
4. The television set broke down. I went to bed early.
5. Bob was late. He slipped in quietly through the back door.
6. It was very warm indoors. Everyone worked in shirt-sleeves.
7. George married Sally Brown. Gordon had to find some-one else.
8. Jim had a lot of homework to do. He decided to stay at home.
9. Bob's wife died. He was left with three children to bring up.
10. Bob did not know the time. He had a look at the station clock.
11. There was someone in the next room. Jim did not want to go in.

12. Peter took a degree in English. Harry decided to do the same.
13. You cannot understand Latin. You cannot translate these stories.
14. The telephones were out of order. Nobody knew what was happening.
15. You know this town well. You can take us round. (use: as you do)
16. Jim did not want to make any mistakes. He paid careful attention.
17. You are a heavy smoker. You know how difficult it is to give up the habit.
18. There was no chance of a peace settlement. The Government broke off negotiations.
19. Michael has not been to Russia. He cannot tell you anything about the way of life there.
20. Betty did not have time to go into the town. She asked for the goods to be delivered.

VERBS FOLLOWED BY THE INFINITIVE OR —ing FORM

290 INTERMEDIATE/ADVANCED

VERB + OBJECT + INFINITIVE			VERB + OBJECT + —ING FORM		
I saw	Mary	sit down.	I saw	Mary	sitting down.
I heard	Jill	cry out.	I heard	Jill	crying.
I felt	the car	stop.	I felt	the car	losing speed.
I noticed	Richard	drop a pen.	I noticed	Richard	falling.

Notes:
(i) The use of the infinitive in this pattern indicates that the whole action is perceived. The speaker is interested in its accomplishment.

The use of the —ing form indicates that only a part of the action is perceived. The speaker's interest is in the action rather than its completion.

(ii) Certain verbs are followed by the —*ing* form only.

I **caught** him **trying** to steal my car.

I **found** her **lying** on her bed.

To contrast the use of the —ing *form and the infinitive without* to. *If it is possible to use either, discuss the situation or add context.*

The woman dropped her handkerchief. Jim noticed it.
Jim noticed the woman drop her handkerchief.

John left his car outside my house. I saw him.
You saw John leaving (or leave) his car outside your house.

They had a party in the flat above last night. I heard them.
You heard them having a party in the flat above last night.

1. Peter skated yesterday. I watched him.
2. The doctor examined my knee. I felt it.
3. Mary dropped her watch. Philip saw her.
4. The train began to move. George felt it.
5. The ship left the harbour. Robert saw it.
6. The guard blew his whistle. David heard it.
7. The rope slipped from her grasp. Sue felt it.
8. Paul sprained an ankle. The spectators saw it.
9. The man broke a shop window. Peter noticed him.
10. Peter came out of Sheila's room. Sheila saw him.
11. Mrs Brown came down the stairs. David watched her.
12. David shaved in the next room. Mary could hear him.
13. The singer rehearsed for the show. Richard heard him.
14. Sandra sat down and then got up again. I noticed her.
15. The crowd waited to get into the grounds. John saw it.
16. The conference delegates left the hall. Gordon saw them.
17. Sally burnt the roast beef in the oven. She could smell it.
18. The managing director stood up to speak. Gordon noticed him.
19. A demonstrator was taken to the police station. John saw him.
20. The salesman sat in his car and examined his papers. I watched him.

VERBS FOLLOWED BY THE INFINITIVE WITHOUT 'TO'
(Let, Make and Have)

Compare the following:

VERB + TO-INFINITIVE	VERB + INFINITIVE (without **to**)
I permit Jim **to see** Mary.	**I let** him **see** Mary.
I forced Bob **to stop** smoking.	**I made** him **stop** smoking.
I got Tom **to mow** the lawn.	**I had** him **mow** the lawn.
I helped Sue **to do** her work.	**I helped** her **do** her work.

Note:
(i) There is no significant difference in meaning between the verbs **permit/let, force/make, get/have** in this pattern. The difference is a structural one.

(ii) See Ex. 253 Note on the subject of British–English and the causative use of **have**.

To practise and contrast the above patterns, respond as shown:

John had the day off. His manager let him —
John's manager let him have the day off.

Harry stopped drinking. Elizabeth got him —
Elizabeth got Harry to stop drinking.

Jim cut some flowers for Sue. She made him —
Sue made Jim cut her some flowers.

1. George washed the dishes. Mary got him —
2. Bob gave John's van a push. John asked him —
3. Gordon had to repeat the exercise. I made him —
4. Peter came back from work early. Anne told him —
5. Susan can do anything she wants. David lets her —
6. Paul had to give up smoking. His doctor made him —
7. Peter read the article twice. The teacher let him —
8. Philip redecorated the whole house. Sheila got him —
9. Richard spoke to the Institute. The director got him —
10. Sally can have a holiday now. Mrs Smith will let her —

11. Jane wanted Bill to keep an eye on Paul. She made him —
12. John told his sister the truth. His sister forced him —
13. George drove Bob to the station yesterday. Bob got him —
14. Children can stay out late at night. Parents permit them —
15. Tom wanted John to help him move the piano. Tom got him —
16. Helen got the room ready for the party. Bill helped her —
17. Sheila chose the pattern for the dress. Alice asked her —
18. Pat decided on the kitchen equipment. Her husband let her —
19. Lucy met David at the station with the car. David got her —
20. Mary told Peter to find out the arrival time. She made him —

'Not' Before and after certain verbs

---

292 INTERMEDIATE/ADVANCED

John did	**not try**	to improve his accent.
Jill **tried**	**not**	to make any mistakes.
I	can**not promise**	to arrive very early.
You **promised not**		to repeat that to Sue.

Note:
A double negative may be used:

EXAMPLE:
Jim can**not** promise **not** to make that mistake again.
   (Cf. Jim cannot promise that he will not make that mistake again.)

To practise placing not *before and after certain verbs.*

Isn't Betty in? (seem)
She doesn't seem to be in. (or: . . . seems not . . .)

Will you call in at the grocer's for me? (promise)
I can't promise to call in at the grocer's for you.

Jim's not going to exceed the speed limit, is he? (try)
He'll try not to exceed the speed limit.

1. Did Joe say he would come? (promise)
2. Did Betty answer every question? (try)
3. Isn't Harry coming home next week? (plan)
4. Doesn't Sheila like this exercise? (appear)
5. Don't you like to discuss politics? (prefer)
6. Doesn't Michael understand the lesson? (seem)
7. Will you be at the meeting next week? (promise)
8. Don't you want to visit Canada next year? (plan)
9. Did John get very brown when on holiday? (appear)
10. Does Jim interfere when Mary's in trouble? (learn)
11. Do you think Tom will bother Mary again? (promise)
12. Didn't Peter want to watch the play on TV? (seem)
13. Doesn't Bob wish to stay on at university? (intend)
14. Don't you know where you're going tomorrow? (decide)
15. Isn't Sheila going to play tennis tomorrow? (intend)
16. Doesn't John wish to emigrate to the U.S.A.? (decide)
17. Did the spectators hear what the announcer said? (seem)
18. Isn't Anne going out with Jimmy tomorrow evening? (plan)
19. Did Sandra show Peter that she was angry with him? (try)
20. Can't Paul sail a boat without an instructor yet? (learn)
21. You're not going to forget Bill's birthday, are you? (try)
22. You'll remember to come to the party, won't you? (promise)
23. Does Sandra object when her husband smokes in bed? (prefer)
24. Is Robert going to the office-equipment exhibition? (decide)
25. Does Gordon still make mistakes when speaking English? (try)

The Infinitive Particle 'To' Used Alone

293 INTERMEDIATE/ADVANCED

Jim should work tomorrow, but he doesn't want **to.**
David didn't come to class, but he'd intended **to.**
Mary was planning to leave, but she's decided **not to.**

Notes:
(i) The **to** in this pattern is unstressed but it often has the strong
pronunciation /tuː/, which students are advised to use.

   Paul and Richard don't want to.
   /'pɔːl ənd 'ritʃəd 'dəunt `wɔnt tuː/

   Gordon's decided not to.
   /'gɔːdnz di'saidid `nɔt tuː/

(ii) In the exercise the **to** is always at the end of the sentence. It is
usually at the end of a clause but this need not be the final
clause of the sentence.

   EXAMPLE:
   I travelled first class. I didn't want **to** but I had **to** because
   there were no second-class seats.

To practise this use of the infinitive particle.

Bill hasn't taken Sally out yet. (expect)
Bill hasn't taken Sally out yet, but he expects to.

Richard's going home tomorrow. (want)
Richard's going home tomorrow, but he doesn't want to.

David didn't do any work yesterday. (intend)
David didn't do any work yesterday, but he'd intended to.

(a) 1. I can't play golf well now. (used)
   2. Richard should take the job. (going)
   3. Jill isn't going to Mexico. (supposed)
   4. Gordon couldn't have the day off. (hope)
   5. Bob didn't want to buy a dictionary. (had)
   6. Jane would like to stay out late. (allowed)
   7. Betty couldn't get rid of her old car. (want)
   8. Richard had to go to Canada for a year. (plan)
   9. David didn't want to go to the party. (promise)
   10. Peter doesn't type his business letters. (ought)
   11. Jim doesn't speak English very well. (would like)
   12. Paul made a few mistakes in his composition. (try)
   13. Peter isn't studying French at the moment. (intend)
   14. Michael said that he might take Sally out. (promise)
   15. Jean would like Jim to take her dancing soon. (offer)

(b) *As (a) above (further practice).*

   1. Sandra got the chance to visit New York. (expect)
   2. Jim can't attend the meeting tonight. (would like)

3. Harry hasn't visited his aunt in London yet. (plan)
4. Peter forgot to send in the application form. (mean)
5. Betty wants Jim to help her with her packing. (offer)
6. Peter couldn't see his dentist about a filling. (want)
7. Jim can't travel by hovercraft next week. (would like)
8. Philip studies until 2 a.m. every day. (shouldn't have)
9. Gordon expected John to attend the conference. (prefer)
10. Bob and John passed all their exams first time. (expect)
11. Joe isn't working very hard just at present. (will have)
12. John won't be able to see the director tomorrow. (ought)
13. Allan didn't want to take Sally to the theatre. (promise)
14. Bob makes a lot of mistakes with his pronunciation. (try)
15. Helen wants Richard to give her driving lessons. (refuse)

QUESTION TAGS

STATEMENT	QUESTION TAG		'EXPECTED SHORT ANSWER'*
I'm right,	aren't	I?	Yes, you are.
I'm not wrong,	am	I?	No, you aren't.
She's in the garden,	isn't	she?	Yes, she is.
She's not in the house,	is	she?	No, she isn't.
You're working tomorrow,	aren't	you?	Yes, I am.
You're not free tonight,	are	you?	No, I'm not.
Paul was here yesterday,	wasn't	he?	Yes, he was.
He wasn't at home,	was	he?	No, he wasn't.
They were at the cinema,	weren't	they?	Yes, they were.
They weren't at the club,	were	they?	No, they weren't.
Tom lives here,	doesn't	he?	Yes, he does.
He doesn't live in Rome,	does	he?	No, he doesn't.
You don't smoke,	do	you?	No, I don't.
You like whisky,	don't	you?	Yes, I do.
Mary can swim,	can't	she?	Yes, she can.
She can't dance,	can	she?	No, she can't.
Peter must shave,	mustn't	he?	Yes, he must.
He needn't go now,	need	he?	No, he needn't.

* See Note ii.

Notes:
  (i) Question tags (interrogative additions to statements) are an essential contribution to spoken language since without them normal conversation would not be possible.

 (ii) The number of different meanings that we can give to a single combination of statement + tag by differences of stress and intonation is very great. It is only a very rough guide to say that:

  (a) When the tag has a rising intonation the speaker is uncertain. There is no 'expected answer' but an answer is required.

   EXAMPLES:
   Mary can swim, can't she?
   /ˈmɛəri kn ˈswim ˌkɑːnt ʃi/
     (The answer may be Yes or No.)

   She can't dance, can she?
   /ʃi ˈkɑːnt ˈdɑːns ˌkæn ʃi/
     (The answer may be Yes or No.)

  (b) When the tag has a falling intonation, the speaker thinks that he knows the answer. If he waits for an answer it is for agreement (the 'expected answer'), confirmation or comment.

   EXAMPLES:
   Mary can swim, can't she?
   /ˈmɛəri kn ˈswim ˈkɑːnt ʃi/
     (No answer, or: Yes, she can.)

   She can't dance, can she?
   /ʃi ˈkɑːnt ˈdɑːns ˈkæn ʃi/
     (No answer, or: No, she can't.)

(iii) The examples above show that a negative statement has a non-negative question tag; an affirmative statement has a negative question tag. (but see Exs. 297/8)

---

294 Question tags   E

To practise question tags with the verb be.
Supply the necessary tag:

Jim's at home.
STUDENT A: **Jim's at home, isn't he?**
STUDENT B: **Yes, he is.** or: **No, he isn't.**

Bob was here.
STUDENT C: **Bob was here, wasn't he?**
STUDENT D: **Yes, he was.** or: **No, he wasn't.**

I'm not late.
STUDENT E: **I'm not late, am I?**
STUDENT F: **No, you're not.** or: **Yes, you are.**

1. Mary's English.
2. It wasn't raining.
3. That's a good hotel.
4. I'm usually early.
5. Your car's a Ford.
6. You're not English.
7. You're not a tourist.
8. Susan was in Paris.
9. They weren't in class.
10. John was at a party.
11. You were in New York last year.
12. Those are French magazines.
13. You aren't American.
14. The camera was a good one.
15. Tom and Bob weren't here.
16. Anne isn't good at tennis.
17. There's an old film on TV.
18. Bill was looking for a flat.
19. They are staying in Stockholm.
20. There are some people coming.

---

295 Question tags   E

To practise question tags with 'special' verbs other than be.
Supply the necessary tag:

You often watch TV.
STUDENT A: **You often watch TV, don't you?**
STUDENT B: **Yes, I do.** or: **No, I don't.**

Mary needn't come.
STUDENT C: **Mary needn't come, need she?**
STUDENT D: **No, she needn't.** or: **Yes, she must.**

1. You sleep well.
2. Mary can't swim.

402

3. You can hear me.
4. You needn't go yet.
5. George speaks German.
6. Lucy worked very hard.
7. Jim enjoys a cup of tea.
8. Peter doesn't live here.
9. You haven't been yet.
10. Betty didn't come.
11. Paul must get up earlier.
12. You make a lot of mistakes.
13. Bob doesn't smoke very much.
14. Susan must see the doctor.
15. Henry went to Bermuda.
16. Lucy knows all the answers.
17. Tom wants to have a holiday.
18. Gordon's taken his car.
19. Sandra will leave tomorrow.
20. We shan't be able to go.

---

296 Question tags   I

Give the correct question tags for the following:
(*See the structure and notes above Ex.* 294.)

She should have come yesterday.
She should have come yesterday, shouldn't she?
Yes, she should.

He would have seen him if he'd been here.
He would have seen him if he'd been here, wouldn't he?
Yes, he would.

Mary didn't use to visit New York so often.
Mary didn't use to visit New York so often, did she?
No, she didn't.

1. She needn't have taken that train.
2. He should have done the work last week.
3. John could have taken an earlier flight.
4. Gordon had to spend the weekend at home.
5. Pat could have bought the tickets yesterday.
6. Mary couldn't have been here at 9 o'clock.
7. Sheila can't have learnt English in a month.

8. Allan won't have come back from the shops yet.
9. Jim might have left the contract at the office.
10. Paul will have finished the translation by now.
11. John didn't use to smoke those dreadful cigars.
12. David might not have gone into the restaurant yet.
13. Peter used to spend all his time in coffee bars.
14. Harry would have taken the short cut to the beach.
15. Paul should have taken his car on holiday with him.
16. Joe shouldn't have had to do so much overtime.
17. Brian might have had to look after the office alone.
18. The computer should have come up with the right answer.
19. Susan ought to have been able to understand the letter.
20. Richard would have had to work sixteen hours a day.

---

297 Question tags   **A**

Note:
If the wish of the speaker is to ask for verification, or to express sarcasm, disbelief or surprise, the affirmative statement has a non-negative question tag, and the negative statement has a negative question tag (Cf. Note iii and structure above Ex. 294).

EXAMPLES:
(Oh,) Mary came yesterday, **did she**?
    /ˈmɛəri ˈkeim ˮjestədi ˌdidʃiː/

(So,) you're always right, **are you**?
    /juːr ˈɔːlweiz ˮrait ˌɑːjuː/

(So,) I'm not supposed to go, **aren't** I?

(Oh,) they haven't begun, **haven't they**?

(So,) she's going to see you tonight, **is she**?

To practise the above pattern, respond as shown.
Use a rising intonation for the question tag.

John can play golf.

Oh, he can play golf, can he? Then he can play against David in the tournament.

Mary doesn't want to talk to you.

So, she doesn't want to talk to me, doesn't she? Well, we'll soon see about that!

1. Bob wouldn't pay the bill.
2. John would prefer coffee.

404

3. You must work harder.
4. You haven't done enough.
5. Jim refused to do the job.
6. Your pronunciation's bad.
7. Tom wants the day off.
8. I can't understand you.
9. Mary used to like Peter.
10. Your application's been turned down.
11. I'd like to leave now.
12. We don't want you to come.
13. I saw Sally with Richard.
14. Those clothes don't suit you.
15. You should have got up earlier.
16. Tom couldn't come to class.
17. Your English is improving.
18. You've made a mistake.
19. Bob said that you're slow.
20. Jim expects to learn English in two weeks.

---

298   Question tags   A

Note:
A double short response also indicates surprise, disbelief, sarcasm, etc. Use extra stress and a falling intonation for the response statement and a rising intonation for the question tag. (Students should be warned that a comment of this sort may be very rude—even 'fighting talk' among men.)

EXAMPLES:

I've been using your car.	(Oh,) you **have**, **have** you?
	/⌐əu juː ˅hæv ˌhæv juː/
She's not going to help you.	(Oh,) she **isn't**, **isn't** she?
I don't like your jacket.	(Oh,) you **don't**, **don't** you?
(Cf. I've won a lot of money.	(Oh,) **have** you?)*

* (Here, a rising intonation on the 'have you?' indicates interest; a falling intonation would indicate sarcasm, disbelief, lack of interest, etc.)

To practise the above pattern.

He didn't post the letters.	**Oh, he didn't, didn't he?**
She forgot to do her hair.	**Oh, she did, did she?**
Jim refuses to see you.	**Oh, he does, does he?**
Mary won't leave.	**Oh, she won't, won't she?**

1. You must go to bed earlier.
2. You should speak more slowly.
3. I'm reading your newspaper.
4. John's got your car.
5. I was at the palace yesterday.
6. I haven't booked the seats.
7. Sue couldn't do her homework.
8. Sandra might be late tonight.
9. Peter's lost the money.
10. Susan won't write to me.
11. Bob used to play chess.
12. Mary's getting married soon.
13. Tom caught a cold yesterday.
14. You'll have to do it again.
15. I need to borrow some money.
16. I should like to do it now.
17. I shan't be able to help you.
18. You shouldn't smoke so much.
19. Bob's been away for a while.
20. Gordon had to go to hospital.

PREPOSITIONS

299 ELEMENTARY

QUESTION	ANSWER		
Where are the books?	The books are	**on**	the table.
Where is John?	John is	**in**	his room.
Where are my friends?	Your friends are	**at**	the hotel.
Where is Mary?	Mary is	**with**	John.
Where are my shoes?	Your shoes are	**under**	the bed.
What time is breakfast?	It is	**at**	8 o'clock.
When is the lesson?	It is	**in**	the morning.
What time is tea?	It is	(at) **about**	4 p.m.
When is Bob's birthday?	It is	**on**	Wednesday.

406

When	is your holiday?	It is	**from**	the 10th.
			to	the 20th
				of August.

Note:
As a general rule prepositions are unstressed. Many of the shorter prepositions have weak forms and students should try to use these where appropriate.

To practise the above prepositions, answer the following:

Where's Mary? (Sally)	**She's with Sally.**
When's your birthday? (August)	**It's in August.**
What time's the concert? (8 p.m.)	**It's at 8 p.m.**

1. Where's Barbara? (Henry)
2. Where's John? (the garden)
3. What time's lunch? (1 p.m.)
4. Where's Paul? (the bathroom)
5. Where's the pillow? (the bed)
6. Where are my shoes? (the chair)
7. Where's Jane? (the Savoy Hotel)
8. When's Sheila's holiday? (April)
9. When does Jim do his work? (night)
10. When's the meeting? (the afternoon)
11. When's Richard's day off? (Thursday)
12. When will you see Mary? (the evening)
13. When's Bob's wedding? (the 1st of May)
14. Where's Tom's bedroom? (the first floor)
15. When's the bar open? (11 a.m.–11 p.m.)

Practise also the conversational short answers:

Where's Mary?—with Sally.

/ˈwɪð ˈsæli/

When's your birthday?—in August.

/ɪn ˈɔːɡəst/

---

300 Prepositions   EI

Note:
  In hospital   (a patient)
  At the hospital   (a visitor)
  At school/college/university (a student)

'in the' often indicates a profession: **In the** army/theatre/medical profession, etc.

Choose between at, on *and* in *when responding to the following:* (*also decide if 'the' is required*)

the student (university)	Where's the student? **He's at university.**
the painting (wall)	Where's the painting? **It's on the wall.**
the patient (bed) (hospital)	Where's the patient? **She's in bed. She's in hospital.**

1. the drinkers (bar)
2. the film-fan (cinema)
3. the actress (stage) (theatre)
4. the workers (work)
5. the housewife (shops)
6. the children (school)
7. the school visitors (school)
8. the patients (hospital) (doctor's)
9. the hospital visitor (hospital)
10. your parents (home)
11. the ship (port) (sea)
12. the ship passengers (board) (deck)
13. the diner (dinner)
14. the traveller (airport)
15. the guest (hotel)
16. the tourist (tour)
17. the executive (business)
18. the holidaymaker (holiday)
19. the caller (telephone)
20. the furniture (house)
21. the church-goers (church)
22. the wedding (church)
23. the married couple (their honeymoon)
24. the driver (car) (road)
25. the bus passengers (bus)
26. the taxi passengers (taxi)
27. the pedestrian (pavement)
28. the prisoner (prison)
29. the escaped convict (hiding)
30. everybody (party)

Many verbs are followed by prepositions.

EXAMPLES:

I **listen to** Mary.

I **agreed with** Paul.

I **thought about** going.

Sometimes more than one preposition can follow the verb.

EXAMPLES:

I **looked at** Mary.   (as she was speaking to me)

I **looked for** the pen.   (as it was lost)

I **looked into** the matter. (as it needed investigation)

Use prepositions to connect the following, as shown:

Were you listening? (the music)
Yes. I was listening to the music.

Have they arrived? (the station)
Yes. They've arrived at the station.

Did you stay? (the house)
Yes. I stayed in the house. (or: at the house)

(a)   1. Were you talking? (Jim)
       2. Did you jump? (the wall)
       3. Did you look? (the sky) (the lost pen)
       4. Have you written? (Mary)
       5. Will you wait? (Susan)
       6. Did you stay? (home)
       7. Did you apply? (the job)
       8. Will you succeed? (passing)
       9. Did you lend it? (Allan)
     10. Did you borrow it? (Jim)
     11. Were you dreaming? (food)
     12. Did you ask? (help)
     13. Will you remind him? (it)
     14. Do you agree? (you)
     15. Did you laugh? (the joke)
     16. Will you vote? (Mr Smith)
     17. Did you discuss it? (Jill)
     18. Did you think? (the problem) (asking Peter)
     19. Will they operate? (John)

20. Was she warned? (the danger)
21. Did you apologise? (Mary)
22. Do you approve? (his action)

(b) *As (a) above (further practice).*

1. Is Jim working? (an essay) (that firm) (New York)
2. Did you run? (the bus) (my dog)
3. Did Mary stare? (John)
4. Do you insist? (going)
5. Did you hide? (Allan)
6. Will it protect it? (rust)
7. Does he come? (Canada) (class)
8. Did you receive it? (Bob)
9. Did you speak? (art) (Richard)
10. Will you invest? (the shares)
11. Did he interfere? (my plans)
12. Did you help her? (her work)
13. Did you accuse him? (theft)
14. Do you gossip? (other people)
15. Did you comment? (the story)
16. Did you tell him? (the match)
17. Can you prevent him? (going)
18. Did you thank him? (his help)
19. Did the room smell? (smoke)
20. Will you search? (the ring)
21. Do you object? (his request)
22. Did you defend her? (attack)

---

302 Prepositions

Prepositions follow certain adjectives.

EXAMPLES:

Peter's **good at** swimming.

I'm **satisfied with** my progress.

Jim was **successful in** passing the exam.

As with verbs, more than one preposition may follow an adjective.

EXAMPLES:

Jim was **sorry for** Joe. (as Joe was always so unlucky)

Bob was **sorry about** the mistake. (he regretted having made it)

410

Respond as shown:

Are you lucky? (cards)
I'm lucky at cards.

Are you happy? (the situation)
I'm happy about the situation.

Were you angry? (Peter) (not passing)
I was angry with Peter. I was angry about not passing.

1. Are you ashamed? (Sally)
2. Were you surprised? (her reaction)
3. Were you interested? (coming)
4. Are you sorry? (John) (the accident)
5. Were you ready? (lunch)
6. Was it different? (John's)
7. Is it similar? (mine)
8. Are you good? (tennis)
9. Was Bob reasonable? (the claim)
10. Were you nice? (George)
11. Are you short? (money)
12. Are you busy? (my work)
13. Are you shocked? (the change)
14. Were you polite? (Tom)
15. Is it safe? (thieves)
16. Were you responsible? (Mary)
17. Are you efficient? (my job)
18. Were you patient? (John)
19. Are you certain? (the future)
20. Are you satisfied? (the flat)
21. Are you familiar? (her voice)
22. Were you right? (the number)
23. Were you far away? (home)
24. Were you rude? (Richard)
25. Are you enthusiastic? (golf)
26. Is he famous? (his singing)
27. Were you curious? (her name)
28. Are you quick? (arithmetic)
29. Were you jealous? (Anne)
30. Were you successful? (the exam)

Other common prepositions are:

above	beneath	around	against	along	up
below	underneath	between	across	near	down
under	opposite	among(st)	past	next to	
over	through	beyond	behind	close to	

To practise using the above answer the following questions:

Where did you hang the hammock? (two trees)
We hung it between two trees.

Where will you have the picnic? (some trees)
We'll have it beneath (or near) some trees.

Where have you been for your walk? (the town)
I've been around (or through) the town.

1. Where was the light? (head)
2. Where's the station? (ground)
3. Where's Peter's flat? (his shop)
4. Where did Anne fall? (the stairs)
5. Where did the bus go? (the school)
6. Where does Bob like to sit? (Mary)
7. Where does John live? (the station)
8. Where did Peter walk? (the village)
9. Where was the summit? (the climbers)
10. Where was the valley? (the climbers)
11. Where's the chalkboard? (the teacher)
12. Where did the hostess walk? (the room)
13. Where did the climber go? (the mountain)
14. Where will the visitors walk? (the beach)
15. Where's Bob's house? (Susan's and Peter's)
16. Where did the horses go? (the winning-post)
17. Where did Jim lean his bicycle? (the fence)
18. Where did you look for the watch? (the sofa)
19. Where will the astronauts travel? (the moon)
20. Where did Bob find the letter? (some documents)

To practise further expressions introduced by in *and* on, *respond as shown:*

Did John come by bus? (foot)
No. He came on foot.

Does the museum own that painting? (loan)
No. It's on loan.

Does Jim owe any money at the bank? (credit)
No. He's in credit.

Do Bob and Jim have different likes and dislikes? (common)
No. They have a lot in common.

1. Is Alice safe? (danger)
2. Was John solvent? (debt)
3. Is Mary happy? (a temper)
4. Has my horse lost? (luck)
5. Is Sally laughing? (tears)
6. Is Jane all right? (trouble)
7. Could Jim get past Mary? (the way)
8. Did Joe pay cash for his car? (credit)
9. Did Bob have plenty of time? (a hurry)
10. Did Tom hit Paul by accident? (purpose)
11. Do Tom and Jane hate each other? (love)
12. Was the meeting held privately? (public)
13. Is that wooden building all right? (fire)
14. Is John against the project? (favour of it)
15. Does Jim dislike Peter? (good terms with him)

---

305 Prepositions   IA

At, in and **on** often introduce idiomatic expressions relating to 'time'.

EXAMPLES:
Patricia arrived **in good time**.

Elizabeth came late **on one occasion**.

Fortunately, I arrived **at the right time**.

Choose between at, in *and* on *to introduce the word(s) in brackets, as shown:*

Did Bob know Mary? (the time)
He didn't know her at the time.

Is the 10 p.m. train ever late? (time)
No, it's always on time.

Will John be here soon? (a month's time)
He'll be here in a month's time.

1. Has Paul come? (last)
2. Isn't Bob here? (the moment)
3. Was Peter ever rich? (one time)
4. Couldn't Jim speak very well? (first)
5. Do the buses leave punctually? (time)
6. Does John still make mistakes? (times)
7. Did Sally miss her train? (time for it)
8. Will you be ready soon? (a few minutes)
9. Was Helen living in England? (that time)
10. Did Joe come when you wanted him? (once)
11. Aren't you thinking about Jim? (present)
12. Won't Tom visit Rome now? (a later date)

---

306 Prepositions   A

Examples of the use of **out of, off** and **away from**:
John lives **out of** town.
We live just **off** King Street.
I live some distance **away from** the sea.

To practise and contrast out of, off *and* away from, *respond as shown:*

Are Jane's clothes up to date? (date)
No, they're out of date.

Is Jim using his car at the moment? (the road)
No, it's off the road.

Do you like to be in the city at weekends? (it all)
No, I like to get away from it all.

1. Does Peter have a job? (work)
2. Can I use your telephone? (order)

414

3. Is Joe eating normally? (his food)
4. Can I visit Helen this week? (home)
5. Isn't the new student well? (school)
6. Was Jim breathing normally? (breath)
7. Is John available to serve me? (duty)
8. Isn't Paul at the office today? (work)
9. Is Gordon allowed to see Elizabeth? (her)
10. Was the demonstration an orderly one? (hand)
11. Can I speak to Mary for a moment? (the house)
12. Can the surgeon see me this week? (the hospital)
13. Did Bill appear to be acting normally? (his mind)
14. Is Tom still in the intensive care unit? (danger)
15. Does Tom keep to the subject under discussion?
    (the subject)

---

307 Prepositions   A

At, **in** and **on** may be used with **top, bottom, side, front** and **back**.

EXAMPLES:
There's a hole **in the back of** my jacket.

The car had been left **at the side of** the road.

There was an advertisement **on the front of** the shop.

*To practise the above, find the prepositional phrase that (in your
opinion) best indicates the position of the following:*

Where's the driver sitting? (of the car)
He's sitting in the front of the car.

Where will Jim hide the letter? (of the wardrobe)
He'll hide it on top of the wardrobe.

Where did they find the sunken wreck? (of the sea)
They found it at the bottom of the sea.

1. Where's the hole? (of my pocket)
2. Where's the garage? (of the house)
3. Where's the car park? (of the cinema)
4. Where's the luggage-rack? (of the car)
5. Where was the hitch-hiker? (of the road)
6. Where were the passengers? (of the taxi)

7. Where was the typewriter? (of the typist)
8. Where were the best rooms? (of the hotel)
9. Where was all the luggage? (of the coach)
10. Where's the quietest room? (of the stairs)
11. Where are the lazy students? (of the class)
12. Where were the drugs found? (of the suitcase)
13. Where was the maker's name? (of the TV set)
14. Where did the caretaker live? (of the stairs)
15. Where was the long advertisement? (of the bus)

---

308 Prepositions A

Certain nouns may be preceded and followed by prepositions.

EXAMPLES:
Paul's **in danger of** losing Mary.

You help me **in exchange for** my helping you.

Bob got a second book published **on the strength of** his first.

Rephrase the following as shown:

Paul could swim when he was five. (age)
Yes, he could swim at the age of five.

Mary remarried to give her children a home. (sake)
Yes, she remarried for the sake of her children.

Richard was about to leave when I arrived. (point)
Yes, he was on the point of leaving when you arrived.

1. Mary loved John. (love)
2. Jim spoke for the chairman. (behalf)
3. Paul was running the factory. (charge)
4. Break the glass if there's a fire. (case)
5. Elizabeth usually goes to bed late. (habit)
6. The children need care and attention. (need)
7. I went in although the water was cold. (spite)
8. Joe was fined as well as imprisoned. (addition)
9. I stayed in because of the bad weather. (account)
10. The passengers said that they could see land. (sight)
11. Tom didn't go swimming, as he was afraid of drowning.
    (fear)

PHRASAL VERBS

Introductory note:

The purpose of the following exercises is to provide oral practice in using those common and vital idiomatic expressions with which foreign learners traditionally experience difficulty. These expressions should be taught by demonstration and explanation before the exercises are attempted.

See Exs. 313–322 for idiom tests.

A common form of idiom is an adverb particle used alone.

EXAMPLES:

Steve is **out**. (out of the house)

David is **off**. (not working)

Adverb particles combine with certain 'idiomatic' verbs.

EXAMPLES:

Paul **took off** his hat.   Jean **turned on** the light.

Mary **put on** her coat.   John **switched off** the fire.

If a pronoun is involved, this goes between the verb and the particle.

EXAMPLES:

Paul **took** it **off**.   Jean **turned** it **on**.

Mary **put** it **on**.   John **switched** it **off**.

It is important to remember that adverb particles nearly always bear sentence stress while prepositions are not normally stressed.

EXAMPLES:

	AS ADVERB PARTICLE	AS PREPOSITION
on	He put on his coat.	He put his coat on the bed.
	/hi 'put 'ɔn hiz ˋkəut/	/hi 'put hiz 'kəut ɔn ðə ˋbed/
to	They set to and tidied the place.	They set to work and tidied the place.
	/ðei 'set ˊˋtuːən ˋtaidid ðe ˌpleis/	/ðei 'set tə ˊˋwɜːk ən ˋtaidid ðə ˌpleis/
up **over**	Bob's taken up with Mary now that Betty's thrown him over.	They've just gone up the road and they'll be leaning over the bridge.
	/... 'teikn ˋʌp wið ˋmɛəri ... 'θrəun him ˋəuvə/	/... 'gɔn ʌp ðə ˋrəud ... 'liːniŋ əuvə ðə ˋbridʒ/

417

(a) *To practise using adverb particles, respond as shown:*

Is the tap on? (off)	**No, it's off.**
Is John in? (out)	**No, he's out.**
Is Paul on (duty) today? (off)	**No, he's off.**

1. Is John out? (in)
2. Is the fire off? (on)
3. Is Susan here? (away)
4. Is Mary in? (out)
5. Is the gas on? (off)
6. Is Peter around? (out)
7. Is Mary still upstairs? (down)
8. Is John still on holiday? (back)
9. Is the milk still fresh? (off)
10. Is Paul still in bed? (up)
11. Is the game still in progress? (over)
12. Is the pie still on (the menu)? (off)

(b) *To practise placing the pronoun between the verb and its particle, respond as shown:*

What did you do with the coat? (put on)
I put it on.

What did you do with the children? (take out)
I took them out.

What did you do with the rubbish? (throw away)
I threw it away.

1. the hat (take off)
2. the lights (put on)
3. the towel (hang up)
4. the book (give back)
5. the shoe-lace (do up)
6. the dishes (wash up)
7. the mess (clean up)
8. the sweater (try on)
9. the word (look up)
10. the money (pay back)
11. the form (fill in)
12. the mistake (rub out)
13. the message (take down)
14. the stockings (put on)
15. the telegram (send off)
16. the water (turn off)
17. the luggage (send on)
18. the TV (turn down)
19. the plates (put away)
20. the tape-recorder (turn on)

Ex. 309 gave practice with the 'verb + (pro)noun + adverb particle' pattern. In the following three exercises this pattern is contrasted with:

(i) 'verb + adverb particle'

EXAMPLES:

I **got away**.   The plane **took off**.

John will **carry on**.   Mary's **come out**.

(ii) 'verb + preposition + (pro)noun'

EXAMPLES:

I'll **call on** Mary.   (I'll **call on** her.)

Jim **got over** his cold. (Jim **got over** it.)

(iii) 'verb + adverb particle + preposition + (pro)noun'

EXAMPLES:

Peter **found out about** the changes.

Jane **keeps away from** Richard.

(a) *Use the idiom in brackets in your response to the following:*

Did you return late? (get back)
Yes. I got back late.

Will you support me at the meeting? (back up)
Yes. I'll back you up.

Did something go wrong with your car? (break down)
Yes. It broke down.

1. Will prices increase? (go up)
2. Has Bob stopped smoking? (give up)
3. Did you invent that story? (make up)
4. Did you disappoint Richard? (let down)
5. Will you visit Tom in Canada? (look up)
6. Can you show me who it was? (point out)
7. Have we used all the bread? (run out of)
8. Did Peter postpone the meeting? (put off)
9. Did you continue watching the film? (go on)
10. Will you meet Mary at the airport? (pick up)
11. Did you return the library books? (take back)
12. Did you give John a bed for the night? (put up)
13. Has Elizabeth recovered from her cold? (get over)
14. Has Bob returned the faulty typewriter? (send back)
15. Did Jane learn to play the game last year? (take up)

(b) *As (a) above (further practice).*
1. Did Richard escape? (get away)
2. Did the parcel explode? (blow up)
3. Will your train arrive late? (get in)
4. Are you going to visit Mary? (call on)
5. Have you redecorated your flat? (do up)
6. Did you reach the office early? (get to)
7. Did you have your car returned? (get back)
8. Have you arranged an appointment? (fix up)
9. Did Jim extinguish his cigarette? (put out)
10. Has the operator disconnected you? (cut off)
11. Did you leave Paul at the station? (drop off)
12. Will you go and collect the parcel? (call for)
13. Will you continue with the exercise? (carry on)
14. Did you avoid having to do the job? (get out of)
15. Did you discover who'd taken your pen? (find out)

(c) *As (a) above (further practice).*
1. Did you test the car? (try out)
2. Do you like Susan? (get on with)
3. Did Sheila disturb you? (wake up)
4. Will Jim arrive on time? (turn up)
5. Did you find the answer? (work out)
6. Will you cancel your tour? (call off)
7. Will you reject the offer? (turn down)
8. Have we finished all the paper? (use up)
9. Is Tom educating Jimmy himself? (bring up)
10. Did you have to delay your holiday? (put off)
11. Have you disposed of the rubbish? (get rid of)
12. Will you discuss the matter with Bob? (talk over)
13. Is Jim making progress with his English? (come on)
14. Did you see the plane leave the ground? (take off)
15. Did they have to demolish the old house? (pull down)

---

311 **Make** and **Do**   I

Notes:
 (i) **Make** has the basic meaning of 'construct'.

EXAMPLES:

John's **making** a model aeroplane.

Mary's **making** a basket.

Do has the basic meaning of **perform** or **carry out**.

EXAMPLES:
John's **doing** an exercise.

Mary's **doing** nothing.

(ii) **Make** and **do** may be used idiomatically.

EXAMPLES:
I **made** a mistake.

He's **done** you a favour.

They won't **do** business with us.

You'd better **make** sure of the time.

To practise and contrast make *and* do, *respond as shown:*

What did you do last night? (—my homework)
I did my homework.

Did you do it correctly? (—a number of mistakes)
No. I made a number of mistakes.

1. Are you going to be busy tonight? (nothing to—)
2. Do you think Bob should marry Anne? (—him happy)
3. Has Philip finished his letter? (—a quarter of it)
4. How was Elizabeth occupied after dinner? (—homework)
5. Can we see the director right away? (—an appointment)
6. Why did you go out of the room just now? (—a phone call)
7. Have you checked that all the car doors are locked? (—sure)
8. How was Richard occupied after breakfast? (—a job for Sally)
9. Is there enough room for another person to sit here? (—room)
10. Did Susan mind when David forgot her birthday? (—light of it)
11. Were you busy in class yesterday afternoon? (—oral exercises)
12. What profession would you recommend for Paul? (—a good lawyer)
13. Was Brian any better when you last saw him? (—any improvement)
14. How does Jane spend her morning? (—the washing-up, —the beds)

421

15. How did Tom wake you up when he came in last night? (—a noise)
16. What shall I do now that I've missed my bus? (—the best of it)
17. Should I take my holiday soon? (—you good, —you more relaxed)
18. What's Jim going to do with that alarm-clock? (—good use of it)
19. How's Bob getting on with his essay? (—the first part yesterday)
20. What did you think of Bob when you met him? (—a good impression)

---

312 Idiom Practice   **IA**

Notes:
  (i) Certain 'idiomatic' verbs combine with adverb particles to form single words.

    EXAMPLES:

    Jim **overtook** Bob in his car.

    Bob's **upset** Sally.

 (ii) Verb and particle combinations may also function as adjectives or nouns.

    EXAMPLES:

I'm **worn out**.	Do you use **make-up**?
Mary's **upset**.	An **upset** stomach.
What's your **income**?	A **worn-out** pair of shoes.
Paul's a **drop-out**.	The firm's **output**.

(iii) Certain combinations are quite complicated.

    EXAMPLES:

    I'll try to make it up to you.

    I've got to get down to some work.

    We'll take it up with the director.

In the following three exercises use the idiom in brackets in a negative response.

(a) Did you take it easy last night? (get down to)
    No. I got down to some hard work.

Is business continuing to improve? (fall off)
No. It's beginning to fall off.

Would you say John's particularly modest? (show off)
No. He's always showing off.

1. Is Paul a young man? (get on)
2. Did Anne fall behind? (keep up)
3. Do you feel energetic? (wear out)
4. Did you spot the error? (overlook)
5. Are you going to ring off? (hold on)
6. Do you want me to do the job? (see to)
7. Did they tell Paul to go in? (keep out)
8. Do your shoes last a long time? (wear out)
9. Do you intend to go to bed early? (stay up)
10. Is John staying here this weekend? (go away)
11. Is there enough beer for everybody? (go round)
12. Can you see the number of the house? (make out)
13. Are you sorry you agreed to go? (look forward to)
14. Did you get through the traffic quickly? (hold up)
15. Does that shop have any cigarettes left? (sell out)

(b) *As* (*a*) *above* (*further practice*).
1. Is the milk all right? (go off)
2. Did you make Lucy happy? (upset)
3. Did the dog like Richard? (go for)
4. Will Anne ring Gordon up? (go round)
5. Did your plan come off? (fall through)
6. Did Sheila have her dinner? (go without)
7. Was Judy interested in the lesson? (fed up)
8. Is the weather going to get worse? (clear up)
9. Did John stay ahead of the others? (catch up)
10. Isn't that noise getting you down? (put up with)
11. Is Jim still engaged (to be married)? (break off)
12. Did Paul remain seated when Mary came in? (get up)
13. Do you and Steve still get on all right? (fall out)
14. Did you stay till the end of the meeting? (call away)
15. Does Tom want to put off doing the job? (get over with)

(c) *As* (*a*) *above* (*further practice*).
1. Did Tom overlook Bill's remark? (tell off)
2. Is this a private discussion? (join in)
3. Has Bob told us the whole story? (keep back)
4. Will you be staying up late tonight? (turn in)

5. Will the dentist leave the tooth in? (take out)
6. Do you think we should keep together? (split up)
7. Can the workers take off their jackets? (keep on)
8. Is John helping Jill to make progress? (hold back)
9. Is Jim going to give up learning English? (keep at)
10. Was service included in the hotel bill? (leave out)
11. Did the firm keep the men they'd taken on? (lay off)
12. Is Jim happy about Mary's having left him? (have back)
13. Did the policeman allow the people to watch? (move on)
14. Do the technicians go near the reactor? (keep away from)
15. Was Jim punished for coming home so late? (get away with)

PHRASAL VERBS—ADDITIONAL PRACTICE

ELEMENTARY/INTERMEDIATE

The following ten exercises contain certain verb–adverb, verb–preposition and verb–adverb–preposition combinations, many of which are practised orally in Exs. 309–312. A rough guide to the meaning of each expression is provided by the second column. Each exercise practises ten idioms in the form of a written (or spoken) test. Answers are given on page 434.

313

IDIOMS	KEY WORDS	EXERCISES
(a) back up	: support	1. My car .. miles from anywhere.
(b) be away	: absent	2. It .. you to make the decision.
(c) be back	: return	3. Will you .. me .. at the meeting?
(d) be in	: at home	4. George.. of the office.
(e) be out	: not there	5. Joe's still asleep, but Pat . ..
(f) be over	: finished	6. When will the lesson ..?

(g) be up	: out of bed	7. How long has he . . from home?
(h) be up to	: responsibility	8. If you go now, when will you . .?
(i) blow up	: explode	9. Paul . . not . ., but he'll be back soon.
(j) break down	: fail	10. He lit the fuse and the bridge . ..

314

(a) bring up	: educate	1. Please . . that awful noise.
(b) call for	: collect	2. How should children be . .?
(c) call on	: visit	3. They have . . the electricity.
(d) carry on	: continue	4. He . . the rent on Thursdays.
(e) catch up	: reach	5. I hope our little plan . ..
(f) clear up	: improve	6. The weather is beginning to . ..
(g) come off	: succeed	7. I shall never . . with Richard.
(h) cut off	: disconnect	8. Shall we . . Betty tonight?
(i) cut out	: stop	9. . .! Don't stop because of me.
(j) do up	: fasten	10. Please . . your buttons and zip.

315

(a) do up	: decorate	1. Will the police . . my stolen car?
(b) drop in	: visit	2. I'm going now. I'll . . late.
(c) fall off	: decrease	3. Please . . for a drink any time.

(d) fill in	: complete	4. Sales have begun to . . now.
(e) find out	: discover	5. Would you . . this form, please?
(f) fix up	: arrange	6. That man would . . with murder!
(g) get away	: escape	7. We must . . an appointment soon.
(h) get back	: return	8. I could never . . what he'd done.
(i) get back	: recover	9. The plane . . at 10 p.m. and took off at 11 p.m.
(j) get in	: arrive	10. To . . this flat will cost a lot.

316

(a) get off	: alight	1. We . . the bus at our destination.
(b) get on	: progress	2. I wish you would . . smoking!
(c) get on	: embark	3. I want to . . him . . his money.
(d) get on	: be friendly	4. John . . immediately on waking.
(e) get out	: exit from	5. Here's the train. . . quickly!
(f) get over	: recover from	6. He doesn't . . with his relatives.
(g) get up	: arise	7. How is your English . . ?
(h) give back	: return	8. Susan will soon . . her cold.
(i) give up	: stop	9. Can you help Sue . . of the car?
(j) go away	: leave	10. Peter has . . from home.

426

(a) go on	: continue	1. Slow down! I can't .. with you.
(b) go out	: leave	2. You should .. your English at home.
(c) go round	: suffice	3. ... I won't interrupt you again.
(d) go up	: increase	4. How can we .. all these draughts?
(e) hold on	: wait	5. Train fares are .. this month.
(f) hold up	: delay	6. There's not enough whisky to ...
(g) keep out	: exclude	7. Mary .. of the house an hour ago.
(h) keep up	: maintain	8. ... while I call Sue to the phone.
(i) keep up	: remain level	9. Sally .. Jim .. by marrying John.
(j) let down	: disappoint	10. The traffic-jam .. me ...

(a) look after	: protect	1. Mary .. her face without a mirror.
(b) look at	: regard	2. I'm .. meeting the chairman.
(c) look for	: seek	3. ... ! A car's coming straight at you.
(d) look forward to	: expect (with pleasure)	4. She'll .. it .. in her dictionary.
(e) look out	: be careful	5. Will you help me .. my lost wallet?
(f) look up	: refer	6. It's difficult to .. what he meant.
(g) look up	: visit	7. I hope you're not .. that story ...

(h) make out	: understand	8. Sue . . the picture in the gallery.
(i) make up	: invent	9. I'll . . your cat while you're away.
(j) make up	: apply cosmetics	10. Promise to . . me . . before long?

319

(a) pay back	: repay	1. I made a mistake and . . it . . .
(b) pick up	: collect	2. I shall . . the money to the bank.
(c) point out	: indicate	3. He used a call box to . . me . . .
(d) put away	: stow	4. Shall I . . you . . outside the shop?
(e) put off	: postpone	5. I can't . . her. She's dreadful.
(f) put on	: dress	6. Can you . . me . . for two weeks?
(g) put up	: accommodate	7. I must . . that you're quite wrong.
(h) put up with	: tolerate	8. . . . your books in the cupboard now.
(i) ring up	: telephone	9. You must . . your new dress for Tom to see.
(j) rub out	: erase	10. She . . making the decision.

320

| (a) run after | : pursue | 1. John was . . by her trick. |
| (b) run away | : flee | 2. You'll have to . . that bus. It won't stop for you. |

428

(c) run out of	: finish	3.	The gang . . from the police.
(d) see to	: attend to	4.	The children asked to . . .
(e) sell out	: all sold	5.	The papers were . . by 9 a.m.
(f) stay up	: go to bed late	6.	As the car was no good I . . it . . .
(g) take back	: return	7.	Go to the shop; we have . . beer.
(h) take in	: deceive	8.	. . . your coat and hang it up here.
(i) take off	: remove	9.	The plane . . from runway six.
(j) take off	: leave	10.	I'll do the drinks; you . . the food.

321

(a) take out	: extract	1.	He . . the TV and read a book.
(b) take out	: escort	2.	The dentist . . one of his teeth.
(c) take up	: begin	3.	He was . . through ill health.
(d) think about	: consider	4.	Paul . . Sue . . to lunch yesterday.
(e) throw away	: dispose of	5.	I'm going to . . golf this year.
(f) try out	: test	6.	Wanting to hear a talk, I . . the radio.
(g) turn down	: reject	7.	I . . going, but decided against it.
(h) turn off	: switch off	8.	What time does Bob . . at the office?
(i) turn on	: switch on	9.	Don't . . it . . ! It's still usable.
(j) turn up	: arrive	10.	I'll . . the bed . . before I buy it.

(a) wake up	: awaken	1. You've . . him by being rude.
(b) wash up	: clean	2. I wanted to . . , but I was on a hill.
(c) watch out	: be careful	3. The teacher luckily . . my mistake!
(d) wear out	: exhaust	4. She . . the dishes and lit the fire.
(e) wear out	: finish	5. . . ! There's a traffic-jam.
(f) work out	: calculate	6. I'm afraid my shoes are . . .
(g) overdo	: exceed	7. Can you . . how much I've won?
(h) overlook	: miss	8. I'm . . after doing that overtime.
(i) overtake	: pass	9. Don't . . it. Have a rest.
(j) upset	: anger	10. Jim will . . if you make that noise.

Appendix A

A selection of clauses, prepositional phrases and structural words.

Time

I was there	during before after until/till at the time of	the earthquake.
You can go	as soon as immediately now (that) once	you've finished.
I saw John	when whenever	he came.
I was in bed	while	Mary was making breakfast.
I've been here	since for (for) as long as	Monday. three days. you have.

No sooner had Gordon left **than**
Hardly had Gordon left **when** } Bob arrived.

Place

You can live	where wherever	you wish.

Purpose

I came	so that in order that for the purpose of	I could see Mary. seeing Mary.
I daren't speak	for fear of in case	waking the baby I should wake the baby.

Manner

Mary did	as	I instructed her.
You can do it	how	you like.
Tom behaved	like	a child.
Jim looked at me	as if	he wanted to speak.

Reason and Cause

I stayed in	**because**	it was raining.
	As **Since** **Seeing (that)**	it was raining, I stayed in.
Bob was late	**because of** **on account of** **thanks to** **owing to**	a traffic jam.
The delay was	**due to**	a rail strike.
Bob loves Jane	**and that's why** **and that's the reason**	she's going to marry him.

Result

We came early,	**so** **with the result (that)**	we had to wait.
I'm never	**so** busy **(that)**	I can't help my friends.
I had	**so** many guests **(that)** **such** a lot of guests **(that)**	I couldn't feed them all.
	As a result of	my call, Bob was on time.

Alternative

You can invite	**either**	John **or** Peter.
I must leave now,	**or (else)**	I'll be late.
Go with John,	**or alternatively**	go with Harry.
	Instead of	going out, let's stay in.
	As an alternative	to tennis, why not take up golf?

Condition

I shall come	**if** **only if** **as/so long as** **provided (providing)** **on (the) condition (that)**	you call for me.
	even if	I'm not invited.
	unless	I've got too much to do.
	whether	I'm invited **or not.**

	Suppose (supposing) **What if**	Bob fails, what then? Bob fails?
	If only	I hadn't drunk so much!

Degree

Peter arrived	**earlier than**	we'd expected.
John's	**as** tall **as**	Mary.
I'll be judged	**according to**	how I speak.
You can stay	**as/so far as**	I'm concerned.
	The more difficult	the job, **the better** I like it.

Addition

John spoke	**and** **and**	so did Mary. Mary did **too.**
I saw Susan	**and**	I **also** saw George.
Tom didn't go	**and neither/nor** **and**	did Sally. Sally didn't **either.**
I was late;	**furthermore** **besides** **in addition**	I'd forgotten my books.
	Both	John and Mary drink coffee.

Contrast

Peter came	**although** **though** **even though**	he hadn't been invited.
	in spite of	not having been invited.
Mary drove badly,	**but** **yet**	she passed her test.
I like John;	**nevertheless** **all the same**	I don't trust him.
Reading is easy;	**on the other hand**	writing is difficult.
I like coffee,	**whereas** **while**	Mary likes tea.
I failed the test.	**Still,**	I can always try again.

Fact

I loved her;
$\left\{\begin{array}{l}\textbf{in fact}\\ \textbf{actually}\\ \textbf{the fact is}\\ \textbf{in actual fact}\\ \textbf{as a matter of fact}\\ \textbf{indeed}\end{array}\right\}$
I adored her.

Anyway, etc.

I wasn't asked;
$\left\{\begin{array}{l}\textbf{anyway}\\ \textbf{anyhow}\\ \textbf{in any case}\end{array}\right\}$
I wasn't keen to go.

At Any Rate

John's busy; **at any rate** that's what he says.

Answers

121. 1. data /ˈdeitə/ 2. phenomena /fiˈnominə/ 3. crises /ˈkraisiːz/ 4. media /ˈmiːdiə/ 5. memoranda /meməˈrændə/ 6. criteria /kraiˈtiəriə/ 7. bureaux /ˈbjuərəu/ 8. formulae /ˈfɔːmjuliː/ 9. analyses /əˈnæləsiːz/

313. 1. j, 2. h, 3. a, 4. e, 5. g, 6. f, 7. b, 8. c, 9. d, 10. i.
314. 1. i, 2. a, 3. h, 4. b, 5. g, 6. f, 7. e, 8. c, 9. d, 10. j.
315. 1. i, 2. h, 3. b, 4. c, 5. d, 6. g, 7. f, 8. e, 9. j, 10. a.
316. 1. a, 2. i, 3. h, 4. g, 5. c, 6. d, 7. b, 8. f, 9. e, 10. j.
317. 1. i, 2. h, 3. a, 4. g, 5. d, 6. c, 7. b, 8. e, 9. j, 10. f.
318. 1. j, 2. d, 3. e, 4. f, 5. c, 6. h, 7. i, 8. b, 9. a, 10. g.
319. 1. j, 2. a, 3. i, 4. b, 5. h, 6. g, 7. c, 8. d, 9. f, 10. e.
320. 1. h, 2. a, 3. b, 4. f, 5. e, 6. g, 7. c, 8. i, 9. j, 10. d.
321. 1. h, 2. a, 3. g, 4. b, 5. c, 6. i, 7. d, 8. j, 9. e, 10. f.
322. 1. j, 2. i, 3. h, 4. b, 5. c, 6. e, 7. f, 8. d, 9. g, 10. a.

434

INDEX

437

439